# How to Get the Most Out of CompuServe®

## Revised Fourth Edition

Charles Bowen
and David Peyton

BANTAM BOOKS
NEW YORK • TORONTO • LONDON • SYDNEY • AUCKLAND

*HOW TO GET THE MOST OUT OF COMPUSERVE 4th EDITION*
*A Bantam Book / February 1989*

*We wish to thank the following photgraphers for the use of their work on the front cover:*
*Donnelley Marks, Peter Gridley/FPG International, Chris Margerin/FPG International,*
*Richard Laird/FPG International, Paul Markow/FPG International, Patricia Lanza Field/Bruce*
*Coleman, Inc., and Scala/Art Resource, N.Y. for the use of the art by Georges-Pierre Seurat.*

*Throughout the book, the trade names and trademarks of some companies*
*and products have been used, and no such uses are intended to convey*
*endorsement of or other affiliations with the book or software.*

ISBN 0-553-34707-1

*Published simultaneously in the United States and Canada*

Bantam Books are published by Bantam Books, Inc. Its trademark, consisting of the
words "Bantam Books" and the portrayal of a rooster, is Registered in U.S. Patent and
Trademark Office and in other countries. Marca Registrada, Bantam Books, Inc., 666
Fifth Avenue, New York, New York 10103.

PRINTED IN THE UNITED STATES OF AMERICA

FG    0    9    8    7    6    5    4    3    2

## Dedication

With love and gratitude, this is dedicated to our
fathers: Wilbur Caldwell, Creath Peyton and
Charles E. Bowen Jr.

# Contents

An introduction to the Executive Options and its top-flight business-related features, available for an extra charge.

A look at the wide variety of single-player games available on-line, forums for gamers.

Introducing multiplayer games, visiting the first on-line "quiz show," a forum just for multi-player game enthusiasts.

CompuServe can be used without menus, Profile section. More on EasyPlex, introducing on-line high-resolution graphics. Advanced tips for log-on and alternate terminal settings.

Summarizing other extra-cost services, including the Executive News Service, IQuest, and the Grolier's Academic American Encyclopedia, Microsearch and other features.

Try to enhance the system. Every member is an element; try to give to it sometimes as well as take. Report wrong-doings. Vision and CompuServe's Host Micro Interface (HMI). A look ahead.

Making the connection. Command Compendium. Troubleshooting and Getting Help. Your Electronic Address Book. Further Reading. CompuServe's Operating Rules and Copyright Policy. Reaching Us.

# Preface

It has been nearly six years since the night we sipped a couple of gallons of coffee at Dwight's Drive-In in Huntington, West Virginia, our hometown, and decided to write a book to help people learn about CompuServe. According to Charlie's notes — Charlie doesn't throw *anything* away — what we perceived that night as the primary need of new subscribers was a series of "road maps" that could be used to discover large parts of CompuServe in a systematic way and at a minimum expense. Equally important, we thought, was that the reader should be made to feel less intimidated by this massive computer system, and should come away from the experience eager to become an active "electronic citizen."

Those principles guided the early editions of this book, the first published in the summer of 1984, the updated second and third editions in 1986 and 1987, respectively. That must have been particularly good coffee at Dwight's that night because, looking now at the needs of today's CompuServe subscribers, those ideas seem more relevant than ever, and so they continue to be central in this latest edition.

But there is more, too. Over the past six years, we computer users have done a lot of growing. It used to be that the new on-line subscriber was satisfied with learning the basics of the system. These days, though, newcomers also want to learn about what we used to consider "advanced features." CompuServe has grown, too. Celebrating its 10th anniversary this year, the Columbus, Ohio, consumer information service has seen its subscriber base grow from not quite 100,000 in 1984 when this book's first edition was released to more than 460,000 this year. During the same time, the number of on-line features has more than doubled.

Consequently, this edition is our most ambitious yet. It updates all the material from earlier editions, taking the reader from their very first visit to the system all the way to expert status. Beyond that, it also gives special attention to newer features, including:

Extensive changes in the popular discussion forums. Four chapters are devoted to using the new forum software that was introduced in the summer of 1988.

Enhancements to the Executives News Service (ENS), which offers electronic "clipping folders" to make the service act as your personal news editor. Since our last editions, several exciting new resources have been added to ENS.

Improvements in travel features, the business-oriented Executive Option and the powerful IQuest gateway to more than 700 databases around the world.

Additions and changes to file transfer technologies, including a new faster version of CompuServe's popular "B" Protocol and the Kermit protocol.

More about on-line graphics, including high-resolution, color pictures that can be viewed on-line.

This book also goes farther than previous editions in helping readers learn the system on their own. New with this edition, a feature called "Side Roads" points out opportunities for a little independent study by noting other features that the reader might explore alone to supplement what has been illustrated in the text. This edition also does more to hint at things to come on CompuServe, such as a new user convention called the *host-micro interface* that ultimately will change the way CompuServe sends its data to us. A chapter near the end of the book puts this new development in perspective with other user interfaces.

As always, we have had the support of a number of fine people in bringing this book together. We're fortunate in that we're still being tolerated by two of the world's best editors, our wives — Susan Peyton and Pamela Bowen — who helped edit our work. Much thanks, too, to our agent, Katinka Matson, vice president of John Brockman Associates, and to the great team at Bantam, including Michael Roney and Kenzi Sugihara. Thanks, also, Rich Baker and Doug Branstetter at CompuServe for keeping us up-to-date on the very latest on-line.

Charles Bowen
Dave Peyton
Spring 1989

# Foreword

It seems strange to see this foreword printed on paper. It seems that a foreword to a book about on-line computing should be read on a computer screen — electrons on phosphorous, not ink on paper.

Yet, it is appropriate to use one of the oldest forms of communication to talk about one of the newest forms of communication — on-line computing. You have to reach into the past to understand the future, and sometimes that means using familiar ways to explain new technology.

That's why it's such pleasure to write the foreword to the 4th edition of *How to Get the Most Out of CompuServe*. We learned many years ago at CompuServe that people embrace the new technology through communication channels with which they are comfortable. The series of books from Bantam about CompuServe has helped shape a generation of on-line computer enthusiasts. The books did it by using the printed medium to explain — and work in harmony with — the on-line medium.

I am also pleased to write this foreword because it gives me the chance to thank Charles Bowen and David Peyton. Charlie and Dave launched the series of books about CompuServe and, in turn, helped create Micropolis. Through their words and imagery, they've taken a somewhat intimidating technology and made it reach out to people. they've add the "high touch" to "high tech," as John Naisbitt would say. They also worked closely with CompuServe every step of the way when writing their books. The 4th edition is no exception. The CompuServe books successfully capture a constantly evolving information service. *How to Get the Most Out of CompuServe* continues as a road map for hundreds of on-line communications pioneers finding their way across a new land of instant communication and timely information.

In 1989, the CompuServe Information Service celebrates its 10th anniversary, and much has happened during that first decade. The CompuServe Information Service grew from 1,200 computer hobbyists to half a million members from all walks of life. Our databases expanded from a handful to more than 1,300. Our membership jumped beyond the borders of the U.S. to Europe and the Far East.

Today, thousands of electronic mail messages are exchanged on CompuServe. Dozens of new member-contributed software programs fill CompuServe's data libraries each day. People meet, become friends and even marry over our phenomenally successful CB Simulator. Business leaders, elected officials and opinion makers exchange important documents. Students and educators use Compu-Serve data to move knowledge ahead.

The real excitement is yet to come. The trend toward global information exchange will bring people of varied backgrounds and cultures together to share their thoughts and feelings. Sending electronic mail to someone in Bangkok will be as common as sending it to someone in Boston is today. On-line communications will bridge social barriers as it has already bridged the geographic barrier. At last, information will become knowledge.

CompuServe is pleased to share the adventure on on-line communication with Charlie and Dave and the people at Bantam Books. I think you'll find the 4th edition of *How to Get the Most Out of CompuServe* to be a valuable addition to your library of computer books.

John E. Meier, Vice President
Market Development and Services
CompuServe Incorporated

# CHAPTER 1

# Welcome to Micropolis!

We knew that being a pioneer could be expensive. Nonetheless, six years ago when we heard about CompuServe Information Service, we couldn't resist exploring it. The idea of thousands of microcomputer owners across the country using their machines to *talk* to each other every night was downright fascinating.

If you own a personal computer (PC), you probably have heard of Compu-Serve, the largest "information utility" in the country. But what people are saying about it may sound like promises of a barker at some space-age sideshow. They will tell you that by connecting to CompuServe with a local telephone call, you can:

— Write and post letters electronically and make them available to recipients around the world in a matter of minutes.

— Chat with friends worldwide by typing messages on the keyboard and waiting a few seconds for replies to appear on the screen.

— Do last-minute Christmas shopping without leaving your living room by ordering gifts from computerized stores.

— Join nationwide electronic clubs (called "forums") devoted to everything from gardening and games to specific computer equipment.

— Instantly search massive libraries of on-line resources and references, such as newspapers, other publications, catalogs, and directories.

— Retrieve public domain and shareware programs from thousands of contributors.

— Play original, challenging games, competing in "real-time" against other players around the world.

— Read the latest news dispatches from some of the most respected wire services and newspapers, many reports available within in minutes of their writing.

— Attend electronic conferences with well-known personalities, from rock stars to the leaders of major companies.

At the risk of sounding like electronic evangelists, we are here to tell you that it is all true. In fact, it is just a fraction of what more than 460,000 computer owners have already learned, and many of them are doing these things every day, around the clock.

When we made our first stumbling steps into this electronic world, we were skeptical, leaden-eyed journalists, not easily wowed. At best we expected this "network nation" to prove an interesting diversion. At worst, it would be just so much hype, not exactly an unknown component in the microcomputer industry. Sometime later we emerged enthusiastic from our first trek into this brave new world. And hooked. Both of us had daily habits. We also were considerably poorer. This exploration business is not for fixed incomes. You hold before you the testimonials of two gentlemen who spent hundreds of hours and thousands of dollars prowling the back roads of CompuServe, looking for the "good stuff."

We found it, and along the way, we discovered better roads. Being stubborn sorts, our lessons usually came the hard way. After all, no scout worth his bunions is going to trust the first promising shortcut he comes across. What we have come up with is a good, reliable way to learn about CompuServe. A plan to look at the most territory at the minimum expense and to teach you enough about this remarkable system to enable you to carry on alone.

As tutorial books go, our method is a little unusual. Instead of simply lecturing you, we want you to accompany us on some on-line *tours*. Together, we will look at the major features and see how to make them do their stuff. With this book beside your computer as you log on, we will walk you through some areas of the system that took us months to find on our own. You even see parts of the system that have needlessly intimidated some longtime subscribers. In the end, we expect you to become comfortable with CompuServe because you will have learned how to *customize* it for your own needs. You will be able to use all kinds of time-saving (and therefore, money-saving) options. More importantly, you will be able to go directly to the features you want, by-passing time-consuming menus.

Now, a word to you folks who have been hunkering down in the back of the hall: This guide is not intended *only* for people who have never seen CompuServe before. On the contrary, we hope that some of you who come along on this expedition have tried CompuServe on your own, even if you got tangled in the undergrowth. On the other end of the spectrum, if you don't have a computer but are curious about CompuServe, we have room for you, too. All along the tours of the system, you will see what is taking place on the screen. Of course, the material will be more meaningful if you have access to a computer, but even if you don't have one yet, you won't be left out.

CompuServe is an enormous service. It can be frustrating and just plain boring if you have no idea where you are going. But this book helps in three ways:

1. The real-time tours that begin in Chapter 3 will be your fundamental road maps.

2.  A feature called "Side Roads," new with this edition, has been placed at the end of many chapters to point out areas of the system you can explore on your own.
3.  In the back of this book is a section we call "The On-line Survival Kit" that summarizes the more important features and commands. It will be of continued value to you even after you have finished the tours.

The rest of this chapter gives you a little history of CompuServe and where it is today. Then we have a few words of encouragement to you new guys.

## But First ...

We have to make certain assumptions in this book and we might as well get them out of the way early. We must assume that you know a few things about your computer. You won't need to write programs, but we do expect that you can load a program and run it. We also assume you have a modem and that your computer is capable of telecommunicating. You would be amazed at how many people think they can talk to CompuServe by simply setting a telephone next to their computer. If you are in doubt about the fundamentals of telecommunicating with your system, please check with your computer store and make sure you have all the necessary equipment to go online.

We assume you have some kind of telecommunications program, also called a *terminal program*, a *terminal emulator*, *comm package* or some such. CompuServe sells its own fine communications programs, called *The Professional Connection* (sometimes called *Vidtex* or CompuServe "executive programs"). The company also produces a program called *Navigator* for the Apple Macintosh. This software is available with CompuServe promotional material and users guides, and is excellent for exploring the system.

We also assume that your terminal program can be set to one of CompuServe's suggested configurations: either even parity, 7-bit words, 1 stop bit or no parity, 8-bit words, 1 stop bit. If you are not sure how to configure your program, refer to the manual that came with the software and check with your computer salesperson.

Some of the most frequent questions we hear about CompuServe actually deal with communications software rather than the system itself. Many new subscribers wonder if they can get printouts of what they see on the screen. Others ask if they can write letters off-line and then connect to CompuServe and deliver them at a burst. The answer to both questions is yes, *if* you have the right software. When you're shopping for a communications program, look for "smart-terminal" software such as CompuServe's own *Professional Connection* program. Tell your computer-store representative how you want to use the system, and get their advice.

Hundreds of different computers are on the market with many communications programs available for each. Because all of us are using different computers, different modems, and different software, obviously we won't be able to have much discussion here about problems you might have with any of those specific components. For those problems, we refer you to your owners' manuals and your service representatives at your local computer store. What we *can* talk about is the common ground among us, CompuServe, which treats us all the same, no matter what machines we are using.

## What Is a CompuServe?

CompuServe began in 1969 in Columbus, Ohio, when a small insurance holding company toyed with the idea of using computers to help manage its business. Not sure of what computers could do, the company hired some experts to determine the cost of setting up a data-processing operation. The report, prepared by a 25-year-old engineering graduate, showed the data-processing subsidiary would lose money the first year. "Do it," said the insurance company's president.

Engineer Jeffrey M. Wilkins, after convincing some of his associates to join him in building the fledgling company, began leasing time on local computers. For the first ten years, CompuServe primarily served corporations and governments, providing convenient computer storage for their data. However, in 1979, ten years ago this year, when the personal computer still was more rumination than reality, CompuServe saw the new PC technology's potential and opened its consumer information service, which has been operating ever since. In 1985, after 16 years at the helm during which the small data-processing subsidiary came to national prominence as a leading high-tech company, Wilkins stepped down as president of CompuServe to follow other business interests, and Charles McCall was named the new president.

Today CompuServe, Inc., still headquartered in Columbus, has broadened its scope from the days when it was recognized as a "time-sharing" company. The firm now offers services in videotex, network communication, and education. It employs more than 900 people, and its computer center houses some 40 Digital Equipment Corporation minicomputers. The firm outgrew its parent company in 1975 and "spun off" to become a public company with stock traded over-the-counter. In May 1980 CompuServe merged with H&R Block to become a subsidiary. Currently, CompuServe can be accessed with a local telephone call in more than 500 cities, meaning that about 85 percent of the U.S. population can log on directly. Hundreds more can reach the service through carrier networks like Tymnet, Telenet, DataPac, and others.

# Be an Explorer!

CompuServe is more than buildings, big computers, and telephone connections. From time to time in this book, we will refer to CompuServe as a kind of *community*. This attitude is common among those who regularly visit this on-line world. As you become familiar with the lay of the land, you will have the sensation of traveling from one place to another through your keyboard. On-line features have their own personalities, very much like neighborhoods in a metropolis. In fact, some early subscribers even dubbed this electronic environment "Micropolis."

Unlike real brick-and-mortar communities, however, Micropolis is in a constant state of change. People who work at CompuServe regularly add new features and improve old ones. Although this ever-changing landscape is something we found most appealing in our exploration of the system, it does cause something of a problem for those of us writing books. No matter how quickly we get into print, there is always a chance that some material might be outdated because someone at CompuServe has added a feature or found a better way to do something involving a changed command or simply a new look for an old service. For instance, in the summer of 1988, Compu-Serve introduced a new version of the software running its popular discussion forums. The new program, which goes a long way toward standardizing commands, prompted this new edition and is discussed at length in Chapters 10 through 14.

This edition also contains updated material throughout. As with earlier editions, we have worked closely with the people at CompuServe to make this book as up-to-date as possible. It is only fair to warn you, though, that the system may have changed slightly since your faithful scouts last passed a particular electronic landmark. Still, if you take to heart what we show you here, occasional changes shouldn't upset you. Although we have specific examples of how to navigate Compu-Serve, what we really want to show you is the system's *structure*. The structure won't change significantly, even if a few commands do. In other words, if you get the idea of how to move from one area to another, a small change in commands shouldn't throw you off the trail. And we have noticed that whenever CompuServe makes changes in command structure, it usually allows subscribers to enter either the old commands or the new ones.

So, we hope that, instead of being upset by system changes, you are challenged by them. After all, you too are a pioneer, one of the first one-third of microcomputer owners in the country to immigrate to these shores. Analysts predict that waves of newcomers are right behind you. For that reason, it is our goal not only to show specific commands for reaching popular features, like the CB Simulator, on-line games, and the forums, but to give you enough information to allow you to continue the expedition on your own.

It costs a few dollars; connect time for 300–baud is $6.25 an hour, for 1200– and 2400–baud, the cost is $12.75 an hour. In addition, a surcharge is levied if you are connecting to CompuServe through a carrier network like Tymnet or Telenet.

Let's make a pact. We promise to show you how to save time and money by using the system wisely. You will see how to navigate it quickly so that you won't burn up your time and money in places you don't want to be, or worse, wander aimlessly. In exchange, promise us you won't be a clock-watcher or corner-cutter. We designed our on-line tours to show you key sections of the system. About a half-dozen such field trips are scheduled, each lasting about an hour. At current 300-baud rates, it comes to about $36 worth of time (not counting surcharges for Tymnet or Telenet). We humbly suggest that is less than 5 percent of the costs you would accumulate if you tried to find these areas on your own without a map.

Also, please resist the temptation to skip ahead in the book. Instead, read the chapters in sequence. The tour format we use makes this a tutorial book, not an encyclopedic reference guide. As we go along, new material is introduced to match your experience on-line so far. A chapter often covers more than one feature. It may show you novice features of one service, provide intermediate information about a feature you saw in an earlier chapter and then give you the rundown on advanced commands for still another service. Rather than risk overwhelming you from the outset with scores of commands — from beginner's to advanced — the tours aim to introduce the features' options over a period of time, showing you how to use them as you need them. For instance, CompuServe's electronic mail system, EasyPlex, is introduced in Chapter 3, then elaborated upon in Chapters 5, 9, and 19; each illustrating different aspects of EasyPlex, depending on the level of experience.

Consider the time we spend together in the book an investment. Spend it now and you get it back later in savings.

# CHAPTER 2

## The Bill of Fare at Chez CompuServe

Here is a riddle for you: How is CompuServe like a restaurant?

If your answer is that restaurants serve bites of food and CompuServe serves bytes of information, then you are just too darn clever for us. Actually, the answer we are looking for is that restaurants and CompuServe are both "menu driven." This chapter is about menus, what they mean in computer parlance and how they fit into the scheme of things on CompuServe. If you have had any experience at all with computers, you know about menus. Most modern software uses them to give you a quick overview of the program's structure, telling you at a glance what options are open to you. CompuServe uses them in that way, too.

To see that, let's first talk about menus at a restaurant and how they do more than simply tell you what is available from the kitchen. They also can guide you through the ordering process. Let's say you are on your first trip to a French restaurant and the menu lists some exotic-sounding dish like "Escargot a la Francaise avec pomme de terre a la Normandy." You want to try it, so when the waiter returns, you have three options:

1. Try to say the name as the French do (and hope your pronunciation is better than ours).
2. Translate it into English — "I'll take the Normandy-style snails and potatoes" — and wonder at how much more tempting it sounds in the original language.
3. Look at the little number to the left of the description and whisper discreetly, "I'll take number 3."

The last option has a lot of appeal because it allows you to take advantage of a system already in use in the restaurant. Maybe the chef doesn't understand English,

7

but he knows the number 3 and heads for the pot of snails. When the cashier sees 3 on the slip of paper handed over by the waiter, he knows to ring up $29.95. In other words, those numbers are integrated into the restaurant's delivery system.

CompuServe uses menus — lots and lots of menus — in a similar way. Visiting CompuServe for the first time is a little like your debut in a French restaurant, in that you may be unsure of what or even how to order. But, in the same way, the options are set out in a logical arrangement that the system is programmed to understand.

When you log on, one of the first things you see is a copyright notice like this:

```
CompuServe Information Service
     23:40 EST Wednesday 11-Jan-89


        Copyright (C) 1989
      CompuServe Incorporated
        All Rights Reserved
```

A number menu like this will follow:

```
CompuServe                                    TOP

  1 Subscriber Assistance
  2 Find a Topic
  3 Communications/Bulletin Bds.
  4 News/Weather/Sports
  5 Travel
  6 The Electronic MALL/Shopping
  7 Money Matters/Markets
  8 Entertainment/Games
  9 Home/Health/Education
 10 Reference
 11 Computers/Technology
 12 Business/Other Interests

Enter choice number!
```

All along the path on CompuServe, your options are outlined on the screen in numbered menu form. You don't have to be able to speak the computer's language to tell the system what to do or where to go. You need only to type a number after the exclamation point (which is called a *prompt*) and then press the ENTER or RETURN key. (Incidentally, throughout this book, we use the words ENTER and RETURN interchangeably to mean the *carriage return* or end-of-line key on your keyboard.)

When you see the menu on the screen, think of a waiter standing at your table with pad in hand, patiently waiting for instruction. ("I'll take number 3.") The emphasis is on *patiently*. Don't feel as if the system is tapping its foot and thinking, "Hurry up, dummy. I've got to wait on other tables!" It is waiting for your instructions and will wait, usually up to 15 minutes, between the commands you enter. (After 15 minutes' of silence from your end, it is liable to get edgy and disconnect you from the system. But even if you are disconnected, you need only to call back and all is forgiven.)

Once you enter the number corresponding to your choice, the system starts on the path to your selection, which often leads to another menu. Menu-driven CompuServe allow you to "fine-tune" your request, homing in on what you want by stepping through a series of menus. You can get to any of the services on the system simply by going from the main menu to a submenu to a sub-submenu, and so forth, typing one number after another and pressing the RETURN key after each selection. When you run out of menus, you have arrived.

Sounds complicated? Not really. You see only one menu at a time, and the latest always is related to the previous one, like branches on a tree. The arrangement has been called exactly that, *a tree structure*, each menu branching out into menus of related features.

To see how it works, look again at that top menu. One of the menu items is called Home/Health/Education. These services are many — hundreds, in fact — so if you enter the number for Home/Health/Education, you are taken to another menu that lists only the main home-related services available:

```
+-----------------------------------------------------------------+
|                                                                 |
|   CompuServe                                        HOME         |
|                                                                 |
|   HOME/HEALTH/FAMILY                                            |
|                                                                 |
|    1 Food/Wine                                                  |
|    2 Personal Finance/Banking                                  |
|    3 Health/Fitness                                            |
|    4 The Electronic MALL/Shopping                              |
|    5 Special Interest Forums                                   |
|    6 Hobbies                                                    |
|    7 Arts/Music/Literature                                     |
|    8 Reference Material                                         |
|    9 Automotive Information                                    |
|   10 Education                                                  |
|                                                                 |
|   Enter choice !                                               |
|                                                                 |
+-----------------------------------------------------------------+
```

There are branches from this "Home" menu. If you choose number 6, Hobbies, you receive a menu like this:

```
CompuServe                          HOBBIES

HOBBIES

 1 Photography Forum
 2 Aquaria/Fish Forum
 3 Outdoor Forum
 4 ModelNet Forum
 5 HamNet Forum
 6 Sailing Forum
 7 Comic Book/Animation Forum
 8 Astronomy/Space
 9 Food/Wine Forums
10 Scuba Forum
11 Genealogy Forum

Enter choice !
```

And so it goes. Menus are helpful for new subscribers. Of course, as you continue to use CompuServe, you eventually may consider them tiresome and time-consuming and long for a faster way to get around the system. There *are* faster ways, and we shall show you some great shortcuts and express lanes. (In a later chapter, we'll even show you how to create your own personal menu to list your own favorite features for easy access right from the start of the system.) For now, however, let's use the menus as the guide wires they were designed to be.

Questions so far?

*Isn't it easy to get lost in this labyrinth of menus?*

No, not if you take time in your early experience. Here are several tips about menus:

— Read each menu before entering your selection. If there are nine items on the menu and you have read down to number 3 and it looks interesting, it is tempting to enter 3 and be done with it. But don't enter a 3 until you have read all nine items. The more familiar you become with the menus, the faster you learn what the system has to offer.

— Also read the prompts at the bottoms of menus. Not all prompts say simply "Enter choice." Others says "Enter choice or <CR> (that is, *carriage return*) for more," meaning there are additional features available in a particular category. Often a prompt is written in such a way to give you a tip to elaborate on the commands, such as, "Enter choice or H for Help."

— And here is an important point. As you will see when we begin touring in the next chapter, help is always at hand. In most places on CompuServe, you are only one command away from either a series of statements or options that give you help and background information to explain the alternatives open to you. Furthermore, simply entering a "blank line" at most prompts (that is, pressing the RETURN key once) returns you to a menu. (Occasionally you may have to enter an "M" or another command, and often that is specified in the wording of the prompt as well.)

## So This Is Help??

Now, about the help CompuServe provides. Occasionally in your travels, you won't arrive at a menu when you want one. Instead, you receive a few lines offering you assistance. Think of these "help lines" as the waiter telling you what number 3 really is, in English no less.

Frankly, some help files on-line are better than others because CompuServe still is evolving. Believe us, the on-line instructions these days are light years beyond the primitive ones offered when we were new users. But even some folks at CompuServe admit that today's on-line help system still is imperfect. Part of the reason is the difficulty in finding a common ground for discussion between the system and the brand new subscribers. (To sympathize with the task, sit down sometime and try to describe the back of your hand in a way that would make sense to a space creature who not only has never seen the back of your hand but has never seen a hand.) Beyond that, the people in charge of composing the on-line help files are fighting a constant battle of on-line information versus the time it takes to read it. Time is money on CompuServe. It is a lot less expensive for you to read extensive instructions from a printed page than to read them on-line.

So, think of the on-line help files as short reminders of available options, not as lengthy training manuals.

*But what do you do when help lines don't help?*

One of the best things to do is to get back to a menu somewhere and take another stab at coming in the front door, as it were. Sometimes simply going out and coming in again gives you a new perspective on where you are and what you are doing. If you are still lost, you can get help by dialing CompuServe's toll-free customer-service number (800) 848-8990 outside of Ohio; (614) 457-8650 for Ohio residents). If that still doesn't satisfy your desire to tell someone you are less than impressed with the on-line help, we shall explain later how you can use a feature called Feedback to address an electronic letter to the system that might say, "Dear Compu-Serve: You call THAT help?"

Seriously, CompuServe officials want your comments. After all, it isn't to their advantage to have confused customers. CompuServe folks learned a long time ago that bewildered users don't return to the system. The more satisfied you are, the more likely you are to be a consistent customer. That is why the Columbus crew is constantly reviewing the service and changing it when shortcomings are identified.

That is why you must be prepared for changes in the system, sometimes from one day to the next. Usually these changes are announced appropriately in the section of the system devoted to new things on CompuServe. Sometimes the changes won't be obvious and sometimes they are quite apparent. All of this is part of the excitement of this new way to communicate and retrieve information. There is no chance to blow the whistle and call everything to a halt for a week or two while computer wizards peek, poke, rewire, and grumble their way toward a better system. In fact, they are probably working on it as you are using it, like a mechanic standing on the motor of your automobile and fine-tuning it as you tool cross-country. What excitement! And what more could you ask from this new form of communication?

## Preparing for the First Tour

The next chapter is built around our first on-line tour of CompuServe. In preparation for that, you might want to take a moment now to look at the On-line Survival Kit in back of this book. Please pay particular attention to section VI of the kit, which contains CompuServe's operating rules and regulations. During the on-line sign-up at the beginning of Chapter 3, the system will quiz you about these rules: We will have saved you time if you look over them before we begin the tour.

# CHAPTER 3

# One Small Step (Our First Tour)

With the fundamentals out of the way, it is time for our first on-line tour. This electronic outing, which should take about an hour, will give you an idea of the structure of CompuServe and also show you how subsequent tours in this book are conducted. During this excursion, we shall see an overview of the system, catch up on a little news, write a letter, and even play an on-line game.

Before you log on, we need to take care of a few preliminaries. Start by deciding where to place this book so you can see it easily while keeping your hands free for the keyboard. You need to be able to read the pages and see the screen easily.

We assume you have purchased a CompuServe starter kit (sometimes called an *IntroPak*). All kits include an important envelope with the printed words "Subscription Information." The envelope contains an agreement number, a serial number, terms and conditions of the service, and usually a note that says the package provides a few dollars worth of free time to explore the system. You might take a moment now to look over the terms and conditions of subscribing to CompuServe.

Also contained in the starter kit envelope are:

— A sign-up user ID number that may look something like "177000,624."
— Your sign-up password, two words separated by a symbol (such as "BOAT/TOUCH").

During the on-line sign-up on this first tour, the system automatically issues a new, permanent user identification number and password, which replaces those issued in your starter kit.

Your starter kit also may include a list of phone numbers with which you can make a *local call* to CompuServe from most major cities in the United States. Phone links to the system come in three types; (1) directly through a CompuServe "node," (2) by way of a "packet network" such as Tymnet, Telenet, or Canada's DataPak, or (3) by a "local access transport area" (LATA) network sometimes offered by a regional phone company. Of the three ways, the CompuServe node is best, because it is a direct connection between your town and CompuServe's computers in Columbus, Ohio. If the list includes a CompuServe node for your area, use it. It saves you money, because it is like having an "800" number directly from your city to CompuServe. The other links — data transmission networks Tymnet and Telenet (and in Canada, DataPac) and LATA networks from a local phone company — connect computers to various information services and databases. In addition to CompuServe, you can use them to link up with services like The Source and Dow Jones News/Retrieval. The downside is that they are sometimes a little sluggish, compared with CompuServe's own lines, and they levy a surcharge — usually about $2 an hour — to be added to your CompuServe monthly bill.

If your information packet does *not* include a phone number for logging from your city, check with the store that sold you the startup kit or call CompuServe's customer service department toll-free at (800) 848-8990; in Ohio, call (614) 457-8650. The hours (in Eastern Time) are 8:00 a.m. to midnight, Monday through Friday, 2:00 p.m. to midnight on Saturdays and Sundays, and noon to midnight on holidays.

## A Little Research on Control

Continuing our advance work, you now need to make sure you have found the *control* key on your computer keyboard. On this first tour, we use that key with the system's "control codes" for stopping and starting the display of text. On your keyboard, the word on the control key may be abbreviated ("CTRL" or "CTR" or the like) or it may be a symbol rather than a word. On the Apple Macintosh, for instance, the control key has a symbol that looks like a square with four looped corners. A few systems have no key labeled specifically as "Control," though other key sequences can be substituted. If you can't find the control key on your keyboard, check the manual that came with your computer.

## An Aside to You Old Pros

For the next few pages, we shall assume the reader has never before connected to CompuServe, so we plan to walk slowly and deliberately through the log-on and sign-up procedures. However, if you already have peeked into CompuServe with your current user ID number, you have gone through the following little initiation rite. For that reason, you might want to just skip the next several pages, log on as you already have learned and rejoin us at the section entitled "From the Top."

# A Little Bookkeeping

For the rest of the log-on preliminaries, please get a piece of paper and a pencil. There is a little information we should collect to prepare for questions the system will ask on your initial visit.

The first, alas, concerns money. Decide how you want your monthly Compu-Serve charges to be billed. Unless you are a business, you have two choices: charge the expenses to your credit card (MasterCard, VISA, or American Express) or pay through a Checkfree method. Checkfree is a computer network that links financial institutions for transfer of funds. It is the same method the federal government uses for direct Social Security payments. If you have a checking account in a bank anywhere in the United States (not a savings institution), you may choose the Checkfree method. Then, on the same day each month (the system will tell you when), Check-free asks the bank to pay CompuServe from your checking account. The bank pays the bill and itemizes the amount on your next statement. CompuServe levies a $5 monthly minimum charge for Checkfree. All connect time and other charges count toward the $5 minimum.

If you plan to charge your connect time bill to MasterCard, VISA, or American Express, note the card number and expiration date on your paper, as well as the name of the bank that issued it. If you decide on the Checkfree method, you will be asked a few more questions, so jot down the following information, which can be found on one of your checks:

— The routing transit number, a nine-digit number usually located in the lower left corner of your check. It often is contained within colons or other symbols. (You won't be entering the symbols on-line, however.)

— Your checking account number, which usually follows the routing number. Don't worry about any spaces in your checking account number. Also, if the symbol "===" appears in the number, substitute a single dash. When providing your account number on-line, don't include the check number, which sometimes comes before or after the checking account number.

— The number of the next check in your checkbook, generally found in the upper right-hand or left-hand corner of your printed checks or before or after your checking account number.

— The bank's name and address. (Sometimes CompuServe doesn't need to ask you for this; it has on file addresses of major banks. But if it doesn't have your bank recorded, the system may ask you to provide the address during the on-line signup, so it is a good idea to have it handy before we log on.)

**Note on Business Accounts:**    If you want to become a business account sub-scriber, you must obtain an application and agreement form from CompuServe's customer service ordering department, Box L-477, Columbus, Ohio 43220, or through the on-line Feedback service after subscribing. You can convert to a business account from MasterCard, VISA, American Express, or Checkfree billing. A one-time $44.95 charge is levied for setting an initial business account user ID number and $19.95 is charged for each additional user ID number. If you want to go on-line right now, you can use a credit card or the Checkfree method and later convert it to a business account for a $10 charge.

Also on your scratch paper, you need to note two things about your computer's screen, its *width* and its *depth*. How many characters does your screen display on one line? And how many lines of text does it display at one time?

Finally, assuming you have determined what local to use to connect with the system — CompuServe's own network, a packet network like Tymnet, Telenet, or DataPac, or a LATA offered by your local phone company — turn to our On-line Survival Kit in the back of the book and locate the first section, called "Making the Connection." In that section, you will find a log-on procedure for each type of connection. Please put a bookmark on the appropriate page; we shall use that information in just a moment.

## Fire Up Your Machine

Okay, let's get started. Turn on your computer and run your communications program. While it is loading, let's talk about three things that should go on when your computer says, "Hello, Columbus!"

First, your program should be communicating in *full duplex*, which means that after you are connected to CompuServe, the letters and numbers you type on your keyboard are transmitted to Columbus and echo (or "bounce back") to you and are displayed on your screen. When you are on-line, what you see on the screen is *not* coming directly from your keyboard but is rather an echo of what the system "thinks" you have typed. The value of this full-duplex arrangement (common on most dialup services these days) is that: Sometimes while on-line, especially on very busy evenings, you may type a command that appears on the screen as usual but ... ut-oh, nothing seems to happen. It is as if the system has just ignored you. But it hasn't. The problem is that when many people are on-line at the same time, the system can become sluggish, and several seconds might pass before the system registers your command and reacts to it. However, as long as the system has echoed what you typed, you know that it has taken notice of your command and will get around to it as soon as it can. The echo is then a report on how you are being received on the other end. Therefore, if what you see on the screen is *not* what you typed — is, instead, garbled characters — then you know immediately you have a problem, usually static on the phone line. Break the connection and call again, and you probably will get a better line. If the condition persists, consult the On-line Survival Kit's "Trouble Shooting" section to see if we have addressed your problem. If not, call the customer-service representatives of CompuServe — toll free to (800) 848-8990; in Ohio (614) 457-8650 — because that's why they are there.

Second, your terminal software should be set to 7-bit ASCII, even parity. The stop bit should be set at 1. (As an alternate setting, CompuServe also recognizes 8-bit words, 1 stop bit, no parity. However, we *don't* recommend that setting for this first logon because it generally results in some garbled characters, which are likely to confuse you.) If you are not familiar with these terms, check the documentation for your terminal software. If that doesn't help, call the dealer who sold you the program and ask about setting terminal parameters. You might want to read this parameter to the technician.

Third, if you have a modem that sends and transmits at speeds faster than 300 baud, we suggest you use 300 baud until you become familiar with the system, especially during these first few tours. The faster 1200 baud and 2400 baud are *premium* services, meaning the hourly connect charge by CompuServe is higher when you use them. After you are familiar with the system, these higher baud rates will save you money, because you can travel faster, but if you try to use them while still learning the system, you will just wind up spending more money while getting lost.

After your terminal program has loaded, you need to check the three settings we just discussed and then call the connection number for your area, either CompuServe or an alternative network. If you use an auto-dial modem, type in the number you want called. A note to those with manual modems: wait until you hear the high-pitched modem tone on the other end of the phone line, then switch your modem to the "originate" mode.

## All Together Now

Now consult the "Making Connections" section of the On-line Survival Kit where you placed the bookmark and log on, following the procedure outlined for either CompuServe, Tymnet, Telenet, DataPac or LATA. After the connection is made, you should see the following on your screen:

```
┌───────────────────────────────────────────────┐
│                                                │
│   User ID:                                     │
│                                                │
└───────────────────────────────────────────────┘
```

At this prompt type in the *sign-up user ID number* exactly as it appears in your sign-up information envelope — comma and all — and press RETURN. The screen will show the following:

```
User ID: 177000,624 <RETURN>
```

Note that there is *no space* between the comma and the numbers.

At the next prompt, you are asked to enter your password:

```
Password:
```

You should enter the two words that make up the *sign-up password*. Enter them just as they appear in the starter kit, complete with the character or space that separates them:

```
BOAT/TOUCH <RETURN>
```

Unlike the user ID number, the letters of the password do not appear on the screen as you type them. That is for your protection; if someone were looking over your shoulder right now, they would be unable to see and memorize your all-important secret password.

**Note:**   At this point, if you get a message saying something about an "invalid entry," it is likely the password was entered incorrectly. Try again when prompted. If you get another "invalid entry," recheck the user number you entered above. Perhaps *it* was entered incorrectly. If so, enter a CONTROL-C by pressing the control and "c" keys together; you get another "User ID:" prompt and you can start again.

After the user ID number and password are accepted, you are asked for two more pieces of information from your starter kit: your *agreement number* and *serial number*. When prompted type them in exactly as they appear in the sign-up information envelope and press RETURN. Finally, the door opens for you. When you are officially on-line, you see a welcome message and then a note about the amount of your usage credit with this the starter kit.

Throughout the sign-up procedure and elsewhere in the system, you will see prompts such as:

```
Press <CR> for more !
```

One Small Step (Our First Tour)   19

The screen stops scrolling until you press the return key to see the next screen (or *page*). Don't press RETURN until you have read all the text. The information you see in this sign-up procedure is important. (In fact, if your system can handle it, it is a good idea to turn on your printer and print out everything coming across your screen during this initial stage.) After a few pages of introduction, the system will request your billing address, with a menu like this:

```
┌───────────────────────────────────────────────────┐
│                                                     │
│  Will Your Billing/Mailing                          │
│  Address be from                                    │
│                                                     │
│  1 United States                                    │
│  2 Canada                                           │
│  3 Japan                                            │
│  4 Other                                            │
│  5 Exit Subscription Process                        │
│                                                     │
│  Enter choice:                                      │
│                                                     │
└───────────────────────────────────────────────────┘
```

Notice that the menu includes an option to exit the subscription process (option 5). This option appears on subsequent menus as well, so you can abort the sign-up process at any point. If there is some reason you can't finish the sign-up now, use the exit option, then log on again later and start over again.

At the colon prompt, enter the number of your mailing address chosen and press RETURN. After that, you are shown this menu from which you are to select a billing method:

```
┌───────────────────────────────────────────────────┐
│                                                     │
│  Please Select the Desired                          │
│  Billing Method                                     │
│                                                     │
│  1 Visa                                             │
│  2 MasterCard                                       │
│  3 American Express                                 │
│  4 Checkfree                                        │
│  5 Explanation of Charge Card                       │
│  6 Explanation of Checkfree                         │
│  7 Exit Subscription Process                        │
│                                                     │
│  Enter Choice:                                      │
│                                                     │
└───────────────────────────────────────────────────┘
```

Based on our earlier discussion make your selection, CompuServe will advise you:

```
Be sure to read and understand
our Service Agreement Terms and
billing options.  The current
Service Agreement terms may be
different from the ones printed
in your subscription material.
You will be asked to agree to
our Service Terms in a moment.

Press <CR> for more !
```

When you press RETURN here, you are given the options to continue the subscription sign-up, read the service terms on-line, choose a different billing method, or exit:

```
Do You Wish to

1 Review Service Agreement
  Terms
2 Review Operating Rules
3 Proceed With Subscription
4 Select a Different Billing
  Option
5 Exit the Subscription Process

Enter Choice:
```

If you already have read the printed version of the terms, you can proceed with the subscription by choosing option 3, and entering AGREE asked at the next prompt.

Once the agreements have been made, you are confronted with a question that sometimes confuses new arrivals. It is:

```
┌─────────────────────────────────────────────────────────┐
│                                                         │
│   Do You Wish to                                        │
│                                                         │
│   1 Select the Executive Option                         │
│   2 See a Description of the                            │
│     Executive Option                                    │
│   3 Proceed with the Standard                           │
│     CompuServe Subscription                             │
│   4 Exit Subscription Process                           │
│                                                         │
│   Enter choice:                                         │
│                                                         │
└─────────────────────────────────────────────────────────┘
```

**Here Is the Background:**   The Executive Option offers additional services, particularly business-oriented features, that you may find useful in time. They are "value-added" — that is, extra-cost — services that you will read about in Chapters 16 and 20. Frankly, we doubt a new subscriber, who is unfamiliar with CompuServe as a whole, is ready for the additional features of the Executive Option. Therefore, despite the fact you get a break on the fees by signing up for the option when you first log on ($5 the last time we looked), we suggest you pass up the opportunity until you become familiar with CompuServe at-large. You can always sign up later, after you have looked over our discussions of what the Executive Option offers. To follow that strategy, just enter 3 at the colon prompt.

CompuServe now gets down to collecting some basic billing information, last name, first name, middle initial, address, zip code, phone numbers, Social Security number, and so forth. (Incidentally, you may notice you are prompted for your zip code but *not* for your city's name; this "smart computer" can figure out the city and state once you have supplied the zip code information.)

After you have filled in the blanks, the system gives you a chance to review the information. If any changes are necessary, just enter the number of the incorrect item and, when prompted, enter the new information. When everything is correct, enter OK at the colon prompt.

Next we come to the data for the credit card or the Checkfree banking method. In entering the information, just refer to notes you jotted before we logged on. After the data has been entered and verified, the system has three more questions for you:

1. Would you like to be on the mailing list for *Online Today*, CompuServe's monthly magazine? If you don't already receive it, by all means, answer

yes. After all, it is free and you can cancel anytime after receiving the first issue.

2. Would you like your name, city, and state included in CompuServe's on-line Subscriber Directory? That is up to you, of course, but we suggest you give the system the go-ahead on this item as well. The directory is a kind of electronic phone book that makes it easier for on-line friends to write you electronic mail. In a few minutes we shall stop by the area where this directory is located. If, in the future, you decide you want your name removed from the directory, CompuServe will comply.

3. What kind of computer equipment are you using? CompuServe displays a menu of computer types and asks you to select the number that describes your machine. CompuServe later uses this information to help format the text it sends to your screen in various features.

CompuServe now generates two very important pieces of information: your new *permanent user ID* (usually a seven- to nine-digit number beginning with a "7" such as 71735,1025 or 70475,1165) and another *temporary password* (again, two un-related word connected by a symbol). As we pointed out before you logged on, the ID number and password provided in the starter kit were intended to be replaced at this point by the system; they are no longer needed. Write down the *new* ID and password on two separate sheets of paper (and be sure to obliterate this information from your printout if you have turned on your printer). No one else should ever have this information. If anyone else obtains your account number and password, they have the keys to your on-line account and can log on under your name. Before you know it, the intruder can perhaps run up a horrendous bill on your account.

After the system produces your new permanent ID and temporary password, it gives you a little test to make sure you know them, prompting:

```
Please verify that you have
copied the User ID number and
password down correctly by
entering them at the following
prompts.

User ID Number:

Password:
```

A new permanent password will be sent to you in the mail once your sign-up information has been verified and processed. When it is sent, you will be told the date when the temporary password is discontinued and your new password becomes effective.

**Notes on Two Other Points:**

1. Until that second, permanent password becomes effective, a few services on CompuServe will not be open to you. Generally, you cannot contribute material on-line, such as public messages, until the permanent password is implemented. During our tours, we shall point out those times when a permanent password is needed to use a particular feature.
2. Once the permanent password has been mailed to you, you probably will receive an electronic message from CompuServe that officially welcomes you to the neighborhood. We will have more on that later.

Well, the sign-up procedure has taken several minutes, but here's some good news: none of this time is subtracted from your usage credit; it has been free time on the system.

In a screen or two, you will see another prompt for your user ID and password. Enter the new set, the ones just issued to you, and you will be greeted by:

```
CompuServe Information Service
  15:15 EDT Thursday 12-Jan-89

     Copyright (C) 1989
    CompuServe Incorporated
     All Rights Reserved

Thank you for subscribing to
CompuServe.

Since this is the first time
you have logged on using your
permanent User ID, we need to
exchange some information which
will help you get the most out
of your subscription.
```

Read the few introductory pages that follow. After that, CompuServe will ask about *terminal emulation*, with a menu such as:

```
┌─────────────────────────────────────────────────────────┐
│                                                           │
│   Terminal emulations are                                 │
│                                                           │
│   1 ANSI (VT-100)                                         │
│   2 CompuServe VIDTEX                                      │
│   3 CompuServe Professional                               │
│     Connection                                            │
│   4 CRT                                                    │
│   5 VT-52                                                  │
│   6 Other (general purpose)                               │
│   7 Help/Descriptions                                     │
│                                                           │
│   Enter choice:                                           │
│                                                           │
└─────────────────────────────────────────────────────────┘
```

The emulation you are using depends on your terminal software. A number of major communications programs — *Smartcom*, *Crosstalk*, *Symphony*, and *Jazz* — all have ANSI (VT100) terminal emulation available. *PCTalk* uses CRT emulation. There are also emulations for CompuServe's *VIDTEX* and *The Professional Connection* programs. (Incidentally, if you are using *VIDTEX* or *The Professional Connection*, there is a good chance that CompuServe will have sensed that and automatically set the terminal emulation for you.) Now, don't let this menu unsettle you if you are unfamiliar these terms. Just choose option 6, the general purpose "Other," for now. In a later chapter you will see how to change this setting.

At last we come to those questions we anticipated regarding screen width and depth. The system asks if you need help in determining this information. Probably not, since our previsit rundown tipped you off about this one. All you need do is to enter the number of characters per line for your terminal when prompted and then, at the next prompt, the number of lines for your screen.

A few screens follow with information about CompuServe's prompts and commands. You may notice that the system now is giving you a full screen of information — no more and no less — before it presents its "Press <CR>:" prompt. Because you have told the system how wide and deep your screen is, CompuServe has adjusted the text accordingly.

As you read, don't try to memorize all the commands, prompts, and control codes you see whizzing by. Notice that, as the instructions say, at certain times during the presentation you can play with some of the commands. If you're printing the information to your printer, that's fine. If not, it is no problem, because we plan to tell you about the features in upcoming chapters. Just consider this on-line introduction as an opportunity to see how versatile the system really is.

Finally, you will be asked if you want to take a "mini–tour" of the system or go directly to the CompuServe Information Service. Let's go directly to the service. You can take the tour any time by logging on and entering GO TOURS at any prompt on the system.

Now you are likely to see CompuServe's main menu. Congratulations! You have arrived.

## From the Top

Okay, everyone should be at the menu labeled "TOP," which looks like this:

```
CompuServe                                TOP

   1 Subscriber Assistance
   2 Find a Topic
   3 Communications/Bulletin Bds.
   4 News/Weather/Sports
   5 Travel
   6 The Electronic MALL/Shopping
   7 Money Matters/Markets
   8 Entertainment/Games
   9 Home/Health/Education
  10 Reference
  11 Computers/Technology
  12 Business/Other Interests

  Enter choice number !
```

If this menu looks familiar, it is because we used it in the previous chapter as an example of a typical CompuServe menu. The exclamation point at the bottom of the menu is the prompt at which the number or command will appear when you enter it. (Incidentally, when a letter or a series of letters is to be entered, it makes no difference if they are capitalized or lowercase; the system understands both.) Depending on your system and terminal software, the exclamation point prompt may be at a different location on your screen, such as two or three lines up from the bottom of the screen to the right of the menu. Similarly, the word TOP may appear in a slightly different position on the screen. Regardless of slight differences in format, all the elements of the menu in the example should appear on your screen. You might want to take a moment now to locate them.

TOP is the menu from which all CompuServe services spring. You can follow it to any feature on the system, because it is the trunk of the menu tree we described in Chapter 2. All features are listed on a submenu of this main menu or sometimes on several submenus. The topics on TOP represent the dozen main branches of the system. We shall travel on several of these branches on this tour. Here is a brief overview of them:

*Subscriber Assistance* leads to an assortment of articles and programs on billing, changing your password, and so on. Also included is a particularly useful area called "What's New," a menu of brief articles about new developments on the system; a feature that is updated weekly.

*Find a Topic* helps you find features on the system, seeking them by specific subjects.

*Communications/Bulletin Boards* contains an electronic mail service, a real-time CB Simulator, a national bulletin board, and more, such as a Feedback feature that lets you leave messages for the customer service department.

*News/Weather/Sports* provides reports from wire services, major newspapers, and newsletters from various sources.

*Travel and Leisure* contains airline schedules and reservations, and related travel services.

*The Electronic Mall* is CompuServe's exclusive on-line shopping center, and the area also has other electronic shopping features.

*Money Matters/Markets* is the financial area of the service, featuring stock market quotes and information, as well as banking and brokerage services and so on.

*Entertainment/Games* is the corner for on-line games and games-related information. Some allow you to play against the computer, others let you match wits with other subscribers.

*Home/Health/Education* offers a wide range of services, from cooking and health topics to personal finance and home banking.

*Reference/Education* leads to electronic reference materials such as an electronic encyclopedias and government publications as well as services for teachers, parents, and students.

*Computers/Technology* offers information about, and programs for, specific kinds of computers and software.

*Business/Other Interests* is for various corporate executives and other professions and trades, such as law, health, aviation, engineering, data processing, and others.

## Two Ways to Get Where We Are Going

We can reach the submenus for these features by simply entering the appropriate number at the prompt. For instance, we mentioned that in the Subscriber Assistance part of the system there is a service called "What's New," which details new developments on CompuServe. Let's find it. At the TOP menu currently on your screen, enter 1 (to select the Subscriber Assistance option) and the system displays:

```
r--------------------------------------------------------------,
|                                                              |
|  CompuServe                                         HELP     |
|                                                              |
|   1 Tour/Find a Topic                                        |
|   2 Online Today                                             |
|   3 Command Summary/How to Use                               |
|   4 What's New                                               |
|   5 Telephone Access Numbers                                 |
|   6 Ask Customer Service                                     |
|   7 Change Your User Profile                                 |
|   8 Billing Information                                      |
|   9 Order From CompuServe                                    |
|  10 Rules of Operation/Copyright                             |
|  11 Subscriber Directory                                     |
|                                                              |
|  Enter choice !                                              |
|                                                              |
L--------------------------------------------------------------J
```

Looking over this new menu, we see that What's New is option 4, so enter 4 at the "!" prompt, and the system displays a menu like this:

```
r--------------------------------------------------------------,
|                                                              |
|  What's New This Week                              NEW-1     |
|                                                              |
|   1 Electronic Mall News                                     |
|   2 Subscriber Directory Coming                              |
|   3 IQuest Offers Free Searches                              |
|   4 Investors' Forum Has Contest                             |
|   5 Chess Game Now Available                                 |
|   6 Terrain Added to ATC Game                                |
|   7 Nodes in NJ, CA, NV, TX, CT                              |
|   8 Online Today                                             |
|   9 CompuServe Community News                                |
|  10 Uploads: New Forum Files                                 |
|                                                              |
|  Enter choice !                                              |
|                                                              |
L--------------------------------------------------------------J
```

Stop a minute and notice that each page we have looked at has had a different word in the upper right-hand corner. The current page has "NEW-1." The previous page was "HELP," and the first page was "TOP." These page addresses often are called *quick reference words*, and we shall use one of them in a moment. But first, at this point you have several options. If any of these articles on the NEW-1 page look interesting, you could enter its number at the prompt and see the contents. Here is a new command, if you want to return to the TOP of the system, you could enter T. Try that. Enter T (for TOP) at the "!" prompt, and the system returns you to:

```
CompuServe                                      TOP

    1 Subscriber Assistance
    2 Find a Topic
    3 Communications/Bulletin Bds.
    4 News/Weather/Sports
    5 Travel
    6 The Electronic MALL/Shopping
    7 Money Matters/Markets
    8 Entertainment/Games
    9 Home/Health/Education
   10 Reference
   11 Computers/Technology
   12 Business/Other Interests

  Enter choice number !
```

That is one way to get around CompuServe, enter a numbered selection from the current menu and then more numbered selections from subsequent menus. But there also are other, more efficient ways of getting around. The key to fast travel is the "GO" command. If you enter GO (or simply G) followed by the identifying word the system understands as one of its services, you jump several layers of menus and land at the feature you have specified. The fast way to get to the "What's New" feature we just saw is to enter the GO command followed by its page address. Try that. Enter:

```
r--------------------------------------------------,
|                                                  |
|   G NEW-1 <RETURN>                                |
|                                                  |
L--------------------------------------------------J
```

Suddenly, jumping across several menus, you come back to:

```
r--------------------------------------------------,
|                                                  |
|   What's New This Week                 NEW-1     |
|                                                  |
|    1 Electronic Mall News                        |
|    2 Subscriber Directory Coming                 |
|    3 IQuest Offers Free Searches                 |
|    4 Investors' Forum Has Contest                |
|    5 Chess Game Now Available                    |
|    6 Terrain Added to ATC Game                   |
|    7 Nodes in NJ, CA, NV, TX, CT                 |
|    8 Online Today                                |
|    9 CompuServe Community News                   |
|   10 Uploads: New Forum Files                    |
|                                                  |
|   Enter choice !                                 |
|                                                  |
L--------------------------------------------------J
```

Once again, if you were to choose one of the numbered options, you would see a brief article about the topic described.

**Time Out for More about What's New:**   First, of course, you aren't seeing exactly the same menu that we are displaying in our example. What's New is revised weekly by CompuServe; what's on your screen is the latest version. Second, as a subscriber, you will be seeing What's New regularly. The feature is so important for keeping users up to date on new services that it is *automatically* displayed at logon twice a week. In other words, although you can visit it directly, as we have just done, What's New also will come looking for you from time to time.

After this tour, we suggest you come back for another look at What's New so that you can read some of the current articles. For now, let's continue exploring the menu and command structures. Enter the T command to get back to TOP:

```
┌─────────────────────────────────────────────────────┐
│                                                       │
│   CompuServe                              TOP         │
│                                                       │
│    1 Subscriber Assistance                            │
│    2 Find a Topic                                     │
│    3 Communications/Bulletin Bds.                     │
│    4 News/Weather/Sports                              │
│    5 Travel                                           │
│    6 The Electronic MALL/Shopping                     │
│    7 Money Matters/Markets                            │
│    8 Entertainment/Games                              │
│    9 Home/Health/Education                            │
│   10 Reference                                        │
│   11 Computers/Technology                             │
│   12 Business/Other Interests                         │
│                                                       │
│   Enter choice !                                      │
│                                                       │
└─────────────────────────────────────────────────────┘
```

This command, now used twice, has taught us an important lesson: From virtually any exclamation mark (!) prompt in the system, you can enter T to return to this TOP menu. Thus, if you are following a menu trail and think you have gotten lost, T will bring you back quickly.

## Checking Out the News

Questions so far?

*Yes. Why bother with traveling the slow menu route when you can get there faster with the GO command?*

Obviously, for the new subscriber, menus are the ideal means of transport, simply because you don't yet know many quick reference words to use with the GO command. But even after you become familiar with the system, you still will use the menu approach sometimes, particularly when you are interested in browsing in the system.

To illustrate, let's suppose we take another trip from this main menu to read some news, but you haven't decided on what resource to use. Instead, you want to browse. From the TOP, you decide to visit the area of "News/Weather/Sports," option 4. Enter 4. You are moved to the next menu level:

```
┌─────────────────────────────────────────────────┐
│                                                  │
│   News/Weather/Sports                    NEWS    │
│                                                  │
│    1 Executive News Service (E$)                 │
│    2 Newsgrid                                    │
│    3 AP Online                                   │
│    4 Weather                                     │
│    5 Sports                                      │
│    6 McGraw-Hill News SNAPSHOT                   │
│    7 OTC NewsAlert (sm)   (E)                    │
│    8 The Business Wire                           │
│    9 St. Louis Post Dispatch                     │
│   10 Entertainment News/Info                     │
│   11 Online Today Daily Edition                  │
│                                                  │
│   Enter choice !                                 │
│                                                  │
└─────────────────────────────────────────────────┘
```

That was easy. Now you see a submenu of TOP that offers news services. Some mention specific services — *The St. Louis Post-Dispatch*, AP Online — while other menu selections are more general ("Weather" and "Sports"). If you were to choose one of latter group, you would be taken to another menu where specific services would be listed.

Notice that the quick reference word or page address for this menu ("NEWS") is located in the usual place, on the upper right hand corner. If you wanted to reach this page from *anywhere* in the system, you could enter "G NEWS." Most menus on the system have their addresses located in that position. Sometimes it is a word ("TOP" or "NEWS"), sometimes it is a word and a number ("NEW-1").

One other thing about this menu. Notice that some of the options are followed by symbols. On menu, three symbols are possible:

1.  A dollar sign ($) means it is a surcharged service. Accessing it costs an extra fee besides the standard connect charges. (We won't be touring any extra-cost features.)
2.  An "E" means it is a feature available only through the Executive Option, described earlier.
3.  A "W" stands for "wide" and signifies that the information displayed in that particular service requires more than 32 characters per line.

Going on, suppose while browsing this menu, your eye is caught by the entry for *Online Today*, an electronic daily newspaper and magazine produced by Compu-Serve. Deciding to look at it, you enter 11 and see:

```
┌─────────────────────────────────────────────────┐
│                                                   │
│   One moment please ...                           │
│                                                   │
└─────────────────────────────────────────────────┘
```

To understand this message, you need to begin thinking of CompuServe in a new way, not as a single giant computer, but rather as a string of connected *host* computers. This message indicates that the feature you request is located on another computer and you are being switched to that system. It takes a few seconds, then you see something like:

```
┌─────────────────────────────────────────────────┐
│                                                   │
│                                                   │
│   :::::::::::::::::::::::::::::::::                │
│   :          Online Today        :                │
│   :        Electronic Edition    :                │
│   :::::::::::::::::::::::::::::::::                │
│                                                   │
│   Thursday, January 12, 1989                      │
│                                                   │
│   *IBM Prepares Strategy/GO 360                   │
│   *Fortune Sys. to Be Sold/GO 503                 │
│   *IBM Exec Dies in Fire/GO 500                   │
│   *Monitor Week In Review/GO 506                  │
│   *Jan. Product Reviews/GO 200                    │
│   Today's News: 90/ Week's: 20                    │
│   CompuServe News: 50/ Forum:69                   │
│                                                   │
│   Press <CR> for more !                           │
│                                                   │
└─────────────────────────────────────────────────┘
```

The introductory page to *Online Today* always contains headlines pointing to the news that has been posted most recently. Note the scrolling stops when the "Press <CR> for more !" prompt appears. You have seen this prompt several times already, and now know what it means. When you press the return key, you continue to the next page:

```
r--------------------------------------------,
|                                            |
|  Online Today                     ONLINE   |
|                                            |
|  ONLINE TODAY MAGAZINE                      |
|                                            |
|  1 Guide to Online Today                    |
|  2 Monitor Daily News                       |
|  3 CompuServe This Week                      |
|  4 Columns/Special Reports                   |
|  5 Hardware/Software Reviews                  |
|  6 Advertisers/Online Inquiry                 |
|  7 Online Today Readers' Forum                |
|                                            |
|  Enter choice !                             |
|                                            |
L--------------------------------------------J
```

Like many publications, *Online Today*'s electronic edition is made up of a number of separate sections, including the latest news about the happenings in the system's forums and conferences ("CompuServe This Week"), as well as daily news from the computer industry as a whole ("Monitor Daily News"). Let's look at the daily news. Enter 2 and see:

```
r--------------------------------------------,
|                                            |
|  Online Today                    OLT-160   |
|                                            |
|  MONITOR                                    |
|                                            |
|  1 About This Section                       |
|  2 Today's News                             |
|  3 This Week's News                          |
|  4 Behind the Screens (sm)                   |
|  5 Send a Letter to Monitor                   |
|                                            |
|  Enter choice !                             |
|                                            |
L--------------------------------------------J
```

Still following the menu trail, we arrive at the Monitor Daily News section of *Online Today*. Now choose option 2 from this menu ("Today's News") and see something like:

```
┌─────────────────────────────────────────────────────┐
│                                                       │
│   Online Today                         OLT-90        │
│                                                       │
│   TODAY'S MONITOR NEWS                                │
│                                                       │
│   1 IBM Readies 'Clone' Strategy                      │
│   2 Men Accused of Selling to Cuba                    │
│   3 IBM Exec, Wife Die in Fire                        │
│   4 Fortune Systems to Be Sold                        │
│   5 Monitor Week in Review                            │
│   6 Yesterday's Late News                             │
│                                                       │
│   Enter choice !                                      │
│                                                       │
└─────────────────────────────────────────────────────┘
```

Of course, this menu is different on your screen than it is in our example, because it changes daily.


## Putting the Brakes on CompuServe

In a moment, we will want you to read story No. 1 from the menu on your screen but, before we start, let us introduce some new features. *Control codes* can assist you in reading material here and in other features on CompuServe. Before we logged on, we asked you to locate the control key on your keyboard. Now we shall use that key to create a pair of important control codes:

CONTROL S: This code freezes a display. If you are in the middle of a file and enter CONTROL S, the upcoming text will halt abruptly, giving you a chance to read it as slowly as you like and even reread it. Remember it as CONTROL S for *stop* the displays.
CONTROL Q: This code resumes the display right where it left off. Remember it as Q for *quit stopping*, that is, resume.

If you have never used control keys on an on-line system, the way they are entered may seem a little strange at first, because you *don't* use RETURN. Instead, just hold down your keyboard's control key (or its equivalent) and letter indicated, in this case, either S or Q.
Here is how to test the control keys: first, we shall enter 1 <RETURN> to start the text of the first news story displaying, then quickly press CONTROL S to freeze the display. Ready? try that much.

Okay? If all went well, the display stopped when you pressed the control and S keys together. (Note that if you are logged on through one of CompuServe's own nodes, the halt was instantaneous; however, if you are visiting via an alternative network, there probably was a slight hesitation between the CONTROL S and the actual stopping.)

Now try CONTROL Q. The scrolling of the text should continue. Just like the brake and accelerator on a car.

## Scrolling Stories

If the story you chose from the menu is long enough, eventually you will come to the "Press <CR> for more!" prompt, which is similar to others you have seen so far. This time, *don't* press RETURN just yet; we want take this opportunity to try out another new command, *S* for "scroll." The S command allows material to scroll on your screen to the end of the file. Scrolling means that new lines of information appear at the bottom of your screen, while the top lines disappear. In other words, all the lines move up the screen to make way for a new line at the bottom. Once you enter S at the prompt, you will not get another "Press <CR> for more!" message; the scrolling won't stop until the entire story has been displayed and the end is signaled by a prompt that says "Last page !" (CONTROL S and CONTROL Q can be used to stop and start the display as needed.)

Time out. If the story you selected from the menu was not a particularly long one, then there probably wasn't a "Press <CR> for more!" prompt; instead, the first prompt you saw was "Last page !." In that case, press RETURN at the "Last page !" prompt to get back to the previous menu and pick another story. Keep trying until you find one that is long enough to pause with a "Press <CR> for more!" prompt so that you can do the experiment by entering S <RETURN> there. If all else fails, just keep the information about the Scroll command in the back of your mind and try it the *next time* you see a "Press <CR> for more!" prompt in a text file.

The S command is particularly useful when you are capturing text to a buffer or a disk, because it eliminates the need to press RETURN at the bottom of every screen, as it suppresses the "Press <CR> for more!" prompts.

## Back to the Menu

At end of a story, the prompt appears as "Last page !" and you can enter a number of navigation commands. Among them is M (for "Menu"), which takes you back to the *previous menu*. Try that. Enter menu at the prompt and you should return to the OLT-90 menu of stories, something like this:

```
r---------------------------------------------------------------
|
|   Online Today                              OLT-90    |
|                                                        |
|   TODAY'S MONITOR NEWS                                 |
|                                                        |
|   1 IBM Readies 'Clone' Strategy                       |
|   2 Men Accused of Selling to Cuba                     |
|   3 IBM Exec, Wife Die in Fire                         |
|   4 Fortune Systems to Be Sold                         |
|   5 Monitor Week in Review                             |
|   6 Yesterday's Late News                              |
|                                                        |
|   Enter choice !                                       |
|                                                        |
L---------------------------------------------------------------
```

You could backtrack even further. Another M command would take you to the menu that led to this one, and so on. But let's take the express. Enter T (for TOP) and in an instant, you are back to:

```
r---------------------------------------------------------------
|
|   CompuServe                                TOP       |
|                                                        |
|    1 Subscriber Assistance                             |
|    2 Find a Topic                                      |
|    3 Communications/Bulletin Bds.                      |
|    4 News/Weather/Sports                               |
|    5 Travel                                            |
|    6 The Electronic MALL/Shopping                      |
|    7 Money Matters/Markets                             |
|    8 Entertainment/Games                               |
|    9 Home/Health/Education                             |
|   10 Reference                                         |
|   11 Computers/Technology                              |
|   12 Business/Other Interests                          |
|                                                        |
|   Enter choice number !                                |
|                                                        |
L---------------------------------------------------------------
```

The difference between M and T should be apparent now. Entered at a "!" prompt, M steps back to the previous menu (the branch from which the current menu originated); T takes you back to the TOP of the system, working from just about *anywhere* in the system for a quick escape to the system's front door.

## Looking at Our First Database

Now we are ready to see one of CompuServe's many searchable databases. At the same time, we want to show you that you are not alone on CompuServe. Our destination is the Directory of Subscribers, the feature we described earlier as the system's phone book, where subscribers are listed along with their user ID numbers and the names of the cities in which they live. The directory is found under the "Communications/Bulletin Bds." option, so enter 3 to see:

```
CompuServe                          COMMUNICATE

COMMUNICATIONS/BULLETIN BOARDS

1 EasyPlex Electronic Mail
2 CB Simulator
3 Forums (SIGs)
4 National Bulletin Board
5 Directory of Subscribers
6 Ask Customer Service
7 CB Society
8 The Convention Center (tm)

Enter Choice !
```

Are target is option 5 on this submenu, so enter 5, and after a "One moment please..." message, you see:

```
CompuServe                            DIRECTORY

SUBSCRIBER DIRECTORY

1 Explanation
2 Subscriber Directory Search
   (U.S.and Canada)
3 Subscriber Directory Search
   (International)
4 Include/Exclude This User ID

Enter choice!
```

As a new user, your own user ID probably hasn't been added yet, but it will be shortly. Meanwhile, we can learn how to search for another subscriber. Begin the search by choosing option 2 on this menu and see:

```
Last name (<CR> to exit):
```

The colon (:) prompt is the same as the prompt used frequently during the sign-up procedure at the beginning of the chapter. Often CompuServe uses the colon prompt to signify that you are to enter a word or portion of a word. The text of the prompt specifies that, telling you the system is expecting a last name. Let's look for Charlie Bowen's user ID. Enter BOWEN at the prompt. You will find there are many Bowens on-line; we know that because the system next asks us to be more specific by providing a first name as well:

```
First name begins with (e.g. JOH):
```

Uh, we have a problem. Wonder if Bowen is listed as "Charles Bowen" or "Charlie Bowen"? As the prompt tells us, it makes no difference. All we have to do is enter the first few letters of the first name. Try that — enter CHARL at the prompt — and you will see a list of people named Charles, Charlie (and maybe Charlotte) Bowen, something like this:

```
BOWEN, CHARLES E.     HUNTINGTON, WV      71635,1025
BOWEN, CHARLES L.     WINSTON-SALEM, NC   70000,0001
BOWEN, CHARLES X.     COLLEEN, KY         70000,100
```

Incidentally, by the time you are taking this tour, the number of Charles Bowens and Charlie Bowens may have grown too large for one screen, and the system may ask you to further specify the search by entering a state designation. If that happens, enter the postal code WV for West Virginia to narrow the search even more.

Notice that after the display, the database returns to:

```
┌───────────────────────────────────────────────────────────┐
│                                                           │
│  Last name (<CR> to exit):                                │
│                                                           │
└───────────────────────────────────────────────────────────┘
```

This prompt means that all is set for another search. A press of RETURN will go back to the directory menu. Please do that — press RETURN and come back to:

```
┌───────────────────────────────────────────────────────────┐
│                                                           │
│  CompuServe                      DIRECTORY                │
│                                                           │
│  SUBSCRIBER DIRECTORY                                     │
│                                                           │
│  1 Explanation                                            │
│  2 Subscriber Directory Search                            │
│     (U.S. and Canada)                                     │
│  3 Subscriber Directory Search                            │
│     (International)                                       │
│  4 Include/Exclude This User ID                           │
│                                                           │
│  Enter choice!                                            │
│                                                           │
└───────────────────────────────────────────────────────────┘
```

Before we leave, take note of option 4. It allows you to include or exclude your name, city, and user ID. Unless you specifically request that this personal information not be included, it automatically *will* be listed (just as you have to request an unlisted number from the telephone company). The "unlisting" process can take a couple of weeks. We suggest that you not request removal of your name from the directory. The free flow of information in this electronic community depends, to a great extent, upon people knowing how to contact other people and the directory is a key to this.

Now let's again take the fast lane to the TOP menu. Enter T at the prompt to reach:

```
┌─────────────────────────────────────────────────────────────┐
│                                                               │
│  CompuServe                                        TOP        │
│                                                               │
│   1 Subscriber Assistance                                     │
│   2 Find a Topic                                              │
│   3 Communications/Bulletin Bds.                              │
│   4 News/Weather/Sports                                       │
│   5 Travel                                                    │
│   6 The Electronic MALL/Shopping                              │
│   7 Money Matters/Markets                                     │
│   8 Entertainment/Games                                       │
│   9 Home/Health/Education                                     │
│  10 Reference                                                 │
│  11 Computers/Technology                                      │
│  12 Business/Other Interests                                  │
│                                                               │
│  Enter choice number !                                        │
│                                                               │
└─────────────────────────────────────────────────────────────┘
```

## A Side Trip to Nowhere

You have seen the value of the T command for getting back to familiar territory (the TOP menu) if you get lost in your travels. Before going on, there is a similar command you should meet. CONTROL C is a kind of system emergency brake. It, too, comes in handy if you find yourself on unfamiliar backroads.

To add a little realism to our exercise, please enter PRO at the prompt on your screen. What you see next may surprise you.

```
┌─────────────────────────────────────────────────────────────┐
│                                                               │
│  OK                                                           │
│                                                               │
└─────────────────────────────────────────────────────────────┘
```

What is this? No familiar prompt. Just an OK. Who says it's OK? It is never OK when you find yourself stuck in strange surroundings. Maybe if you enter "HELP," you can find a way out. Do that.

```
┌─────────────────────────────────────────────────────────┐
│                                                           │
│  Help is available for:                                   │
│                                                           │
│                                                           │
│        New_Features    Reader_Comments   ALTER            │
│        APPEND          BINDMP            BYE              │
│        CATALOG         CHANGE            COMBINE           │
│        COPY            CREATE            DAYTIME           │
│        DELETE          DIRECTORY         DOCUMENT          │
│        EDIT            ENTER             EXTRACT           │
│        Filcom         FILGE             Filtrn           │
│        FIND            FULLD             GO               │
│        HALFD           HEAD              HELLO             │
│        HELP            ICS_Editor        INSERT            │
│        JOB             KEY               LENGTH            │
│        LEVEL           LINES             LIST             │
│        LOCATE          LOGIN             MAKE             │
│        MERGE           MONTH             MOVE             │
│        NEW             NEWS              OFF              │
│        OLD             PACK              PROTECT           │
│        RENAME          REPLACE           REPNN             │
│        REQUEST         RESEQUENCE        SAVE             │
│        SAVENN          SCRATCH           SEARCH            │
│        STATUS          SUBSTITUTE        TAIL             │
│        TAPE            TECO              TERMINAL          │
│        TIME            TWITCH            TYPE             │
│        USTATUS         Vidtex            WEAVE             │
│                                                           │
│  Topic?                                                   │
│                                                           │
└─────────────────────────────────────────────────────────┘
```

Ahem. Well, some of these certainly look interesting (TWITCH? SCRATCH?), but there seems to be no help for getting out of this mess.

The part of the system into which you have fallen *is* important, and later we shall introduce you properly. For the time being, we simply wanted to use this unfamiliar area to illustrate how CONTROL-C really can come to the rescue, acting as a sort of special *Break* key to interrupt whatever is going on between you and the system. It is a clear signal to the system to "Get me outa here the best and fastest way possible."

Try it at the "Topic?" prompt now on your screen. Enter CONTROL-C (that is, hold down the "Control" and "c" keys together). This will take you back to the "OK" prompt.

```
┌─────────────────────────────────────────────────┐
│                                                   │
│   OK                                              │
│                                                   │
└─────────────────────────────────────────────────┘
```

Now do it again; enter another CONTROL C and up pops:

```
┌─────────────────────────────────────────────────┐
│                                                   │
│   ^C Interrupt. H for Help,                       │
│   T for TOP, M for prior MENU !                   │
│                                                   │
└─────────────────────────────────────────────────┘
```

At last, something familiar, a "!" prompt. The lesson here is that no matter where you are in the system, entering a CONTROL-C usually will get you back on firmer ground, a common prompt, or this "CONTROL-C interrupt !" prompt. Sometimes, it requires entering a couple of these control codes, as above. In nearly all cases, though, CONTROL-C works as a lifeline to bring you back to familiar territory. In this case, the message tells you to enter T to get back to the top of the system. Do that and you will be home again at the TOP menu.

Now that your out of the "OK Corral," you probably are wondering what all that the OK business was about. Consider it a preview of coming attractions. We are coming back to that area in Chapter 7 to show you what you can do there. You will find it isn't as mysterious as appears.

## A Little Adventure

You've been working hard, so it is time for a little relaxation. Let's take a side trip now to play a computer adventure game. Choose option 8 from TOP to go to the Entertainment/Games area of the system:

```
┌─────────────────────────────────────────────────────┐
│                                                       │
│   CompuServe                              GAMES        │
│                                                       │
│   ENTERTAINMENT/GAMES                                 │
│                                                       │
│    1 Intro to CompuServe Games                        │
│    2 Adventure Games                                  │
│    3 Board/Parlor Games                               │
│    4 Fantasy Role-Playing Games                       │
│    5 Multi-Player Games                               │
│    6 Simulation/Sports Games                          │
│    7 Trivia/Thought Games                             │
│    8 War Games                                        │
│    9 Entertainment News/Info                          │
│   10 Entertainment/Games Forums                       │
│   11 Order CompuServe Games Manual                    │
│                                                       │
│   Enter choice !                                      │
│                                                       │
└─────────────────────────────────────────────────────┘
```

CompuServe's games are divided into more than a half dozen different types. Let's head straight to option 2, Adventure Games.

```
┌─────────────────────────────────────────────────────┐
│                                                       │
│   CompuServe                             ADVENT       │
│                                                       │
│   ADVENTURE GAMES                                     │
│                                                       │
│    1 British Legends                                  │
│    2 CastleQuest                                      │
│    3 House of Banshi                                  │
│    4 Original Adventure                               │
│    5 New Adventure                                    │
│                                                       │
│   Enter choice !                                      │
│                                                       │
└─────────────────────────────────────────────────────┘
```

Lots to choose from here, too. The one we want to play is New Adventure, option 6.

*Why is it called New Adventure?*

Because it is a hybrid of option 5, the Original Adventure, one of the oldest, perhaps *the* oldest, computer text adventure around. The Original Adventure was developed in the late 1970s at the Massachusetts Institute of Technology by precocious computer students. The New Adventure is a modification of this original game.

After choosing option 6 from this menu, you see an introductory menu for New Adventure:

```
CompuServe                               NEWADV

NEW ADVENTURE

1 To Read Instructions
2 To Play New Adventure

Suggested Age             :12 & Up
Classification            :Adventure
Players (min/max)         :1/1
Special Requirements      :None
Minimum Screen Width      :Any
Direct Access Page        :GAM-201

Enter choice !
```

Nearly all on-line games are prefaced with a menu like this, which is helpful in determining what games you might want to play. Choose 2 to enter the game-playing area. After a couple of announcements, you see:

```
Welcome to ADVENTURE!!   Would
you like instructions?
```

Enter N for No. We are here to look after you this time. Next comes an opening scene for this adventure:

```
You are standing at the end of
a road before a small brick
building. Around you is a forest.
A small stream flows out of the
building and down a gully.
```

As in most text games, you give commands to your "alter ego" and direct this persona through the adventure. The object of the game is to collect as many treasures as you can without getting killed by a horrible monster that awaits you in an underground labyrinth. Many commands begin with a verb such as GO, GET, THROW, etc., while the second word is often a direction or a noun. So that we all can stay together on this journey, we shall suggest commands. Of course if you were playing this by yourself, you would make your own choices.

When the screen stops scrolling, you won't see a prompt. There are no prompts in this game. Simply enter GO BUILDING (telling the system you want your character to go inside the building). After that, you see:

```
You are inside a building, a
well house for a large spring. Off
to one side is a small storeroom.
There is a shiny brass lamp nearby.
There is a leather sack here.
Taped to the wall is a faded poster.
There is a small matchbox here.
```

Were you an unguided neophyte, you might be inclined to get all the items you see here, thinking you would probably need them later in the adventure. You would do that with such commands as GET LAMP, GET SACK, and GET MATCHBOX. You also probably would want to read the poster with the command READ POSTER.

But your trusty scouts already have scoped things out and are here to expedite matters for you. All you *really* want is the lamp. To fetch it, enter GET LAMP and you should see:

```
Taken.
```

Just as a fishing guide can show you the best place to fish, we can show you how to get to the exciting part of the adventure quickly. You might wander around for hours trying to figure out how to get underground where the treasures lie. But we know a secret word, it is XYZZY, your next command should be SAY XYZZY.

```
It is now pitch dark.  If you proceed
you will likely fall into a pit.
```

Now you know why we told you go get that lamp. Enter LIGHT LAMP.

```
Your lamp is now on.
You are in a debris-filled room with
stuff washed in from the surface.A
low, wide passage with cobbles becomes
plugged with mud and debris here,
but an awkward canyon leads upward
and west.  A note on the wall says
"Magic Word XYZZY." A 3-foot
black rod with a rusty star on an
end lies nearby.
```

Hmmmm! A debris-filled room. Looks just like Dave's son's bedroom, in fact. By the way, if you said the magic word we told you about at this point, you would be taken back to the building. Remember this when you want to take your treasures up top. Okay. Now enter GO WEST (or WEST).

```
You are in an awkward sloping
east/west canyon.
```

Keep going WEST in the canyon by typing WEST again.

```
You are in a splendid chamber thirty
feet high.  The walls are frozen rivers
of orange stone.  An awkward canyon and
a good passage exit from east and west
sides of the chamber. A cheerful little
bird is sitting here singing.
```

Don't try to catch the bird. We have tried and found it a slippery little sucker. It may be pretty here and there may be lots of things to look at, but let's continue to GO WEST.

```
At your feet is a small pit breathing
traces of white mist. An east passage
ends here except for a small crack
leading on. Rough stone steps lead down
the pit.
```

Follow those steps down into the pit. Enter GO DOWN.

```
You are at one end of a vast hall
stretching forward out of sight to the
west. There are openings to either side.
Nearby, a wide stone staircase leads
downward. The hall is filled with wisps
of white mist swaying to and fro almost
as if alive.  A cold wind blows up the
staircase. There is a passage at the top
of a dome behind you. Rough stone steps
lead up the dome.
```

Can't you almost smell the treasure nearby? We *must* be getting close now. Enter GO WEST again.

```
You are on the east bank of a fissure
slicing clear across the hall. The mist
is quite thick here, and the fissure is
too wide to jump.
```

"Too wide." It's probably a trick. Throw caution to the wind. Nothing ventured, nothing gained (and cliches of like import.) Enter JUMP.

```
You didn't make it.
Oh dear, you seem to have gotten
yourself killed.  I might be able to
help you out, but I've never really done
this before.  Do you want me to try to
reincarnate you?
```

Rats and darn! We had hoped you would be the one who could jump that fissure. Oh, well, guess not. If it is any consolation, thousands have met their doom here, before you.

You could type Y (for yes) and find yourself "reincarnated" and back in the building, but we'll let you continue the adventure alone. Enter N to the prompt.

```
You scored 15 out of a possible
751, using 10 turns. You are
obviously a rank amateur. Better
luck next time. To achieve the
next higher rating, you need
31 more points.


CompuServe                              ADVENT

ADVENTURE GAMES

1 British Legends
2 CastleQuest
3 House of Banshi
4 Original Adventure
5 New Adventure

Enter choice !
```

## The Find of the Century

If you read the instructions as you were logging on after the sign-up procedure, you probably saw a discussion of FIND, one of the handiest commands on the whole system. Entering FIND at any "!" prompt followed by a descriptive word causes Compu-Serve to search all its features. It builds a special menu of those services for which you are looking. As we are now at a "!" prompt, try it out. The next stop on this tour is the EasyPlex electronic mail service, where we shall see how to write a letter. So, at the prompt, enter:

```
Enter choice ! FIND MAIL <RETURN>
```

After a moment, the system constructs a menu something like this:

```
CompuServe

1 EasyPlex (MCI Mail)              [ MCIMAIL ]
2 EasyPlex (TELEX)                 [ TELEX ]
3 EasyPlex Electronic Mail         [ EASYPLEX ]
4 FAX-EasyPlex                     [ FAX ]
5 Play-By-Mail Games Forum         [ PBMGAMES ]


Last menu page, enter choice   !
```

This is a kind of index of services pertaining to "mail." Options 1 and 2 refer to areas where you can go to get explanations of how to send MCI Electronic Mail through CompuServe's EasyPlex system and how to send and receive a Telex through EasyPlex. (We talk about this and more in Chapter 19.) Option 3 is the EasyPlex service area itself where you can both send and read mail. (Option 4 is the listing for a forum for those interested in playing games by mail, which also will be discussed in a later chapter.)

Those words at the right are the quick reference words or page addresses that can be used with the GO command for direct access. And there is another way to get there. Because this list forms an actual customized menu, you can now get to Easy-Plex by entering 3 at the prompt. Do that; enter either 3 to G EASYPLEX. In a moment, you arrive at the following introductory page:

```
EasyPlex

Welcome to EasyPlex, your new
electronic mail system.
Features of EasyPlex include:
-an online Address Book
-REPLY, FORWARD, RECEIPT options
-UPLOAD and DOWNLOAD support
-Access to over 500,000 EasyPlex,
 InfoPlex and MCI mail users
-Switchable modes for using
 EasyPlex: Menu, Prompt, Command
-Switchable modes for editing.
*Type: HELP for more assistance*
Do you wish additional
information (Y or N)!
```

Answer N to this question. We'll be learning more about EasyPlex in the next few chapters. Next, you will see the main EasyPlex menu:

```
EasyPlex  Main Menu
   *** No mail waiting ***

2 COMPOSE a new message
3 UPLOAD a message
4 USE a file from PER area
5 ADDRESS Book
6 SET options

Enter choice !
```

Since you are new to these parts, it isn't surprising that there is no mail waiting for you to read. For that reason, option 1 on this menu — which is READ MAIL — is missing.

## Sit Right Down and Write Yourself an EasyPlex

Choose option 2 from this main EasyPlex menu so you can write a letter that you will post to yourself as a practice. In a moment, you see:

```
EasyPlex  Compose

Enter message. (/EXIT when done)

1:
```

The "1:" is where you start writing your message. You may put up to 79 characters on each line before pressing RETURN. When you press RETURN, you will get the next line number. Here is what we want you to do. Type exactly what we show you to type in the following example, pressing RETURN as indicated.

```
1: Hi! Welcome to CompuServe <RETURN>
2: Information Service. <RETURN>
3: You've made amazing progress so <RETURN>
4: far. But there's much more to <RETURN>
5: learn. <RETURN>
6: /EXIT  <RETURN>
```

The slash that precedes the "EXIT" on the last line tells the system that what follows is a command rather than text. The /EXIT command tells the system you are finished writing and wish to exit the text-writing area. Next, you see the Send menu.

```
EasyPlex   Send Menu

For current message

1 SEND
2 EDIT
3 TYPE
4 FILE DRAFT copy
5 SEND with /RECEIPT   ($)

Enter choice !
```

These options will be explained later. For now, choose option 1. (Don't worry if you've made a typographical error in your test; after all, the letter is going to yourself.) After you enter 1, the system says:

```
EasyPlex

Send to (Name or User ID):
```

When the system asks for a name or user ID, enter in your *own* permanent user ID (the one you jotted down when it was issued at the beginning of this tour). Next, the system asks:

```
r--------------------------------------------------¬
¦                                                  ¦
¦   Subject:                                       ¦
¦                                                  ¦
L--------------------------------------------------
```

Enter WELCOME. After that, EasyPlex asks for your name. Enter your name, first, last, or both. Finally, you should see a message like this:

```
r--------------------------------------------------¬
¦                                                  ¦
¦   Would you like to save this name               ¦
¦   as your EasyPlex name so you do not            ¦
¦   have to type it in the future?                 ¦
¦     (Yes or No):                                 ¦
¦                                                  ¦
L--------------------------------------------------
```

Decisions, decisions.... For the time being, answer NO to this one. If you answer YES, the name you have just typed will be automatically added to every EasyPlex note you send. You are probably not ready to give yourself a permanent EasyPlex name. You can do that at any time by adding it to your Address Book, which will be covered in Chapter 9. For now, let's leave that blank. When you answer "NO," you will see something like this:

```
r--------------------------------------------------¬
¦                                                  ¦
¦   You may add your EasyPlex                       ¦
¦   name on the Address Book menu.                 ¦
¦                                                  ¦
¦   To:  71635,1025                                ¦
¦   From: Charlie Bowen                            ¦
¦   Subj: WELCOME                                  ¦
¦                                                  ¦
¦   Is this correct? (Y or N)!                     ¦
¦                                                  ¦
L--------------------------------------------------
```

Check the user ID, making *sure* you have entered it correctly. If so, enter Y for yes. If it isn't — that is, if you have made a typo while entering your user ID number — enter N for no and you will be allowed to re-address the message. Finally, you will see confirmation that your EasyPlex has been sent:

```
r--------------------------------------------------¬
¦                                                  ¦
¦   Message sent to 71635,1025                     ¦
¦   Press <CR>!                                    ¦
¦                                                  ¦
L--------------------------------------------------
```

And that wraps up the first tour. You have been to a lot of places and seen a lot of things. You have learned the principal control codes and commands in the system and seen how menus are organized. It is time to log off the system. To do that, simply enter OFF or BYE at the "!" point, and off you go.

```
Thank you for using CompuServe!


Off at 16:15 EST 12-Jan-89
Connect time = 1:00
```

This message tells you the time you are logging off, the date, and your total connect time. You will see this message every time you log off. If you want to keep track of your on-line time, just jot this down for exactly how many hours and minutes you were connected. By the way, always try to log off with the BYE or OFF command, rather than simply turning off your modem or computer. Without the correct log off, you may be charged for several extra minutes.

## Side Roads

From time to time, in the book, we shall suggest possible "self-guided tours" you might want to take between chapters to see features that are similar to some we have just used. If you would like to log little independent study time before the next chapter, here are a few other features that might be of interest. (Incidentally, when you log on, you probably will see a message that says "you have an EasyPlex message waiting." That shouldn't be a surprise, as we just wrote one to ourselves. Please resist the urge to look at the test message; we plan to use it again when we go back on-line in Chapter 5.)

Some other features of interest:

*The INDEX Database* — We saw how option 1 on the TOP menu was "Find a subject." During the tour, we found EasyPlex using the FIND command from a "!" prompt. The INDEX program (accessible by option 2 on TOP or by entering G INDEX) allows you to search a database of subjects and quick reference words.

*The PHONES Database* — CompuServe also maintains a database of telephone access numbers for its own network and for packet network services. To reach it, enter G PHONES at any prompt. This service also is discussed in the On-line Survival Kit in the back of the book. See the "Making Connections" section.

*The Business Wire* — We got a brief look at news features with our trip to *On-line Today*'s electronic edition. You might also be interested this service, which is a collection of press releases and statements from various companies. To reach it, enter G TBW at any prompt.

*AP Online* — The Associated Press provides a specially edited report, usually containing between 250 and 300 stories that make up the top national, international, Washington, financial, and sports news of the day. Also available is a summary of the top stories of the hour. The feature is transmitted around clock every day. To see it, enter G APO.

*What's New* — CompuServe's weekly collection for news items. To reach it, enter G NEW at any prompt. Actually, when you log on again, What's New probably will be waiting for *you*. As noted, the system automatically displays the feature to all subscribers twice a week.

*CompuServe's On-line Tours* — You saw them mentioned following the sign-up procedure. If you would like to see more, enter G TOURS at any prompt on the system. Actually, you won't find much additional information on the tours, but it will give you a change to practice your commands, such as CONTROL S, Q, and C, and the S, M, and T navigation commands.

*Checkfree Transfer Account* — If you decide to pay your CompuServe bill by the Checkfree method discussed earlier, note that your current Checkfree transfer amounts can be viewed on-line free of connect-time charges. To access the information, enter G CHECKFREE at any CompuServe prompt.

# CHAPTER 4

---

# Electronic Rendezvous

If the on-line tour in the previous chapter was your first small step into CompuServe, you may well have a new question now:

*Where were all the 460,000 other subscribers that these yahoos have been telling me about?*

Granted, it may have seemed a little strange. We went in the system's front door, strolled all up and down the main corridors, and didn't run into another living soul. It was almost as if no one were home.

If what you saw in the last chapter were all that was available on CompuServe, you would not be reading a book like this. There probably would not be national excitement about electronic information services, and what CompuServe had to offer could be covered in a comprehensive magazine article.

What makes this dialup community exciting is not just electronic mail and on-line adventure games, it is something more old-fashioned than that — it is people talking to other people. In the rest of our visits together, much of our time will be spent showing you the numerous ways CompuServe has come up with to let you talk, play, and work with people all across the country. Starting in the next chapter, we shall take our first look at electronic conferences, where any number of subscribers can chat together by simply typing their messages on the screen and reading the replies. Down the line, we also discover electronic clubs called "forums" (sometimes called by their older name, "SIGs," that is, "special interest groups").

First, though, we want to get you in the right frame of mind with a few stories from Micropolis, tales intended to illustrate the potential of interactive computing for creative fun and for serious work.

---

## The Electronic Stone Age

CompuServe was an innovator in developing real-time electronic conferencing. It allows any number of computer users to type messages to each other as if on some enormous telephone party line. We have watched this feature evolve from a novelty to a sophisticated, imaginative medium that is the heart of computer networking.

In the early days — that is, the late 1970s — when programmers in the fledgling consumer wing of CompuServe added real-time conferencing to its services, they didn't really know what they had. As one long-time employee told us, "We called it 'CB' [the whimsical name stuck] and we thought it would be an interesting diversion." Most subscribers in those days were computer professionals or serious hobbyists interested in on-line programming tools. It was not at all unusual, he said, to be logged in to the new conference area for an hour or more, waiting for someone else to come along to talk. After a long wait, finally a message like this might appear:

```
(FRED:)  WHAT KIND EQUIP U USE?
```

Those clipped messages, mostly technical in nature, were the CompuServe equivalent of "What hath God wrought?"

Many things, indeed.

Each new wave of electronic immigrants has contributed a little of its own imagination to conferencing until it has evolved from a computer toy to a powerful tool that can be used for play and work.

*What kind of play?*

Consider the time that Charlie became the first on-line holdup victim...

## Shoot-Out on Channel 10

It was three in the morning and Charlie had just discovered the CB Simulator. He had chatted with a fellow who called himself PECOS BILL from Washington State who had given Charlie and other insomniacs a firsthand account of Mount St. Helen's latest tremors. PECOS said something about how the latest eruption had knocked out telephone service for a few days, interrupting his on-line time, but "at least it saved me some money in CompuServe bills."

"I know what you mean," typed someone named SWEETCAKES. "Boys, I don't know what I'm going to do about these bills. I'm hooked, and it's getting expensive!"

A Texan, whose CB "handle" was GUNNER added: "Guess we're going to have to rob a bank."

"Hey, you want to?" said COWPOKE, another Texan. "I got the horses."

The idea appealed to SWEETCAKES and for the next few minutes, everyone who logged on to that particular channel of CB was issued an imaginary hat — a black one or a white one. (SWEETCAKES was in charge of assigning the colors.) Newcomers did not know what was going on, but it took just a moment for each to realize from the context of the conversation that they were being conscripted into a gang of Old West outlaws.

"Can I have feathers in my hat?" asked BRIGHT EYES.

"Girls!!" groaned PECOS BILL.

When SWEETCAKES decided the gang was big enough, she asked her lieutenants, "Banks or trains, boys?"

Charlie had been "lurking" up until then. (*Lurking* is on-line jargon for a CB wallflower who listens but does not participate. A philosophical argument can be made that in this medium, you don't exist if you don't speak up.) To announce his presence, Charlie offered, "Why not rob the data banks?"

"Naw," said GUNNER, "we've got plenty of data. We need cash."

SWEETCAKES directed GUNNER to take part of the band up the west side of the river, while she and PECOS took the east. As they rode off, looking for an unsuspecting bank, Charlie said, "Folks, if I don't have a hat, does that mean I'm a victim?"

GUNNER: "Put your hands in the air and don't say a word."
CHARLIE: "Is a buck and a quarter going to save my life?"
GUNNER: "Fork it over."
PECOS BILL: "Hey, I like that watch!"
SWEETCAKES: "I want his wallet ... I'm into leather!"

Things got a little confusing then. As the desperadoes smelled fresh loot, everyone typed at once, and the story line the group was composing together got a little convoluted. When things settled down again, SWEETCAKES' gang was encamped and GUNNER had out his harmonica. (To supply the soundtrack on the silent computer screen, GUNNER waxed poetic as he typed: "Long lonesome sound mingles with the prairie winds ...")

"Pardon me," Charlie then piped up, "but could someone tell me if I got killed."

"Nope," said SWEETCAKES. "You're a repeat customer. We figured we'd rob you again next week."

"Who's tending the horses?" asked PECOS BILL.

"BRIGHT EYES is," said SWEETCAKES.

"No. Sorry about that," said GUNNER, "but I'm tending BRIGHT EYES. Hehehehe."

The peacefulness of the on-line "camp" was not to continue. About that time, a stranger rode onto the channel, calling himself INJUN. His simple message was:
"(Arrow). Sssssssssst!"

SWEETCAKES narrated the action, informing all (and him) that PECOS BILL had been wounded, and she ordered the gang to head for the horses. Then Charlie got his revenge. "Sorry, turkeys," he typed, "but I was the one tending the horses. Bye-bye," and he rode off, leaving the Injuns to do what Injuns do.

## The Stuff of On-line Friendships

That little bit of on-line horseplay was the beginning of a long friendship between Charlie and the other members of the gang. They eventually issued him a hat for being a good sport, and let him ride with them. They even formed an imaginary ranch (called the "Seedy Weed Funny Farm") in a private area of the CB channels, where they could meet and chat regularly when they felt playful. It grew beyond play. Like any friendships, the regulars shared each others' triumphs and defeats, and celebrated birthdays and holidays together on-line. And off-line. Today, years later, Charlie still communicates by phone and letter with some of the original gang members. They have exchanged Christmas presents and even have visited each other on vacation, though, as it turns out, they live thousands of miles apart.

That is not unusual. Many on-line friendships are later supplemented by other kinds of communications. CB aficionados host parties in major cities across the country. Friends fly in from all directions to meet, face-to-face, the people they may have been talking with for months or years by computers. Such meetings have become so common that CompuServe has given some of its on-line space to regular reports of CB parties, part of a feature called "Cupcake's CB Society." Located at page CUP-1, the feature, written by a New York CBer named Terry Biener, also includes profiles of new CB fans, interviews with regulars, and general "social news" of this community.

There *is* a sense of community here. EasyPlex is the postal service. There are marketplaces we shall see later. The forums become the on-line neighborhoods that have their own characteristics. In that context, the CB Simulator is the town square, a common ground, a meeting place where folks come to chat, compare notes, ask for help and directions, and more often than not, just play. After all is said and done, CB is there for the fun of it. You can communicate anonymously if you like, as you can use a handle rather than your real name, letting your imagination run wild.

## Lights, Camera, Action!!

Newcomers to CB often are surprised to find out how much can be communicated with what is really a rather limited medium. After all, you are dealing with mere words that appear at the bottom of the screen then scroll to the top and disappear as more words come to take their places. There is no sound, no body language, no exchange of meaningful glances. But for diehard CB fans, the limitations add to the excitement, requiring them to figure out new ways to get across subtle ideas.

Most CBers try to communicate sounds and actions as well as comments (as GUNNER transmitted the sound of his harmonica). It is common on CB for users to transmit laughs ("hahahahahaha" or "hehehehehe" or occasionally, "Har har har," or "tee hee"). If someone makes a bad pun, the comment from the listeners usually is "*GROAN!*" Some regulars enjoy playing with the medium itself. Once upon a time, a very popular CB citizen was a fellow in Boston who called himself "****(<>)****." He enjoyed having a handle that was instantly recognizable but that no one could pronounce.

## Hard Times for Reality

As you might imagine, in a world of handles and "playlike" games, reality sometimes comes across as fiction. There is a CB legend of a famous science-fiction writer who once logged in to the CB Simulator using his real name instead of a handle. He reportedly spent 15 minutes trying to convince skeptics that he was indeed who he said he was, only to leave in disgust unable to persuade anyone.

CB's other famous visitors have not always been so unlucky. Professional games programmer Scott Adams logged on to CB in late 1983. His computer adventure games are played very much like the adventure we saw in the previous chapter, by directing the action through the use of two-word commands such as GO EAST, EXAMINE CAVE, GET TREASURE, OPEN DOOR, WAVE SCEPTER. Each game is played in an exotic setting such as a pyramid, mysterious island, haunted castle. These text adventures made his company, Adventure International, one of the legendary game developers in the early days of personal computing.

Who knows why Adams chose to enter CB with his real name, but when he did, it did not take long for people to find him. After a few sessions, the regulars on CB spread the word that it was, in truth, the *real* Scott Adams, creator of "Adventureland" and other game favorites, who was using CB as a diversion. Many who met him could only type their excitement. "WOW!" and "I can't believe it!" was typed time and again.

Adams took it all in stride. "Calm down," he usually said.

Dave (whose CB persona is "HERMIT DAVE") watched with amusement as Adams' fans gathered around him. Finally, PATTI wandered onto the channel with a familiar "Hi Folks!" After a few minutes, while others offered Adams phrases of adoration, PATTI seemed perplexed.

> HERMIT DAVE: "Scott, watch this! Hey, PATTI! Does the name Scott Adams sound familiar?"

PATTI: "Scott Adams? Never heard of him until just now!"
SCOTT ADAMS: "Thanks, HERMIT. I needed that."

It was not long until on-line Adams admirers had given PATTI a short history of the game creator's work. Later PATTI became serious about Adams' adventure games. A few nights later, she and others gathered on channel 23 for another meeting of the Scott Adams Fan Club.

PATTI: "Hi Scott! Going crazy over your first game."
SCOTT ADAMS: "Good crazy or bad crazy?"
PATTI: "Desperate crazy. Stuck!!!! The bear in Adventureland is driving me bonkers!"
SCOTT ADAMS: "Did you use the honey?"
PATTI: "If I use it, then how do I get my honey back?"
HERMIT DAVE: "Write your honey a note and tell him all is forgiven. Hehehe."
PATTI: "**GROAN**"
SCOTT ADAMS: "Don't use the honey. Get mad at the bear instead."
PATTI: "And do what to him? Hit him? Kill him?"
SCOTT ADAMS: "No, PATTI, what do you do when you get mad at some-one?"
COMPUNUT: "Yell at him!"

This is a typical conversation on open CB. All the time PATTI was communicating with Adams, others were carrying on conversations with Adams and with each other, a form of verbal ping-pong that some say is hard to follow. That night it left one newcomer with the handle MOUNTAINEER wailing, "Is this the way it goes all night?" Yes, all night and well into the wee hours of the morning. People come and go and many return again and again. Some prowl the channels for old friends. Others look for new relationships. Some are looking for adventure. Some are looking for someone with whom to pass the time.

# But Seriously, Folks ...

A medium this powerful obviously has more applications than merely electronic horse operas and on-line fan clubs. Dave knows that. After developing a friendship with Scott Adams on the public CB channels, Dave persuaded Adams to join him in a private area of the system to be interviewed for an article Dave and his son were writing. Adams, at home at a computer keyboard, later said he found the interview more comfortable than many more conventional meetings with journalists.

Meanwhile, "across town" there is a segment of the community that seldom goes near CB and yet uses electronic conferencing every day. They are the members of the forums, gathered for discussion of specific topics. Whereas the commands are virtually the same as CB's, the forums' use of conference facilities often is markedly different. A forum might have a guest conference with a news-maker. Members of CompuServe's MAUG (the Micronetworked Apple Users' Group) have had on-line interviews with Apple President John Sculley and Apple co-founder Stephen Wozniak. The conferences often end up being newsworthy. Excerpts of one Wozniak conference were quoted for three straight weeks in the prestigious *InfoWorld* computer newspaper.

Other forums have had guest conferences with established programmers, writers and editors, rock stars, and politicians. Still others seek to explore the medium in new ways. The game-oriented forums have held on-line, real-time role-playing adventures, a kind of electronic Dungeons and Dragons, and the Literary Forum has tried writing an experimental group novel, with conferencing used for planning sessions.

Some forums have even been the setting for truly historic gatherings. Just ten minutes after the tragic explosion of the space shuttle Challenger in January 1986, members begin gathering in the Space Forum to share their shock, grief, and frustration. That spontaneous conference continued nonstop for more than 18 hours, with members coming and going.

The same forum has been the site of happier events, too. In the spring of 1985, it hosted what probably was the first truly international real-time conference. The guest was science-fiction author Arthur C. Clarke. That was quite appropriate, since many credit Clarke with having the first vision of the telecommunications satellite that made it all possible. For that conference, Clarke sat in his home in Sri Lanka near the Indian Ocean and typed messages on his keyboard that were seen simultaneously on several different continents.

Usually, in formal forum conferences, the members adopt a protocol for questions and answers, having found that guests are overwhelmed if everyone "talks" at once. A protocol might simply require asking to be recognized by the discussion leader before posing a question. But don't think forums are stuffy and humorless. Other conferences in forums are just for fun. A few years ago, in a usually rather staid corner of the system, we engaged in an evening of puns with a group of respected writers and editors. Because we are nice guys, we shall refrain from identifying them. Suffice it to say that for two hours this verbally inclined assembly bandied about puns on the word "Spam." (Our personal favorites were "Lady of Spam I adore you" and "I think, therefore I Spam.")

But we are getting ahead of ourselves. We talk a great deal about forums in later chapters. (If you want to take a peek at things to come, look ahead to Chapter 14, where we list most of the popular forums. But, as interesting as they may look to you, please wait for the rest of us to catch up before you go exploring.)

For now, we hope we have convinced you of the need to learn about conferencing, whether you plan to play or to work on the system. If you don't give the conference facilities a try, you miss out on a big part of what CompuServe has to offer.

## Business Conferences

Some people are exploring conferencing in still other ways, as a medium for business. We have used real-time conference facilities for business meetings and, in one case, even for contract negotiations on a book project when all the parties could not be in the same town at the same time. There have been on-line auctions using conference facilities, and often people in computer-related businesses use the medium to stay in touch with their customers. Andrew Fluegelman's story is a good example.

Fluegelman, a writer and programmer in San Francisco, created the idea of *freeware* for distribution of his famous IBM-PC program, *PC Talk*. This terminal program was distributed free to customers, who paid him $35 for it. But only if they liked it; they paid nothing if they didn't. In a 1982 interview (on-line, of course), Fluegelman told Charlie that communications networks like CompuServe were essential to his optimistic experiment in software distribution. He used the systems, including conferencing, to talk with customers and to spread the word. The on-line community has embraced Fluegelman's ideas; a whole genre of low-cost "user-supported software," now generically called *shareware*, has sprung up around the system. Many programmers distribute their works through the data libraries of the forums. Before his untimely death in 1985, Fluegelman had attracted such a broad following on the system that a group of experienced programmers gathered on-line to assist him in writing enhanced versions of *PC Talk*.

In other uses, programmers sometimes send advance copies of their commercial software to friends around the system for "beta testing," then hold a private conference with them to compare notes on possible problems.

## What Is Compusex?

Before we take our first field trip into CB, we need to tell you about other uses to which the medium is being put these days, including several that make some newcomers blush. You won't find the word *compusex* in any dictionary — not yet, anyway — but you ought to be aware that this mysterious "art form" is another part of CB.

*What the heck is compusex?*

Some call it a sexual fantasy role-playing game. One CB'er described it as "sort of like a dirty book that talks back to you." Here is how it works: On-line User A (with a masculine handle) meets User B (with a feminine handle). The two agree to form a private communication linkup called "TALK." Once in that mode, their two-way conversation cannot be seen by anyone else. Officials say that TALK is completely private and not even CompuServe employees can monitor private conversations. It is in this TALK mode where fantasy sex can be played out to various stages. Because CompuServe has decided that whatever goes on between two consenting adults in TALK is okay, nearly anything can happen, or at least can be TALKed about.

Now, of course, don't assume that just because two people are in TALK, they are engaged in this electronic form of heavy petting. Many people simply enjoy the privacy of talking one-on-one. Still, if you are not interested in exchanging frank sex talk with a stranger, you should be cautious about going into a private, two-way conversation with anyone whom you don't know — or at least you ought to send the kids out of the room first. The sweet, polite fellow on the public channels of CB might have a different tune in TALK.

Fortunately for the timid, there is a quick and easy way out of any TALK that gets uncomfortable. As you see in Chapter 6, a single command (/BREAK) whisks you out of TALK and back to the public channel whence you came. Remember that and you should not have to contend for long with anything that angers or offends you.

Of course, there are other ways of bringing a halt to unwanted compu-pandering. Our friend Lindsy Van Gelder, a New York writer, tells the story of a gentleman whose TALK session turned into heavy compu-petting and he typed, "I LOVE YOU DARLING. (LONG FRENCH KISS)."

"Phtoooey!" came the reply from his unwilling partner, who entered /BREAK to break connection with the man (leaving him, no doubt, with his tongue hanging out). It turned out that his intended actually were Lindsy's two prepubescent daughters, who were having none of his foolishness.

More than one CB user has compared the CB channels to a series of singles bars where people hang out waiting for everything from companionship to something a little more hardcore. That may be overstating it a bit, but be aware that there is some of the spirit of the singles bar in CB. Each night, however, is different. As Peter Sellers said in *A Shot in the Dark*: "It's all a part of life's rich pageant!"

## Channel 33 and Other Special Places

CompuServe has attempted to designate channels for specific activities and age groups. Channel 1 is supposed to be the adult channel. Channel 7 is supposed to be for youngsters, Channel 17 for teens, and 22 for "seniors." Channel 6 is for those who might want to meet someone to practice writing French messages to each other, and Channel 15 is for those who might want to practice their Spanish. Channel 23 is for the "Knights of Olde," or those folks who are veteran CB users. Channel 16 is called

"The Flamingo Lounge," and Channel 34 is called "The Porch," names which are supposed to indicate the ambience you find there. Honestly, though, this idea of assigned usage has not worked too well because "channel hopping" is fun for people of all ages and all personalities.

There are, however, two channels that are really special. They were not originally designed to be that way by CompuServe, but rather by the subscribers themselves. They are Channel 33, the "Alternate Lifestyles Channel" and Channel 13, the "Alternative Gender Channel." Most of those who use Channel 33 are gay men. It has been the gay channel since 1980. One of the regulars on the channel said he has counted more than 500 gay men who have used the channel for conversation. "We call ourselves 'the family,'" he said. If you are heterosexual and happen to wander to channel 33, you probably will be told quite early that the channel has been dedicated to a special use by its residents (a sort of electronic "home rule," if you will). Those on the channel won't resent your stumbling into what they consider their little corner of the system. What they do mind is people who harass them or preach to them. They simply won't tolerate it, and like all other CB users, they have a way of "turning off" disagreeable transmissions from anyone. Channel 13 is for those who are cross-dressers and transsexuals, those who are planning sex-change operations and those who have already undergone sex-change operations. It is not quite as old as Channel 33, but sometimes it is just as active.

Remember that no one can force you to use Channel 33 and Channel 13 and no one can stop you from going there, just as no one can force you into TALK or keep you there if you want to leave. These decisions are all yours. It is perhaps the purest form of democracy you have going for you. That should be reason enough to look in on the fascinating world of CB.

# CHAPTER 5

# The Electronic Party

We hope we have whetted your appetite for a little conversation, because tonight we shall log on and drop in on the never-ending party that is CompuServe's CB Simulator. As we indicated, CB is where thousands of PC owners congregate daily from coast to coast to chat about a wide range of topics. We plan to party in a minute, but first....

## Picking Up Where We Left Off

You wrapped up your first tour in Chapter 3 by mailing yourself an electronic letter called EasyPlex. On this tour, the first order of business is to see how that letter arrived in your electronic mail, how to read it, answer it, save it in the system, and so forth. So, when you are ready, log on to the system as you did the first time, making the modem connection and then entering your user ID number and password when prompted for them. Once you are connected, you should see the copyright notice, like this:

```
CompuServe Information Service
   14:26 EST Friday 13-Jan-89
   Last access: 16:15 12-Jan-88


        Copyright (C) 1989
     CompuServe Incorporated
       All Rights Reserved
```

One of three possible displays should follow:

1. The main (TOP) menu that we saw many times in Chapter 3.
2. The "What's New" menu of news items about CompuServe. As mentioned, the system automatically displays this menu twice a week. Usually, What's New is updated on Thursdays, so you are shown the menu on your next two log ons.
3. A menu that illustrates that you have received an EasyPlex letter, like this:

```
EasyPlex  Message Menu

  1 Charlie Bowen/WELCOME!

  Last page.  Enter choice
or M for EasyPlex main menu!
```

Of course, your name follows the "1" instead of Charlie's. The reason you are shown a menu like this is that if you are like most subscribers, at log on you want to pick up new mail *before* doing anything else. CompuServe accommodates by always checking to see if you have mail waiting and, if you do, by bringing you directly to the EasyPlex menu as soon as you log on, bypassing TOP.

Two points about this opening display. First, an option exists to change this EasyPlex routine. With it, instead of being brought to EasyPlex when mail is waiting, you are simply notified of pending mail, then shown the TOP menu (or What's New, if you are due for an automatic display of that menu). Later in the book, we'll learn about this and other options when we look at the functions of an area called Profile. Second, if you are eligible to see *both* the What's New menu *and* be notified about waiting EasyPlex, the system first notifies you of the waiting mail (with a message after the copyright notice that says, "You have Electronic Mail waiting"), then displays the What's New menu. If you press RETURN at the prompt following What's New, you then are brought to a menu like the one in the above example.

As we all might be at different displays at this point, we need to get to some common ground. Note that, even if the system has automatically brought you to the menu of EasyPlex or What's New, you don't have to deal with that menu immediately. *You* are in charge here. We already have seen that you can visit What's New at any time by entering "G NEW" at a prompt. Similarly, you can leave your EasyPlex messages for later, visit other features, and come back or even log off entirely and return another day. Either way, your mail will wait for you. Let's examine that. Before we pick up the mail, let's find out where the system has taken us. The best way to get our bearings is to return to the TOP of the system and "walk through" the menus back to EasyPlex. You recall that a T command always takes us back to the TOP of the system. So, at the bottom of the menu on your screen, enter T, causing CompuServe to display this familiar fellow:

```
CompuServe                          TOP

   1 Subscriber Assistance
   2 Find a Topic
   3 Communications/Bulletin Bds.
   4 News/Weather/Sports
   5 Travel
   6 The Electronic MALL/Shopping
   7 Money Matters/Markets
   8 Entertainment/Games
   9 Home/Health/Education
  10 Reference
  11 Computers/Technology
  12 Business/Other Interests

Enter choice number !
```

We have shown you how to zip around the system in the express lane with the GO command to travel directly to a specified page address, such as "OLT-90," a page within *Online Today*'s electronic edition. But you can't really appreciate the convenience of that command until you have navigated the system the way we shall this time, the hard way, the way Granddad used to do it on his old steam-powered modem. From the main menu, select option 3 for Communications and system displays:

```
r---------------------------------------------------------------
!
!   CompuServe                           COMMUNICATE  !
!
!   COMMUNICATIONS/BULLETIN BOARDS
!
!   1 EasyPlex Electronic Mail
!   2 CB Simulator
!   3 Forums (SIGs)
!   4 National Bulletin Board
!   5 Directory of Subscribers
!   6 Ask Customer Service
!   7 CB Society
!   8 Public File Area (ACCESS)
!   9 The Convention Center (tm)
!
!
!   Enter choice !
!
L---------------------------------------------------------------
```

The quick reference word (COMMUNICATE) reminds us that if you ever need to reach the menu in a hurry, just enter G COMMUNICATE. It also says that option 1 is electronic mail. Choose it now, and CompuServe sends you something like this:

```
r---------------------------------------------------------------
!
!   EasyPlex  Main Menu
!
!   1 READ mail, 1 message pending
!   2 COMPOSE a new message
!   3 UPLOAD a message
!   4 USE a file from PER area
!   5 ADDRESS Book
!   6 SET options
!
!   Enter choice !
!
L---------------------------------------------------------------
```

When we saw this menu on our first tour, there was no option 1, READ mail, because you had no mail waiting. Because there is a letter in the mailbox, option 1 has been restored. Choose it by entering 1 at the prompt, and your letter is displayed, something like this:

```
EasyPlex

Date:  12-Jan-89 16:05 EDT
From:  Charlie Bowen [71635,1025]
Subj:  WELCOME!

Hi! Welcome to CompuServe
Information Service. You've made
amazing progress so far. But
there's much more to learn.

Last page. Enter command
or <CR> to continue!
```

Okay, troops. Let's wait for everyone to catch up. Some of us may want to savor our words. By the way, this letter probably is one of more than a million Easy-Plex will deliver this month. In 1987, the Electronic Mail Association estimated that CompuServe's EasyPlex processed at least 1.1 million letters a month. In fact, CompuServe attracts many businesses to its electronic mail services — EasyPlex and a customized service called InfoPlex — and actually manages the mail features under a separate business service divison that is profitable in its own right. As we shall see in Chapter 19, EasyPlex interconnects with InfoPlex and MCI Mail, as well as with telex and facsimile (FAX) machines.

Now, ready? Everybody press RETURN until you reach this menu:

```
EasyPlex  Action Menu

** Charlie Bowen/WELCOME! **

1 DELETE this message
2 FILE in PER area
3 FORWARD
4 REREAD message
5 REPLY
6 SAVE in mailbox
7 DOWNLOAD message

Enter choice or <CR> to continue!
```

This busy and important screen is called an *action* menu. With it the system finds out what action you want to take regarding this piece of correspondence. The menu lists your alternatives. Some are quite clear. Selecting 6 saves the letter in the mailbox, meaning it would be there the next time you visited EasyPlex; option 4 would display the message again, and option 1 would delete it.

**Note:**   An undocumented, but handy EasyPlex command is UNDELETE. It allows you to recover messages you inadvertently delete. However, it can be used *only* during the EasyPlex session in which the message was deleted. Once you leave EasyPlex, there is no way to recover deleted messages. To use the command, simply enter the word UNDELETE at the prompt and system displays a menu of the deleted messages and prompts you to specify those that should be restored.

Two main ways exist for answering a EasyPlex message: to REPLY to it (option 5) and to FORWARD it to someone else on the system (option 3). The more common response is a REPLY, and the system makes it easy. You need only enter 5 at the prompt and you are whisked away to your work space, where you can write your message, just as you did on the first tour when you COMPOSEd this letter. Let's try that. Enter 5 at the prompt, and you see:

```
EasyPlex   Compose

Enter reply. (/EXIT when done)

1:
```

The top line reminds you that you now are in the "compose" mode so, following the 1:, type "This is a reply to the first message I wrote." and press RETURN. At the next prompt (2:), enter /EXIT or just /EX, and the system displays:

```
r--------------------------------------------------¬
¦                                                  ¦
¦   EasyPlex   Send Menu                           ¦
¦                                                  ¦
¦   For current reply                              ¦
¦                                                  ¦
¦   1 SEND                                         ¦
¦   2 EDIT                                         ¦
¦   3 TYPE                                         ¦
¦   4 FILE DRAFT copy                              ¦
¦   5 SEND with /RECEIPT   ($)                     ¦
¦                                                  ¦
¦   Enter choice !                                 ¦
¦                                                  ¦
L--------------------------------------------------┘
```

This menu should look familiar too. It is the same *send* menu you saw at the
end of Chapter 3 when you wrote your original letter. On it, option 3 displays your
message, try that, enter 3 (or the word TYPE) and see your message with its line numbers, then come back to the send menu. Let's suppose that while TYPing your message with the last command, you saw typographical mistakes that you now want to
correct. Enter 2 at the send menu (or the word EDIT) now, and the system produces
this *edit* menu:

```
r--------------------------------------------------¬
¦                                                  ¦
¦   EasyPlex   Edit Menu                           ¦
¦                                                  ¦
¦   1 CHANGE characters in line                    ¦
¦   2 REPLACE line                                 ¦
¦   3 DELETE line                                  ¦
¦   4 INSERT new line(s)                           ¦
¦   5 TYPE all lines                               ¦
¦                                                  ¦
¦   0 SEND message                                 ¦
¦                                                  ¦
¦   Enter choice !                                 ¦
¦                                                  ¦
L--------------------------------------------------┘
```

The first four options allow for the major operations in editing. When selected,
each prompts for the *number* of the line (1) in which you wish to change characters,
(2) replace, (3) delete, or (4) after which you wish to insert lines. We shall have a
workout with this editing menu in a later chapter; for now, let's suppose you just have
finished your corrections and are ready to send the letter on its way. Enter the word
SEND (or option 0 at this prompt); the system will ask you for your name. After you
enter it, you receive word that "Message sent to ..." Note that because this is a reply,

the system *remembers* the user ID of the other party and doesn't trouble you to enter it again. By contrast, if this were an original message, the system would need you to enter the user ID of the intended recipient.

Questions?

*How long can an electronic message wait in a recipient's mailbox?*

Presently, EasyPlex messages are held for the addressee up to 90 days. If a message is not picked up after 90 days, the system automatically deletes it.

Now press RETURN at the prompt and up comes the action menu again:

```
EasyPlex   Action Menu

** Charlie Bowen/WELCOME!  **

1 DELETE this message
2 FILE in PER area
3 FORWARD
4 REREAD message
5 REPLY
6 SAVE in mailbox
7 DOWNLOAD message

Enter choice or <CR>
to continue!
```

In other words, REPLYing to a message does not remove it from your mailbox, so the system still offers you alternatives for dealing with it.

FORWARDing a message (option 3) works a little like a REPLY, but it lets you send your comments along with a copy of the original message to someone on the system. Suppose that "WELCOME!" actually was an invitation to correspond with someone about a hobby or business venture and you knew someone else on-line who also would be interested. To see how that works, enter 3 at this prompt and you are taken to compose mode again, with the cursor stopping at the "1:" prompt. Type this:

```
1: This time I'm forwarding <RETURN>
2: the message to myself. <RETURN>
3: /EXIT <RETURN>
```

After you complete the composing with the /EXIT signal, the system displays the same *send* menu you saw earlier:

```
EasyPlex   Send Menu

For current reply

1 SEND
2 EDIT
3 TYPE
4 FILE DRAFT copy
5 SEND with /RECEIPT   ($)

Enter choice !
```

However, this time when you choose the SEND option (option 1 on this menu), the system needs a little more information. As you are supposedly forwarding this message to someone else, the system must ask you for the user ID of the recipient. When you see "Send to (Name or User ID):" type in your *own* ID number for this experiment. (Obviously, if you were *really* forwarding the message to someone else, you would enter their ID number at the prompt.) The system now summarizes the address, something like:

```
To:  71635,1025
From: Charlie Bowen
Subj: WELCOME!

Is this correct? (Y or N)?
```

Enter Y and the message is sent on its way.

By the way, also notice that item 5 on the send menu, is a second send option; one that allows you to send any EasyPlex with a *receipt*. This option means that you receive a brief acknowledgment via EasyPlex when the recipient has retrieved the letter, like registered mail from the U.S. Postal Service. At this time, this is an extra-cost service of EasyPlex; 25 cents is charged to your account for each receipt.

The next time we are on-line together, we shall contrast how replies and forwarded messages appear when you *receive* them. For now, we have one more little EasyPlex exercise; press RETURN to get back to the action menu:

```
EasyPlex  Action Menu

** Charlie Bowen/WELCOME! **

1 DELETE this message
2 FILE in PER area
3 FORWARD
4 REREAD message
5 REPLY
6 SAVE in mailbox
7 DOWNLOAD message

Enter choice or <CR>
to continue!
```

We mentioned that option 6 saves this letter in the mailbox. Selecting it causes the letter to remain for reading another time. We also have pointed out that messages can remain in a mailbox for up to 90 days before the system automatically deletes them. However, you can use this save-in-mailbox option to renew that 90-day period. To do that, simply read the message again and select option 6, Save in Mailbox.

However, a better way is available for saving old letters, one that doesn't clutter up your mailbox. Notice option 2 allows you to "FILE in PER area." As you will see in Chapter 7, PER is your "personal file area," a private part of the system where you can keep your own files on-line. Sounds good, so for now let's tuck this letter away in the PER area for future use. Choose option 2 and the system asks:

```
Name of file:
```

CompuServe needs to know what you want to call this particular file when it is placed in your storage area. It can be a word up to six letters. Let's call it MYMAIL. Enter that and the system reports, "Message filed in MYMAIL." By the way, there is still one more item on the action menu, option 7, "DOWNLOAD message," but let's defer discussion of that one for the time being.

**Note:**   If a week or so has passed since your reading of Chapter 3, then a few other CompuServe-related events may have happened to your household. First, you may have received a letter from CompuServe's Columbus, Ohio, office that provides your permanent password. If so, you also may have another message in your Easy-Plex mailbox, one that officially welcomes you to the system, gives you a quick run-down of commands, and perhaps mentions a few new features.

## On to the Party!

Enough of this sitting around reading letters from ourselves. We promised you a party. To get to it, use the express lane by entering G CB (for Go CB Simulator) at the prompt. You will go right to the front door, where you should see a list of options something like this:

```
CB SIMULATOR                        CB-10

1 Guidelines and Instructions
2 Access CB Band A
3 Access CB Band B
4 Special Pricing — The CB Club
5 Cupcake's CB Society Column
6 CB Forum — CB Bulletin Board and
  Data Libraries
7 CBer Pictures
8 Nodes — Updated December

Enter choice !
```

From here, we want to take option 4 to go to "Band A" of the CB Simulator. Enter 2 and the system replies:

```
CB Simulator                        CB-1

One moment please...
```

Somewhere in Columbus, Ohio, we are being moved to the host computer that contains the CB Simulator, and, finally ...

```
CB II — CB Simulator(sm) v2G(74) Band A
++++++++++++++++++++++++++++++++++++++++++++
The CB Club  makes good sense. Type
 /GO CBCLUB for details.
++++++++++++++++++++++++++++++++++++++++++++
What's your handle!
```

CB starts with a little commercial for its discount CB Club (we talk about in the next chapter), then asks for your "handle," that is, what you want to call yourself. Your handle is necessary because once in the real-time conference area, every message you send will be preceded automatically by your name, as it might appear in the script of a play. Therefore, be sure to enter your handle the way you want it to appear to people with whom you will be talking.

Some people spend hours dreaming up just the right handle. Charlie uses the handle "Bluegrass" because he grew up in Kentucky and likes to play guitar. Dave picked "Hermit Dave" because he has always had a fondness for the arts, particularly classically ribald old limericks. Just pick a handle that says something about you, but one that *doesn't* hint at your password. (As we shall continue to say, your password is the key to your account number. Guard it!) Your handle can be up to 19 characters long, but a few characters are reserved; you may not use either an asterisk (*) or a pound sign (#) in your handle.

After you have entered your handle, the system checks its files to make sure your choice isn't a handle already *reserved* by someone else (more about that later as well). If it finds a problem, the system will ask you to pick another handle. Once you have entered an accepted name, CompuServe gives you a quick accounting of how many people are on the 36 "channels" of CB with a message like this:

```
(channel) users tuned in
  (1)21 (3)4 (5)2 (6)2
  (7)8 (10)1 (11)2 (12)1 (13)2
  (14)1 (16)8 (17)5 (18)3 (21)2
  (22)1 (23)1 (24)1 (27)2 (29)1
  (30)1 (33)12 (34)9 (36)3 (Tlk)50
```

This message means there are 21 participants on channel 1, 4 on channel 3, 2 on channel 5, 2 on channel 6, and so on. The "(Tlk)50" at the end of the line means that 50 users are in the private TALK area we mentioned in the previous chapter. As you will see later, there are other ways to get user information and several ways to "talk" publicly and privately on CB. We save details of many of those for the next chapter, when you are off-line again. No use spending your connect time reading instead of doing.

CB now asks what channel you wish to visit (that is, on which channel you want to begin sending and receiving messages). Look at the report on your screen and pick a channel where there are four or five people, such as channel 3 in our example, and enter that number. (Obviously, the report — called a "status" — is different on your screen than it is here, as we are all visiting CB at different times. However, the commands are the same for all of us.) As you choose your channel, remember what we said in the previous chapter about some channels being dedicated for specific uses. Channel 1 is called the adult channel, but that doesn't mean it is intended to be pornographic. Channel 7 is the young adults channel, Channel 13 is the "gender alternatives" channel (primarily for cross-dressers and those who have had sex change operations), Channel 17 is the youth center, Channel 22 is the seniors channel, Channel 23 is the Knights of Olde channel (for CB old-timers), and Channel 33 is the "alternative lifestyles" channel, primarily for gays. All other channels are unassigned.

Once you have entered a number, you probably will start seeing messages right away from other people tuned to that channel. (Incidentally, you may see some handles enclosed in asterisks, even though we told you not to use asterisks or pound signs in your own handle. In this case, the asterisks mean the handle-owners are members of that discount CB Club that we shall talk about in Chapter 6.) If you would like, continue watching the messages come in for a minute, but *don't* try to talk to anyone yet, not until you have read the next few pages. The others on the channel won't mind. They were talking to each other before you arrived; they talk now; and some of them probably will continue talking long after you have logged off.

When it is time, you will be able to communicate with others logged in to your channel by simply typing your messages, ending each by pressing the RETURN key. A message can be up to 139 characters long. (If you try to send a line longer than that, the system will cut off the message when the limit is reached.) Also, no one can see what you are typing *as you type it*. Only after you press RETURN is your message transmitted to the others.

The system always handles the introductions. Suppose you were to enter "Hello, all" and press RETURN. To everyone else tuned to the channel, your message would appear as:

```
(A3, Bluegrass) Hello, all
```

Of course, your handle would appear in place of "Bluegrass." You, however, wouldn't see your own messages scrolling across the screen with your handle in front of them. You would see only what you typed, no channel designation nor handle. Everyone else tuned to that channel would see both in addition to your message.

Now, about trying to get a word in edgewise on CB. When a channel is particularly active and a new user's message a little long, it can get confusing. Some new users have the mistaken notion that they must type all they have to say in between the messages arriving on the screen from other subscribers. That is *not* true. Remember what we just said about nothing you type being transmitted *until* you press RETURN? That means that everything you type (up to 139 characters) is stored in a memory "buffer" in CompuServe's computers until you press the RETURN key; the RETURN signals the system to send your message out to the others on the channel.

To see how that works, let's say you wanted to send a line that said, "It's great to be here. It's my first time on CB, and it's really exciting." However, while you are typing it, suppose others on the channel are sending their own messages. In that case it could appear, to you, as something like this:

```
It's  gre(A3,Virginia Gentleman) How is it on river
                              at to be here.
(A3,NightMan) Isn't that interesting!
(A3,Honey Bear ) I am new!!!! It's my first time
on CB, and (A3,NightMan) hehe
(A3,*Stormie Normie*) You have a staff? and it's
 really exciting.
```

Your message *is* in there, but you have to look carefully for it, because your words are woven among the messages from others on the channel. If this happens to you as you begin to communicate on this tour, don't panic and don't start retyping what you have already typed.

As one old CB'er used to say, "Just put your head down, son, and type!" In other words, when you finally type what you want to appear and you press RETURN, your message will be displayed in its entirety to the others — not chopped up as it may have appeared to you during the writing of it. Later, we'll have some hints about how to see what you have typed *before* you send it and how you can solve the verbal traffic jams, like the one in the example, by using a special kind of terminal program.

Incidentally, the "3" in our examples refers to channel 3. As there are two bands of the CB Simulator — bands A and B — the letter refers to the band. You may remember that the CB menu offered two bands. The bands are identical in operation, but people using one band can't talk to those on the other. If you want to meet a friend on CB, be sure to specify in advance what band you will be using.

Before we get too far along in our visit, please take a moment now to enter this command on your keyboard:

```
/NOTALK <RETURN>
```

Note that a slash (/) precedes it; all commands on CB are preceded by a slash. (As with EasyPlex's /EXIT command, the slash tells the system that what follows is a command, not text.) Note, too, that it is one word, all run together, /NOTALK.

*All right. What was that all about?*

We reported in the previous chapter how CB offers a popular option for private "talks" between just two subscribers. We have quite a bit to say about TALK and other forms of private chatting in the next chapter. However, until we have that later discussion, we suggest you not accept any TALK requests on this visit. The command you have just entered directs the system automatically to turn down such requests for you during the current session. Handy, that.

By now, you may have received greetings from others on this channel. We don't want to interrupt, so we shall keep the rest of this brief. Now keep an eye on the screen and be ready to answer questions that others may ask. It is common for CB regulars to ask newcomers where they are from, what they do for a living, whether they are male or female ("You M or F?"), etc. Listen to some of the chatting, and when there is a lull in the conversation read on.

## Conferencing Commands

Oh, hi, again. Having a good time? While there is a pause in the action, here is a rundown on some other features of CB.

If you have tried to do any serious conversing, you probably have noticed that the messages you are typing sometimes get interrupted by incoming messages. Don't say we didn't warn you. It can get a little confusing, and you may find that you have forgotten what you've typed so far. CompuServe provides a useful control code for these times. If you enter a CONTROL V, the system redisplays what you have typed before you actually send it with the RETURN key. Of course, it works only on your *current* message, not those that you have already sent when you pressed RETURN.

Another valuable control code, CONTROL U, erases everything you have just typed (that is, *if* you haven't pressed RETURN yet). Thus, if you type a message and decide before you press RETURN that you don't want to send it after all, just press CONTROL U and it is erased from the CompuServe's memory buffer.

As noted, aside from those control codes, all commands in the real-time conferencing area are preceded by a slash (/) and must be typed flush left on the screen (the first position of a new line).

Here are some important commands:

/STATUS is the command for a status report and it displays the number of users on each channel, just like the report you saw when you first came to the CB area. Try it. On a new line, type /STATUS. The system shows you something like this (the # sign indicates the channel to which you are tuned):

```
(1) 5  (3) 5#  (6) 3  (30) 10  (Tlk) 8
```

/CHANNEL lets you move to another channel. If you want to leave channel 3 and go to channel 1, you enter /CHANNEL 1 flush left on the screen. Now a /STATUS command shows you something like this:

```
(1) 6#, (3) 4, (6) 3, (30) 10, (Tlk) 8
```

In this example, there would be one more person on channel 1 (you) and one fewer on channel 3 (you again), and the # sign would be moved from 3 to 1.

**Important Note:** All commands in CB can be abbreviated to the slash and the *first three* letters (sometimes fewer), so instead of typing /CHANNEL, you can type /CHA. Similarly, either /STA or /STATUS works.

Also, you can eavesdrop. Sometimes the best part of a busy party is that you can stand in the middle of the room and listen to several conversations at once. You can do that here in this imaginary room as well. With the /MON command you can monitor up to two other channels without actually tuning to them. You may send messages on only one channel, but you can listen to (well, okay, see) the messages being sent on up to three, that is, the channel you are tuned to and the two you are monitoring. Here is how it works. Suppose you were tuned to Channel 1 and you still wanted to see what was being said on channel 3. You enter the command:

```
/MON 3
```

Now when you enter a /STA command, the channels you are monitoring are noted with an asterisk (*), making the status report appear:

```
(1)6#  (3)4*  (6)3  (30)10  (Tlk)8
```

If you decided to monitor channel 5 or channel 30 in addition to channel 3, an asterisk (*) would appear beside the new channel as well. Try that.

Monitor a channel with the /MON command followed by a channel number, and watch the conversation for a minute or so. You should see comments coming from both the channel to which you are tuned and the one you are monitoring. Preceding each comment is the number of the channel on which it is being typed.

Also, enter /STA to look at where the "#" and the "*" are placed. Remember, whatever you type in CB is transmitted to *only* the channel to which you are tuned, *not* to the ones you are monitoring. (It leads to embarrassing results if you forget that and start trying to converse with people on other channels. To the people on your channel, it will look as if you are electronically talking to yourself.)

If you want to stop monitoring a channel, the command is "unmonitor," that is, /UNM, such as:

```
/UNM 3
```

You can get a list of the handles of all the people currently on CB by requesting a "user status" report. The command is /USERS. It gives you a list of all the users on all the channels. On a busy night, though, hundreds of people might be on the channels so that can be quite a list! Therefore, you also can use the /USERS command followed by a channel number to get a list of users on just one specific channel. Right now try that one. Enter /USERS followed by a channel number, like:

```
/USERS 6
```

The computer responds with a list something like this:

```
Job    User ID       Nod  Chn  Handle
----   -----------   ---  ---  -----------
  19   71635,1025    NYN   6   FALCON
 114   70000,111     HWV   6   Lady
 203   77777,375     QAK   6   Bluegrass
 214   70000,1331    ALT   6   Hermit
```

In the user-status list, the number on the left is a job number. (The *job* is a one-, two-, or three-digit number the computer automatically assigns to each user when they log in to the CB area. You need to use job numbers in some special features of conference that we will see in the next chapter.) Following the job number is the user ID number, the node, the channel to which the user is tuned, and the handle of each user. The *node* (the "NYN," "CWV," "QAK" business) is a code for the cities from which the users are calling. (And if you are thinking of a wonderful pun — "I've got a code in my node" — save your breath; it has been done.) If you want to become a node-watcher and figure out where some of the other people are calling from, you can get a list of the nodes and the cities sometime when you are not in CB by entering G NODES any "!" prompt. Or, you can use the /NODE command. Try that. Let's say you would like to know where the node HWV, in the example above, is located. To that, enter:

```
/NODE HWV
```

The system should report:

```
NODE = Huntington WV
```

This message means a person identified with the HWV node is located in Huntington, West Virginia. Sometimes, the location of a node isn't given. For example, if you asked for the node location of QAK, the system would respond with:

```
NODE = Tymnet
```

This message means the caller is using the Tymnet packet network and could be calling from one of hundreds of locations served by this network.

Wrapping up our quick summary of major commands is the one for changing your handle. You can do it with this command.

```
/HAN
```

The system asks:

```
What's your handle?
```

Now you simply enter your new handle, and the system will verify that your handle has been changed.

Enjoy yourself! We leave you with several commands for leaving CB. If you want to leave and log off CompuServe, enter /OFF. If you want to leave CB and return to the CB menu, enter /EXIT. Also /TOP or /MAIN leaves CB and goes to the TOP of the system. If you would like to use the GO command to leave CB and travel directly to another page of the system, just precede it with a slash. For instance, /G OLT whisks you out of the CB Simulator and puts you in the fast lane to the *Online Today* publication. If you want to find a page address, enter /FIND followed by a keyword, such as /FIND IBM.

When you are ready to log off the system, remember that you should always disconnect with an appropriate log-off command rather than simply breaking the phone connection. That is because it can save you money. It may take CompuServe's computers one to seven minutes to detect that you are gone, and if that happens, you are charged for that additional connect time. However, if you end the session by entering the BYE or OFF commands (or /OFF in CB) to log off, the disconnection is immediate and no additional charges are levied.

Incidentally, along the same lines, CompuServe always watches for input from your computer and is prepared to automatically log you off if it doesn't receive any input in a certain number of minutes. On *most* of the system, this is a 15-minute time limit. In other words, if for some reason you sit at a menu for 15 minutes without typing anything, CompuServe assumes you meant to log off and take care of business. Note, though, that on CB, that time limit on inactivity is one hour, not 15 minutes.

## Quick Reference on Major CB Commands

If you plan to stay on CB a little while longer, here is a list you may find useful. It recaps the basic CB commands you need for general use on your first visit.

/STA — gives you a list of the number of users on each channel.

/CHA — tunes to a new channel. For example, /CHA 6 would move you to channel 6.

/MON — monitors a channel other than the one you are on. You can monitor up to two channels at a time. /MON 1,2 would monitor channels 1 and 2.

/UNM followed by a channel number — unmonitors a channel you are monitoring.

/USERS — displays a list of all users by job number, name, node, and user ID number. If followed by a channel number, it gives the information for that channel only.

/NODE followed by a three-letter node code — tells you the location of a specified node represented by the three letters.

/NOTALK — stops talk requests from others.

/HAN — allows you to change your handle.

/OFF — exits CB and logs you off the service.

/EXIT — exits CB and returns you to the CB menu.

/G followed by a page number — leaves CB and takes you to a specified menu, such as /G OLT-10.

/TOP or /MAIN — leaves CB and goes to the TOP of the system.

/FIND followed by a keyword — finds specific subjects, just as FIND without the preceding slash does elsewhere in the system.

CONTROL V — redisplays what you have typed before you actually send it.

CONTROL U — erases everything you have just typed if you haven't tapped RETURN yet. Of course, once you press the RETURN key, everything you have typed is transmitted.

# CHAPTER 6

# After the Ball: More about CB

You can put away your party shoes now. We won't be going on-line in this chapter. Instead, we shall sit back and reflect a little on what we have learned so far about electronic conferences and what we can learn to tailor this powerful service to fit your needs. In this chapter, you will find out how to have private talks with one or more friends at the same time and how to set aside a private area where only those who know a specific code word will be able to enter. Also, you will get some hints on how to be a good citizen of this new medium, and what to do about those who aren't particularly good citizens. Finally, we'll offer some tips from the Sadder-but-Wiser Department about how to avoid the wolves and vipers in this neck of the woods and how to sidestep that minority that always seems to want to abuse a good thing.

In the previous chapter, you saw only half of the 72 channels available to CB users, the half on Band A. At the CB page of the system (G CB), you have the option of going to Band A or Band B.

*But what if I'm already on one of the bands and I want to go to the other? Do I have to /EXIT back to the menu?*

Not at all. The command /BAND B from Band A will get you to the other set of 36 channels. Likewise, the command /BAND A entered on Band B will get you quickly back to Band A. No matter what channel you are on, you will be taken to the corresponding channel on the other band.

Even with your brief exposure to real-time conferencing channels, you have seen their potential. You can use such a facility for a free-wheeling national party. And, being able to talk with any number of people at the same time, you can use CB for meetings of people of similar interests to set up discussion groups, business sessions, seminars. Of course, the service would be even *more* useful if you could alter it to meet your own needs.

As it happens, you can. For instance, one of the most popular features of CB is TALK, which allows you to communicate privately with one other person. Here is how it works. Suppose you are on one of the public channels and, by entering the /USERS command, you see that your old friend, Boston Slim, is on the system. As you recall, the /USERS command lists, among other things, each participant's "job number" (assigned by the system each time you log on), and you use those job numbers with the TALK feature. From the list, suppose you see that your friend's job number is 166. To invite him into a private conversation, you enter on any channel:

```
/TALK 166
```

This tells the system, "Send a talk request to job number 166." After you press RETURN, this message appears on your screen:

```
Job 166 has been notified, please wait
To stop waiting, enter /BREAK
>
```

You will no longer see the conversations on the public channel to which you were tuned. That's because with the /TALK command, you have gone into a kind of limbo, waiting for Job 166 to reply. As the second line of that message says, you can enter /BREAK (or a CONTROL P, incidentally) to stop waiting and return to the public channels. It is up to Boston Slim to accept or to decline your invitation for a private conversation. On his screen (while you are in limbo) is a message like this:

```
*** Please /TALK with Job 32 [70000,010]
Old Fella
To do so, enter /TALK 32
```

Your job number, user ID, and handle all are displayed in a message that appears on his screen only; others on the channel do not even know he has received a TALK request. If he decides to TALK to you, he enters:

```
/TALK 32
```

This message means, "Talk to job number 32"; then you both receive messages something like this:

```
Job 32 [70000,010] Old Fella is now
in contact. To break contact, enter /BREAK
>
```

Again, /BREAK (or CONTROL P) is the way to break off the TALK and return to the public channels. Also, notice the ">" below the message. That is the prompt for TALK mode. CompuServe assumes you know to whom you are "talking," so it doesn't supply handles in TALK; instead, all your messages are automatically preceded by the ">" prompt.

As long as you both want to continue the TALK, your messages are seen by only the two of you. Some of your commands from the public channels — particularly /STATUS and /USERS — also can be used while in TALK. This feature allows you, for instance, to have a brief /TALK with one friend while watching the /USERS list for another's arrival.

TALK, because it allows some privacy in your real-time conversations, is popular with CB regulars who have developed friendships on the system. Many subscribers use EasyPlex to set dates for TALK sessions later.

Now, a word about manners. Had you been on-line just now and followed our instructions to the letter, you might have offended some CB regulars. In these circles, it is considered good manners to use the public channels to invite someone to TALK *before* entering the /TALK command. Many regulars simply ignore TALK requests from people they don't know, particularly requests that aren't previously announced. The etiquette, then, would have you seek out Boston Slim on the public channel and ask him there if he would like to talk. If yes, *then* you would enter a /TALK 166 command. (Of course, old friends might, by mutual consent, develop a more casual procedure.)

Also, it is a good idea to know your *own* job number. It is polite to save a TALK partner that hassle by simply saying, "Call job 23," or whatever your job number is. As we have seen, you can find job numbers on the USERS list, but on a busy night around the system, that can be quite time-consuming. Fortunately, a faster way is available. On a public channel, enter:

```
/JOB
```

The system then reports a one-, two-, or three-digit number that is your "job."

Something else about TALK — we noted in the previous chapter that when you issue a /USERS command on an open channel, you probably will find some on the list with "Tlk" beside their names. This notation means they are "in talk" with someone. And, if you would like to see a list of users currently in talk, you can enter /USERS TLK.

It used to be (several years ago) that if you tried to talk to someone who was already in TALK, you would receive a system message saying that person was unavailable and suggesting you try later. However, more recent improvements now make it possible for you to send a /TALK request to a person already /TALKing. If the recipient of the request then enters /TALK followed by your job number, the system automatically disconnects the original talk partner and initiates the new talk session with you.

More questions?

*Let's say that the person with whom you are talking breaks off suddenly or otherwise is disconnected from TALK or the system. What happens?*

You remain in TALK, but the system informs you that the person with whom you were talking has disconnected and that you should type /BREAK if you want to return to the public channel. Remember, you are not returned to the public channel from TALK unless you first type /BREAK or CONTROL P.

Finally, if you sometimes don't want to be bothered by /TALK requests, you can enter a /NOTALK command, as we did during the tour in the previous chapter. That causes the system to decline automatically (and politely) any TALK requests directed your way. The /NOTALK is in effect for the current session only. To turn off /NOTALK, you enter /TALK <RETURN>.

## Finding and Paging Your Friends

With such a busy, popular feature, there has to be faster ways to locate your friends in all those crowded electronic rooms. You have already used one major locating command, /USERS, which gives you a list of handles, user IDs, and job numbers. However, if hundreds of people are on-line (which can easily happen on weekend nights), it could take quite a while to display and sift through the list. Even entering /USERS with a specific channel number, such as /USERS 6, could produce a long list. Fortunately, CompuServe's programmers have come to the rescue with a command called /WHO. (It used to be called /WHERE, and /WHERE still worked at the time of this edition, but /WHO is the preferred command. It also works with a simple /W instead of spelling out entire word.) /WHO (or /W) works this way. Suppose you know that a friend with user ID 71635,1025 is somewhere on CB, but you don't know the handle or channel being used. You enter:

```
/WHO 71635,1025
```

The system scans the CB channels and, if it finds the user ID you have specified, it reports something like:

```
  23   71635,1025   HWV   1   Bluegrass
```

Look closely and you see that is the same format as entries in the /USERS list. The first number (23) is your friend's job number, followed by the user ID number, node, the number of the channel to which the friend's tuned (1), and the handle (Bluegrass). /WHO also works if you know your friend's current job number, as in /WHO 23.

Another command the wizards have come up with allows you to *page* or signal an acquaintance from across a crowded CB. Enter /PAGE followed by the other person's current job number, as in /PAGE 23. On the other end of the floor, your friend sees what amounts to the CB version of a beeper:

```
  *** Job 40 [70475,1165] Hermit Dave
  has just /PAGE'd you
```

You might then send your friend a /TALK request or just look him up on the public channels with the /WHO command (/WHO 40 in this example) to see where he is.

Of course, there may be times when you don't want to be interrupted by /PAGEs. You can turn off your own beeper by entering /NOPAGE. That tells the system you are not accepting /PAGE requests at the moment. Anyone who tries to page you then will be told you aren't available. When you are ready to turn the beeper back on, type /PAGE <RETURN>.

## When Three Isn't a Crowd

The advantage of TALK is that it is private and it is one to one. You don't have to "shout" to get your messages across over all the other conversations on a public channel. The disadvantages are that you are out of touch with the rest of the channels during the private session and that it is for only two people at a time. If you wanted to have a three-way private conversation, you couldn't use TALK mode. But the system does provide ways for multiuser privacy. The next time you are on-line, try some *scramble* options.

Suppose you have agreed to meet four friends on channel 16, and you want to have a private chat with them all at the same time. You could decide, in advance, on a code word, say, "Violet." First, you would all tune to channel 16 and then each of you would enter:

```
/SCR VIOLET
```

That message means, "Scramble on the word VIOLET." In a second, the system responds with:

```
** SCRAMBLE is ON **
```

From this point, your transmissions would be scrambled, readable only by those who have entered the same code. Other subscribers on that channel see none of your conversation.

Participants in a scrambled conversation do not have to enter the code at the *same time*. If one of your friends is late arriving, the friend need only tune to the proper channel and then to enter the /SCR VIOLET command to join you. Note, though, that all the participants on a scrambled conversation do have to be tuned to the same channel. It does no good to know the right code word if all your associates have scrambled on channel 1 and you are on channel 16.

To leave scramble and return to the regular CB public channels, you "unscramble" by entering the command:

```
/UNS
```

Anything you type after entering this command is readable on the public channel.

*But where do you "go" when you scramble? Is it a separate area of the system, like TALK?*

Not really. In scramble, you are still on the public channels, but in a special encrypted area. It is as if you are invisible to everyone except those with the correct code word. You might think of scramble as going "upstairs" to private chambers. CB regulars even have standing code words for their groups of friends. Remember in Chapter 4 when Charlie shared his story about the "Seedy Weed Funny Farm" cowpoke gang? Their "ranch" was channel 10 scrambled on the code SWFF, the first letters of each word.

Because scramble doesn't really remove you from the public channels, all regular features of CB still are available to you when you are scrambled. You can enter a /USERS command and get a list of other users. You also can enter a /STA and see the number of users on each channel. Not only that, you also can monitor what's happening "upstairs" *and* "downstairs" during a scrambled conversation. Suppose you decide to scramble, but all your participants haven't arrived yet. The late arrivals might not know you have scrambled. You would want to monitor the public channel (as well as the scrambled channel on which you are transmitting). The command /SMC followed by a code means "scramble and monitor clear." Enter this command when you want to see the messages from those users on the open channel who aren't scrambled and at the same time communicate with those who are scrambled. For example, you could enter:

```
/SMC VIOLET
```

This entry produces the message:

```
** SCRAMBLE is ON **
** Receiving both clear & scr **
```

CompuServe is telling you that everything you type from now on will be scrambled on the code word VIOLET, receivable only to those people who also have scrambled on that code. However, you will be receiving messages from *both* the scrambled channel ("upstairs") and the public channel ("downstairs").

The flip side of this command is /XCL. It means "transmit clear." Use it when you want to monitor the scrambled conversation while still communicating with those who aren't scrambled. For example, you might enter:

```
/XCL VIOLET
```

Now the system tells you:

```
** Receiving both clear & scr **
**CAUTION: sending clear text **
```

With /XCL, you see what's going on in a scramble. Remember, though, that any text you send appears on the public channel. To get out of this mode, enter:

```
/XCL
```

Now the system responds:

```
** SCRAMBLE is OFF **
```

Finally, your /USERS list can tip you off about others on the channels who are using scramble code words. Suppose you are on channel 5 and the /STA report says there are three people on the channel with you, but you aren't seeing any communications from them. If you enter /USERS 5, you might see a report like this:

```
Job   User ID      Nod   Chn   Handle
---   ----------   ---   ---   --------------
 1    70000,012    NYJ   5s    H. Ross Perogi
 2    70000,0010   IND   5s    C.Y.Borg
 3    70007,411    CWV   5     Bluegrass
 4    70000,100    PNX   5s    Izod
```

The "s" after the channel number for three of the four users is your answer. You guessed it; "s" means "scrambled."

# A Profile of CB Users

One of the newest features of CB is Profile, a way to find out a little something about those who are using CB. It also lets others know something about you without clogging the public channels with those basic questions. A CB Profile is completely voluntary, a public file that contains your handle, user ID, birth date and age (computed from your birth date), city and state, computer you are using, occupation, and interests.

To install your own CB Profile, enter G CBPROFILE at any system prompt or /G CBPROFILE while on a CB channel. This entry takes you to the CB Profile menu:

```
CB SIMULATOR              CBPROFILES
CB Profiles
1 Description
2 Enter/Change your Profile
3 Delete your Profile
```

It is a good idea to read the rules and caveats of CB Profiles (option 1) before entering your own profile (option 2). Notice you can delete your profile at any time by choosing option 3.

Once your profile is on file, other CB'ers have instant access to it. Let's say you are on a CB channel and you see the handle *LooLoo*. You note that the user ID is 70006,522 and the job number is 52. By entering /PR followed by either the user ID (/PR 70006,522), handle (/PR *LooLoo*), or job number (/PR 52) you might see:

```
Handle:      *LooLoo* [70006,522]
Birth:       1/30/41  48
From:        Columbus, Ohio
Using:       IBM PC
Job:         Electronic Conferencing Mgr.
Interests:   Flying, fishing, jazz, painting
```

A CB'ers profile is available only while the user in the CB Simulator. If the CB'er has chosen not to profile himself or herself, only the first line of the profile is presented.

Incidentally, you can double-check your own profile by typing /PR followed by your own handle, user ID, or job number while on a CB channel.

## Manners, Morals, Etiquette, Cranks, and Crazies

You now know most of the major commands for the real-time conference feature. You will learn several more important ones before this chapter ends, commands that let you to block out (or "squelch") messages from other users.

*Why in the world would I choose not to hear someone else's comments on an open channel?*

One reason is convenience. When you are tuned to a public channel on which 20 to 30 people are trying to talk simultaneously, you may find it useful to squelch certain users just to better follow a conversation in which you are interested. Sometimes you might want to squelch a person whose language or comments you find distasteful. CompuServe frowns on the use of vulgar language and even threatens immediate disconnection of offenders, who then have to pay $10 to reconnect. Still, the channels are public and, just like in the CB radio fad of the 1970s, conversations sometimes get a little racy. Squelching another subscriber's messages simply informs the system that you want to see no further messages from him or her. It has no effect on the squelched party; he or she won't even know you have stopped listening (unless for some reason you decide to announce it publicly). To use the command, enter /SQU followed by the handle, user ID, or job number of the subscriber in question. For instance:

```
/SQU HARPO
```

or

```
/SQU 23
```

or

```
/SQU 70000,010
```

The system then tells you that a particular user ID number has been squelched:

```
% Squelching [70000,010]
```

To "unsquelch," enter /SQU with no handle, and the system says:

```
% No longer squelching
```

You can squelch as many as ten users, one at a time for any CB session. The system keeps track of those of whom you aren't interested in listening. A single /SQU command (that is, /SQU without any data following it) lifts the ban against *all* you have squelched. Once you have squelched a user, he or she remains squelched during your current CB session, even if he or she changes his or her handle. Also with this command, you don't have to be on the same channel with a particular user to squelch.

## Is There an Echo in Here?

We have talked a little about how CompuServe sends back to you the characters you enter. It is called *echoing* and you have seen an example of it on CB. As you enter characters, they are echoed (or "bounced back") to you before you press RETURN to send the message to other users on the system. But there is a way to turn *off* the echo in CB: the command /NOECHO.

There are advantages and disadvantages to turning off the echo. The advantage is that you won't see your message being mixed up with those of others as you type. (You remember that "traffic jam" of messages in our example in the previous chapter.) Also, you won't see your message until others see it and you will see it exactly the way others see it, complete with the band, channel, and your handle.

The disadvantage, of course, is that you cannot see what you are typing at the moment you are typing it. If part of your typing routine is to check the screen to see what character you just typed, then /NOECHO probably is not for you. Just experiment with the /NOECHO command and, if it is not your cup of tea, use the /ECHO command to return to the echo.

## Electronic Civics Lesson

Before calling it a night, let's talk a minute about the kinds of conversations you might hear on the CB Simulator, the good guys, the bad guys, and you.

Being a good citizen in this new medium is more than just avoiding offensive language on public channels. Some of the real CB stars are those who have made a name for themselves by being helpful. Back when we were learning about the system, we were fortunate to find a number of good, helpful people who were willing to take greenhorns under their wings and show them around. These people are still out there answering questions every day about all kinds of things, from navigating the system to technical computer questions to advice for the lovelorn. As you become experienced at this kind of communication, you can repay that debt of kindness by watching out for newcomers. We are all still very much in the pioneer stages of this kind of communications and you can make a memory for some frustrated electronic immigrant if you take a few minutes to help them along.

Those are the good guys. The bad guys fall into general categories: the obnoxious, the vandals, and the crooks.

Among the bad citizens of conferencing are the Buffer Dumpers. Most good terminal programs these days have a facility for transmitting the contents of a buffer. That is a useful feature for preparing electronic mail off-line and dumping it to Easy-Plex in a burst. But for some reason, Buffer Dumpers think they are the only subscribers who have this feature; they take satisfaction in capturing a large amount of data — their current term paper, grocery list, even a portion of earlier CB transmissions — and dumping it *back* to CB. They try to tie up communications for everyone else until the buffer is empty. The best recourse against this character is to either /SQUelch the offender, or to tune to another channel. CompuServe, by the way, has been quite effective lately in fighting Buffer Dumpers. CB software detects buffered transmissions that are sent quickly (with little pause between the transmitted lines) and usually is successful in blocking them after a line or two.

Of course, if this offense (or any of the others we talk about here) is serious enough that you want to file a complaint, CompuServe wants to hear about it. Just look up the offender's user ID number and you can file your report in a special area of the system called Feedback by entering G FEEDBACK at any "!" prompt. All reports are kept confidential. Remember, you'll need the offender's user ID number, which you can get with the /USERS or /WHO command.

Also, if you would like to see all user ID numbers displayed as messages are being received, here's another useful command. It is /DISPLA UID (that is, "Display user IDs"). Enter /DISPL UID in the conference area, and you are shown the user IDs along with incoming messages, such as:

```
(A1,Bluegrass) [71635,1025] Had a good time!
```

To turn off this function, you enter /DISPL NOUID. You can also use the /DISPL command to have job numbers automatically displayed. /DISPL JOB turns the function on; /DISPL NOJOB turns it off. To have both user ID and job number displayed, type /DISPL ALL. To get rid of both of them, type /DISPLAY NONE.

Now back to the bad guys. Another electronic jerk is the one who likes to use the public channels to try to offend strangers, hiding behind the partial anonymity of a handle. This antic is a kind of obscene phone call with an audience. Newcomers, particularly those with feminine handles, are often the prankster's victims. He likes to lure them into TALK. Again, if this kind of thing offends you, use your /SQU option, and remember, /BREAK gets you out of any TALK session immediately, and typing /OFF from TALK will log you off the system without going back to the public channels.

**A Reminder:**    A more "legitimate" form of this is what some people think of as "compusex." Though this is a relatively new phenomenon, some CB'ers have developed it into a full-fledged electronic recreation. They cruise the system looking for partners who want to go into TALK and have a dual fantasy. As one user said, "It's sort of like a really erotic book that talks back to you." A case can be — and has been — made that compusex can be a serious, useful psychological release for people who have difficulty talking about sexual matters or who fear real intimate contact. Make up your own mind about whether this sort of thing appeals to you. But remember, serious compusex enthusiasts frown on those who trick others into a session. If talking about sex with strangers is not your idea of a good time, just politely decline.

By far, the most serious offender you might run across is the Password Thief. As we already have said several times (and will say several more times), NEVER GIVE YOUR PASSWORD TO ANYONE ON THE SYSTEM. You would be surprised how many people forget that simple rule when confronted by an official-looking message. That is precisely what the Password Thief hopes, that you will let down your defenses. Password thieves work in several ways. One popular ploy is to invite a newcomer into TALK and after a few minutes of routine conversation, suddenly transmit a message something like this:

```
%NTSWRK Communication problem — please wait
```

This message is quickly followed by:

```
PASSWORD:
```

But *you* now know enough to see through that one, right? Even though there are no handles present in TALK, you now know that all messages there are preceded by a ">" prompt, which makes this alleged "systems message" look pretty suspicious. All you have to do in this situation is enter /BREAK. If it is indeed a ruse, then it causes you to exit TALK and return to the public channels. Even if there is a system problem (and error messages and systems messages *are* sent from time to time), the best approach when in doubt is to hang up and redial. Do not enter your password!

In a variation on this theme, the Password Thief sometimes changes his handle to something like "CIS Supervisor" and then tells an unsuspecting newcomer that he is "running a check" and needs for you to "verify" your password. Bunk! Compu-Serve doesn't do that. Yes, there *are* CompuServe employees who regularly visit most features. Most of them have user ID numbers that start with 7000 (such as 70001 or 70003 or 70006), but a CompuServe employee will never ask you to enter your password. So just make a note of the user ID number of anyone who ever asks for your password. The good folks at Feedback will want to talk to the offender.

We mean none of this to scare you away from CB and the other conferencing features. On the contrary, it is our hope that by knowing about some of the wolves in these woods and how to deal with them, you will be more confident in your explora-tion. We have had many rewarding, exciting, amusing, satisfying experiences in electronic conferencing. We urge you to test your new knowledge on-line. You now know more about CB than we did in our first year on the system.

# Reserving Your CB Handle and Getting a Discount to Boot

CB can be addictive. There is a fascination with the idea of being able to chat with people throughout the world. Subscribers have told us how they spent night after night and hour after hour talking to new-found friends on CB. Or at least, they did until that first bill arrived and reality came home to roost. A regular CB habit can get expensive at $6 an hour. CompuServe has provided frequent CB users with a way out. It is called the CB Club, and it offers an optional pricing plan for those who use the feature frequently.

The CB discount plan works this way. Each month you pay a monthly fee, and the hourly charges for your use of CB are reduced. At this writing, you could pay a $100 monthly fee and be charged only $1 an hour for the time you spend on CB. An alternate plan offers a $4 per hour rate for a $25 monthly fee.

In addition, those who sign up for the special CB pricing also may reserve a CB handle, meaning that no one else may use it. If you have been on CB, you have probably seen handles enclosed in asterisks. These are handles reserved by those who are members of the CB Club.

You can check out details of the CB Club by choosing option 4 from the CB Simulator menu (G CB) or you can enter G CBCLUB at any "!" prompt. The CB Club menu offers a complete description of the club, the procedure and rules for reserving a handle, and an on-line CB Club sign-up area.

## Finally, Split Screens for Civilized Conferencing

In your firsthand experience with conferencing in the previous chapter, you probably noticed one of its frustrations: With so many people trying to talk at once, you may have felt you couldn't get a word in edgewise. As you tried to type your messages, you were constantly interrupted by incoming messages appearing in the middle of what you were trying to compose.

These days, many modern terminal programs offer a solution in the form of a *split-screen* feature (sometimes called "chat," "talk," or a "conference" option). It provides a special, protected area at the bottom of the screen where you can compose your messages for transmission, away from the distraction of incoming messages. You write the message in its entirety, edit it if you like, then transmit it with the RETURN key. If you become a conference enthusiast, we recommend a communications program with this split-screen option. When buying communications software or considering public domain programs, ask the salesperson or study the documentation to see if it has a built-in split-screen. Or check with others on CompuServe to see what they are using in the way of split-screen terminal programs.

## Side Roads

If you plan some more on-line exploration before starting the next chapter, here are three features you might want to look into:

*Cupcake's CB Society (G CUP)*. This feature is the CB Simulator's society pages. Cupcake, a New York CB enthusiast named Terry A. Biener, has been writing monthly columns for several years about the CB goings-on. On her menu, you can read the current issue and back issues, take part surveys and tell her your own news.

*CB Node List (G NODE)*. This feature is the translation of those location codes that show up in the /USERS and /WHO lists. It is a long list, but confirmed CB'ers often get a printout of it to hang near the computer. (As noted earlier, you also can search the list from a CB channel by enter /NODE followed by a code, such as /NODE CWV.)

*CB Club (G CBCLUB)*. This feature is a way to get discounts on connect time charges for CB usage. You don't have to be a member of the club to use the CB channels, but as noted earlier, those with confirmed CB habits find it helpful when the bill comes.

# CHAPTER 7

---

# Introducing Databases

*Databases* are great repositories of information and programs and CompuServe has many of them. In fact, much of the entire service could be thought of a colleection of databases with a wide variety of applications.

This time, in our third on-line tour, we will visit one kind of database, the National Bulletin Board, the system's classified ad section, where subscribers can post free notices to buy or sell all kinds of things. Also during this tour, we will look at the system as we have never seen it before — and in a way that even some experienced subscribers have never seen it — when we take our first steps into the Twilight Zone, the mysterious personal file area (also called PER). And we'll find out that it is not nearly as scary as some people seem to think. One purpose of this tour is to show you neighborhoods in CompuServe that don't use the menus of options you have gotten familiar with. Some of the best services in the system have different screen displays and their own sets of commands. You shouldn't let these features frighten you away just because they are different. Finally, we will see the Feedback area of the system, where you can you find answers to frequently asked questions about CompuServe and pose your own questions free of charge.

Before getting on the system, get a pencil and paper and put it beside your computer. Then, to get an idea of where we are going on this trip, look back to chapter 5 at the place in which we took our first visit to the CB Simulator and find the Communicate menu. Looking at that again, you see other selections available there, including the National Bulletin Board. We see, then, that this session's destinations are in the same general neighborhood as CB. Also while in Chapter 5, please locate our examples of EasyPlex's *action, edit* and *send* menus in the first part of the chapter and place a bookmark on those pages. We will compare those menus with others we see during this tour.

---

## Unfinished Business

Once you have a feel for on-line geography, log on to the system as you usually do and CompuServe will remind you of a little unfinished business left over from the previous outing. After the usual greeting, you should be taken to the EasyPlex menu and see something like this:

```
EasyPlex  Message Menu

1 Charlie Bowen/WELCOME!
2 Charlie Bowen/WELCOME!

0 READ ALL 2 messages

 Last page.  Enter choice
or M for EasyPlex main menu !
```

These, of course, are the messages you posted to yourself on your previous tour, one as a "reply," the other as a "forwarded" message. We did that so you can see what it is like to be on the receiving end of these options. Notice, too, that EasyPlex is giving you a special option to let you read *all* the messages in your mailbox with a single command. Let's do that. Enter a zero at the prompt and you will see the one-liner you sent as a reply. It says simply, "This is a reply to the first message I wrote."

Press RETURN and you find a familiar menu:

```
EasyPlex  Action Menu

** Charlie Bowen/WELCOME! **

1 DELETE this message
2 FILE in PER area
3 FORWARD
4 REREAD message
5 REPLY
6 SAVE in mailbox
7 DOWNLOAD message

Enter choice or <CR>
to continue !
```

Delete this first message (option 1), and the system then displays the next message in your mailbox. As you recall, this one was FORWARDed, so it has your note attached to the top, then the original, like this:

```
Date:   13-Jan-89 16:20 EST
From:   Charlie Bowen [71636,1025]
Subj:   WELCOME!

This time I'm forwarding the message to
myself.

--- Forwarded Message ---

Date:   12-Jan-89 16:05 EST

From:   Charlie Bowen [71635,1025]

Enter command or <CR> for more!

EasyPlex

Subj:   WELCOME!

Hi! Welcome to CompuServe Information
Service.
You've made amazing program so far. But
there's much more to learn.

Last page. Enter command
or <CR> to continue!
```

When you press RETURN, you are shown another Action menu. Delete this message, too, by entering 1 at the subsequent prompt. After that, EasyPlex displays its main menu:

```
EasyPlex  Main Menu

*** No mail waiting ***

2 COMPOSE a new message
3 UPLOAD a message
4 USE a file from PER area
5 ADDRESS Book
6 SET options

Enter choice !
```

As you now know, this is the menu you ordinarily see if you enter G MAIL or G EASY at any prompt, and from this one you can write and send letters.

## The Big Bullet

The first stop on this chapter's tour is the National Bulletin Board. When you glanced back at Chapter 5, you saw how to get there by the Communicate menu. However, we generally save time by using one of CompuServe's quick reference words. At the prompt on your screen, enter G BULLET. The system displays the "One moment please" message, followed by:

```
NATIONAL BULLETIN BOARD

The information appearing in this
bulletin board is provided by persons
who are not affiliated with
CompuServe. Persons using such
information do so at their own risk.
Any person who elects to provide
information agrees by doing so to
indemnify and hold CompuServe harmless
from all claims with respect to the
information provided. CompuServe
reserves the right to remove any
information.

Press <CR> !
```

Take a moment to look over this disclaimer, then press RETURN and you see a menu that sets forth the major commands available in the National Bulletin Board:

```
National Bulletin  Main Menu

1 COMPOSE a bulletin
2 SCAN bulletins
3 BROWSE through bulletins
4 READ a bulletin
5 KEYWORD list
6 AGE of bulletins to view
   ( currently 14 days)
7 New features


Enter choice !
```

These are some — but not all — of the commands BULLET recognizes. Here is an important point. As we travel these roads together, you will find that many services have more options than are outlined on the menus; you often can see the complete list of commands by entering HELP or a question mark (?) at the prompt. Try that. Enter HELP at this prompt, and you should be shown:

```
BULLET


More information is available for:

Instructions    AGE            BROWSE    BYE      CHECK
COMPOSE         DOCUMENTATION  EDIT      ERASE    EXIT
HELP            OFF            POST      READ     REPLY
SCAN            SET            TYPE

Enter HELP selection or
<CR> to continue :
```

Seventeen words (the capitalized ones) are in the National Bulletin Board's vocabulary, that is, 17 commands that it recognizes. The prompt tells you that we are currently in BULLET's "Help mode," and at the colon (:) prompt you could type in any one of those commands and receive a description of how it works. (Or at the "!" prompt on the previous menu, you could enter HELP READ or HELP BROWSE, and so forth.) No need to go through the help files now; we shall be going over that ground together. Just remember that here, and on most features of the system, help is available for the asking. Let's return to BULLET's main menu by pressing RETURN at the colon prompt and up comes:

```
National Bulletin   Main Menu

1 COMPOSE a bulletin
2 SCAN bulletins
3 BROWSE through bulletins
4 READ a bulletin
5 KEYWORD list
6 AGE of bulletins to view
  (14 days)
7 New features


Enter choice !
```

The National Bulletin Board is CompuServe's classified ad section, where there is a national audience for three kinds of messages: general NOTICE, items for SALE, and items and services WANTED. The easiest way to read this material is to BROWSE. To do that, enter 3 at the menu, which causes BULLET to display these three categories:

```
National Bulletin   Section

1 SALE    (339)
2 WANTED  (273)
3 NOTICE  (367)

Enter choice !
```

This menu tells you how many messages exist in each category, and then asks you to make a selection. We shall browse the SALE category — enter 1 here — and the next choice is:

```
Enter keyword (e.g. book)
or <CR> for all :
```

A person who writes a message on the bulletin board assigns it a *keyword*, a word that describes the bulletin's general subject. If you wanted to read all the bulletins in the SALE category, regardless of keyword, you would leave this option blank by just pressing RETURN at the prompt. However, that would lead to a pretty long session for you. In our example, 347 bulletins are in the SALE category alone. It is probably smarter, then, to take the system up on its offer to get specific. Therefore, let's enter the keyword IBM <RETURN>.

Now BULLET gets down to business, rounding up the SALE messages that have "IBM" as a keyword. It then draws the column headers and displays the first bulletin it has found:

```
#        From:     Date:      Keyword:

312    71635,1025  12-Jan-89   IBM
-- Read? (Y or N)! Y
```

Obviously, the numbers and dates on your screen are different, but the format should be the same. On the left is the message number (each bulletin has its own unique number), followed by the user ID number of the person who posted it, the date of the posting, and finally the keyword. The prompt after that line asks whether you want to read this message. Type Y (for yes) if you do, or N (for no) and continue to the next message the system has found for you. On the message you find in your search, enter Y and let's take a look at a bulletin's style. The one displayed on your screen probably looks something like this:

```
FOR SALE
       --------


Tandy 1000 with 640k RAM
768k RAM disk/print spooler
2 ea 5-1/4" drives - 360k each
10 Meg external hard disk
CM-2 RGB hi-res color monitor

All manuals and cables included.
Best offer takes it

  ** 296    [71635,1025]   12-Jan-89   IBM-PC


Last page. Enter REPLY
or <CR> to continue!
```

Note the prompt. The REPLY command entered at this point makes it easy to answer to any message you find on the bulletin board. If you enter REPLY, the system prompts you to write your answer, using numbered lines as you have seen in EasyPlex; BULLET then automatically sends your reply to the submitter of the original bulletin. (You also can enter the REPLY command at BULLETIN's main menu. If you enter REPLY at the main prompt, the system asks for the number of the message to which you wish to reply.)

Let's continue on by pressing RETURN. Now you are taken to next SALE IBM message that the system has located, something like this:

```
346    70475,1165   13-Jan-89   IBM/EGA
-- Read? (Y or N)!
```

And so it goes. You display or pass up messages by entering yea or nay, and eventually you run through all the SALE IBM bulletins and are returned to the main Bulletin menu. But — flash! — if you want to abort the BROWSE session earlier, there is another command available that is *not* mentioned in the "Read? (Y or N)!" prompt. Just enter X at that prompt and you are whisked back to the main menu of the bulletin board.

Take your time and browse a while, and when you are done meet us back at the main menu:

```
National Bulletin  Main Menu

1 COMPOSE a bulletin
2 SCAN bulletins
3 BROWSE through bulletins
4 READ a bulletin
5 KEYWORD list
6 AGE of bulletins to view
  (14 days)
7 New features

Enter choice !
```

There is another way to look through these messages, by combining SCAN (option 2) and READ (option 4). Some subscribers think that using those two commands together is faster than the BROWSE option.

Without actually typing on the keyboard, let's see how that works. If you were to select option 2 (SCAN), you would be prompted in the same way you were in the BROWSE option. The system would ask first for a category (SALE, WANTED, or NOTICE), then a keyword. After that, it would show you the list of bulletins it found but, *unlike* BROWSE, the SCAN option does not pause after each message to give you a chance to read it. The list would look something like this:

```
 ┌ ─ ─ ─ ─ ─ ─ ─ ─ ─ ─ ─ ─ ─ ─ ─ ─ ─ ─ ─ ─ ─ ─ ─ ─ ─ ─ ─ ─ ┐
 |                                                          |
 |    #        From:      Date:        Keyword:             |
 |                                                          |
 |   48     70000,001   12-Sep-87    IBM                    |
 |  339     70000,111   03-Sep-87    IBM                    |
 |  345     70007,411   03-Sep-87    IBM/GRAFIX             |
 |  346     76703,375   03-Sep-87    IBM/EGA                |
 |  471     70001,1025  05-Sep-87    IBM-AT                 |
 |  524     70475,1165  10-Sep-87    IBM/XT                 |
 |  567     71635,1025  07-Sep-87    IBM                    |
 |  718     70007,2141  13-Sep-87    IBM                    |
 |  804     76703,375   14-Sep-87    IBM                    |
 |                                                          |
 └ ─ ─ ─ ─ ─ ─ ─ ─ ─ ─ ─ ─ ─ ─ ─ ─ ─ ─ ─ ─ ─ ─ ─ ─ ─ ─ ─ ─ ┘
```

Do we hear mumbling? A question, perhaps?

*You bet. What good is SCANning the messages if you can't stop and read them?*

As you have seen, each message has its own unique number (the code in the left-hand column), so you could use a quick SCAN to get the numbers of messages that look interesting (such as "IBM/GRAFIX" in the example, which is number 345), then return to the main menu and use the READ command (option 4). The READ command subsequently prompts you for the number of the message you would like to read, at which you could specify 345.

In addition, you have a lot of flexibility in entering commands by *anticipating* prompts before you get to them. Suppose you want to SCAN the SALE category for messages about IBM. Because you know precisely where you are going, you don't have to wade through the menus. Hands back on the keyboard; let's give that a try. You should be at the main menu of BULLET. At the "!" prompt, enter SCAN SALE IBM and see what happens. The system should bypass the prompts for category and keyword (as you have already supplied that information) and get right down to the scanning. Similarly, if you already knew from a previous SCAN that you wanted to read message 345, you could take care of business at the "!" prompt of the main menu by entering simply READ 345.

Time out. We have just learned two important things about BULLET, things that will apply later to other features on the system:

1. At a "!" prompt, you often can substitute *word commands* for the numeral options suggested on the menu.
2. You can often skip subsequent menus by *anticipating* the prompts.

**Note:**    Another handy command for quickly finding notes to read is option 5 on BULLET's main menu. It produces a KEYWORD list, a fast, easy way to check for messages that carry a specific topic. Option 5 lets you list of ALL the keywords used in messages currently on the bulletin board, or lets you search to determine how many messages uses a specific keyword.


## Writing Your Own Bulletins

To learn how to write bulletins, we need to get back to the main menu:

```
National Bulletin   Main Menu

1 COMPOSE a bulletin
2 SCAN bulletins
3 BROWSE through bulletins
4 READ a bulletin
5 KEYWORD list
6 AGE of bulletins to view
   (14 days) 7 New features

Enter choice !
```

As you see, COMPOSE is option 1. At the "!" prompt, you could enter the number 1 or the word of the command, in this case COMPOSE. Or, as you've see elsewhere on the system, you can abbreviate. Like most CompuServe features, BULLET accepts commands abbreviated to their first three letters, so, you can get into Compose mode by entering either 1, COMPOSE, or COM, and your next prompt is:

```
┌──────────────────────────────────────────────────┐
│                                                    │
│   National Bulletin   Compose                      │
│                                                    │
│   Enter bulletin. (/EXIT when done)                │
│   1:                                               │
│                                                    │
└──────────────────────────────────────────────────┘
```

Look familiar? Like the composition mode of EasyPlex, perhaps?

**Note:**    There is a chance that you *didn't* get that display, but instead received a message that says, "This service is available only to subscribers who have received their permanent (2nd) password." This statement merely means that you can't write messages on BULLET until you receive your permanent, second password in the mail. If that has happened to you, just read over the next few pages and rejoin us at the section called "Having It Your Way."

As it turns out, this is the same editing program that is available in EasyPlex, and it works just the same way as it did in Chapters 3 and 5. One of two editors available on CompuServe, called LINEDIT, a line-numbered editor, because you are prompted with a number at the beginning of each new line. In the next chapter, we shall compare this with the unnumbered editing program called simply EDIT. In many CompuServe features, you have a choice of using either EDIT or LINEDIT and, of course, later we shall show you how to flip the switches necessary for changing from one editor to the other.

Right now let's reexamine this LINEDIT editing program by writing a brief bulletin that we can post on the National Bulletin Board. (Never mind if you think you have nothing worthy to say to the nation right now; we shall delete the message before we leave.) At the prompt, type this, pressing RETURN at the end of each short line:

```
┌──────────────────────────────────────────────────┐
│                                                    │
│   1: This is a test to see if I can                │
│   2: post this message on the                      │
│   3: National Bulletin Board.                      │
│   4: /EXIT (or /EX)                                │
│                                                    │
└──────────────────────────────────────────────────┘
```

When you enter /EXIT or /EX (in either uppercase or lowercase), the file is closed, just as it was in EasyPlex. This time you are taken to a menu that you may compare with your bookmarked example of the EasyPlex *send* menu:

```
r---------------------------------------------------------┐
|                                                         |
|   National Bulletin   Post Menu                         |
|                                                         |
|   For current bulletin                                  |
|                                                         |
|   1 POST                                                |
|   2 EDIT                                                |
|   3 TYPE                                                |
|                                                         |
|   Enter choice !                                        |
|                                                         |
L---------------------------------------------------------┘
```

You have three alternatives: (1) POST puts it on the bulletin board, (2) EDIT lets you, uh, edit it (surprise!), and (3) TYPE displays the message again. Enter TYPE, or 3, at the prompt, and you will see the three lines you just wrote, with their assigned line numbers. The display is followed by the message, "Press <CR> !" Press RETURN and you are back at the Post menu. Now let's try the EDIT option. That produces this menu:

```
r---------------------------------------------------------┐
|                                                         |
|   EDIT                                                  |
|                                                         |
|   1 CHANGE characters in line                           |
|   2 REPLACE line                                        |
|   3 DELETE line                                         |
|   4 INSERT new line(s)                                  |
|   5 TYPE all lines                                      |
|                                                         |
|   0 END editing                                         |
|                                                         |
|   Enter choice !                                        |
|                                                         |
L---------------------------------------------------------┘
```

Again, notice the similarities to the bookmarked example of the EasyPlex *edit* menu. As we saw in EasyPlex, choosing any of the first four options causes the system to prompt you for the number of the line on which you want to make changes. For that reason, before you start editing, it's always a good idea to TYPE the message out (either from the previous menu or here, with option 5). That way, you can find the numbers assigned to each line. Let's practice with LINEDIT's editing feature by inserting two lines at the bottom of the messages. At the "!" prompt, enter 4 (or the word INSERT or the letters INS) and the system says:

```
┌────────────────────────────────────────────────────┐
│                                                      │
│   Insert after which line (0 if at top):             │
│                                                      │
└────────────────────────────────────────────────────┘
```

To insert the material at the bottom, that is, *after* line 3, enter 3 at the colon (:) prompt, and see:

```
┌────────────────────────────────────────────────────┐
│                                                      │
│   Enter lines to be inserted.                        │
│   4:                                                 │
│   (/EXIT when done)                                  │
│                                                      │
└────────────────────────────────────────────────────┘
```

Let's add these lines:

```
┌────────────────────────────────────────────────────┐
│                                                      │
│   4: We'll delete this before                        │
│   5: leaving the bulletin board.                     │
│   6: /ex                                             │
│                                                      │
└────────────────────────────────────────────────────┘
```

Keep your bulletins concise. You can have up to 50 lines, with no line longer than 64 characters. In other words, on each line, you must press RETURN before you reach the 64th character.

Now you are back at the Edit menu, so choose option zero to END the editing session. That returns you to the Post menu:

```
┌────────────────────────────────────────────────────┐
│                                                      │
│   National Bulletin  Post Menu                       │
│                                                      │
│   For current bulletin                               │
│                                                      │
│   1 POST                                             │
│   2 EDIT                                             │
│   3 TYPE                                             │
│                                                      │
│   Enter choice !                                     │
│                                                      │
└────────────────────────────────────────────────────┘
```

Let's post it by entering 1 (or typing the word POST or POS); the system asks you to indicate the category in which you wish the message to appear (SALE, WANTED, or NOTICE.) Choose one — for this exercise, it doesn't matter which one

— and BULLET then asks for a keyword. Pick something short, like "TEST." Your keyword can be up to ten characters.

Finally, the system posts your message and tells you something like, "Message recorded as # 111." On your scratch pad, note the number reported on your screen. We shall use that information in a moment. Now press RETURN, and we are back at BULLET's main menu:

```
National Bulletin   Main Menu

1 COMPOSE a bulletin
2 SCAN bulletins
3 BROWSE through bulletins
4 READ a bulletin
5 KEYWORD list
6 AGE of bulletins to view
  (14 days)
7 Additional Features

Enter choice !
```

Messages stay on BULLET up to two weeks, then are automatically deleted by the system. Subscribers who use BULLET regularly often have more than one notice on the board at a time, so there needs to be an easy way to keep track of them all. There is, but it is another one of those commands *not* shown on the main menu. Try this. At the "!" prompt, enter the word CHECK and the system shows you something like this:

```
You have posted the following messages:
   #        Date:     Keyword:
  SALE
  WANTED
  NOTICE
   111       16-Jan-89      TEST
Last page !
```

The reference is, of course, to the message you just posted. Pressing RETURN takes you back to the main menu.

You also can read your message (number 111, in our example), either by following the menu options or by simply typing READ 111 at the "!" prompt.

Now let's delete your message. (No use cluttering up BULLET with test messages. Your on-line neighbors appreciate your refraining from electronic litter.) At the "!" prompt, enter the word ERASE followed by your message number, such as ERASE 111. The system takes care of business, then brings you back to the main menu. Now if you now try to READ 111, you are informed, "That message number does not exist!"

## Having It Your Way

As noted, messages stay on the bulletin board for 14 days, and after you enter a SCAN or a BROWSE command, you are shown messages posted during that entire period. However, if you would like to look at a smaller age group of messages — say, just those posted in the past *five* days — you can use the AGE option, (option 6 on the main menu.) When you select option 6 or the word AGE, the system prompts with:

```
┌─────────────────────────────────────────────────┐
│                                                 │
│   Enter # of days (1-14)                        │
│                                                 │
└─────────────────────────────────────────────────┘
```

If you enter 5, then all subsequent reading and browsing commands will show only those messages posted in the past five days. If later in the session, you want to broaden the field to older messages, just reenter the AGE option and set a higher number. When you leave the National Bulletin Board and then return, the AGE automatically is reset to 14 days. This automatic resetting is referred to as a *default*. We shall have much more to say later about the setting of defaults in various places in CompuServe.

There are two commands for leaving the National Bulletin Board, EXIT and BYE, and they work very much as they did in the CB Simulators. The first takes you out of the BULLET program and lands you on a menu; the second logs you off the system. (In fact, as you will see, from nearly *anywhere* in the system, BYE is the log-off word.)

As we have more touring to do, type EXIT and we meet up at the Communicate menu:

```
r---------------------------------------------------------1
|                                                         |
|                                                         |
|   CompuServe                      COMMUNICATE           |
|                                                         |
|   COMMUNICATIONS/BULLETIN BOARDS                        |
|                                                         |
|   1 EasyPlex Electronic Mail                            |
|   2 CB Simulator                                        |
|   3 Forums (SIGs)                                       |
|   4 National Bulletin Board                             |
|   5 Directory of Subscribers                            |
|   6 Ask Customer Service                                |
|   7 CB Society                                          |
|   8 The Convention Center (tm)                          |
|                                                         |
|   Enter choice !                                        |
|                                                         |
|                                                         |
L---------------------------------------------------------J
```

## Introducing the Personal Area

Our next stop is an important one called the "personal file area." Here is an opportunity to exercise the FIND command we learned earlier. At the "!" prompt, type this: FIND Personal File Area. The system does the searching, then displays:

```
r---------------------------------------------------------1
|                                                         |
|                                                         |
|   CompuServe                                            |
|                                                         |
|   1 Personal File Area    [ FILES ]                     |
|                                                         |
|   Last menu page, enter choice !                        |
|                                                         |
L---------------------------------------------------------J
```

This feature gives us yet another quick reference word (FILES) to tuck away. From anywhere, we can take the express lane to the personal file area by entering G FILES. So, enter that at the prompt, and you will see its introductory menu:

```
r------------------------------------------------7
I                                                  I
I  Personal File Area PER                          I
I                                                  I
I   1 Brief CATALOG of files                       I
I   2 Detailed DIRECTORY of files                  I
I   3 Create & edit files                          I
I   4 TYPE a file's contents                       I
I   5 DELETE a file                                I
I   6 RENAME a file                                I
I   7 COPY a file                                  I
I   8 Change a file's PROTECTION                   I
I   9 Upload or download a file                    I
I  10 PRINT a file ($)                             I
I  11 Enter command mode                           I
I                                                  I
I  Enter choice !                                  I
I                                                  I
L------------------------------------------------J
```

Here we are, but — ahem....

*Where precisely are we, guys? What is this personal file area, anyway?*

For a hint, take a good look at the menu on your screen. Most options seem to deal with manipulating files through catalogs, directories, renaming, and deleting. If that sounds similar to the functions you use with your word processor or the operating system of your computer when you are off-line, then you are on the right track. The similarity is no coincidence. The personal file area is the private storage section for your on-line files. Using this menu, you can read files, change them, create new ones, and so on. Most importantly, you are the *only* subscriber who can see what is in your personal file area. As a matter of fact, you already have stored a file here, though you might not remember it. Let's find it by doing a catalog of everything in your file area. Select option 1 from the menu on your screen. The system should respond with:

```
r------------------------------------------------7
I                                                  I
I   MYMAIL                                         I
I                                                  I
L------------------------------------------------J
```

Ah, *that* one. Back in Chapter 5, you saved your EasyPlex under the file name "MYMAIL." EasyPlex automatically stored your message away in your PER area with the name you assigned it at the time. The catalog option gives you a quick look at everything you have stored in your private area.

Now get back to the Personal File Area menu — you need to press the RETURN key to continue — and select the "detailed directory" option (option 2) and compare that with the brief catalog. You should see something like this:

```
Name          Blocks        Creation         Access
MYMAIL.         3         14:32 13-Jan-89   13-Jan-89 (4)
TOTAL           3
Last page !
```

Notice that the simple catalog gives you only the file names, while the directory provides more information, such as the length of the file (in block of space), date and time when you created the file, date you last looked at it, and so on.

As you probably have already figured out, option 4 on the menu (TYPE) displays a file by typing it on your screen. If you would like to reread MYMAIL, enter 4 and the system asks for the name of the file you want to display.

Most of the other options are clear enough. Option 3 allows you to write a new file (which we will look at in Chapter 8). The option to delete a file (option 5) asks for the name of the file to remove and then zaps it. The renaming option (option 6) asks for the existing file name and the new name you want to give the file. Copy (option 7) does just that, duplicates an existing file under a new name.

Option 8, changes a file's *protection*; this option requires some explanation. CompuServe automatically sets a protection level when a file is created and placed in disk storage so that only you (or, more specifically, anyone using your user ID number) may display or modify it. There are two protection levels you may find useful:

1. Protection 4 allows you to read, modify, or delete the file. The system automatically assigns this the protection level to all files. It is indicated by the "(4)" listed after the file name when you ask for a directory of the PER area.
2. Protection 7 allows you to read the file, but not to modify or delete it. You may wish to set a protection level of 7 on important files to avoid the possibility of accidentally deleting them. Of course, should you later wish to delete the files, you would need first to lower the protection to 4.

**Note:** Changing protection levels had more significance back in the days when all subscribers' files were located on a single mainframe computer and files could be transferred easily from one personal file to another. It was done simply by the sender's "lowering" the protection level on the file or files then telling the sendee the file name to copy. These days, it is not that simple. If your personal file area *happens* to be on the same mainframe computer as someone else's, you would be able to lower protection on your own files and allow another user to copy those unprotected files from your own area, once that user knows the file name. In reality, though, odds of your being on the same mainframe as your friends are slim. This particular function, then, has limited use for the average user. (Besides, there are other easy ways of submitting files invisibly to a public access area where they can be retrieved, and we shall discuss this procedure in the next section.)

For the time being, let's not worry about option 9, upload or download a file; we shall be talking about that later.

Now, pay particular attention to option 11 — enter command mode — because this is one of the reasons we wanted to bring you here. We told you earlier that menus in CompuServe are a wonderful way to learn the system, but that a time would come when you might tire of them, like training wheels on a bicycle after you have learned to ride. Throughout the system, opportunities are offered to turn off menus and save time (and money) by operating in a sort of expert mode. Command mode is one such invitation. To see what it looks like, select option 11 (command mode) and you should see "OK." No menus, no friendly message advising the next step. Just OK.

The terseness of that prompt (which probably looks familiar, because we saw "OK" briefly on our first tour in Chapter 3) has confused and upset many new subscribers who felt lost without their familiar menus. It's as if they had fallen over the edge of the system. That is why CompuServe's programmers constructed the Personal File Area menu in the first place. However, once you are comfortable with the neighborhood, you might choose to use command mode instead of the menus, just for the speed and convenience. Everything you could do from the menu, you can do from this "OK" prompt. Want to catalog your files? Enter CAT. Want a detailed directory? Enter DIR. Would you like to have the system type out MYMAIL again? Enter TYP MYMAIL. If you wanted to create a new file, say one called TEST1.TXT, you could enter CREATE TEST1.TXT at the "OK" prompt, and it would work just as well as option 3 on the Personal File Area menu.

**Historical Note:**   By the way, in your electronic conversations with other CompuServe users, you may hear the "OK" prompt referred to by a number of different names. Some veteran subscribers still call this area "MicroNet," even though the term has been out of vogue for several years. It is not unlike the varying language of different neighborhoods in a metropolitan area. Subscribers here tend to cling to the terms that were fashionable when they arrived.

The "OK" prompt gives us an opportunity to show you something about the menus to which we have become so attached. It is time you learned the truth: those handy lists of options are just part of a a program or user interface called *Displa* (standing for "display"), which is being operated by CompuServe itself from an area not unlike the "OK" prompt. In fact, most of the system's features we have seen can be visited directly from the "OK" prompt in your personal file area. The truth is that menus are a convenience, not a necessity. When you log on, the system assumes you want the menus; however, some experienced users find menus a bore and a bother. Once they think they can navigate the system without them, they turn off the menus permanently on their account numbers. It may seem impossible to you now that anyone could navigate CompuServe without menus, but it actually is quite common. Before we finish this book, you will see how you can turn Displa on and off for yourself.

But for now, that isn't the problem. The menus are gone and we want them back.

*Okay, if Displa is a program, we should be able to "run" it, right?*

Right you are. Let's "Request DISPLA." At the "OK" prompt, you enter R DISPLA. Viola! The system shows us its TOP menu:

```
CompuServe                                    TOP

    1 Subscriber Assistance
    2 Find a Topic
    3 Communications/Bulletin Bds.
    4 News/Weather/Sports
    5 Travel
    6 The Electronic MALL/Shopping
    7 Money Matters/Markets
    8 Entertainment/Games
    9 Home/Health/Education
   10 Reference
   11 Computers/Technology
   12 Business/Other Interests

 Enter choice number !
```

Now, rejoin us at the "OK" prompt. To do that, type G FILES at this menu. That returns you to the personal file area. When you reach that menu take option 11 again, the one that will, as the screen says, "Enter command mode." (By the way, if you wanted to reach the PER menu again from the "OK" prompt, you wouldn't have to go around the horn by way of TOP. Just enter PER and you will return to menu mode.)

Okay, troops, we have covered a lot of territory in this session and you probably want to take some time to think about it. Let's all log off now. At the prompt on your screen, enter BYE or OFF and the system will sign you off with something like:

```
Thank you for using CompuServe!

Off at 19:26 EST 14-Jan-89
Connect time = 0:55
```

After that, make yourself comfortable as we spend the remaining pages of this chapter talking about Feedback, a place where you can get help with many of your on-line questions.

## Visiting Feedback

From anywhere in the system, you can reach Feedback with the GO command followed by its page address or quick reference word. For instance, if we were still on-line and at the OK prompt, you could enter G FEEDBACK and your next menu would look something like this:

```
ASK CUSTOMER SERVICE

  1 Questions and Answers
  2 Feedback
  3 Calling Customer Service

Enter choice !
```

As you see, this area of the system offers answers to frequently-asked questions as well as gives you an opportunity to leave your own questions or comments. Let's start by seeing the range of answers to existing questions. If you were to select option 1 in our example, you would see something like this:

```
┌─────────────────────────────────────────────────┐
│                                                 │
│  CompuServe                          OQA-6      │
│                                                 │
│  QUESTIONS AND ANSWERS                          │
│   1 Billing                                     │
│   2 Logon/System/Access                         │
│   3 EasyPlex/MCI Mail                           │
│   4 Forums                                      │
│                                                 │
│                                                 │
│   5 Personal File Area                          │
│   6 Service Options/Terminal Settings           │
│   7 Executive Option                            │
│   8 CompuServe's Online Ordering                │
│     Service/Shoppers Advantage                  │
│   9 CB Simulator                                │
│  10 Market Quotes                               │
│                                                 │
│                                                 │
│  MORE !                                         │
│                                                 │
└─────────────────────────────────────────────────┘
```

Already we find among the subjects an area we just visited. Let's see what questions the system is prepared to raise (and answer) about the Personal File Area. If we entered 5 at the prompt, we would see something like this:

```
┌─────────────────────────────────────────────────┐
│                                                 │
│  CompuServe                          QAPER      │
│                                                 │
│  PERSONAL FILE AREA                             │
│                                                 │
│   1 How Do I Access My Personal                 │
│     File Area?                                  │
│   2 Some of My Files Are                        │
│     Missing                                     │
│   3 Forgot a File Name?                         │
│   4 Are There Storage Charges?                  │
│   5 Where Can I Find Help Using My              │
│     Personal File Area?                         │
│   6 File Protection Levels                      │
│   7 Feedback                                    │
│                                                 │
│  Enter choice !                                 │
│                                                 │
└─────────────────────────────────────────────────┘
```

To see the kind of details Feedback can provide for a question, let's say you've forgotten the name of a file you have placed in your PER area. Coming here, you enter 3 at the prompt. Feedback replies with something like this:

```
CompuServe                        OQA-625


Q:  I have a letter stored in a file in my
Personal File Area.  The problem is that I
can't remember the name of the file.  How
can I get a listing of the files that are
stored in my Personal File Area?


A:  Enter GO PER at any ! prompt and, once
the menu below displays, choose the option
"Brief catalog of files" or "Detailed
directory of files."

            FILE MANAGEMENT
    1 Brief catalog of files
    2 Detailed directory of files
    3 Create & edit files via EDIT (FILGE)
    4 Type a file's contents
    5 Delete a file
    6 Rename a file
    7 Copy a file
    8 Change a file's protection
    9 Upload or download a file
   10 Print a file ($)
   11 Enter command mode

Additional notes:


* You have 128K (or 192K if you have the
Executive Option) in online storage space
available to you in your Personal File Area.


* Files not accessed in 30 days (or six
months if you have the Executive Option)
are automatically deleted.


    !
```

Notice:

1. The system uses an approach that is similar to one we use in this this book, giving an illustration of the correct menu, in this case, the main menu of the Personal File Area.
2. It has provided an answer you probably expected, since we saw earlier in this chapter how the "Brief catalog" and "Detailed directory" option work to show the names of files in the PER area.
3. Finally, the system also provides some additional information on the maximum amount of storage space available in the Personal File Area and the fact that files must be accessed regularly to avoid their being automatically deleted. We shall have more to say about both these aspects of the PER area in Chapter 9.

If you were to press RETURN at the ! prompt in this example, the system would return you to the QAPER menu, like this:

```
CompuServe                              QAPER

PERSONAL FILE AREA

  1 How Do I Access My Personal
    File Area?
  2 Some of My Files Are
    Missing
  3 Forgot a File Name?
  4 Are There Storage Charges?
  5 Where Can I Find Help Using My
    Personal File Area?
  6 File Protection Levels
  7 Feedback

Enter choice !
```

Pressing RETURN again would bring you back to the main questions menu:

```
r----------------------------------------------------------,
I                                                          I
I  CompuServe                                    OQA-6     I
I                                                          I
I  QUESTIONS AND ANSWERS                                   I
I   1 Billing                                              I
I   2 Logon/System/Access                                  I
I   3 EasyPlex/MCI Mail                                    I
I   4 Forums                                               I
I   5 Personal File Area                                   I
I   6 Service Options/Terminal Settings                    I
I   7 Executive Option                                     I
I   8 CompuServe's Online Ordering                         I
I        Service/Shoppers Advantage                        I
I   9 CB Simulator                                         I
I  10 Market Quotes                                        I
I                                                          I
I  MORE !                                                  I
I                                                          I
L----------------------------------------------------------J
```

And pressing RETURN at this MORE ! prompt provides the rest of the listed questions addressed in this portion of CompuServe:

```
r----------------------------------------------------------,
I                                                          I
I  CompuServe                                   OQA-709    I
I                                                          I
I  QUESTIONS AND ANSWERS (Cont'd)                          I
I                                                          I
I  11 National Bulletin Board                              I
I  12 VIDTEX/Professional                                  I
I        Connection                                        I
I  13 Uploading/Downloading Files                          I
I        To/From CompuServe                                I
I  14 Graphics                                             I
I  15 Games                                                I
I                                                          I
I  Enter choice !                                          I
I                                                          I
L----------------------------------------------------------J
```

## Types of Questions Answered in Feedback

Obviously, some of these questions deal with topics we haven't discussed yet — forums, uploading and downloading, graphics and so on — so you should simply note this section of the system for later reference. For now, here are the kinds of questions covered in this part of Feedback:

Billing: reviewing charges on-line, changing your billing options, advice to new subscribers, how you are billed in various features, description of surcharges and minimums and so on.

Logon/System/Access: what to do about garbled text after log-on, what to do when there is no local CompuServe number in your area, overseas access, dealing with call-waiting services, trouble with 1200-baud access, etc.

EasyPlex/MCI Mail: finding/reading/sending messages, deleting unread messages, uploading/downloading mail, and so on.

Forums: Finding and joining forums, reading messages, finding information about other members, using the data libraries and so forth.

Personal File Area: How to Access and use the PER, about storage charges and protection levels, etc.

Also, similar questions are answered about setting options in the Terminal Profile area of the system and the extra-cost Executive Option, how to use the shopping services and the CB Simulator, the ins and outs of the financial market features and more.

## Writing a Message to Feedback

Finally, what if you can't find an answer to your particular question? Perhaps it is something that doesn't happen frequently to other users of the system. In that case, you may want to write a letter directly to the customer service people at CompuServe, using the same Feedback feature. Selecting the "Feedback" option from the main menu or any of the sub-menus causes this message to be displayed:

```
Welcome to FEEDBACK. We appreciate any
comments, ideas, problems, or suggestions
you send us. Your connect time is credited
while you are in FEEDBACK (any FBK page),
although you will be charged for
communication surcharges. A Customer
Service Representative will answer via
Easyplex Electronic Mail as quickly as
possible.

Instant answers to hundreds of the most
frequently asked questions can be found in
the Online Questions & Answers area.  Enter
GO QUESTIONS to exit to this area.

MORE !
```

Note that you are not charged for the time you spend in writing the message. Press RETURN and you are prompted with:

```
CompuServe Feedback                 FBK-208

Please enter your name
(Last name, First name)
 :
```

After you have entered your last and then your first name, the system reports:

```
Please enter your message (press your
carriage return key to end each line). You
may enter up to 43 lines. When done, enter
EXIT at the beginning of a new line.

 1:
```

From here, it just as if you were writing a message on EasyPlex. You have up to 43 lines for your message. At the end, enter EXIT at the start of a new line and message automatically is sent to the appropriate people at CompuServe's customer service department. Usually, a reply is sent to your EasyPlex mailbox.

# CHAPTER 8

---

# Writing and Contributing On-line

You have now been around the block on CompuServe. You have seen behind the curtain of the menus and learned that they actually are part of a program called Displa. When you go to the personal file area, you can even turn off the menu program temporarily and run around the system in a kind of expert mode. However, you are new on this system and not having the menus probably is a little disconcerting. Our reason for showing you this OK area so early is twofold:

1. We don't want you to be afraid of the "OK" prompt. Many new subscribers report they did "something wrong," fell into this section, and panicked. We want you to know that if it happens, you can get back to the menus from the "OK" prompt by simply entering R DISPLA (meaning "Request the Displa program").
2. More importantly, we want you to know, and keep in the back of your mind, that there are many shortcuts once you are familiar with the terrain. Intermediate subscribers sometimes complain (rightly so) that the menus are slow, repetitious, time-consuming, and costly in connect-time dollars. Nonetheless, the menus serve their purpose: to keep new arrivals from getting tangled in the undergrowth. By the time we finish our tours, you will be so comfortable with the system's layout that you'll be pretty darn sick of menus. Then we shall delve deeply into the part of the system we identified as Profile, where you can set the "expert mode" permanently for yourself and be done with menus for good. (In fact, Profile is so important to our enterprise that you will have a preliminary look at it in the next chapter.)

We go back on-line in this chapter to take a second look at the personal file area, this time to see behind another curtain: CompuServe's other text editor. You recall that whenever you have written something on-line, we have mentioned that there are two editors available, one with line numbers and one without. So far, we have concentrated on the line-numbered editor, called LINEDIT. However, you may find you prefer the nonnumbered editor, called EDIT. (Incidentally, some on-line veterans still call EDIT by its old name, FILGE, for File Generator and Editor). This time we shall get an introduction to this different editing program.

## Logging On

When you are ready log on as usual, at the bottom of the main menu enter G FILES to go directly to the personal file area (PER) menu. As we told you, whatever you file in this part of the system can be viewed by no one other than you (or anyone else who has access to your ID number and password). This section, considered to be your on-line disk storage area, is introduced by this familiar PER menu:

```
Personal File Area PER

  1 Brief CATALOG of files
  2 Detailed DIRECTORY of files
  3 Create & edit files
  4 TYPE a file's contents
  5 DELETE a file
  6 RENAME a file
  7 COPY a file
  8 Change a file's PROTECTION
  9 Upload or download a file

 11 Enter command mode

Enter choice !
```

Just as the numbered editor (LINEDIT) is routinely used in EasyPlex and the National Bulletin Board, the unnumbered editor, EDIT, is available here. To see that, let's write something into a file we shall call TEST.TXT. At the PER menu, select the "Create & edit" option by entering 3 at the prompt. In a moment, the system asks for a file name. Enter TEST.TXT and the system displays:

```
New file TEXT.TXT created--ready
```

Having requested the EDIT program and opening a file called TEST.TXT, the system is ready to receive your words. Notice, though, that there is no "1:" prompt on the screen; that prompt is an exclusive feature of LINEDIT. By contrast, EDIT has *no* line numbers. So, below the "New file created" message type the following lines, but please take care to enter them *exactly* as they are presented here, mistakes and all. (We worked overtime to imbed those typographical errors — "tht," "gtwhen," " ,it," and "driectly" — so that you can see how the editor part of this different text editor works.) Incidentally, we also are deliberately making the lines short in this example to accommodate those of you with computers that have only 40-character screen widths. Even if you have a computer with a larger screen width, please humor us here and type in the lines as we have them. It will make it easier for you to follow this exercise. And remember to press RETURN at the end of each line as indicated.

```
    Notice that the heading here <RETURN>
tells us you are opening a fresh <RETURN>
file. The key word in tht message <RETURN>
is "new." If TEST.TXT already <RETURN>
existed, the message you'd gtwhen <RETURN>
you typed the file name would be <RETURN>
"File TEST.TXT -- ready." <RETURN>
    We'll use this file to learn about <RETURN>
the nonnumbered editor, because, as <RETURN>
we noted ,it is the same program <RETURN>
we have an option to use in other <RETURN>
features, except this time we are <RETURN>
running it driectly <RETURN>
from the personal file area.<RETURN>
/EX <RETURN>
```

EDIT uses the same command as LINEDIT (/EX or /EXIT) at the bottom of the message to close the file. Put a bookmark on this page; we will refer back to the text of the example.

Once /EX is entered, the system returns to the personal file area menu:

```
Personal File Area PER

  1 Brief CATALOG of files
  2 Detailed DIRECTORY of files
  3 Create & edit files
  4 TYPE a file's contents
  5 DELETE a file
  6 RENAME a file
  7 COPY a file
  8 Change a file's PROTECTION
  9 Upload or download a file

 11 Enter command mode

Enter choice !
```

Before we go on, let's make a *copy* of this file, so we can use the original error-ridden version in another exercise later. To make a copy, enter the word COPY (or 7 at this menu) and the system asks for "File name:" meaning the name of the file you want to copy. Enter TEST.TXT. After that, the system asks, "Destination file:" meaning the name of the new file we are creating that contains the copy. Let's call it MISTAK.TXT (to mean "mistakes"). So enter MISTAK.TXT at the destination prompt. After the system accepts that information, press RETURN at the "Last page !" prompt to get back to the main menu.

Questions so far?

*Yes. Where are these files. Where is the message I just wrote?*

Both have been filed in your storage area, along with any other files you already have placed there. To see them, you use the directory option (enter DIR or 2) and the system shows you something like this:

```
Name         Blocks      Creation        Access

MYMAIL.       3        14:32 13-Jan-89   15-Jan-89 (4)
TEST.TXT      3        09:00 15-Jan-89   15-Jan-89 (4)
MISTAK.TXT    3        14:08 15-Jan-89   15-Jan-89 (4)
```

There is MYMAIL, the letter we saved on an earlier outing, along with TEST.TXT and MISTAK.TXT, the files created moments ago.

Now that you have finished composing and have closed your file, suppose you want to see it again. What we need to do is to type it to the screen, just as you did in the last chapter. In other words, the TYPe command, option 4 on the menu. Enter 4 or TYP at the prompt and, when asked for a file name, enter TEST.TXT. This command causes the system to begin to display your text.

As it is scrolling by, let's take a minute to understand how the editing program, EDIT, works, and how it differs from line-numbered LINEDIT. As an unnumbered editor, EDIT uses the idea of an *invisible line pointer* that keeps your place in the text. As the lines scroll by, the invisible pointer drops down one line at a time.

*Great, but how can I correct the errors in the file? The TYP commands just shows them to me again.*

First we need to reopen the file to edit. To do that, you select option 3 ("Create & edit") and the system displays the message: "File TEST.TXT--ready." Notice the subtle difference between this message and the one we received when you first created the file; the word "New" is missing this time. This signals that EDIT isn't creating a new file, but rather is editing an existing one, that is, reopening TEST.TXT. It is now ready to receive your editing.

*But where is the message I composed?*

Remember what we said about the *invisible* line pointer and how it points to each line in the file, one at a time? Right now, the line pointer is just above the first line of text. To see that, enter this:

```
/P 1
```

Note the syntax: a slash, followed by the letter P and the numeral one. (The space is not required; you may also enter it as /P1./) As soon as you press the RETURN key, the system prints:

```
Notice that the heading here
```

/P 1 means, "Print one line of the text." In the process, the line pointer has moved down a line, from just above the text to the first line. Try it again, but this time enter /P 2. The system prints:

```
┌─────────────────────────────────────────────┐
│                                               │
│   Notice that the heading here                │
│   tells us you are opening a fresh            │
│                                               │
└─────────────────────────────────────────────┘
```

Take a minute to think about the concept. When you first entered the /P command, the line pointer was on the first line of the text. Because you wanted two lines displayed, the system printed the line to which it was pointing, then moved the pointer down one line and printed the next line. So when it finished executing your command, it left the line pointer on line 2. (If this seems at all confusing, hang in there. It will become clearer as we begin to work with EDIT.)

Now enter the command /P 1000. Obviously, we are asking the impossible by commanding, "Print the next 1,000 lines of text," knowing all the while that there aren't a 1,000 lines in TEXT.TXT. Nonetheless, the program will give it a valiant try. Look at what happened. It printed "tells us you are opening a fresh" (the second line of the file, which is where we had the line pointer when we issued the command). That is followed by "file. The key word in tht message" (the third line), and so forth, down to the end of the file. When it runs out of text, the EDIT program (realizing it's been had) reports, "% FLGEOF-- End of file." This final item is an *error message*, meaning, "I tried, boss, but I couldn't complete that last instruction." But, of course, we didn't expect it to find 1,000 lines to print.

*Where are we now?*

Well, let's see. You haven't returned to the PER menu; that must mean you are still in the editing program and working on TEST.TXT; except that now the line pointer has reached the bottom of the file. If you were to type in a line or two here and close the file again (with the /EX instruction), you would have added some new lines to the bottom of your original TEST.TXT file.

Let's go back to the top of the file — that is, move the line pointer to the top of the file — with a /T command. *All* the editing commands are preceded by a slash (/), just as the commands in CB are. Any new line that starts with a slash is interpreted by EDIT as a command rather than text. So, enter /T now and ... uh-oh. Hmmmmm, nothing appears to have happened.

*Maybe it didn't work.*

Not to worry. Because the line pointer is *invisible*, the /T command doesn't change anything on the screen itself. But the invisible pointer has indeed moved to the top of the file. If you doubt that, enter /P 1 and you see the system display "Notice that the heading here," which is our first line. And, if /T takes you to the top, you can bet that /B takes you to the bottom of the file. But let's not get ahead of ourselves. While we are at the top of the file, let's get down to some serious editing.

The first task is to move the pointer to the line containing our first typo. Checking your bookmarked example, you see that the first error is *tht* in the third line. Of course it should be *that*. If we were in the numbered LINEDIT program, we could select a menu option and be prompted to enter the number of the line we want to change. However, EDIT has no line numbers so we have to tell the system to find — or "locate" — the first occurrence below the line pointer of the letter combination *tht*. This concept probably isn't foreign to you if you use an off-line word processing program; it is the same as the search-and-replace function you probably use all the time. In the on-line EDIT program, the search command is /L (for Locate). So, enter:

```
/L/tht
```

Notice the syntax, especially the second slash between L and *tht*. Also note that there are no quotation marks around the word we are looking for.

Again, nothing *seems* to have happened on the screen, but EDIT has moved its invisible line pointer to the first line containing the "string" for which we are looking. If you enter /P 1, it displays the line "file. The key word in tht message."

Now we are ready to correct the word in this line. We need to tell the system to /CHANGE *tht* to *that*. The command is:

```
/C/tht/that
```

To the EDIT program, this means "change tht to that." If you want to make sure the change was made, enter /P 1 again. What appears on your screen now is "file. The key word in that message."

Moving on, let's find and fix the next error. Referring again to the bookmarked example, you see the error is in the fifth line. It is *gtwhen* when it should be *get when*. So, enter:

```
/L/gtwhen
```

This entry locates the "gtwhen" string and moves the pointer to that line. To fix it, enter:

```
/C/gtwhen/get when
```

When you enter /P 1 now, the system shows you the corrected line: "existed, the message you'd get when."

The next error we need to find is a subtle one in line 10. Find it in the printed example. Line 10 says "we noted ,it is the same program" — the space and the comma are reversed — so let's look for "it." Enter:

```
/L/it
```

Okay, let's take a look at the line we have found by entering /P 1 and ... Oops. We have found the wrong *it*! The line on which the pointer has stopped is "the non-numbered editor, because, as" but there is nothing *wrong* with that line.

*Okay, wise guys, what's going on here?*

The point here is that EDIT always looks for the *first* occurrence of the specified string below the current position of the line pointer. It found *it* all right, but it was the wrong *it* — the *it* in the word "edi*t*or" in this line. As it isn't the *it* we are looking for, we need to tell EDIT to continue searching for it (as it were). To do that, enter /L (because you are looking for the same "it" string, you don't have to specify it again; EDIT "remembers" the last string for which it was searching. This time when you /P 1 the line, you should have: "we noted ,it is the same program."

To change the sentence, enter:

```
/C/,it/, it
```

Notice here that the editing program considers a space to be just another character, so you can replace spaces as if they were letters. (Incidentally, a faster way to have found this incorrect string in the first place would have been to search for *,it* rather than just *it*. When searching, think in terms of the *uniqueness* of the string for which you are looking.)

The final error in the file is the misspelling of *directly* (as *driectly* ). Locate it (with /L/driectly, or just /L/drie), and change it (with /C/drie/dire).

Now that we are finished, we must close the file. Enter /EX at the bottom on the file and up comes the PER menu again:

```
Personal File Area PER

  1 Brief CATALOG of files
  2 Detailed DIRECTORY of files
  3 Create & edit files
  4 TYPE a file's contents
  5 DELETE a file
  6 RENAME a file
  7 COPY a file
  8 Change a file's PROTECTION
  9 Upload or download a file
 10 PRINT a file ($)
 11 Enter command mode

 Enter choice !
```

This signifies that you are no longer running the editing program.

## More On PER Functions

Now that you are back at the PER menu, we can use a few more of the file area commands. For starters, please request a DIRECTORY (by entering 2 or the letters DIR at the prompt). After this, you should see something like this:

```
 Name          Blocks   Creation        Access

 MYMAIL.       3 14:32 13-Jan-89 15-Jan-89 (4)
 TEST.TXT      3 09:15 15-Jan-89 15-Jan-89 (4)
 MISTAK.TXT    3 09:02 15-Jan-89 15-Jan-89 (4)
```

Notice that this is precisely the same display we saw earlier in the tour, right after we copied the TEST.TXT file to a new one called MISTAK.TXT.

*Uh. Question. Since there is no change in this display, could that mean our editing in TEST.TXT didn't "take?"*

There's an easy way to find out. Press RETURN to get back to the PER menu:

```
Personal File Area PER

 1 Brief CATALOG of files
 2 Detailed DIRECTORY of files
 3 Create & edit files
 4 TYPE a file's contents
 5 DELETE a file
 6 RENAME a file
 7 COPY a file
 8 Change a file's PROTECTION
 9 Upload or download a file
10 PRINT a file ($)
11 Enter command mode

Enter choice !
```

Now at the prompt, select the TYPE option (that is, option 4) and, when prompted for a file name, enter MISTAK.TXT. This causes the system to show us:

```
   Notice that the heading here
tells us you are opening a fresh
file. The key word in tht message
is "new." If TEST.TXT already
existed, the message you' gtwhen
you typed the file name would be
"File TEST.TXT -- ready."
   We'll use this file to learn about
the nonnumbered editor, because, as
we noted ,it is the same program
we have an option to use in other
features, except this time we are
running it driectly
from the personal file area.
```

Of course, this is the copy of our original file. Since the copy was made *before* we edited TEST.TXT, it is complete with all those well-planned typos ("gtwhen," "driectly," "tht" and all).

Now press RETURN, getting get back to the PER menu. Again select the TYPE option and, when prompted for a file name, this time enter TEST.TXT. Now the system displays:

```
    Notice that the heading here
tells us you are opening a fresh
file. The key word in that message
is "new." If TEST.TXT already
existed, the message you'd gtwhen
you typed the file name would be
"File TEST.TXT -- ready."
    We'll use this file to learn about
the nonnumbered editor, because, as
we noted, it is the same program
we have an option to use in other
features, except this time we are
running it directly
from the personal file area.
```

Comparing the two, it is easy to see that TEST.TXT contains the edited changes we made. From this little exercise, we learn two things:

1. Entering the /EXit command causes the system to *replace* the original file with the latest version, in this case, the newly edited one.
2. Editing a file on CompuServe *does not* does not change its file *name*. So in our example, /EX caused CompuServe to replace the older TEST.TXT with the newer one, but to keep the same file name.

*But what if I do want to change a file name?*

Glad you asked. Press RETURN to get back to the menu:

```
r---------------------------------------------------------¬
|                                                         |
| Personal File Area PER                                  |
|                                                         |
|  1 Brief CATALOG of files                               |
|  2 Detailed DIRECTORY of files                          |
|  3 Create & edit files                                  |
|  4 TYPE a file's contents                               |
|  5 DELETE a file                                        |
|  6 RENAME a file                                        |
|  7 COPY a file                                          |
|  8 Change a file's PROTECTION                           |
|  9 Upload or download a file                            |
| 10 PRINT a file ($)                                     |
| 11 Enter command mode                                   |
|                                                         |
| Enter choice !                                          |
L---------------------------------------------------------┘
```

Earlier on the tour, you saw how to *copy* a file, using option 7 here to create a new file (MISTAK.TXT) that contained exactly the same material as the original (TEST.TXT). As you see now, the PER menu also offers an option for giving a file a new name. Let's try it. At the prompt, enter RENAME (or REN or 6) and the system responds with:

```
r---------------------------------------------------------¬
|                                                         |
| File name:                                              |
L---------------------------------------------------------┘
```

Enter the TEST.TXT at the prompt, and now the system says:

```
r---------------------------------------------------------¬
|                                                         |
| Destination file name:                                  |
L---------------------------------------------------------┘
```

What this means is the the *new* name you want to give the existing TEST.TXT file. It may be any name of up to six letters with an optional extension of up to three letters. Let's enter NEWONE.TXT.

When the system returns you to a prompt, press RETURN to get back to the PER menu. Then enter DIR to get a directory of your files and notice the difference:

```
 Name          Blocks   Creation      Access

 MYMAIL.      3 14:32 13-Jan-89 15-Jan-89 (4)
 NEWONE.TXT   3 09:15 15-Jan-89 15-Jan-89 (4)
 MISTAK.TXT   3 09:02 15-Jan-89 15-Jan-89 (4)
```

Obviously, the file name TEST.TXT is gone from our list and in its place is NEWONE.TXT.

Before we log off, let's try one more PER command. Press RETURN to see the menu again:

```
 Personal File Area PER

  1 Brief CATALOG of files
  2 Detailed DIRECTORY of files
  3 Create & edit files
  4 TYPE a file's contents
  5 DELETE a file
  6 RENAME a file
  7 COPY a file
  8 Change a file's PROTECTION
  9 Upload or download a file
 10 PRINT a file ($)
 11 Enter command mode

  Enter choice !
```

Suppose you no longer need the TEST.TXT file and you want to remove it from the personal file area. The command is DELETE, which, of course, is option 5 on this menu. Enter that at the prompt and the system asks:

```
 File name:
```

Enter TEST.TXT.

Note that CompuServe usually will not delete a file — here in the personal file area or elsewhere on the system — without confirming your choose. This time, the system asks:

```
┌─────────────────────────────────────────────────┐
│                                                 │
│   Are you sure you wish to delete TEST.TXT?     │
│                                                 │
└─────────────────────────────────────────────────┘
```

When you enter Y (meaning yes), CompuServe reports, "File TEST.TXT deleted." Now if you return to the PER menu and enter a DIR or CAT command, you won't find TEST.TXT among your files. Of course, you also could use the same procedure to delete MISTAK.TXT, but let's leave it for the time being. We shall use it again at the end of this chapter.

That's it for this tour. Please log off now and settle back so we can go over a few more points about editing on-line.

## More on Editing

This chapter has taken a running leap at EDIT, CompuServe's *other* editing program. EDIT is available as an option in features throughout the system. Later we shall see how you can specify EDIT rather LINEDIT in EasyPlex, for instance, and as the message-writing system for use in the forums, which we will meet in Chapter 10. Some experienced subscribers prefer EDIT to the numbered editor, believing it is faster and more flexible. Therefore, we need to take a few more minutes for a closer look at the commands. Here, in one neat package, is an overview of the EDIT system for quick reference. Included here are some commands that we didn't use on the tour. The next time you are exploring the system on your own, give them a try.

First, a few rules and terms:

— In writing messages, every command begins with a forward slash. If a line does not begin with a slash, EDIT assumes it is text.

— In the following command definitions, the word *string* means one or more consecutive pieces of text on a line. A string can contain letters, spaces, tabs, punctuation marks, and numbers. *Current line* means the line on which you are working.

— When you are using EDIT, it is helpful to think in terms of an invisible pointer that marks the position of the current line. You can direct the line pointer to move up or down your file. The pointer can be directed to move downward line by line from the first line of your text file, searching for information to be displayed, changed, or erased.

## Editing Commands

/EX exits EDIT and returns you to the menu or command mode.

/T positions the line pointer at an imaginary line just before the first line of the file. This feature allows you to insert new lines above the current first line of the file.

/P*n* displays a specified number (*n*) of lines in the file. If *n* is omitted, only the current line will be displayed. For example, /P3 will display three lines starting with the current line. (*Tip:* Entering /T followed by /P1000 will display the entire contents of any file, unless, of course, it is more than a 1,000 lines long.)

/L/*string* scans the lines following the current line one by one until the first occurrence of the specified string is located. To display the line located give the /P command. Example: If you were to type in "This is an easy projeckt" in your text file, and you find this typo when you are proofreading your file, you can search for a unique string by entering /L/projeckt.

**Caution: Your pointer must be on a line *above* the line you are searching for in order to use /L/*string*. It always searches downward in the file. (*Tip:* If you give the /T command just before the /L/*string* command, you will be able to locate a string above the current line.)**

/C/*old string*/*new string*, the change command replaces any specified string in the current line with a new string: *old string* = the string to be replaced, *new string* = the replacement string. (If the new string is omitted, then the old string will be erased.) For example: "This is an easy projeckt." To change the spelling of *projeckt*, enter /C/ckt/ct. The /P command issued after the change command will display the line in its changed form. "This is an easy project."

/A/*string* adds the specified string to the *end* of the current line. The line pointer will remain on that line after the command is executed.

/D*n* deletes the number of lines specified starting with the current line; *n* is the number of lines to be erased. If omitted, only the current line is erased. The pointer will be positioned at the line following the last line erased.

/B moves the line pointer to the last line (bottom) of your file.

/N, meaning next, moves your line pointer down the file a specified number of lines from its current position.

/N*n*. If you enter *n* as a positive number such as 2, the line pointer advances down your file two lines (it would look like this: /N2). Conversely, if you enter *n* as a negative number such as -3, the line pointer backs up the file -3 lines and the command would look like this: /N-3.

In addition to these, there is a handy global search and replace command that takes a little explaining. First, the syntax is a little strange. It is:

```
/(GC/old string/new string
```

Note the use of the single parenthesis and the fact that there are no spaces in the command. This command is the same as the /CHANGE command, except that it alters *all* occurrences of the old text on the current and following lines. If you wanted to search an entire document, replacing *Bill* with *Will*, you would first go to the /TOP and enter:

```
/(GC/Bill/Will <RETURN>
```

That would change all instances. Note, too, that if you do not include the left parenthesis after the slash, the editor will change only the first occurrence of the old text.

Finally, here is a tip. If you have an ESCAPE key on your keyboard, you can put it to good use in EDIT as a kind of super RETURN key. Using the ESCAPE key rather than RETURN causes the system to make the specified changes and then display the corrected line. It saves you from having to enter a subsequent P to see the fixed line. Suppose you type:

```
/C/the/this <ESCAPE>
```

The effect is the system changes *the* to *this* and automatically displays the edited line.

## Independent Study

Before our next chapter, you might want to go back on-line now to compare editing with EDIT and with LINEDIT. During the tour we copied our original error-filled TEST.TXT file, so all you need to do is go to a LINEDIT feature and call the copy (MISTAK.TXT) into your work area. If you want to do that, log on and go to Easy-Plex (G EASYPLEX):

```
,-----------------------------------------,
|                                         |
| EasyPlex   Main Menu                    |
|                                         |
| *** No mail waiting ***                 |
|                                         |
| 2 COMPOSE a new message                 |
| 3 UPLOAD a message                      |
| 4 USE a file from PER area              |
| 5 ADDRESS Book                          |
| 6 SET options                           |
|                                         |
| Enter choice !                          |
|                                         |
L-----------------------------------------J
```

At the main EasyPlex menu, option 4 allows you to USE a file from the PER area. Enter USE (or 4) at the prompt and system asks:

```
,-----------------------------------------,
|                                         |
| Name of file to use:                    |
L-----------------------------------------J
```

Enter MISTAK.TXT. EasyPlex then searches your PER area, loads MISTAK.TXT into your work area, and displays its Send menu:

```
,-----------------------------------------,
|                                         |
| EasyPlex   Send Menu                    |
|                                         |
| For current message                     |
|                                         |
| 1 SEND                                  |
| 2 EDIT                                  |
| 3 TYPE                                  |
| 4 FILE DRAFT copy                       |
| 5 SEND with /RECEIPT   ($)              |
|                                         |
| Enter choice !                          |
|                                         |
L-----------------------------------------J
```

Obviously, we aren't planning to SEND this file anywhere, but we can use the EDIT functions, so enter EDIT or 2, which produces the Edit menu:

```
EasyPlex   Edit Menu

1 CHANGE characters in line
2 REPLACE line
3 DELETE line
4 INSERT new line(s)
5 TYPE all lines

0 SEND message

Enter choice !
```

First, use option 5, TYPE, to see your original file, but with LINEDIT's exclusive line number, like this:

```
 1:   Notice that the heading here
 2: tells us you are opening a fresh
 3: file. The key word in tht message
 4: is "new." If TEST.TXT already
 5: existed, the message you'd gtwhen
 6: you typed the file name would be
 7: "File TEST.TXT -- ready."
 8: We'll use this file to learn about
 9: the nonnumbered editor, because, as
10: we noted ,it is the same program
11: we have an option to use in other
12: features, except this time we are
13: running it driectly

Press <CR>!
```

Of course, all of our original errors — "tht," "gtwhen," " ,it," and "driectly" — are there needing to be fixed. Pressing RETURN, you come back to the edit menu:

```
┌─────────────────────────────────────────────────┐
│                                                   │
│   EasyPlex  Edit Menu                             │
│                                                   │
│   1 CHANGE characters in line                     │
│   2 REPLACE line                                  │
│   3 DELETE line                                   │
│   4 INSERT new line(s)                            │
│   5 TYPE all lines                                │
│                                                   │
│   0 SEND message                                  │
│                                                   │
│   Enter choice !                                  │
│                                                   │
└─────────────────────────────────────────────────┘
```

Selecting option 1 (or entering CHANGE or just CHA) causes the system to prompt:

```
┌─────────────────────────────────────────────────┐
│                                                   │
│   Which line #:                                   │
│                                                   │
└─────────────────────────────────────────────────┘
```

If you entered 13, it would lead to a dialog such as this:

```
┌─────────────────────────────────────────────────┐
│                                                   │
│   Current line:                                   │
│   13:  running it driectly                        │
│                                                   │
│   Text to replace: dri <RETURN>                   │
│   Replacement text: dir                           │
│                                                   │
│   New line:                                       │
│   13:  running it directly                        │
│                                                   │
│   Press <CR>!                                     │
│                                                   │
└─────────────────────────────────────────────────┘
```

When you are ready to quit the practice, you might want to return to the PER area and delete the MISTAK.TXT file. Then log off by entering BYE or OFF at a "!" prompt.

# CHAPTER 9

# Interlude: Taking Stock and Restocking

If you were a mountain climber and CompuServe were your challenge, you would be about halfway up the face by now. In our first eight chapters, you have seen how to:

— Navigate the system with the menus.
— Take express routes with the powerful GO command.
— Use the FIND command to search for specific services and general topics.
— Send and receive electronic mail.
— Party with other subscribers on the popular CB Simulator, talking publicly, privately, and semiprivately.

In addition, you have looked behind the curtain to find that menus are all part of a program called Displa, which actually can be turned off and on. You are a step ahead of many new subscribers in that you have met the "OK" prompt, and it doesn't intimidate you. You have learned how to use both editing programs — EDIT and LINEDIT — and you have explored some of the wonders of the massive Public Access database, and have used your own storage space, the personal file area.

By now, however, you have every right to be a little overwhelmed by the electronic world in which you are traveling. It is probably larger than you thought it would be and you might feel a little shaky about commands used in the various corners of the system. Our tours have taken you through the middle of CompuServe at a rather rapid clip. Remember that we have your pocketbook in mind and want you to see as much in as little connect time as possible. If there are sections of the system of which you are unsure, take a break now, reread portions of those chapters, and explore a little on your own. Use our On-line Survival Kit at the back of the book to remind yourself of commands. This independent exploration will be helpful to you. We have said all along that we don't intend our words to be a summation of Compu-

Serve, but rather to be your starting point. The fact that the system constantly is changing makes it even more important that you get used to tooling these byways on your own. It is likely that between the time these words leave our word processors and reach your eyes, CompuServe's programming wizards will have added new features here and there and modified older ones. If we have sold you on the importance of having an explorer's spirit, then you will be excited by these unexpected changes, not upset by them.

In the coming chapters we will show you the wide assortment of on-line games available, from traditional fare, like the adventure game we played in Chapter 3, to exciting multiplayer games in which you compete against friends and strangers around the world. We will look at business and financial features, from stock quotes to shop-at-home services. And, beginning with the next chapter, we will look at what some consider to be the most satisfying part of all CompuServe, the forums, which in many ways represent the culmination of all that is intriguing about the system's conferencing, databases, and bulletin boards.

## But First ...

Before we start the climb again, we devote this chapter to elaborating on what you have learned so far with a potpourri of additional commands, services, features, and shortcuts. We look at:

— The story on uploading and downloading, a feature available in EasyPlex, the personal file area and such places as the forums' data libraries, which you will see later.

— Handy additional information about EasyPlex, including how to upload letters written off-line and how to use the built-in Address Book, as well as how to mail letters to more than one person at a time and how to use to prewritten form letters.

— How you can change some of what is being displayed on your screen through an area called Profile. Our first encounter with a powerful feature that will be increasingly important as we go on.

— The easy way to change a password.

— A few more important control codes and navigation commands.

## The Story on Downloading and Uploading

So far we have communicated with CompuServe in a very direct sort of way. When we have had something to say, we typed it on the keyboard; when CompuServe has had a message for us, we read it on the screen. However, sometimes you will want to communicate with the system differently from your disk to CompuServe and from CompuServe to your disk. In other words, you will:

1. Have information stored on a disk — a text file, a prewritten EasyPlex letter, an original program — that you want to send (*upload*) to the system for someone else to retrieve, either a specific recipient or the public in general.
2. Find files in the various nooks and crannies of CompuServe that you want to retrieve (*download*) and store on a disk for later use.

These terms sometimes confuse people who are new to on-line services, but they aren't so obscure. *Uploading* simply means sending something from your computer to the computers at CompuServe. *Downloading* means going the other way, taking something from CompuServe and storing it on your computer. (To keep the terms straight, you can think of CompuServe's big computers as being on top, while your little micro is always on the bottom. To transmit something to CompuServe, you send it *up*; to get something, you need to bring it *down*.)

We have seen one or both terms on several menus in our tours so far, such as option 3 on the EasyPlex menu:

```
EasyPlex   Main Menu

1 READ mail, 1 message pending
2 COMPOSE a new message
3 UPLOAD a message
4 USE a file from PER area
5 ADDRESS Book
6 SET options

Enter choice !
```

Option 9 in the personal file (PER) area:

```
r----------------------------------------------------------------------1
I                                                                      I
I                                                                      I
I    Personal File Area                           PER                  I
I                                                                      I
I     1 Brief CATALOG of files                                         I
I     2 Detailed DIRECTORY of files                                    I
I     3 Create & edit files via FILGE                                  I
I     4 TYPE a file's contents                                         I
I     5 DELETE a file                                                  I
I     6 RENAME a file                                                  I
I     7 COPY a file                                                    I
I     8 Change a file's PROTECTION                                     I
I     9 Upload or download a file                                      I
I                                                                      I
I    11 Enter command mode                                             I
I                                                                      I
I    Enter choice !                                                    I
I                                                                      I
I                                                                      I
L----------------------------------------------------------------------J
```

In addition, you will see later that file transfer also plays an extremely important part in the data libraries of the forums.

In all cases, downloading and uploading represent a special, more intimate kind of communication, with CompuServe, that depends largely on your own communications software. If you are new to file transfer, you would do well to take a break at this point and consult the manual that came with your communications program. Look for details of how your software is prepared to handle uploading and downloading. Pay particular attention to the specific command sequences used for those operations. Also of interest to us is what file transfer *protocol* or *protocols* (sometimes called "error-checking protocols" or "binary file transfer protocols") your software supports.

A *protocol* is a set of rules that allows computers to send and receive data between each other without the errors caused by static on the phone lines. Computers do this by carrying on a clever little conversation of their own during the file transfer, periodically checking to see if the data received is identical to what was sent. We humans usually don't have to be involved directly in this digital dialogue. Most communications programs allow the computers to handle it all by themselves, following the rules set forth in the protocol. Here is how they do it:

— The computer *sending* the file (CompuServe when you are downloading, *your* computer when you are uploading) transmits a certain amount of data called a *block* that the receiver catches.

— The computers then do some calculations. The sending computer analyzes the digital representations of the block and comes up with a number called a *checksum*. The receiver does the same calculation on the received block. Then the sender and receiver compare checksums. The only way the two numbers can match is if exactly the same block was received as was sent. The difference of a single byte of data will result in different checksums.

— If the checksums don't match, the receiver throws away the block it received, and the sender tries again. If they do match, the receiver saves the block on the disk and prepares to receive the next transmission. The procedure continues until the entire file is sent and confirmed, then the computer lets you, the human, know that the deed is done.

One of the differences among various transfer protocols is simply in the size of that block of information that is passed between the two computers. Some protocols send blocks of 256 bytes of data before comparing checksums, whereas others use larger or smaller blocks. Because of those different block sizes, it is essential that both the sending and receiving computers use the same protocol during a transfer. Obviously, chaos reigns if one computer chooses a protocol that transmits 512-byte blocks while the receiving system is using a protocol that wants to compare checksums every 128 bytes. That is why CompuServe asks you to specify which protocol to use before starting a download or an upload.

Fortunately, CompuServe supports an assortment of different protocols for file transfer, so check your communications program's manual to see if your terminal software also supports any of the following:

**CompuServe's B Protocol and Quick B Protocol** were developed specifically for CompuServe. They are supported in a number of communications programs, including CompuServe's own *Professional Connection* packages, CompuServe *VIDTEX* (for Apple IIe, Tandy Color Computer, and Commodore computers), *Crosstalk Mk4*, *Lotus Symphony 1.2*, *ProComm*, and others. Incidentally, a few terminal programs still support CompuServe's older A Protocol (which still is listed on some menus around the system) but their numbers rapidly are dwindling.

**Xmodem** (also called MODEM7) is a well-known public domain protocol that was developed in the late 1970s by Ward Christensen of Chicago. A great many communications programs support Xmodem. In fact, if your communications program supports only one kind of transfer protocol, chances are it is Xmodem. However, each program may support a slightly different version. For instance, in some parts of CompuServe a "Macintosh Xmodem" is listed on protocol menus, indicating a Xmodem installation for the Apple Macintosh computer.

**Kermit** is a protocol that was developed at Columbia University for file transfer. It is becoming increasingly popular in communications software.

## Using Protocols for Downloading

To see how transfer protocols work, let's think again about the TEST.TXT file you created during the past chapter. Suppose that instead of being a simple exercise to learn the non-numbered editor, this actually had been an important file. Perhaps before deleting it, you wanted to retrieve the file from your Personal File Area and save it on a disk on your microcomputer. It sounds like a job for a protocol. You start by visiting your file area, entering G PER to reach this menu:

```
Personal File Area PER

 1 Brief CATALOG of files
 2 Detailed DIRECTORY of files
 3 Create & edit files
 4 TYPE a file's contents
 5 DELETE a file
 6 RENAME a file
 7 COPY a file
 8 Change a file's PROTECTION
 9 Upload or download a file
10 PRINT a file ($)
11 Enter command mode

Enter choice !
```

Notice that option 9 handles both downloading and uploading. Since you want the former operation, which produces this menu:

```
File Transfer

Protocol

 1 XMODEM (MODEM7) protocol
 2 CompuServe 'B' protocol
 3 CompuServe 'A' protocol
 4 DC2/DC4 (CAPture) protocol
 5 MACintosh XMODEM protocol
 6 CompuServe Quick 'B' protocol
 7 Kermit protocol

Enter choice !
```

(Please bookmark this example. The only protocol listed here that was not mentioned earlier is option 4, "DC4/DC2 CAPTURE protocol," to which we shall return in a moment.)

If you have already familiarized yourself with the manual of your own communications software, you know what protocols are available — Xmodem, Kermit, B Protocol, and so on. All you have to do is enter a number to tell CompuServe which one it should use in the coming file transfer.

**Time Out #1:**    If you are using one of CompuServe's own terminal programs, such as *The Professional Connection*, *VIDTEX*, or *Navigator* for the Apple Macintosh, the system might *not* display this menu of transfer protocol selections. Instead, if the system already has recognized your communications program as one of its own (and there are options we shall discuss in a later chapter to allow the system to do just that), CompuServe may automatically select B or Quick B protocol and initiate the transfer for you. In other cases, you will need to indicate your preferred transfer protocol with a selection from the menu. The system then will prompt you to initiate the transfer, and you must enter the appropriate commands for your software. Obviously, it is here that you will need to have done your homework by studying your software's manual. For instance, if the manual tells you that your program supports the Xmodem protocol, you will need to select 1 from this menu, then, when prompted by the system, initiate the download with whatever command sequences your software requires.

Most communications programs also pause before the download begins in order to prompt you for the name you want to assign the file as it arrives on your disk during the download. This name does not have to be the same name as exists in the database. Although the file in our example is called TEST.TXT, you may call it anything you like on your disk, so long as it is a legal file name for your computer. (Also, if you have a hard disk and use directories and subdirectories to organize it, make sure you enter the full pathway name when specifying the file name.)

Now the actual download begins. CompuServe sends data and your machine captures the data comparing checksums to verify what has been received and saving it on your disk. With some communications software, the screen displays numbers and plus signs during the download, something like:

```
1+++++++2++++++3++++++4+++++ etc.
```

This display is just to assure you that nothing is broken and that the transfer is going on properly. Other terminal programs do not display this string of numbers and symbols, but offer their own screen displays to report the progress of the file transfer. See the manual with your terminal program for specifics.

After the download is finished — the file has been transmitted from Compu-
Serve, confirmed, and saved on your disk under the specified name — the system
notifies you. Later, when you log off, you can use the file you have retrieved, reading
it if it is text, running it if it is a program.

If you were to download a second file at this point, the system would not
prompt you for a transfer protocol; it would skip that menu, assuming you were using
the same protocol as you used on the first transfer.

Questions?

*Sure, I'll bite. What about this "DC4/DC2" stuff?*

Okay, let's back up a moment to the file transfer menu to discuss our missing
option. Until now, we have sidestepped a discussion of the option 4 on the transfer
menu. "DC4/DC2 CAPTURE" is *not* an error-checking protocol; it does not compare
checksums like B and Quick B Protocol, Xmodem, and Kermit. Instead, DC4/DC2,
sometimes referred to as an "ASCII" (American Standard Code for Information Interchange) transfer, is similar to what you would receive if you simply used the REAd
option instead of DOWnload, that is, an ASCII display of the file. Some communications programs have what is called an "ASCII dump" or a "buffer capture." You can
use this option for such capturing. However, it should be used only for capturing *text
files*; by contrast, program files should always be downloaded or uploaded with an
error-checking protocol.

*Okay, but what does "DC4/DC2" mean, anyway?*

Uh-oh, some jargon is creeping up on us. It means "Device Control 4/Device
Control 2." Uh-huh. Clear as mud, right? Well, fortunately, we need not have a long
technical discussion. Suffice it to say that some communications programs have an
option to use a buffer to receive and send ASCII files; a buffer that is regulated by
these device control blocks. Of course, check your software's manual to see if such a
thing is available to you. If so, you can select this option, and you will receive a message something like this:

```
 ┌──────────────────────────────────────────────────┐
 │                                                    │
 │   This protocol supports ASCII                     │
 │   file transfer only.                              │
 │   Is this an ASCII file (Y or N)?                  │
 │                                                    │
 └──────────────────────────────────────────────────┘
```

The system is reminding you that one of the other protocols should be used for binary files, such as programs. If you answer this prompt with Y for yes, the system pauses a moment to open your capture buffer and sends the file in ASCII.

## Uploading Made Simple

Transmitting — uploading — material to the system works in the same basic way, but because you are sending rather than receiving data, you usually have to supply CompuServe with a little more information. To see how uploading works, suppose you have an original file on a disk in your microcomputer that you want to save in your personal area on-line, such as a form letter for EasyPlex (using a technique we shall discuss in next section). As with downloading, you specify your desire to upload at the main PER menu, selecting option 9 in this example.

```
Personal File Area PER

  1 Brief CATALOG of files
  2 Detailed DIRECTORY of files
  3 Create & edit files
  4 TYPE a file's contents
  5 DELETE a file
  6 RENAME a file
  7 COPY a file
  8 Change a file's PROTECTION
  9 Upload or download a file
 10 PRINT a file ($)
 11 Enter command mode

Enter choice !
```

After that, you'll be prompted for a file name.

**Time Out #2:**   About *file names.* Various parts of CompuServe — the personal file area and data libraries of the forum — as you will see use names to identify files. A name always can be one to six characters with an optional four-character extension (though the extension's first character must be a period), as in NAME.EXT. You may use alphabetic or numeric characters and/or hyphens in the name, but the first character must be a letter of the alphabet. When the system prompts for a file name, it means the name under which the data should be stored on CompuServe; what you enter does *not* have to be the same name that exists on your disk. By the disk. By the way, sometimes extensions on file names are used in special ways in parts of CompuServe, particularly in the data libraries of forums. We shall talk about that at length in Chapter 13.

Once the file name has been specified, the system will want to know which transfer protocol you want to use and will display its menu of available protocols — B Protocol, Xmodem, Kermit, etc. — just as in downloading. (Again, if you are using one of CompuServe's own terminal programs, such as *Professional Connection*, the system may skip that menu and assume you will use B or Quick B Protocol.)

After the transfer protocol is specified, the system will need another piece of information, one that it does not require in downloading. This time it will need to know *file type*, and will inquire with menu like this one:

```
Transfer types available -

1 ASCII   (7 - bit)
2 Binary (8 - bit)
3 Graphic:RLE
4 Graphic:NAPLPS
5 Graphic:GIF

Enter choice !
```

This screen refers simply to the format in which the file should be *saved* on CompuServe. We shall defer discussion of the last three options here (Graphic:RLE, Graphic:NAPLPS, and Graphic:GIF) until a later chapter when we talk about graphics. The first two options on the list require some translation. As we have said, ASCII usually means text, including letters, documents, or source codes of programs; binary means computer programs, primarily. Generally speaking, you should specify the same file type for the file as it is currently stored on your disk. In other words, if the file you are uploading is a binary program (machine language or tokenized BASIC), you should specify that it be saved in binary format on the CompuServe end of the connection; on the other hand, if it is an ASCII text file, such as an article or letter, it should be saved in ASCII on the receiving end.

**Time Out #3:**    About text files and ASCII. A confusion about text files sometimes arises because many commercial word processors routinely store documents, not in ASCII, but in a binary format to save space on your disk and to imbed commands for printers and so on. It is a mistake to upload one of these *compressed* binary files and have it saved as ASCII on CompuServe. Since it is not ASCII, it will not be readable by those who download it. Fortunately, your word processor itself usually offers the solution. Most good word processors have an option for saving files in a plain vanilla ASCII rather than their own compressed format. Check the users manual of your word processor and use that option to save your text files in true ASCII before uploading them.

After the file type has been specified, the system prompts you to begin the transmission. The manual of your own communications program should tell you the command sequence for uploading. Usually, the terminal software prompts you for the name of the file on your disk that you want to upload. After that, your computer and CompuServe begin that clever digital comparison of checksums until the entire file has been transmitted.

Two more points:

1. As in downloading, if you were to upload a second file, the system wouldn't prompt again for a file transfer protocol, but would assume you were using the same protocol you used for the first upload.
2. If for any reason you need to stop an upload or a download before it is finished, press CONTROL C or the ESCAPE key several times. Usually, CompuServe displays a message reporting the transfer was aborted and allows you to return to a menu.

We have more to say about uploading and downloading in Chapter 13 where we discuss the data libraries of forums.

*Is uploading with DC4/DC2 different from uploading with an error-checking protocol?*

Yes, a little. When you select the DC4/DC2 options from the protocol menu for uploading, the system displays:

```
This protocol supports ASCII
file transfer only.
Is this an ASCII file (Y or N)?
```

Again, the system is reminding you that an error-checking protocol, rather than DC4/DC2, should be used for uploading binary files. If you answer this prompt with Y for yes, meaning your file is indeed ASCII, the system then prompts with:

```
No error detection protocol in use.
Do you wish to be prompted for each line (Y
or N)?
```

If you answer Y to this question, the system asks you to enter the prompt
character to use. (For instance, if you enter a question mark, the system will prompt
with a "?" at the beginning of each new line.) If you answer N to the prompt in the example, the system will not prompt you at the beginning of each new line. After that,
the system reports:

```
Begin sending your data.  Use a
control-Z (1A hex, 032 octal) to
indicate the end of your data.
```

Now you may tell your software to fire away and begin its ASCII transmitting.
(Also with the DC4/DC2 option, you can even type in your file directly from your
keyboard.) When you are finished, signal CompuServe with a CONTROL-Z.

Just keep in mind that DC4/DC2 is fine for transmitting text files, but cannot be
used for binary files, such as programs.

## Uploading Files for EasyPlex

You also can use uploading techniques to save time in EasyPlex by (1) storing *form
letters* in your personal file area and (2) uploading to the system directly with new letters that you have written off-line with your usual word processor. For either application, you need to keep these three points in mind in composing letters for uploading:

1.  Have your off-line word processor save the text *in ASCII* format with a car-
    riage return at the end of each screen line. This rule is the most important
    one to remember. As noted, most modern word processing programs
    routinely save text in their own compressed binary formats, but can be
    directed to save in ASCII instead. Check your users manual for details of
    this important ASCII option, and always use it for text you intend to upload.

2. A single EasyPlex can be no longer than 50K (about 50,000 characters). If you are preparing a letter with your word processor for later uploading, keep an eye on the length.
3. EasyPlex message lines may be no longer than 80 characters. Just as you must press RETURN at the end of each line you type on-line, those carriage returns must be in place as your file is transmitted. Make sure there is a *line feed* entered after each carriage return in the file. This task is most conveniently done while typing the letter in the word processor, but sometimes it can be done by using your editor to insert the carriage return/line feeds with a search-replace function before the uploading begins.

**Now, about Form Letters:**   Some subscribers have regular introductory EasyPlex messages they send to new friends they meet on the system. They don't have to type in the EasyPlex each time; they simply load it in from their PER area.

Suppose you have a letter of introduction you have written with your word processor and saved in ASCII following the above tips. Now you can store it in your PER area by logging on and entering G FILES, which brings you to the opening menu:

```
Personal File Area                      PER

   1 Brief CATALOG of files
   2 Detailed DIRECTORY of files
   3 Create & edit files via FILGE
   4 TYPE a file's contents
   5 DELETE a file
   6 RENAME a file
   7 COPY a file
   8 Change a file's PROTECTION
   9 Upload or download a file
  10 PRINT a file ($)
  11 Enter command mode

Enter choice !
```

By selecting option 9 at the menu, you cause the system to ask about the protocol you will use, with a menu something like this:

```
File Transfer

Protocol

1 XMODEM (MODEM7) protocol
2 CompuServe 'B' protocol
3 CompuServe 'A' protocol
4 DC2/DC4 (CAPture) protocol
5 MACintosh XMODEM protocol
6 CompuServe Quick 'B' protocol
7 Kermit protocol

Enter choice !
```

Enter your choice; the system then asks:

```
File Transfer

Direction

1 DOWnload from CompuServe
2 UPLoad to CompuServe
3 Exit

Enter choice !
```

A 2 entered here specifies uploading. The PER then needs to know the format of the file, either ASCII or binary. Specify ASCII, because it is text that you have saved in the ASCII format from your word processor. Then the system prompts for the file name. Enter up to six letters with an optional three-letter extension, such as FORM.LET. Finally, the system prompts you to begin the transfer, and signals you when it is completed.

Once you have stored a form letter, you can mail it from EasyPlex with an option on the main menu, one that we saw at the end of the previous chapter:

```
EasyPlex  Main Menu
   *** No mail waiting ***

2 COMPOSE a new message
3 UPLOAD a message
4 USE a file from PER area
5 ADDRESS Book
6 SET options

Enter choice !
```

(Please bookmark this page. We will refer to it several times in the next few minutes.)

Option 4, "USE a file from PER area," instructs the system to load a file from your PER area into your EasyPlex work space, just as if you had typed it in. If you enter 4 at the prompt, the system responds with:

```
Name of file to use:
```

It is waiting for the name of the file you gave the letter when you created it in the PER area, such as FORM.LET. (Incidentally, to save time you can combine the commands by entering USE FORM.LET at the "!" prompt.) Now a copy of the file is loaded into the EasyPlex work space and you advance to the *send* menu:

```
EasyPlex  Send Menu

For current message

1 SEND
2 EDIT
3 TYPE
4 FILE DRAFT copy
5 SEND with /RECEIPT  ($)

Enter choice !
```

From here on, it is just as if you had typed this letter into EasyPlex during the current session. With the TYPE option, you can display the file; with EDIT you can open the work space and change the file, in case you want to customize it. Some subscribers leave the top of their form letters blank and edit in a salutation. You then can close the file with the /EX command, and when you are ready to mail it, use the Send option 1, as always.

**About Directly Uploading.**   You can save time by directly uploading to EasyPlex with a message you have written off-line. Simply choose option 3 from the bookmarked example of the main EasyPlex menu, or enter UPL at the prompt. As always, the system quizzes you about which transfer protocol you want to use and the file type (ASCII or binary); then it begins that intimate, machine-to-machine dialogue. The same rules apply: the file must have been saved in ASCII, be less than 50K and have lines of no more than 80 characters each. Once the file is transferred, you are taken to the send menu, as always.

**Tip:**   Another little time-saver for messages prepared off-line is the imbedding of the header information in the letter you intend to upload. You have seen that routinely after you instruct the system to send a message, and you are prompted with "To:" and "Subject:" You can bypass these prompts by simply including them at the top of the letter on the first two lines, like this:

```
To: 71635,1025
Subject: Upcoming conference
(Begin the text)
```

When the system processes your letter for mail, it checks the first lines and, if it finds "To:" and "Subject:" already supplied, it doesn't bother to ask you for them again.

## Sending and Receiving Binary via EasyPlex

A recent enhancement of EasyPlex actually allows you to send and receive program files — binary — through the mail as well. To upload a binary file, you follow the above procedure, but choose the binary file type option rather than ASCII when prompted.

Although it isn't displayed on the menus in our bookmarked example, you can download from your EasyPlex mailbox by simply entering DOW at the main prompt. You then will be asked for the file transfer protocol and so on.

When uploading binary files, remember the length restrictions; EasyPlex messages cannot exceed 50K. Also, for the convenience of the recipient, it is a good idea to precede binary files with a brief ASCII message that says something to the effect, "Dear John, About the NEXT letter in your mailbox. It is a copy of my new program. Note it is a BINARY file so to get it, enter DOW at the EasyPlex prompt and choose a transfer protocol..."

## Using Your Little Black Book

Another great time-saver in EasyPlex is your on-line Address Book; option 5 on the bookmarked example. ADDRESS book is an electronic file in which you can keep the names and user IDs of up to 50 of your regular on-line correspondents. At the main menu, you enter 5 (or the word ADDRESS or the letters ADD), and the system shows you:

```
EasyPlex  Address Book

1 INSERT an entry
2 CHANGE an entry
3 DELETE an entry
4 LIST Address Book
5 Enter/Change your NAME

Enter choice !
```

If you choose option 1 (INSERT), the Address Book prompts for a name and then a user ID, like this:

```
Address 1
Name: Charlie Bowen <RETURN>
Charlie Bowen's User ID: 71635,1025 <RETURN>

Address 2
Name: Dave Peyton <RETURN>
Dave Peyton's User ID: 70475,1165 <RETURN>
Address 3
Name:  <RETURN>
```

After a name has been saved in the Address Book, you can save time when mailing letters. When prompted with "Send to:," you can enter the name as recorded in the book rather than the user ID. In this example, if you were writing an EasyPlex message to Dave Peyton, you would need only type "Dave Peyton" when you came to the "Send to:" prompt; the system would look him up in your Address Book and find the ID number, 70475,1165, and supply it itself.

The other options on the menu let you change, delete, and list the entries in your book.

Notice, too, that you can place your own name in a special place in the Address Book, so that the system can automatically sign your outgoing messages for you. (For instance, Charlie uses "Charlieb" as his EasyPlex signature, by filing that spelling in his Address Book.) If you select option 5 of the Address Book menu, the system asks for the name you wish to have signed automatically to all your letters. The first time you use this option, the system displays:

```
Enter a period to erase this
name, or <CR> to leave it
unchanged.


Your EasyPlex name
   Old: *NONE*
   New:
```

From then on, if you use option 5 to change your signature, the system displays the old name and prompts you for the new.

## Multiple Mailings

Continuing with EasyPlex tips, it is possible to send the same electronic letter to more than one on-line acquaintance. In fact, you can send a message to up to ten different subscribers at the same time. Here is how. As you have seen, when you select the SEND option, the system prompts with:

```
Send to (Name or User ID):
```

Simply type in the recipients' user ID numbers (or their names as listed in the Address Book) with each entry separated by a semicolon (;). For example:

```
r--------------------------------------------------------------------¬
I                                                                    I
I   Send to (Name or User ID): CHARLIE BOWEN;70000,00;DAVE PEYTON;71635,1025   I
I                                                                    I
L--------------------------------------------------------------------J
```

As you see, user ID numbers and names filed in your Address Book can be used at the same prompt.

A ten-cent surcharge is levied for each destination after the first to which your message is sent. In this example, a 30-cent fee would charged, as the message is going out to four people.


## Preserving Data in the Personal File Area

We have seen that using EasyPlex can result in the addition of files in your PER file area. As early as Chapter 5, we used EasyPlex's FILE option to store a letter in the PER area as MYMAIL. We also have seen how to upload a form letter to the PER for EasyPlex use (FORM.LET). Not only that, when you begin using your Address Book, you actually are causing the system to create, automatically, a file called EMAIL.ADR and to store it in your PER area.

All of these files, including the form letters and the EMAIL.ADR file, remain in the PER area as long as you use them regularly. However, if a file in the PER area isn't accessed in a 30-day period, it is subject to being deleted automatically by the system, in its continuing efforts to provide ample storage space for all subscribers. Avoiding this purge is easy:

— To protect the EMAIL.ADR file, you should use the Address Book feature at least once a month, using one of the menu options (to insert, delete, or list Address Book names) or one of the names in the "Send to:" prompt in mailing.

— To secure other PER files, such as the text of a form letter saved for use in EasyPlex, try this: Once a month, visit the file area (G FILES) and use the menu option to *edit* the file. This tactic will "open" the file in question; then, without making any changes, you can close it again with the /EX command. Your file will be secure for another month.


More points about PER files:

— For subscribers to the Executive Option, discussed in Chapter 16, the time limit on PER files is six months rather than 30 days.

— The PER recognizes some file name and extensions as temporary files. Any file whose name begins with a number or has an extension of BAK, CRF, LST, or

TMP (as 2FILE, FILE.BAK, FILE.TMP, etc.) automatically is deleted when you log off the system.

— All CompuServe subscribers get at least 128K (that is, about 128,000 bytes) of storage space in their PER areas. All files you save in the PER area — whether you create them yourself, save them after receiving them in EasyPlex, or copy them from Public Access — use up part of that 128K. For that reason, some subscribers want more than the minimum storage in the PER. CompuServe offers additional disk space in units of 64K at a surcharge of $4 a week per 64K unit. You can request additional storage space by entering G FEEDBACK at any prompt and choosing the category "Request additional services." (More about Feedback later this chapter.)

— If the total size of the files saved in the PER area exceeds the limit, you may be charged an additional storage fee.

— The Executive Option also offers users an addition 64K of online storage space, bringing the standard to a total of 192K.

## Changing the Rules through Profile

So far, an underlying theme of this chapter has been *rules*. We have talked about different kinds of rules, from those that computers understand for uploading and downloading (as established by a transfer protocol) to the rules for preparing text for uploading to the different kinds of rules that CompuServe itself sets up for matters such as retaining or deleting data in your personal file area. As in life, rules exist throughout the on-line system, but at least some rules are determined by you. Setting your own rules is especially important in the area of the system called Profile, which is primarily concerned with the way information is displayed on your screen.

It is possible that the way CompuServe has been presented on your screen just hasn't looked quite right. Sure, you can read it, but maybe while your computer can display both capital and lowercase letters, all you get from CompuServe are capital letters. Or maybe everything you type appears in ALL CAPITAL LETTERS, even though you haven't pressed the shift key. Or perhaps the length of your lines look funny. Maybe your screen can accommodate 80 characters on each line, but the system is sending lines to you that are only half that width. You may have a computer with a 32-character width but are getting a couple of lines that fill up the screen entirely, followed by a third line that is a few characters long, followed by more lines that fill up the screen width again. Or maybe you have more than one computer to take on-line, one that has an 80-character screen and another that has a 40-character screen; the system always seems to be "wrong" for one machine or the other.

In cases such as these, there need to be procedures for changing the way CompuServe displays the information it is sending to you. By manipulating your on-line User Profile, you can change how your computer interacts with the one at CompuServe's headquarters.

When you first logged on, the system asked you what kind of computer you had and what kind of terminal program you were using. The answers you gave on that first session helped CompuServe determine how you wanted the information delivered to your screen. Maybe you inadvertently gave the wrong information or perhaps couldn't determine the correct answers at the time. CompuServe took its best shot, but it may not have been the perfect shot. We now can fix that.

From anywhere in the system, you can enter G PROFILE to visit the area where you can change the technical information on file about your computer. That command takes you to:

```
CompuServe                          PROFILE

CHANGE YOUR USER PROFILE

1 Terminal Settings
2 Change Your Password
3 Password Security Guidelines
4 Change Your Billing Options
  or Credit Card Information
5 Change Your Billing Address

Enter choice !
```

Several pieces of handy information are contained herein. We shall come back to one of them — Change Your Password — in a minute. For starters, option 1, "Terminal Settings," allows you to alter and fine-tune the way information is being delivered to your screen. Selecting it takes you to this menu:

```
TERMINAL SETTINGS/SERVICE OPTIONS

Use this area to change your terminal
type/parameters and/or service options.

Note: Your permanent and session
settings do not match.

1 Instructions
2 Change permanent settings
3 Explanation of session vs. permanent
4 Show session vs. permanent
5 Change current session settings

Enter choice!
```

Two notes right off the bat: (1) This screen has two quick reference words. You can reach it directly by entering either G TERMINAL or G OPTIONS. (2) Historically speaking, this feature used to be called "Default," and as you talk to other subscribers on the system, you may come across old-timers who still speak of "setting defaults" on the system. Don't be put off if the terminology is unfamiliar; they are talking about this Terminal Setting feature.

TERMINAL/OPTIONS control a variety of settings, some of them with obscure names such "real form feeds" and "simulated form feeds," tabs, parity, and a variety of semitechnical settings. However, for the time being, we shall look at only a small portion and wait until a later chapter to look more closely.

Option 1 on this menu is instructions, which gives an overview of the specific things you can do here. If you are somewhat familiar with computer terms, you may have no trouble at all understanding the text. The rest of the menu deals with "permanent" and "session" changes.

**Time Out #4:**   People get confused about computers when new concepts are introduced that don't quite fit their older names. For instance, in the Real World, the words "permanent" and "temporary" have precise meanings. A thing is permanent if it is constant, unalterable; temporary things are momentary, provisional. As far as English and logic are concerned, the difference comes down to whether the thing in question can be *changed*. Computers, however, have come along with a new idea: "permanent" things that can be changed; "temporary" things that might remain unchanged forever (or might change in the next minute). The concept, sandwiched between those Real World definitions, is: some things are "permanent" until the user changes his or her mind about them, that is, "permanent — until further notice."

On CompuServe, this new perspective on permanent/temporary is most evident in the way these *default* settings in TERMINAL/OPTIONS are handled. To see how it works, suppose you came to this menu and selected 2 "Change permanent options." This causes the system to display:

```
PERMANENT SETTINGS

1 Explanation
2 Logon/Service options
3 Display options
4 Terminal type/parameters
5 Transfer protocol/graphic support
6 Make session settings permanent

Type EXIT when done
```

Both problems we want to address in this chapter — screen width and depth and capitalized text — are managed under the "Terminal type/parameters" section of this menu. If we entered 4 at this prompt, we would see something like:

```
TERMINAL TYPE/PARAMETERS

 1 TERMINAL type                    [OTHER]
 2 Screen WIDTH                      [32]
 3 LINES per page                    [16]
 4 Form FEEDS                   [SIMULATED]
 5 Horizontal TABS              [SIMULATED]
 6 Chars. received (CASE)          [U/L]
 7 Chars. sent in CAPS             [YES]
 8 PARITY                          [EVEN]
 9 Output DELAYS                     [1]
10 ERASE when backspacing           [NO]
11 Micro inquiry sequence at logon  [NO]

Enter choice!
```

Let's say you have a computer that has an 80-character screen width and all the lines you have been receiving so far are too short. In this example, you see the problem by looking at the current setting for "Screen WIDTH," option 2. The information in the square brackets is the current setting, in this case "[32]," which means 32 characters per line. To change it, enter 2 at the prompt and the system displays:

```
SCREEN WIDTH

Permanent setting =                    [32]

This determines the number of characters
per line.

Type H for help.

WIDTH:
```

The system's "WIDTH:" prompt is, of course, asking for your new setting of this parameter. If you wanted to leave it unchanged, you could simply press the RETURN key. However, if you have an 80-character screen and this parameter were set to 32 as it is in the example, you should type 80. Entering a new number here corrects the problem of short lines. On the other hand, if you have a couple of long lines and a short one, it is probably because you have a computer with a 32-character or 40-character display and CompuServe is sending 80-character lines. In that case, you should go to the same menu and set the line lengths to suit your computer.

**Note:**  Some subscribers report that the system sometimes give them occasional extra blank lines in the display of text files, even though they have correctly entered their screen width dimensions at this prompt. The problem is that some terminal software disagrees with CompuServe on how to handle word-wrap on long screen lines (when, for instance, a line is precisely 80 characters long on an 80-character screen.) Often the problem can be solved simply by setting this default on one character *less than* the actual size, that is, setting 79 for an 80-column screen. If you are finding occasional extra line feeds in text received on the system, try this easy solution.

After you enter the new screen width, you will be returned to the main TERMINAL TYPE menu:

```
r----------------------------------------------------------------¬
¦                                                                 ¦
¦   TERMINAL TYPE/PARAMETERS                                      ¦
¦                                                                 ¦
¦    1 TERMINAL type                          [OTHER]             ¦
¦    2 Screen WIDTH                              [79]             ¦
¦    3 LINES per page                            [16]             ¦
¦    4 Form FEEDS                         [SIMULATED]             ¦
¦    5 Horizontal TABS                    [SIMULATED]             ¦
¦    6 Chars. received (CASE)                   [U/L]             ¦
¦    7 Chars. sent in CAPS                      [YES]             ¦
¦    8 PARITY                                  [EVEN]             ¦
¦    9 Output DELAYS                              [1]             ¦
¦   10 ERASE when backspacing                    [NO]             ¦
¦   11 Micro inquiry sequence at logon           [NO]             ¦
¦                                                                 ¦
¦   Enter choice!                                                 ¦
¦                                                                 ¦
L----------------------------------------------------------------
```

Note that whenever the system returns to the menu, it reflects the latest change you have selected, in this case, the value in option 2.

Option 3 on this menu controls the number of lines per screen. In this example, CompuServe has recorded that our screen is 16 lines deep. Why does the system care about the depth of the screen? As you have observed, when you read long files on the system, the display stops from time to time with a prompt to:

```
r----------------------------------------------------------------¬
¦                                                                 ¦
¦   Press <CR> for more !                                         ¦
¦                                                                 ¦
L----------------------------------------------------------------
```

This message is calling *paging*. (Ideally, the system fills your screen with a page of information, then stops to wait for carriage return to signal that you are ready for the next page.) Of course, the problem is that CompuServe has no way of knowing the dimensions of your particular screen; you have to tell it how many lines your screen can accommodate. In this example, the system has been told that if it sends 16 lines of no more than 79 characters, it will fill one screen's worth, then can send a "Press <CR> for more !" message. If you choose to change this option by entering 3 at this menu, the system will ask you for the new value. Your page can be between 0 and 63 lines. (If you selected 0, the system simply passes up the opportunity to "page" at all.)

Finally, what about all those uppercase letters? You know your computer can generate lowercase, but perhaps the system doesn't seem to want to cooperate. That is controlled by options 6 and 7 on the TERMINAL TYPE/PARAMETERS menu:

```
TERMINAL TYPE/PARAMETERS

 1 TERMINAL type                   [OTHER]
 2 Screen WIDTH                       [79]
 3 LINES per page                     [16]
 4 Form FEEDS                  [SIMULATED]
 5 Horizontal TABS             [SIMULATED]
 6 Chars. received (CASE)           [U/L]
 7 Chars. sent in CAPS              [YES]
 8 PARITY                          [EVEN]
 9 Output DELAYS                      [1]
10 ERASE when backspacing            [NO]
11 Micro inquiry sequence at logon  [NO]

Enter choice!
```

To see how option 7, "Chars. sent in CAPS," works, let's say your computer can create and receive both capital and lowercase letters but is currently sending only capital letters. In other words, all the menus are received in both upper and lowercase, but what you type is coming out in capital letters only. Looking at the example here shows us why. Following option 7, the information in the square brackets tells us that the current setting is "[YES]," meaning, yes, send data in CAPital letters only. This instruction needs to be changed to NO. If you select 7 at this menu, the system displays:

```
CHARACTERS SENT IN CAPS

Permanent setting =                    [YES]

1 NO - normal mode
  (Whatever you input will be in the
  case you send it.)

2 YES
  (Whatever you input will always be
  in CAPS regardless of how you send
  it.)

Enter choice or <CR> to leave unchanged!
```

Again, the message at the top tells us the current default, [YES], meaning uppercase only. So, as the prompt indicates, selecting option 1 would revise your record to "normal mode," having the system expect uppercase *and* lowercase letters.

But this option doesn't affect the case of letters sent *to* your screen. That characteristic is controlled by previous settings on this menu, option 6. There are three possible settings for characters received (CASE): (1) U/L (normal mode) means that the text you receive from CompuServe will be in capital and lowercase letters as available on the host computer; (2) UPPER means you'll receive the text from host in capital letters only; (3) LOWER means you will receive the text in lowercase only.

This has been a cursory look at the TERMINAL/OPTIONS area. More than 25 settings are controlled here and we shall be looking at them more closely in Chapter 19. Nonetheless, feel free to experiment with your Terminal Settings. When you are ready to leave this area, you are asked if you want to record the changes you just made for future sessions, or implement them for the current on-line session only. If you are communicating with the computer you normally use, go ahead and make the changes permanent. That way, you won't have to worry about these defaults the next time you log on. But if you want to just "try on" some terminal setting changes, make them effective for the present session only and drive them around the block a while. You can always come back and make the changes permanent if they seem to fit the bill. As noted, in this on-line world, *permanent* means merely "keep them that way until I change them again."

Using Profile's TERMINAL/OPTIONS proves a very important thing about CompuServe: Nothing is engraved in stone as far as your relationship to the system is concerned. Flexibility is the keyword. It just takes time to learn how to make the system suit your needs.

## The Set Command

Speaking of flexibility, the system supports another powerful command — SET — that lets you make quick adjustments to your screen display without having to go all the way to Profile. At nearly any "!" prompt on the system, you can enter SET and the system prompts you with "SET sub-command:" Several options can be adjusted with the SET command, including "WIDth."

Suppose you have logged on and found the screen displays are being received in 80-character column, while you currently are using a computer with a 64-column screen. As you saw, you could truck all the way over to the TERMINAL/OPTIONS and reset that screen WIDTH default. Alternatively, to save time, you could enter SET and then WID at the "Sub-command:" prompt. The system then asks you to enter a new screen width, a number between 16 and 255 characters. After that, all information you receive *during that session* will conform to the screen width you have specified. (In fact, you can save even more time, because you can link the commands by anticipating upcoming prompts. Entering SET WID 64 at any "!" prompt would do the job.)

Here are some other options you can manipulate with the SET command:

LINe — remember what we were saying a minute ago about "paging?" At TERMINAL/OPTIONS, you can specify the number of lines your screen can accommodate. You can use the SET command to change that quickly. With SET LIN you can enter a number between 0 and 63. Entering SET LIN 16 at a "!" prompt would tell the system you want pages of no more than 16 lines at a time.

PAGe — this paging business can be turned on and off. If you decide that you temporarily *don't* want your text interrupted by the messages like "Press <CR> for more !" you can enter SET PAG OFF. That means that for the current session, the system would avoid paging, no matter how your defaults were set in the TERMINAL/OPTIONS area. To turn paging back on — you got it — SET PAG ON.

Many other options can be manipulated with the SET command. In fact, virtually every parameter controlled by the TERMINAL/OPTIONS menu also can be set temporarily by the SET command. But we shall defer discussion of all those other options until later chapters. For now, let's concentrate on the concepts introduced by the SET command, especially these three things:

1. It's a time-saver, a shortcut for changing your screen display without having to go to the Terminal Settings area of Profile. Everything you can do with SET also can be done at the Terminal Settings feature. SET is merely faster.
2. But SET is temporary. Unlike the Terminal Settings feature, which lets you specify the changes as either for the current session or for all future sessions, the changes made with SET always apply to only the *current session*. Once you log off and back on, the screen display is reset to the defaults on file in the TERMINAL/OPTIONS area.
3. As a practical matter, probably the most useful of these will be the SET WID command and the SET LIN and SET PAG ON or OFF options.

## The Public and the Private You

As far as CompuServe is concerned, your name is your user ID number. The reason is obvious. How many John Smiths do you think are CompuServe subscribers? And when John Smith logs on CB or any other place in the system, he may call himself anything he would like, from Abbott to Zorro. Thus, the assignment of a number to each user isn't only for the system's record-keeping purposes; it also is a means for subscribers to identify each other, no matter what name is connected to that number.

Every other subscriber has the opportunity to know your user ID. People use it when they send you electronic mail. When you wrote yourself letters in Chapters 3 and 5, the system asked to which user to send it, you didn't enter a name; you entered the ID number. When you called up a list of people who were on the CB channels at the same time you were, they were listed by their user ID numbers. In this community, your user ID is the public part of your identification.

Your password, on the other hand, is the private part of your identity and *should be kept that way.* If your user ID is the worst-kept secret, your password should be the best-kept one. You received a password when you got your start-up kit. After you completed the on-line sign-up information, a second password was generated for you. It is the personal pass-key that unlocks the door. Keep it a secret! There is no reason anyone else should know your password. If you suspect that someone else knows your password, change it immediately. In fact, you ought to change your password once a month as a matter of habit, just in case someone has discovered the word or words that let you into the system.

As you saw earlier, "Change Your Password" is an option listed on the Profile menu. Selecting it carries you off to a menu entitled Password. (For quick access, enter G PASSWORD.)

Once there, you are prompted to "Type your current password:." (Except at log-on, this is the *only* time the system ever asks you to reenter your password.) When you have entered your present password, the system says, "Now type a new password:" After you have typed it in, CompuServe will want to confirm the change (and guard against typing errors) by having you enter it a second time. Then you should receive the message, "Password change successful." The new password is in effect immediately and must be used at next log-on.

Many say the most secure password is made up of two unrelated words with a symbol between them. In one of its booklets, CompuServe gives the example BOAT%TOUCH. Probably the password that came with your starter kit contained two unrelated words separated by a nonletter symbol. A password can be up to 24 characters, and no fewer than eight characters. One of those characters must be something other than a letter of the alphabet, such as a punctuation mark.

Your password should be kept in a secure place.

*What if it is so safe and secure I can't find it? And I can't remember it?*

Don't ask CompuServe to help you remember it. No one you can call at CompuServe will know it either. What CompuServe *can* do is this: If you lose or forget your password, call Customer Service — (800) 848-8990 or, in Ohio, (614) 457-8650 — and ask that a new password for your user ID be generated and mailed to you at the address on file for your account.

## On-line Product Ordering

An area of interest to most subscribers is the on-line product ordering feature (G ORDER). Here you may order and have charged to your bill a number of CompuServe-related products, including user manuals for various features, gifts and computer accessories, books and software, including CompuServe's communications programs, such as *The Professional Connection*.

Like Feedback, which we discussed in Chapter 7, there are no connect charges for the time you spend in this part of the system, where you may read ordering instructions, view descriptions and place orders for various merchandise and check on orders placed earlier.

It's a good idea to thoroughly read the descriptions of products before ordering because all sales are final. At anytime while in the On-line Ordering Service, you may view items ordered so far during the current session by enter DISplay at a prompt. At that point, you will be asked if you want to make a change. Once you've competed your visit and you issue a command to leave, your order automatically will be displayed for your verification. You may then change it or verify its accuracy. An order number will be displayed for you to write down. Use it to check on your order's status later.

Generally speaking, allow three to four weeks for delivery (longer if the items are being shipped outside the United States.)

## Control Commands

In earlier chapters we introduced you to some valuable CONTROL codes, including:

CONTROL C interrupts any program you are running on the system, like a "bailout" key.
CONTROL S freezes the display.
CONTROL Q resumes the display.

There are a few more CONTROL keys, including a real time saver, CONTROL P. You can use CONTROL P to interrupt the menu and take you immediately to the next prompt. This feature is handy if you know precisely where you are going and don't want to waste time reading familiar menus.

Suppose you wanted to read daily computer industry news from the *Online Today* feature. If you are a regular reader, you already know that G OLT takes you directly to the front page of the service; you can use CONTROL P to get you there even faster from the top of the system.

```
r-----------------------------------------
|
|  CompuServe                          TOP
|
|  1 Subscriber Assistance
|  2 Find a Topic
|  3 Commu^P
|
|  ^P Interrupt. !
|
L-----------------------------------------
```

Here we have entered a CONTROL P right after the beginning of the TOP menu and the system has stopped the menu, acknowledged the CONTROL P interrupt, and given us the prompt. Of course, that is the prompt that would have appeared at the bottom of TOP (so to speak), but we have said, "Hey, don't bother — I know what it looks like. Just give me the prompt." At the prompt, we would enter G OLT (for "Go to Online Today.").

After a "One moment please" message, the system displays the publication's title page, and we could continue our speeding through the next menu displays:

```
r-----------------------------------------
|
|  Online Today                    ONLINE
|
|  ONLINE TODAY MAGAZINE
|
|  1 Guide to Online Today
|  2 Monitor Daily News
|  3 CompuServe Daily Update
|  4 Comm^P
|
|  ^P Interrupt. !
|
L-----------------------------------------
```

We enter a CONTROL P right after we see the feature we want, in this case, option 2, "Monitor Daily News." Again, the menu is stopped, and the prompt is given. We can then enter 2 and the system continues:

```
┌─────────────────────────────────────────────────────┐
│                                                       │
│   Online Today                            OLT-160     │
│                                                       │
│   MONITOR                                             │
│                                                       │
│   1 * About Monitor *                                 │
│   2 Today's News                                      │
│   3 Recent News^P                                     │
│                                                       │
│   ^P Interrupt. !                                     │
│                                                       │
└─────────────────────────────────────────────────────┘
```

This time we apply the brakes to the menus because we have seen the option we want, "Today's News." The point is, if you are familiar with the territory, you don't have to sit and watch menus go by.

While we are at it, you may have noticed by now that CompuServe supports what is called a *type-ahead* capability. That means that you can enter your command *before* the prompt is displayed and CompuServe will honor it when it gets to the prompt. Suppose you have a menu of ten items and you know you want option 2, you can enter the 2 before the prompt appears. The system displays the rest of the menu and the prompt; then it will go right on to execute your request for option 2.

**Note:**   About both CONTROL P and the type-ahead capabilities, they work best when you are connected to the system through a direct CompuServe node, rather than Tymnet or Telenet. The latter networks are sometimes noticeably slower than the regular CompuServe nodes. In using hurry-up commands like CONTROL P, you will notice that it takes a little longer for the system to receive the instructions. Experiment with them and see if they are useful to you.

Other control codes are also recognized by the system, some are more useful than others. For a complete list, see the control code section of the Command Compendium in the On-line Survival Kit at the back of the book.

## More Navigation Commands

There are some additional navigation commands you should know about as well. You have seen how the S command at the menu prompt scrolls a message, how T takes you to the TOP of the system, and M returns you to the menu page. Here are a few more specific commands in this family that you might try out the next time you are on-line:

N — NEXT can be entered at any prompt within related pages of information. This command selects the next menu item from the most recently used menu without redisplaying the menu.

F — FORWARD displays the next page in a series of pages. A single RETURN key will do the same thing.

B — BACKWARD returns to the page preceding the current page.

P — PREVIOUS goes to the previous item from the last selected menu. For example, if 5 was the last choice, P will display item 4.

R — RESEND displays the current page. This command is useful if the current page has scrolled off the screen.

Also, CompuServe menus are more sophisticated than we have led you to believe so far. The "Enter choice !" prompt, at the bottom of menus, actually can accept a number of different kinds of instructions, such as multiple menu choices. For example, had we continued our trek into *Online Today's* "Monitor Daily News" area, we would eventually have come to a list of stories, like this:

```
Online Today                         OLT-90

TODAY'S MONITOR NEWS

1 Online Auction Raises $25,000
2 Phoenix Settles BIOS Suit
3 AIDS Database on Disk
4 Woman's Phone Bill Cleared
5 Dow Jones Buys Quote Service
6 Wang Predicts Revenue Climb
7 Monitor Week in Review
8 Yesterday's Late News

Enter choice !
```

Suppose we want to read all the items from this menu. We could enter 1 at the prompt, wait to read that item to the end, then enter 2 at the next prompt, and so forth. Or we could simply enter ALL at the prompt and the system would interpret that to mean "display all the articles on this menu."

Suppose you want to read only article 2, "Phoenix Settles BIOS Suit," and article 6, "Wang Predicts Revenue Climb". To do that, we could enter:

```
┌─────────────────────────────────────────────────┐
│                                                   │
│   Enter choice ! 2,6 <RETURN>                     │
└─────────────────────────────────────────────────┘
```

You also can enter a range of options connected by a hyphen, such as 1-4, 3-6, and so forth. You may even mix the two approaches; entering 1-3,5,7 would display articles 1 through 3, 5 and 7.

**Note:**   As we have seen, some items on menus aren't displayable text, but rather pathways to other menus. In our example here, item 8 obviously is not a text article but rather an option to a menu of the previous day's stories. If you include such an option in a multiple display command like this, the system simply informs you that the item isn't an article and moves to the next specified selection.

Another navigation command feature involves an enhancement of the Scroll command. As you have seen, the S command can be used alone. Entered at the first occurrence of a "Press <CR> for more" prompt in a long file, S will override any sequence "pauses" until you reach the end of the file. In addition, S can be used with one or more menu option numbers.

If you know that you are going to want to scroll the stories you select (that is, to bypass the paging option), you can specify that as you select your story. For instance, entering S 1 would scroll the "Online Auction" story, showing you the entire story without the "Press <CR> for more" messages along the way.

Also, you don't have to return to a menu to use the S command this way. Suppose you had read the auction story and now you wanted to read the Wang story. Because you remember that it was option 6 on the menu, you don't *have* to return to the menu to retrieve it. At the bottom of the auction story, you could enter S 6 at the "!" prompt and the system would know you mean, "Find item 6 on the menu I'm dealing with and scroll it for me." In addition, S can be used with multiple menu options, such as S ALL, S 1-7, S 1,4,5-6.

Finally we come to an idea called "command stacking." A while back we told you that CompuServe had a type-ahead buffer, meaning that you can enter a command, such as a numbered menu selection, *before* you get to a prompt and the system will "remember" it. This concept has been used in some of the recent refinements to the system, and it actually lets you skip some menus. Suppose you were in a familiar area of the system and, from experience, you knew that to reach a favorite feature you needed to take option 1 from the menu on your screen and then take option 4 from the subsequent menu. You could enter 1 <RETURN> at the first prompt, quickly followed by 4 <RETURN>, and in many cases CompuServe actually would skip the subsequent menu and take you directly to the target feature of option 4.

By the way, some of these commands are recent additions, developments of CompuServe's programming wizards who are trying to make your life on the system easier. To stay up-to-date on future enhancements, you should periodically check the

"What's New" bulletins and the Community News section of the *Online Today* electronic publication.

## Side Roads

Among this chapter's themes was the idea of taking care of your own on-line files, such as those in your personal file area. Meanwhile, CompuServe itself manages some files for you, such as your billing information. A number of areas are available for you to look at own records, to check the latest surcharges, and so on. Here are some on-line addresses for news about the bill. For general billing information, enter G BILL or CHARGES. For answers to frequently asked billing questions, enter G QABILL. To look over various billing options, try G BILOPT. To see the limits on CheckFree and Direct billing options, as discussed in Chapter 3, enter G LIMIT. For information disk storage charges, try G STORAGE and for connect time and other rates, enter G CONNECT and G RATES. For specifics on surcharge and transaction program charges, enter G SURCHARGES and G TRANSACTION. And finally, for miscellaneous billing charges, the command is G MISC.

# CHAPTER 10

---

# The System's Neighborhoods — The Forums

Newcomers generally are awed by CompuServe's size and by the variety and quality of its information and features. Some, in fact, are overwhelmed and throw their hands up in frustration. There's just too much. It is too big, too impersonal, just too difficult to understand. Those who give up probably haven't explored enough to find the islands in the CompuServe stream that provide personal, even friendly, service.

One of the ways CompuServe has made its system friendly, as well as helpful, is to create discussion forums (features still known to some long-time subscribers by their older name, "special-interest groups" or SIGs.) Now numbering more than a hundred, the public forums are electronic clubs of sorts that probably are the system's innovative services. They are devoted to a number of subjects, ranging from specific computer systems to general-interest topics like music, games, comic books, ham-radio operators, literature, sports, and so on. There is, more than likely, a forum focusing on one or more of your own interests, and if not, then just wait, because several new forums are brought on-line each month.

Unlike many clubs, forums generally aren't exclusive in their membership. They are places where people of similar interests gather to share information, and everyone is welcome. All the forums have identical commands and features, so learning how to use one opens the door to all of them. Despite this technical sameness, each forum is a little different from all the others in terms of content, style, and approach, they are always changing. In fact, the forums are perhaps the most fluid part of the system. It is their changing nature that makes this new form of communication so exciting.

In the next chapter we shall tour a forum, but before we go, let's use this chapter to prepare you for some of the things you will find there.

---

## All Forums Are Divided into Five Parts

The most popular feature in most forums is the *message board*. It is similar to electronic mail, but with an important exception. Most messages left to someone in a forum may be read by everyone else who visits.

*Wait a minute! That sounds slightly sinister, doesn't it? After all, messages are private, aren't they?*

Well, not in forums. At least not ordinarily. You will find that the public nature of the messages is not only the forums' charm, but is also essential for their designed purpose: On-line places where people can learn about their special interests by reading other people's messages and by asking the whole group for help. Think of a forum's message area as a big public bulletin board or a question-and-answer section of a magazine. Sometimes the messages are posted for all to read. Sometimes they are posted for a specific individual but may contain information that is helpful to others besides the intended recipient. Because these messages are public, not only does the recipient benefit but all the other readers learn as well.

In general, members can reply to any message left on the board. From this a chain of related messages develops. This chain is called a *thread*, as all messages in the group are connected by the thread of a single idea.

**Example:**   User A joins the Alphabyte Computer Users' forum (not a real forum, nor a real computer, for that matter) and leaves a message to all other members asking what word processor he should purchase. User B writes a reply recommending one called Crunch-A-Word. User C also leaves a reply to the original message saying he thinks a program called Alpha-Writer is best, then leaves a message to User B saying he once used Crunch-A-Word and found it to be too slow. User B then responds to C's criticism saying that he still feels Crunch-A-Word is superior and that it has nothing to do with the fact that his brother-in-law, who owes him money, published it. This series of messages, involving three people, forms a thread, a long-distance conversation that takes place over hours, days, or even a week or two.

If you later happened into the Alphabyte forum, you might find that you had the same question, or at least you were interested in the same topic. You could read all the messages in the thread and get some idea of the pros and cons of various word processors available for the Alphabyte computer. Or, if you had a different question about the Alphabyte, it is likely you would find an answer by leaving it in a message addressed to "All."

Message boards also can have specialties, being divided into as many as 17 sections or *subtopics* devoted to specific topics. The Alphabyte message board might be divided into topics such as "Alphabyte News," "New User Questions," "Alphabyte

Programming Tips." This division allows the forum visitor to zero in on a specific subjects instead of having to wade through all the messages on the board.

For immediate real-time on-line discussions, each forum also has its own version of the CB Simulator, called the *conference area*. The conference area has multiple channels (or "rooms" as they are sometimes called). Most CB commands also work in the forum conference channels. However, these channels aren't always used for CB-type conversations. They are meant for discussions related to specific forum topics (although friends who have been brought together by the forum have been known to "get crazy" on the forum channels from time to time). Mutually consenting forums members can do what they please....

Forums usually offer two kinds of conferences: (1) informal gab sessions and (2) more formal guest conferences featuring an electronic lecture by an expert in a particular field. In the latter, the forums often try to follow a structured kind of question-and-answer session. Rather than having all the members "talk" at once, as in CB, the conference has a moderator who recognizes questioners one at a time. Usually in advance of a major guest conference, forums post messages outlining the protocol for questions and answers. In addition, many forums have regular weekly or monthly conferences. There are usually several going on every night somewhere in the system. Topics for these more informal gatherings range from esoteric computer-related subjects to general-interest to out-and-out on-line parties. Dave holds a weekly get-together in the conference area of his service, The Good Earth Forum. Regular conferences elsewhere on the system deal with politics, puns, philosophy, and so forth. Newcomers almost always are welcome to drop into these electronic gabfests. While you tour the system, you should be on the lookout for conference groups on subjects of interest to you. In the next chapter, you will even find a place to locate the schedules of regular conferences.

Each forum also contains databases (known as *libraries* or data libraries). This area is filled with a variety of specific information related to the interests of the group. Our make-believe Alphabyte Forum's data libraries, for example, might contain public-domain programs specially written for that imaginary computer. There could be reprints of news articles about the Alphabyte. A particularly good thread from the message board on some hot topic might be saved in a database. In fact, the libraries could contain anything the administrators want to save for long-term reference.

Each forum also has its own *announcements* where the administrators post information that the general forum memberships need to know. Some of the announcements are more or less static, presenting general information about the forum; others change quite often, especially the "News Flash," which lets those running the forum provide up-to-the-minute information about what is happening at any hour of the day or night. These announcements actually are text files and reading them is as simple as reading any text that scrolls up on your screen. We shall look at some announcements in our forum tour.

Finally, every forum also has a *member directory*. The feature is similar to the Subscriber Directory you saw in Chapter 3, except that the member directory is used exclusively by forum visitors for listing their interests. Once listed, they are added to a database within the forum that can be searched by name, user ID or interests. The member directory is more important in some forums than in others. One of the best uses of the member directory is in the Genealogy Forum where members list the surnames that they are researching. Other members can go to the member directory and type in a family surname as a keyword to see if other forum members are reaching the same family name. It makes for a fast and efficient way to find others on the system with the same interests, and is a big help to the sysop.

## The Scoop on Sysops

*Sysop*? Hmmm, that may be a strange word to you. What, in the name of all that's subtly threatening, is a sysop?

A sysop is the person in charge of a forum. The word means "system operator." (CompuServe prefers to call them *forum administrators*, but the term "sysop" is rooted in recent telecommunications history and seems to have staying power.) A large forum usually has more than one sysop, a chief and several assistants. Sysops usually are not CompuServe employees, but rather independent contractors who keep the forums going. They are paid a small percentage of the connect-time dollars each user spends while in their forums. (As additional compensation, sysops may get free time on the system or free time while doing necessary tasks in their forums.) So, if you devote an hour in a forum, you spend $6.30 under the current rates and the sysop gets a percentage of that. That should answer the question "will I be welcome in the forum?" The sysop is going to make you feel welcome as long as you are civil, because you are, in a sense, a customer.

Questions so far?

*What kind of special on-line powers does a sysop have?*

The sysop has a few extra options necessary for maintaining the message boards and data libraries and operating the conferences. He or she can delete messages found to be in poor taste, can bar unruly members from the forum, and can even "gag" a person who might be disrupting a real-time conference (though, in realty, these drastic steps happen very rarely).

*If I decide to frequent a particular forum, what does the sysop know about me?*

Very little, actually. Not even enough to send an insurance salesman to your door. All the administrator really knows is your user ID. (This number, of course, can be common knowledge around the system anyway.) The sysop doesn't have access to your CompuServe sign-up record, meaning he or she does *not* know your U.S. Postal address or and how you are paying your bill.

Basically, the sysop has the power to keep the forum running, to keep it informative, and to keep it on the right track. But the sysop is not an all-knowing seer who keeps files on members' private lives, nor a censor who passes judgment on all messages.

## Make Yourself at Home

We can think of each forum as a sort of microcosm of the entire CompuServe system, because it has all of the most powerful features of the larger network: messaging, libraries, real-time conferencing and more, as we shall see in Chapter 11. However, unlike the system as a whole, a forum usually is devoted to a single, specific subject or group of closely related topics. Talk there tends to be more personal, but also sometimes more serious than with the casual acquaintances made on CB. Also, most forums urge (some even require) that members use real names, rather than CB "handles," when leaving messages. Perhaps that's the reason some new users seem standoffish about forums, feeling threatened by them, afraid they won't be welcome, as if they were gate crashers. It is a common attitude, one that gives sysops gray hair. We hope you will see that most sysops are happy to have new members and will go out of their way to be helpful. You will be surprised how quickly you will be regarded as a friend.

As a new member, don't be afraid to ask questions. After all, questions and answers are the life's blood of the message board. Also, if you have information you think other forum visitors would like to have, by all means, leave a message. If you have a comment on one of the raging debates that often breaks out in the forums, jump in! You are encouraged by most sysops to add your two cents' worth (or $6.30 worth, if you want to spend an hour there).

On the other hand, expect to do a little exploring on your own. Remember, there always is ongoing communication taking place. Unless you visit a new forum within a day or two of the time it is announced, you are *always* joining in the middle of things. You can't expect everything to come to a halt until you catch up. Like any other club, a forum is dynamic, changing its pattern of messages, information, and conversations. Most sysops we know quietly grind their teeth every time they find a message from a newcomer that reads: "What's this forum all about?" Goals and purposes of each forum are posted on-line, for anyone to read, in the announcements and messages. Don't ask the sysop or anyone to give a 20-line summary. Instead, explore and find out for yourself. The next three chapters will show you how.

## Some Other Questions?

*Where are these forums located in the system? Are they in an area that we have already visited?*

Forums are all over the system and each has its own address, that is, a quick reference word. There are several broad categories of them, such as computer-related (including groups interested in specific computers, such as the IBM and compatibles, Apple and Macintosh, for TRS-80 enthusiasts, Atari users, Commodore owners including those who have the Amiga, and some more general forums devoted to programming), general-interest (about topics ranging from games to space to music) and professional forums (for the lawyers, doctors, aviators, and so on). We have a detailed rundown of most current forums in Chapter 14.

*Are all forums public?*

No; but most are. The forum software, with its sophisticated message boards, libraries, and real-time conferences, can be a valuable tool for business, and some firms have private forums for their own use. These do not appear on any menu. Only people who know its unpublished page address in the system can find a private forum and, if you should stumble on to this address by accident, you won't be allowed in unless you are already on the membership logs.

*Are all public forums free of surcharges?*

Again, most are. In 95 percent of the public forums, your only charge is the cost of your connect time, the standard $6.30 an hour through a CompuServe node. In those rare forums that do charge extra, you are notified of the additional fee before you are invited to join.

*What kind of people become sysops?*

Many are private citizens who have a special interest in a particular subject and they devote a portion of their day to running the forum. In other cases, companies, such as computer manufacturers or software publishers, run public forums usually with employees as the sysops. In either case, the average sysop isn't getting rich on your connect-time dollars. A sysop's share is small; for most it is, at best, the income of a part-time job. Instead of money, the sysop's motivation more often is similar to the drive in some people to take part in civic work in a community.

We have spent many hours exploring forums and can report that nearly all of them have good sysops in charge and friendly members willing to help newcomers with simple or complex problems. A single issue or single interest has brought people together, in this place called a forum, from all over the world. An exciting thought in itself, and the result can be an enriching experience for all.

# CHAPTER 11

# Getting to the Forum

Enough *talk* about forums, let's visit one. In this chapter, we shall tour the Good Earth Forum, one of CompuServe's general-interest home-related services. Why the Good Earth Forum? As mentioned at the end of the last chapter, Dave runs the forum. He is the sysop (administrator) of Good Earth and likes new users to come to his neck of the system and... Uh-oh. Do we hear grumbling?

*Hmm! It's a cheap trick to get me to spend time and money in his forum!*

Wait. Before you revolt, consider this: First, there is nothing cheap about our tricks, and second, it is not a trick if you are told in advance what's going to happen (they said sheepishly). Besides, we thought at this point in your travels, you ought to learn about places in the system where you can find us. Dave's forum is one of them. (In the On-line Survival Kit, at the back of the book, we have included our user ID numbers with which you can write us electronic mail if you would like.) Another reason for visiting Dave's forum is that we didn't think it would be polite to fellow sysops to lead the tour group through their homes. We shall use Peyton's stomping ground for your quick peek at these special on-line neighborhoods, because Ol' Dave doesn't mind you tracking up his electronic hallway.

*Okay, then. What is the Good Earth Forum, anyway?*

It is a service devoted to gardening, natural nutrition, herbs, and more. Members' interests range from organic gardening and vegetarianism to solar heating. (At least, those were the interests when this book was updated. Who knows what topics will be on the agenda by the time you tour it....)

*So, what if I'm not interested in vegetarianism or rammed-earth houses or the "secret oath of the sacred tofu"?*

That's okay. You are taking an educational tour, not committing yourself to a future as a neohippie. We shall use Dave's Good Earth to learn about forums in general; after that, you can explore other forums to find some in which you are more interested. As noted, all forums use the same commands, even though their content and subjects are vastly different. Learning to use one opens the door to more than a hundred others. Let's see.

## The First Stop

Crank up the computer now and place your modem call. Log on as you always do and get the TOP menu on your screen.

```
CompuServe                              TOP

   1 Subscriber Assistance
   2 Find a Topic
   3 Communications/Bulletin Bds.
   4 News/Weather/Sports
   5 Travel
   6 The Electronic MALL/Shopping
   7 Money Matters/Markets
   8 Entertainment/Games
   9 Home/Health/Education
  10 Reference
  11 Computers/Technology
  12 Business/Other Interests

Enter choice number !
```

Two ways exist for reaching the Good Earth Forum by the menus. If you chose option 3, "Communications/Bulletin Boards," you would find Good Earth eventually, though you would need to see about four more menus after this one. Suppose you were just browsing the menus for home-related features and you chose option 9, "Home/Health/Family." Do that now and you will see:

```
┌─────────────────────────────────────────────────────┐
│                                                      │
│  CompuServe                              HOME        │
│                                                      │
│  HOME/HEALTH/EDUCATION                               │
│                                                      │
│   1 Food/Wine                                        │
│   2 Personal Finance/Banking                         │
│   3 Health/Fitness                                   │
│   4 The Electronic MALL/Shopping                     │
│   5 Special Interest Forums                          │
│   6 Hobbies                                          │
│   7 Arts/Music/Literature                            │
│   8 Reference Material                               │
│   9 Automotive Information                           │
│  10 Education                                        │
│                                                      │
│  Enter choice !                                      │
│                                                      │
└─────────────────────────────────────────────────────┘
```

Now the idea of home-related forums strikes your fancy, so you choose option 5, after which the system begins displaying a list:

```
┌─────────────────────────────────────────────────────┐
│                                                      │
│  CompuServe                              HOM-48      │
│                                                      │
│  SPECIAL INTEREST                                    │
│                                                      │
│   1 Religion Forum                                   │
│   2 Working From Home Forum                          │
│   3 National Issues/People Forum                     │
│   4 Space Forum                                      │
│   5 Good Earth Forum                                 │
│   6 Consumer Electronics Forum                       │
│   7 Military Veterans Services                       │
│                                                      │
│  Enter choice !                                      │
│                                                      │
└─────────────────────────────────────────────────────┘
```

Notice they cover various topics, including religion, space, veterans, issues, and so forth. Choose option 5 from this menu to go to the Good Earth Forum's front door.

```
CompuServe                          GOODEARTH

One moment please...

Welcome to the Good Earth Forum!
```

What follows this welcome line is a visitor's introduction to the forum. The administrator of each forum decides what this announcement contains, usually a little about what the forum is about, reasons for joining, something of the forum rules, and so on. Once you join a forum, you won't see this visitor's announcement again. So, take a moment to read the visitor's announcement, pressing RETURN when prompted. In time, you see:

```
Welcome to Good Earth Forum, V. 4D(40)

Forum messages:  29952 to   31340

News Flash:
```

Two notes here:

1. First comes a notice about the *lowest* message number and the *highest* message number in the forum. Most forums hold more than a thousand messages, though some busier ones may hold 2,000 or 3,000. Each message has its own unique number and as new messages are posted, the oldest ones are deleted automatically by the system.
2. Next, you see "News Flash," a message from the sysop that reports the latest forum highlights, such as new files added to the data libraries in recent days, upcoming special conferences, perhaps a note about the latest raging debate on the message board. The sysop changes this News Flash announcement as needed; whatever it is updated, the new version usually is automatically redisplayed to the membership. On your first visit to any forum, the News Flash always is automatically displayed. It isn't automatically displayed again until it is updated.

Following the News Flash, you get your first glimpse of the Good Earth Forum main menu, which is the same menu you see in all forums:

```
┌─────────────────────────────────────────────────┐
│                                                   │
│   Good Earth Forum Menu                           │
│                                                   │
│    1 INSTRUCTIONS                                 │
│    2 MESSAGES                                     │
│    3 LIBRARIES (Files)                            │
│    4 CONFERENCING (0 participating)               │
│    5 ANNOUNCEMENTS from sysop                     │
│    6 MEMBER directory                             │
│    7 OPTIONS for this forum                       │
│    8 JOIN this forum                              │
│                                                   │
│   Enter choice !                                  │
│                                                   │
└─────────────────────────────────────────────────┘
```

We have already briefly discussed most of these options. We shall look at all of them in detail in this and next two chapters. First, though, we want you to JOIN the forum.

*Ah-hah! I thought they were up to something.* **Why should I join?**

Because most forums distinguish between "visitors" and "members" by restricting most features for members only. By joining Good Earth and most other forums, you won't be charged extra. In fact, you are not committing yourself to anything. Dave promises there will be no initiation; you won't be asked to wear any bizarre organic vegetables from his garden. JOINing simply enables you to use all the forum's functions.

To JOIN, enter 8 (or the word JOIN) at the prompt, which begins the sign-up process:

```
┌─────────────────────────────────────────────────┐
│                                                   │
│   Please enter your name:                         │
└─────────────────────────────────────────────────┘
```

Enter a first name and last name, or at least a first initial and last name. Although Good Earth doesn't require that all members use full names, other forums do. After that, you see your name displayed and are asked:

```
┌──────────────────────────────────────────────────┐
│                                                    │
│   Is this correct (Y or N)?                        │
│                                                    │
└──────────────────────────────────────────────────┘
```

You verify by entering Y, and you see:

```
┌──────────────────────────────────────────────────┐
│                                                    │
│   Inserting name and ID...                         │
│                                                    │
└──────────────────────────────────────────────────┘
```

Now comes another announcement to your screen. This one is called the New Member announcement and reports what the sysop thinks new members ought to know about the forum. This is another announcement that you automatically see only once, immediately after you join a forum. (However, there is a way to have any announcement redisplayed, as we shall see later in the tour.) Usually the New Member announcement gives you a rundown on the use of the message board and the libraries, etc. After that, you are returned to the forum's main menu:

```
┌──────────────────────────────────────────────────┐
│                                                    │
│   Good Earth Forum Menu                            │
│                                                    │
│   1 INSTRUCTIONS                                   │
│   2 MESSAGES                                       │
│   3 LIBRARIES (Files)                              │
│   4 CONFERENCING (0 participating)                 │
│   5 ANNOUNCEMENTS from sysop                       │
│   6 MEMBER directory                               │
│   7 OPTIONS for this forum                         │
│                                                    │
│   Enter choice !                                   │
│                                                    │
└──────────────────────────────────────────────────┘
```

Notice the difference? Option 8 has disappeared because it is no longer a viable option. You can't JOIN this forum anymore because you are already a member.

**Note** this important concept: forum menus are designed to display only those options open to you. Routinely, menus revise themselves to accommodate to this goal. We shall see this idea at work again in a moment.

## Reading the Message Board

The best way to get involved in any forum's activity is to read some messages, which is the next stop on this tour. The main menu makes it clear how to do that, because option 2 is clearly labeled MESSAGES.

> **Note:** About forum menus. On this and other menus in the forum, you will notice that some words are capitalized, as MESSAGES, CONFERENCING, LIBRARIES, and so on. As on other menus in the system, this capitalization is a signal to mean that you can enter these words instead of the numeric menu items, and you can abbreviate them. Word commands are particularly important in forums as we shall see.

> To start to read a message, choose option 2 or enter MESSAGES or MES at the prompt, which takes you to the Messages Menu. Note that one forum menu usually leads to another, just as one menu on the main CompuServe system often leads to a submenu.

```
Good Earth Forum Messages Menu

Message age selection = [All]

  1 SELECT (Read by section and subject)
  2 READ or search messages
  3 CHANGE age selection
  4 COMPOSE a message
  5 UPLOAD a message

Enter choice !
```

> Many options here. Press on toward option 2, the READ option. It leads you to the Read menu:

```
Good Earth Forum Read Menu

Read
 1 [ALL] messages
 2 Message NUMBER
 3 WAITING messages for you (0)

Search [all] messages
 4 FROM (Sender)
 5 SUBJECT
 6 TO (Recipient)

Enter choice !
```

By now, you probably are getting the idea that there is more than one way to read or search for forum messages. You are exactly correct. The message board is the most sophisticated part of the forum, so sophisticated, in fact, that we shall devote the entire next chapter to reading and writing forum messages. For now we want to see a single message. To do that choose option 1.

*But doesn't the menu say that will "Read [All] messages?"*

Not to worry. You won't be compelled to read *all* 1,000 messages on the Good Earth board. You will see how to end the reading session a little earlier than that.

When you choose option 1, the system finds the public message with the lowest message number — that is, the oldest message on the board — and displays it. Of course, we can't tell what message you see on your screen, but it should look something like this:

```
#: 29952 S2/Vegetable Gardening
    20-Jan-89  03:11:38
Sb: Large carrots
Fm: Jeff Smith 70000,999
To: Mike Jones 70101,010

Hi Mike!
Remember those carrot seeds you sent me?
They are three quarters grown now and so
big I can't get them out of the ground. I'm
making plans to rent a ditch-digger to
harvest them. Do you know if these carrots
are mean-spirited? I wouldn't want to make
them angry if they are.

There is 1 Reply.

Press <CR> for next or type CHOICES !
```

This message gives us a chance to examine the various parts of all messages on all forum boards:

— The first line gives the message's unique number ("29952" in our example) and the *section* of the message board where it is located. In the previous chapter, we pointed out that message boards usually are subdivided into sections or subtopics to help members find subjects of interest? (The message in our example in section 2 called "Vegetable Gardening".)

— The second line gives the date and time the message was posted.

— The third line states the subject ("Large Carrots"). By the way, if a number precedes the subject, such as "#29940 Large Carrots", it means it is a reply to a previous message (in this example, a reply to message 29940.)

— The next line, preceded by "Fm:," is the name and user ID of the sender.

— After that, preceded by "To:," is the person to whom the message is sent. Usually, the recipient's user ID is displayed as well. Sometimes, though, a message isn't written to a specific person, but rather "All" is written in the "To" field, meaning the note is addressed to all readers. In addition, some messages are addressed to "Sysop," the forum administrator.

— Then comes the message, which may be one line or perhaps 30 or more lines.

— The last line before the prompt tells you there is one reply to this message. As noted, forum messages form *threads* of conversations, that is, a chain of messages and their replies. The forum's MESSAGES option allows you to easily view those messages in terms of replies, as Chapter 12 will demonstrate.

The prompt that follows the message tells you that if you want to see the next message available, you should press RETURN. Or, to get more choices for actions on this message, enter CHOICES. Do that now. Enter CHOICES (or just CHO) and see a new menu, one called the Read Action Menu:

```
Good Earth Forum Read Action Menu

 1 REPLY with same subject
 2 COMPOSE with new subject
 3 REREAD this message
 4 NEXT reply
 5 NEXT SUBJECT
 6 READ reply
 7 DELETE this message

Enter choice !
```

The system is saying; "Okay, now that you have read this message, what do you want to do next?" If you choose option 1 (or enter REPLY or REP), you could write an answer to this message and it would be stored as a new part of the thread with the same subject header. If you choose 2 (or COMPOSE or COM), you could reply to the sender of the message, but with a new subject header. (Sometimes reading a message on one subject makes you think of something else; this option allows you to take advantage of this impulse.) Option 3 (REREAD) simply displays the message again. Option 4 (NEXT) allows you to display the next message in the thread (that is, skipping replies to the current message). If you choose Option 5 (NEXT SUBJECT), you skip all unread messages in the current thread and move to the first message in the next thread (or subject). Option 6 (READ) shows you the next reply in the thread. And Option 7 (DELETE) lets you delete this message.

*Now, wait just a minute, guys! The menu on my screen doesn't look like that!*

There is a good reason for that. Remember the concept we discovered after JOINing the forum? The JOIN option was then removed from the main menu. Forum menus are designed to display *only* those options currently open to you. Our example shows the complete Read Action Menu, but all options won't be shown to you at all times. Everyone always sees the first three options, but options 4, 5, and 6 are displayed only if the message you just read is part of several multimessage threads. There is no need to offer you the NEXT or NEXT SUBJECT options if the message you have just read is among such threads. In addition, the only time you are offered the DELETE option is when the message is either (1) addressed to you or (2) was written by you. Unless you are a sysop in this forum, you can't delete other people's messages. We shall see other cases in which the smart forum software customizes menus for us.

These are the basic steps in reading messages on any forum board. We shall go into greater depth about the forum commands later. For now, enter T at the prompt to take you back to the Main Menu:

```
Good Earth Forum Menu

  1 INSTRUCTIONS
  2 MESSAGES
  3 LIBRARIES (Files)
  4 CONFERENCING (0 participating)
  5 ANNOUNCEMENTS from sysop
  6 MEMBER directory
  7 OPTIONS for this forum

Enter choice !
```

**Note:** Depending on the kind of menu at which you enter it, the effect of the T command is a little different in a forum that in the main system. If you enter it at a forum submenu (as we just did), T takes you to the "top" of the forum, the main menu; if you enter it at the forum's main menu, T takes you to the TOP of the system itself. Also, if you enter a GO command at a forum "!" prompt, you are whisked out of the forum to another service.

# Bulletins from the Sysop

At the beginning of the tour, you saw how the sysop provides special messages through announcements to visitors and new users. Other announcements also are on file from the management, bulletins you ought to look at in the forums that you regularly visit. In the previous chapter, we observed that it is unnecessary — and rather rude — to leave a message asking a sysop to explain what the forum is all about because such information is already on file. You see that such background is contained in the ANNOUNCEMENTS from sysop section, option 5, on the main menu. Enter ANNOUNCEMENTS, ANN or 5 at the prompt and you see:

```
Good Earth Forum Announcements Menu

  1 News flash
  2 General
  3 Messages
  4 Conference
  5 Library
  6 Membership
  7 Sysop roster
  8 New member
```

Sysops file bulletins for most major features in their forums. Several of the options lead to bulletins you already have seen. Option 1 (News Flash) is one of them. If you missed some information that was displayed in the News Flash when you entered the forum, you can come to this option and reread it. The same is true with the New Member announcement (option 8), which is the announcement you saw immediately after you JOINed the forum. Some of the other announcements you haven't seen before and you might want to look at them now:

— General Announcement (option 2) is basic news about the forum, information that has more lasting interest to the group than that contained in the News Flash.

— Messages Announcement (option 3) may tell you about current hot message threads or may outline the various message sections and the subject matter in each.

— Conference Announcement (option 4) tells of regular real-time conferences held in the forum or reports upcoming special conferences.

— Library Announcement (option 5) may summarize what each data library contains or it may list files recently uploaded to libraries in the forum.

— Membership Announcement (option 6) usually contains additional information about membership.

— Sysop Roster (7) details the sysops' backgrounds, with information on how they came to be here in the first place.

Have a look around here, then meet us back at the main menu, by pressing RETURN at the "Enter Choice !" prompt:

```
┌─────────────────────────────────────────────────┐
│                                                   │
│   Good Earth Forum Menu                           │
│                                                   │
│   1 INSTRUCTIONS                                  │
│   2 MESSAGES                                      │
│   3 LIBRARIES (Files)                             │
│   4 CONFERENCING (0 participating)                │
│   5 ANNOUNCEMENTS from sysop                      │
│   6 MEMBER directory                              │
│   7 OPTIONS for this forum                        │
│                                                   │
│   Enter choice !                                  │
│                                                   │
└─────────────────────────────────────────────────┘
```

## Finding out about Fellow Members

You are drawn to forums because of particular interests, and one option on the main menu helps you find like-minded people. MEMBER directory, option 6, allows you to view the forum's membership log, where forum users voluntarily place information about themselves. The feature also allows you to add information about your own interests. To see it, you enter MEMBER, MEM, or 6 at the prompt and the system displays:

```
┌─────────────────────────────────────────────────┐
│                                                   │
│   Good Earth Forum Directory Menu                 │
│                                                   │
│   Your current entry                              │
│    1 ADD/modify                                   │
│    2 LIST                                         │
│    3 DELETE                                        │
│                                                   │
│   Search by                                       │
│    4 USER ID                                      │
│    5 NAME                                         │
│    6 INTEREST                                     │
│    7 AGE                                          │
│                                                   │
│   Enter choice !                                  │
│                                                   │
└─────────────────────────────────────────────────┘
```

The first three choices deal with your own entry. You can add your own information by choosing option 1. You might not want to do that yet, but here's a rundown on what you will see when you do. The first display is:

```
Your entry in the Member
Directory consists of your name,
User ID, and your specified list
of interests. You may change
your existing Member Directory
entry by entering new interests,
one per line, at the "*" prompts
below. Pressing <CR> at the
first "*" prompt will leave your
current entry unchanged.
Otherwise, the new entry will
replace the old one.
An entry's list of interests may
be up to 149 characters long.
To end your list of interests,
press <CR> at any "*" prompt.
*
```

You can begin entering your interests at the asterisk. If you were interested in gardening, you might type "Gardening" and press RETURN. You would then be told you had 140 characters left and another asterisk would appear. When you finish entering your interests, you press RETURN at the asterisk and you are taken back to the Directory menu:

```
Good Earth Forum Directory Menu

Your current entry
 1 ADD/modify
 2 LIST
 3 DELETE

Search by
 4 USER ID
 5 NAME
 6 INTEREST
 7 AGE

Enter choice !
```

Option 2 lists your own entry, and option 3 deletes it. Once you have added your own entry, you can modify it by choosing option 1 again.

When it comes to finding other members and their interests, you can search by a member's user ID (option 4), a member's name (option 5), or an interest (option 6). Also, if you want to check the additions made to the directory in recent days, you can choose option 7 and specify a number of days at the subsequent prompt (this feature works much like the AGE functions in the National Bulletin Board and Public Access). Entering 5 at the prompt would give you information about all members who have added their interests to the director in the previous five days.

To try out the Member Directory, you should do this: Enter NAME or 5 and, when prompted for the name, enter PEYTON. Now the system should show Dave's entry in the directory, something like this:

```
Dave Peyton    76703,244
Writing / Gardening / Good Earth
Forum Sysop / Co-Author of How To
Get The Most Out Of CompuServe
/ Folk music / Folk Culture
```

The entry provides Dave's name, his user ID, and one of his interests such as gardening or sysop or folk music.

Enter T or just press RETURN at the "!" prompt to return to the main menu:

```
Good Earth Forum Menu

  1 INSTRUCTIONS
  2 MESSAGES
  3 LIBRARIES (Files)
  4 CONFERENCING (0 participating)
  5 ANNOUNCEMENTS from sysop
  6 MEMBER directory
  7 OPTIONS for this forum

Enter choice !
```

## Helpful Lists

Now let's get ready for some help. As with most of CompuServe, help always is available. In this case, help with all forum commands is located at this main menu prompt. Type 1 (or INS for INSTRUCTIONS) and press RETURN.

```
Forum Instructions

   The menu that follows contains
   instructions on the various
   areas of a Forum.  To find out
   more about a particular area,
   select it from the menu on the
   next page.  For general Forum
   Instructions, type "ALL" at the
   Instructions menu.

   Press <CR> !
```

Press RETURN to see the Instructions Menu:

```
Good Earth Forum Instructions Menu

Instructions are available for:
 1 Overview
 2 Messages
 3 Libraries
 4 Conferencing
 5 Announcements
 6 Member directory
 7 Options
 8 Miscellaneous
 9 Complete HELP facility
10 Forum Reference Card
11 Forum User's Guide

Enter choice !
```

Here is the on-line place you can come for help with the forum commands as well as for overview of the various parts of the forum. Options 1 through 8 summarize the specified forum features. Most of these help files are only a few lines long. If you want to see a complete essay on all parts of the forum, along with all the commands available in the forum, choose option 9, but be prepared for information overload. Choosing this one presents page after page of instructions about all commands you can use on the forum. Don't try to read this one on the screen. It would be best to send it to your printer or a disk file to read and digest off-line. Option 10 gives you a shorter look at the available commands, much like the command reference card you might get with a software package. Be advised that it is still several screens worth of information; it is adviseable to download it to your printer or disk. Option 11 gives you an overview of forums in general, as well as a brief overview of the functions of a CompuServe forum.

Fortunately, you don't have to memorize all this information before you use the forums. The more you visit forums, the more you will need some of these special options, most of which are explained in the next chapters and in the On-line Survival Kit at the back of the book. When you need them, you can search them out, ask others for help, consult or print out this list, or order a manual from CompuServe where the words remain stationary on a page instead of jumping all over a screen.

After you have looked at this help section, press RETURN to come back to the main menu:

```
Good Earth Forum Menu

  1 INSTRUCTIONS
  2 MESSAGES
  3 LIBRARIES (Files)
  4 CONFERENCING (0 participating)
  5 ANNOUNCEMENTS from sysop
  6 MEMBER directory
  7 OPTIONS for this forum

Enter choice !
```

We are making progress. Looking over this menu, we see that we have briefly examined four of these seven options — INSTRUCTIONS, MESSAGES, AN-NOUNCEMENTS, and MEMBERS — and we shall discuss one more (CON-FERENCING, option 4) after we log off. Chapter 12 presents an in-depth look at the MESSAGES options. Chapter 13 focuses on LIBRARIES and Users OPTIONS (options 3 and 7). But note, as elsewhere on CompuServe, not *all* the options are on the menus. For instance...

## The ULOG: It's Not Fuel for a Holiday Fire

Once you find one or more forum homes, you get to know the people who check in regularly. ULOG, a command not on the menu, lets you find out who has been on the forum in the past day or so. Enter ULOG (or simply U) at the prompt, and you should see something like this:

```
Enter control-P to stop

Harry Greene
01-Jan-89   21:09:09

Ken Salyers
01-Jan-89   21:07:39

Sam Feinberg
01-Jan-89   21:04:09

Dave Peyton
01-Jan-89   20:49:52

Lisa Duncan
01-Jan-89   20:40:30

Howard Maculsay
01-Jan-89   20:39:21

Michael Harris
01-Jan-89   20:29:09

Kathleen Davis
01-Jan-89   20:27:30
```

The list begins with the most recent forum visitor. Each entry contains the date the member was on the forum as well as the time (in military format). It usually records about 24 hours worth of visits. As it says at the top, if you want to interrupt the listing and go back to the menu, you enter Control P.

It is now time to log off. You can log off directly from a forum by entering OFF or BYE at any forum "!" prompt. Notice the exit message as you leave, which gives you the highest message you retrieved and a thank you for visiting, something like this:

```
r-----------------------------------------------------------
|
|   Exiting at 20-Jan-89  16:11:31
|   Thank you for visiting Good Earth Forum
L-----------------------------------------------------------
```

# A Backward Glance at Forum Conferencing

Now that we are off-line and the money meter has been turned off, let's look at another major forum function, CONFERENCING. The forum's main menu tells you if anyone is using the conference area at the time you are on-line. Notice option 4 here:

```
r-----------------------------------------------------------
|
|   Good Earth Forum Menu
|
|    1 INSTRUCTIONS
|    2 MESSAGES
|    3 LIBRARIES (Files)
|    4 CONFERENCING (5 participating)
|    5 ANNOUNCEMENTS from sysop
|    6 MEMBER directory
|    7 OPTIONS for this forum
|
|   Enter choice !
L-----------------------------------------------------------
```

If you saw this menu, you could join the five talkers by entering CON (or CONFERENCING or 5) at the prompt. In most forums, you would be greeted by a Conference Announcement (the same announcement you could see at the Announcement Menu if you chose Conference option). The conference announcement may contain news about an upcoming gathering or perhaps a brief text file explaining conference commands.

After the announcement, you are shown the conference room or rooms available in the forum. These "rooms" are the same as "channels" on the CB Simulator. At the time of this writing, the Good Earth Forum had opened only one room, so the conference room menu looked like this:

```
┌──────────────────────────────────────────────────────┐
│                                                        │
│   Good Earth Forum CO Rooms Menu                       │
│                                                        │
│   Conference Rooms Available:                          │
│    1 General Conference                                │
│                                                        │
│   Enter choice !                                       │
│                                                        │
└──────────────────────────────────────────────────────┘
```

Forums may have up to 18 different conference rooms for public use. The conference announcement may give suggestions on how the various rooms should be used. After choosing the conference channel you want to use — not exactly an arduous task when only one is offered — you are taken to the conferencing area. Unlike CB, you aren't prompted to enter a "handle"; instead, the system uses the name under which you joined the forum.

Now, there is good news tonight, friends, because you *already* know how to use this portion of all forums. Forum conferences are virtually the same as the CB Simulator, with these two notes:

1. The content of forum conferences is often markedly different from CB; usually a bit less freewheeling and sometimes even quite formal.
2. A few additional conferencing commands are available in forums as well as alternative words for commands you are familiar with from your CBing. For instance, in forum conferences, you can enter /ROOM followed by a channel number. It works the same as /CHANNEL (which also is recognized in the forum conference mode). Similarly, /NAME can be used instead of /HANDLE.

Also, the /USERS command in a forum conference area produces a list that looks a little different from the one in the CB simulator. It looks like this:

```
┌──────────────────────────────────────────────────────┐
│                                                        │
│   User    User ID    Nod    Rm    Name / Forum Area    │
│   ────    ─────────   ───    ───   ─────────────────    │
│     73    76703,244   HWV    1     Dave Peyton          │
│     82    70000,010   MON          ACCESS               │
│     94    79999,999   MRT          SIG                  │
│                                                        │
└──────────────────────────────────────────────────────┘
```

If the user is in the conference area, their name appears in the USERS list. If, however, the user is not in the conference area, the USERS list will display the forum area where the user is located, rather than the user's name. For example, the user with job number 82 in the list above is in one of the data libraries and User No. 94 is in message area of the forum. The /USERS command has a few extra features in the forums. In addition to /USERS followed by a channel number and /USERS TLK (to list those in "Talk"), you can enter /USERS CO to list only those members in conference mode or /USERS SIG to list only the members who are "outside" in the main forum area.

USERS has another special function in forums; it also can be used *outside* the conference area. At the forum's main menu, you can enter USERS (no slash this time) and the system displays a list of those currently in the forum, such as:

```
   Job      User ID     Node      Area
    39     70000,020    T01MRT    Conference
    40     76666,3333   T01NOL    Libraries
    42     78888,000    T02KMZ    Conference
    43     70990,414    T06DCJ    Libraries
    48     73999,000    T03DCJ    Libraries
    51     76703,244    T06HWV    Messages
    52     70475,1156   T04SJN    Libraries
```

It is similar to /USERS in CB and the conference area, including the job numbers and nodes of individual subscribers; but it shows only the area in which the user is, whether it is in conference, the library, or the message board.

## Sending out the World in Forums

Sometimes yours is the only name on the list, meaning you are the only person kicking around in that particular forum at that particular time. However, if you do see another user ID on the list (and you are feeling talkative), you can say hello without even entering the conference area by using a command called SEN (that is, SENd). Here is how it works.

Suppose that after entering the USERS command at the forum's main menu, you see the job numbers of the various visitors as in the example above. If you wanted to say a quick howdy to job 51, you could enter the forum at a "!" prompt:

```
   SEN 51 Hi there! I'm new here.
```

The SEN command would send the message to job 51. No matter what the other visitor was doing at the moment — reading messages, writing messages, etc. — he or she would see something like this on the screen:

```
;;GOODEARTH - Job 54: Hi there! I'm new here.
```

If the other subscriber wants to reply, he or she goes to a forum prompt and enters something like:

```
SEN 54 Welcome aboard? Time for a chat in CO?
```

This would cause his message to appear on your screen. Such quick and private messages can be SENt to and from the conference area. If you see from your /USERS command list that a friend with job number 23 is in the Conference area, you can enter:

```
/SEN 23 Hi George. What's happening?
```

It makes no difference if George is "out in the main part of the forum or in the conference area. George will get the message. That means that /SEN can be used as a kind of electronic whisper between people in a conference. Suppose you are attending a gathering and you have something to say to your friend George that you don't want to speak publicly. Aside from being able to go into /TALK or a /SCRrambled conversation, just as in CB, you could just look up his job number and enter /SEN followed by the job and the message.

On the other hand, sometimes when you are in conference, you might want to turn down SEN messages politely. The command to turn off the function is /NOSEND. (/SEND <RETURN> will turn it back on again.) Incidentally, the NOSEND command doesn't work at the main menu prompt, only in the Conference area.

Now that we have told you how to SEN a message, we are going to urge you to not overdo it. Here's why. Some forum visitors get annoyed by being regularly interrupted by SEN messages. Everyone in a forum is doing *something*, whether reading or writing a message, perusing an announcement, or visiting the forum libraries. No one comes in and sits patiently waiting for SEN messages to arrive. SEN is best used as either a quick "hi" to a friend in a message that doesn't require a reply, or as an invitation to drop into the forum's conference area for a chat.

In the same vein, if you ever SENd a message and don't get a reply, it could mean that the other user hasn't yet learned this command. Or, more likely, he or she is in the middle of writing a message on the board. If the user were to stop to answer your SEN message immediately, he or she might have to cut the message short in order to get back to you. (Also, there is at least one forum activity that generally cannot be interrupted by SEN messages. If the intended recipient is downloading or uploading files in the data library when you SENd, you may receive a message that says, "Busy.") In any event, in this forum society, it is *not* considered impolite if SEN messages sometimes go unanswered.

On your forum field trip, if you want to get an idea of how SEN works without disturbing a stranger, you actually can SENd to yourself. Simply enter the USERS command from the main forum menu and find your own job number. Then enter SEN followed by your job and then the message (up to 80 characters). In a few seconds, that message should come bouncing back to you. If that is your idea of a good time, then you probably can stop your CompuServe research right now. But if you think your mother had more in mind for you than talking to yourself electronically via Columbus, Ohio, at $6.30 an hour, check back with us after your field trip. In the next chapter we shall look at some more of the advanced forum commands, including ways to scan the message boards quickly, and a way to save time in the forums.

## Forum Conference Etiquette

Some forums conferences are intended as informal gabfest, just to allow users to chat with each other and have a good time. However, the same conference facilities are occasionally used for more formal "guest" conferences in which a speaker or a panel of speakers addresses the group. On those occasions, you are expected to follow local customs for raising questions. In most forums, the sysops asks that you "raise your hand" before asking a question, by entering a question mark (?) and then waiting to be recognized by the moderator.

When you are called on, enter "OK" to let the others know you are still on-line and that you are composing a question. Then when you have finished your question, let the others know by entering "GA," meaning "go ahead; I'm finished talking."

Also, try not to enter more than 50 or 60 characters on a line at a time, and if your full question is going to take several such lines, end each transmission with "..." (meaning, "I have still got more to say.").

## The Convention Center

In addition to in-forum conferences, a relatively new service called "The Convention Center" allows a large number of subscribers to gather to listen to a prescheduled real-time presentation, such as an electronic lecture or a panel discussion. The service was launched in March 1987 with a convention hosted by Neil Shapiro, sysop of the Micronetworked Apple Users Groups (G MAUG). In it, nearly 300 subscribers gathered to read the real-time transcript of the words of Apple Computer President

John Sculley and others who were appearing on-stage in Los Angeles to announce the latest in the Apple Macintosh line of computers.

These electronic conventions are usually sponsored by a particular forum, but the actual conference runs outside of the forum. To reach the Convention Center, enter G CONVENTION at any prompt. You are greeted by menu like this:

```
Electronic Convention Center

INFORMATION/RESERVATIONS

   1 Instructions
   2 List Conferences/Make Reservations
   3 Review/Cancel Reservations
   4 Conference Etiquette

Enter choice !
```

If a scheduled convention already is going on at the time you access the feature, a fifth option is added to the menu that says, "ENTER A CONFERENCE IN SESSION."

There are three kinds of conventions:

1. A roundtable that permits open chatter throughout the duration of the conference by all participants.
2. A more formal "moderated" conference, in which the guest speaker makes an opening statement, then members of the audience may ask questions in turn. The Convention Center software prevents listeners from transmitting questions except when the moderator authorizes it.
3. A lecture conference, the most formal of the three, which permits no open chatter or questions during the event.

Those conventions that permit questions "from the floor" use the same basic commands of the CB Simulator and forum conferences, all preceded by a slash (/), such as "/STA" for a status report. There are a few extra commands available. For instance, in a moderated conference, the moderator exercises control over who can transmit and when. Speaking is permitted by only one audience member at a time. In those conventions, if you want to ask a question, enter /QUESTION. You are then notified when it is your turn. To see how many questioners are still ahead of you, enter /LOOK. For details of other special convention commands, see the "Instructions" option on the main conference menu.

Some particularly popular conventions require advanced registration to attend. You can read about upcoming conventions by regularly checking option 2 on the main menu, "List Conferences/Make Reservations." Some require a fee to attend, and that bulletin identifies any such surcharged features.

## Keeping Control

One more item before we wrap up, this time about control codes.

— CONTROL P has a special function in the forums. You can use a CONTROL P to interrupt announcements, text files in the database, and messages on the message. Think of CONTROL P in the forums as saying, "Okay, okay, let's get on with it!"

— CONTROL C, the great bailout command, is particularly useful in a forum; it tells the system to stop what it is doing because you have changed your mind. It needs to be used only occasionally, as the menus usually give you handy exit options, but it is nice to know it is there in emergencies. No matter where you are in the forum, you will see the following when you type a CONTROL C:

```
Control-C Intercepted Menu

   1 Continue
   2 Return to menu/prompt
   3 Return to forum top
   4 Exit this forum
   5 Log Off

Enter Choice:
```

Options 2 or 3 return you to the main forum menu. Option 1 allows you to continue (that is, ignore the CONTROL C and go ahead), option 4 exits the forum, and option 5 logs you off the system.

## Side Roads

Now that you have gotten your feet wet in the Good Earth Forum, you might want to start exploring a little in other forum neighborhoods. We ask you to not use the forum message boards, data libraries or the user options until you have read Chapters 12 and 13. However, as you now know everything there is to know about other forum features — especially the real-time CONFERENCING facilities — feel free to begin looking around. Just review the CB commands discussed in Chapters 5 and 6 and check out the forums.

To find out what forum conferences are going on, you should return to the electronic edition on *Online Today*, where page OLT-50 contains stories and features about activities around the system. Enter G OLT-50 at any prompt and see something like:

```
Online Today                          OLT-50

COMPUSERVE THIS WEEK

   1 About This Section
   2 What's New on CompuServe
   3 CompuServe Community News
   4 Forum Conference Schedules
   5 What's New - Previous Weeks
   6 Uploads/Forum Program Updates
   7 Send a Letter To the Editor
   8 Online Today Readers' Forum

Enter choice !
```

Note that some options contain current and previous "What's New" features; another option (3) has additional stories from around CompuServe. Of interest to us currently is option 4. As noted, many forums hold regularly scheduled conferences, where members can get together informally and discuss common interests. A list provided by option 4 contains the names of some such forums, the times of the conferences (all in Eastern time), and their quick reference words. Have a look. Maybe you will find just the group to which you want to talk.

# CHAPTER 12

---

# More About Forums and Messages

If you have reflected on what you saw in the previous chapter and in any of your own explorations, you probably have been struck by the forums' enormous potential. If they seem to be little communities unto themselves, the perception is more than coincidence. The more you learn about forums, the more you see them as microcosms of CompuServe itself — much as states are smaller versions of nations.

Often forum discussions sound like old-fashioned town hall meetings. Forums can have thousands of members, some of whom are so active that they fill their message boards' capacity in an evening or two. By contrast, other forums are quiet, esoteric little corners of the system where the membership, though small, is fiercely loyal. With such diversity, it is little wonder that some subscribers find forums the most appealing part of CompuServe and spend most of their on-line time tooling from one forum to another.

In this chapter, without actually going on-line, we shall continue our look at forums, exploring one of their most powerful features, the message board and how to read and write notes on the board.

## The Message Board, an Overview

We have talked a little about the structure of messages and how message boards are organized. Messages are placed on message boards sequentially, regardless of the subject. If the message posted in the Good Earth Forum just before your arrival was number 2000 and you write a message (either an original note or a reply to someone else's message), your's will be number 2001. The system itself takes care of the numbering (you needn't worry about it), and your message will be the *only* one in that forum with that number.

Although sequential order makes good sense for the system's automatic posting of messages, it is not the best way to read them. On the contrary, though it is possible to read forum messages sequentially, it may be the *worst* way to find out what's happening. That's because subjects usually vary greatly from one message to the next. Message number 1998 might be someone's comments about an earlier boast by Charlie on the success of his wife's tomato plants, whereas message 1999 might be someone else's criticism of the notion that the phases of the moon affect test scores and message 2000 might be a reply in an ongoing discussion about the proper care of dogwood trees. Although you can read those messages sequentially, it doesn't make much sense for you to jump into the middle of three different conversations for which you probably have little understanding.

Fortunately, a number of options are available for reading messages in logical ways, and most of those approaches can be initiated directly from the menus. To see that, let's suppose that you have just logged on to CompuServe and have entered the command G GOODEARTH. Let's recap what you saw first-hand on the last tour. When you arrive in the forum, you may be greeted by a few sysop announcements, then reach this main menu:

```
Good Earth Forum Menu

   1 INSTRUCTIONS
   2 MESSAGES
   3 LIBRARIES (Files)
   4 CONFERENCING (0 participating)
   5 ANNOUNCEMENTS from sysop
   6 MEMBER directory
   7 OPTIONS for this forum

 Enter choice !
```

In Chapter 11 we saw that option 2 takes you to the message board, signaled by this Messages menu:

```
┌─────────────────────────────────────────────┐
│                                             │
│   Good Earth Forum Messages Menu            │
│                                             │
│   Message age selection = [New]             │
│                                             │
│     1 SELECT (Read by section and subject)  │
│     2 READ or search messages               │
│     3 CHANGE age selection                  │
│     4 COMPOSE a message                     │
│                                             │
│   Enter choice !                            │
│                                             │
└─────────────────────────────────────────────┘
```

It is from this menu that we shall start all the tasks in this chapter.

## Selecting Groups of Messages

The first option, SELECT ("read by section and subject"), represents one way in which you can read messages in a manner that is more logical than a simple sequential order.

We have pointed out that each forum's message board is divided into subtopics or *sections* that are, in effect, departments or categories, and that the sysop can assign up to 18 different subtopics. Section 1 might be "General Interest," whereas section 2 is devoted to "News," section 3 to "Help Wanted," and so on. (Some forums start with section 0, others make section 1 their first subtopic. Also, not all subtopics are public; some forums reserve a few areas of the board for sysop-invitation only.) Choosing SELECT (by entering SEL or 1 or the entire word SELECT) causes the system to show you something like this:

```
┌─────────────────────────────────────────────────────────┐
│                                                           │
│   Good Earth Forum Sections Menu                          │
│                                                           │
│   Section names (#subjs/# msgs)                           │
│                                                           │
│    1 Homesteading (4/7)                                   │
│    2 Vegetable Gardening (1/15)                           │
│    3 Ornamental Gardens (1/1)                             │
│    4 Herbology (5/16)                                     │
│    5 Folkways (2/5)                                       │
│    7 Pets (2/2)                                           │
│    8 Help (2/14)                                          │
│   10 General Information (1/1)                            │
│                                                           │
│   Enter choice(s) or ALL !                                │
│                                                           │
└─────────────────────────────────────────────────────────┘
```

This display has two functions: First, it gives you the *names* of the message board's sections (at least, the names of those currently containing messages). In this example, taken from the Good Earth Forum, messages posted on sections 1 and 2 deal with homesteading and vegetable gardening respectively. Second, this menu — through the two numbers in parentheses following each section name — tells you how active each section is. The first number indicates how many different *subjects* are being discussed in the messages posted there and the second is the total number of messages filed. We can, therefore, see that in the Homesteading section there are seven messages covering four different subjects, whereas the Vegetable Gardening section has one subject discussed in 15 messages.

The prompt is waiting for you to indicate the section or sections you want to SELECT for reading which you do by entering a single number, several numbers separated by commas, or the word ALL. Suppose you want to look at the "Herbology" messages, you enter 4 at the prompt. The menu already has told you that there are 16 messages there, divided among five different subjects. Now the system gets more specific by listing the specific subjects, with a Subjects menu like this:

```
┌─────────────────────────────────────────────────────┐
│                                                       │
│   Good Earth Forum Subjects Menu                      │
│                                                       │
│   Subject (# msgs)                                    │
│                                                       │
│   Section 4 - Herbology                               │
│                                                       │
│    1 Rosemary (1)                                     │
│    2 Herb tea (1)                                     │
│    3 Pasta and herbs (5)                              │
│    4 Garden Project (5)                               │
│    5 Wimpy Herbs (4)                                  │
│                                                       │
│   Enter choice(s) !                                   │
│                                                       │
└─────────────────────────────────────────────────────┘
```

The menu starts by reminding you that this list is for "Section 4 on Herbology," and the individual subjects are listed followed by a number in parentheses that tells you how many messages are in each subject. We learned about these "subjects" in the previous chapters and called them *threads*, as in "threads of conversation." In the forums, the terms threads and subjects are used interchangeably. Of course, the numbers in the parenthesis add up to the total we already expected from the previous menu, 16. At this point, you may read one or more of the subjects. Let's say the "Wimpy Herbs" thread catches your eye, so you enter 5 and the forum shows you the first of the messages available in that discussion:

```
#: 30296 S4/Herbology
    15-Dec-88  16:55:05
Sb: #Wimpy Herbs
Fm: Lindsy 70000,100
To: All


    Here's a question I can't find the
answer to in the data library. What happens
to herbs when they're frozen in fish or
meat stock? Do they lose their potency, and
if so, how long does it take? I'm
especially interested in the word on
saffron, garlic, fennel, parsley, thyme,
bay leaf and pepper.


    Thanks!

There are 2 Replies

Press <CR> for next or type CHOICES !
```

Note the *name* of the subject as listed on the previous menu actually comes directly from the "Sb:" line of this initial message. When Lindsy composed her message and closed it, the system prompted her for a subject, thus starting a new thread of conversation called "Wimpy Vegetables."

You have two options at this point: (1) If you want to go directly to the next message in the discussion, you could press the RETURN key. (If there were no more messages, pressing RETURN takes you back to the subject menu.) (2) If you want to see other possible actions on this message, you could enter CHOICES (or simple CHO) and see a Read Action menu, like this:

```
┌─────────────────────────────────────────────────┐
│                                                 │
│   Good Earth Forum Read Action Menu             │
│                                                 │
│   1 REPLY with same subject                     │
│   2 COMPOSE with new subject                    │
│   3 REREAD this message                         │
│   4 NEXT reply                                  │
│   5 NEXT SUBJECT                                │
│   6 READ reply                                  │
│                                                 │
│   Enter choice !                                │
└─────────────────────────────────────────────────┘
```

As noted in the previous chapter, options 1 and 2 offer two ways to answer this message that we shall discuss below. Option 3 lets you reread the current message. Option 4 takes you to the next message in the thread (you would have gotten the same result if you had simply pressed RETURN at the previous prompt.) Option 5 skips unread messages in the current thread and displays the first message in the *next* message thread. Option 6 displays a reply to the message you are currently reading. (This option appears on the Read Action menu only if there is a reply to read.) An option 7 ("DELETE this message") also is displayed on this menu if that option is open to you. You may delete a message only if (1) you wrote it or (2) it was written specifically to you (that is, your user ID number was specified by the sender in the TO: field when the message was written or the message was written as a reply to one you wrote — more about replies later).

Suppose you continue to the next message in the thread — either through option 4 (NEXT) on this menu or by pressing RETURN at the previous prompt — and you see:

```
#: 30301 S4/Herbology
    16-Dec-88  20:13:00
Sb: #30296-#Wimpy Herbs
Fm: Dave Peyton 76703,244
To: Lindsy 70000,100 (X)


    Lindsy: Generally speaking, herbs do
not lose their potency when frozen. But
some of them are, in my opinion, amplified.
Garlic, for example, seems a little
stronger after it has been frozen either
alone or as part of a prepared dish.


There is 1 Reply

Press <CR> for next or type CHOICES !
```

Please look at the "Sb:" information in the third line in this message. The preceding "#30296" means it is a reply to message 30296, telling you that this is not the first message in the thread of conversation, but rather is a reply. The pound sign preceding the subject ("#Wimpy Herbs") means there is at least one reply *to* this message. The X at the end of the recipient user ID number means that he or she has read the message. And, of course, we know this message has a reply because the line at the bottom above the prompt spells it out: "There is 1 Reply."

Again, you press RETURN to see the third message in the discussion:

```
#: 30342 S4/Herbology
    16-Dec-88  22:44:00
Sb: #30296-#Wimpy Herbs
Fm: Don 70000,76
To: Lindsy 70000,100 (X)


    If the dish is frozen rapidly, and
kept covered, little effect on the herbs
should be noticed. If experience shows a
slight loss, just add a little more herb
than normal when preparing a dish that you
intend to freeze.


    There is 1 Reply


Press <CR> for next or type CHOICES !
```

The subject line here ("#30296") indicates this, too, is a reply, not to the previous message, but to Lindsy's original. Pressing the RETURN key once more brings up:

```
#: 30392 S4/Herbology
    20-Dec-88  10:18:04
Sb: #30342-Wimpy Herbs
Fm: Lindsy 70000,100
To: Don Goldberg 70000,76 (X)


    Thanks, Don. I tend to have a heavy
hand with my herbs, but I will just make it
a wee bit heavier.

Press <CR> for next or type CHOICES !
```

Now glance back at the four messages, this time looking at the message numbers (on the first line of each note), and you will see that they are *not* sequential. Far from it. The first message (Lindsy's original) is number 30296, the fourth and last message in the conversion is number 30392. Nearly a hundred messages were posted between the first and last in this particular thread. Those in between were messages covering a variety of topics, nonetheless, the SELECT command has enabled you to quickly find the original and replies wherever they occurred on the board — and you never even have to notice their individual message numbers.

Recapping, then, SELECT allows you to group messages in two ways:

1. By the *section* (or subtopic) of the message board.
2. By *subjects* or threads of the messages.

This second group — subjects (threads) — means the earliest messages and their chains of replies. As you might imagine, threads can be quite elaborate. Suppose you log into the forum and leave a message about a popular topic, and Dave logs in and replies to you, then Charlie logs in and writes one reply to you and a different reply to Dave, then Dave answers Charlie and you answer both of us, then someone whom none of us know comes along and.... Well, before long, we have many branches from that original messages. Fortunately, the system displays threads in the order of replies, so that you see the give and take of a conversation, and read the issues as they develop.

## Staying up with New Messages

The only problem with reading messages by thread is that sometimes the message that started the whole conversation scrolls off the board. Forums have only a limited amount of storage space for messages. (The actual number varies from forum to forum, depending on how active it is). Whenever a new message is posted, an older one, elsewhere on the board, usually is automatically deleted.

**Note:**   There are exceptions. Recent enhancements allow sysops to designate special messages — usually introductions to forum projects or those concerning long-term issues — for permanent storage on the message boards. When a message is so marked by the sysop, the system simply skips it when time comes to delete a message automatically as a new one is posted.

Of course, *all* messages can't be protected in this way, so inevitably some important messages do eventually scroll off into oblivion. For this reason, sysops often preserve popular threads of conversation in the forum library. (We shall have more about data libraries in Chapter 13.)

Meanwhile, smart forum members don't rely solely on the sysop to look after them; instead, they check in with their favorite forums regularly to make sure they don't miss out on the start of hot new conversations. Some message board commands make it easy to see what has been added on the board since the last visit. To see those commands, let's return to the Messages menu:

```
Good Earth Forum Messages Menu

Message age selection = [New]

  1 SELECT (Read by section and subject)
  2 READ or search messages
  3 CHANGE age selection
  4 COMPOSE a message

Enter choice !
```

Option 2 allows us to READ or search messages in several ways. Selecting it, we are shown this Read menu:

```
Good Earth Forum Read Menu

Read

  1 [NEW] messages
  2 Message NUMBER
  3 WAITING messages for you (4)

Search [new] messages

  4 FROM (Sender)
  5 SUBJECT
  6 TO (Recipient)
```

(Please place a bookmark here temporarily.)

Doubtlessly, this menu looks familiar. We used it on the tour in the previous chapter to read messages. We simply selected option 1 here and the system displayed the first message it found on the board and...

*Hey, wait just a minute here! What the...*

Those with keen eyes have noticed a difference. When you made your first tour of the Good Earth Forum in Chapter 11, this option 1 on the menu offered to read "[ALL] message" rather than "[NEW] messages," as it appears in this example. The fact is that when you visit any forum for the first time, the system realizes that all its messages are, technically speaking, *new* messages to you, as you have never visited there before, and couldn't have had an opportunity to read them. However, after you have read at least one message on that forum's board, the system revises its Read menu, changing the option so that from then on it allows you to read "[NEW] messages" with option 1.

*But how does the system know whether I have read any messages? And how does it know what's new to me?*

By "new," the system always means those messages that were posted since your last visit to the forum. Every time you leave a forum, the system automatically stores the number of the *highest* message (that is, most recent message, the one with the highest message number) you read. Then, if on your next visit you ask to see "new" messages, the system checks it files, finds your *high message number*, and displays the messages after that.

Two additional points: first, CompuServe allows you to reset that high message number in your file (we shall learn about that in Chapter 13). Second, words that appear on the menus in square brackets (such as "[NEW]" and "[ALL]") have a special function in the forums. In a moment, we shall see a command that allows you to change those square bracketed words.

Messages gathered by option 1 are grouped automatically in order of threads. This feature is particularly handy if you have been following conversations over several days, as the READ NEW messages function allows you to catch up automatically on each of them. (On the other hand, if some new messages make you regret that you haven't been following a conversation that now looks interesting, all you have to do is go back to the SELECT function on the previous menu and pick up the earlier thread.)

The next option on this menu — NUMBER — displays a message whose number you specify. When you select it (by entering either 2 or NUM), the system displays the range of messages currently on the board, with a prompt something like this:

```
Forum messages:  29777 to   30540
Message #:
```

Messages in this example range from 29777 to 30540. The system waits for you to enter the number of message you want to see.

As a practical matter, you won't use this option as often as others. Instead of reading individual messages by number, it is simply wiser to read messages grouped by threads and age, or grouped in another way. For instance, option 3 here — WAIT-

ING — allows you to read messages waiting *for you*. Messages that have been written to you — either as original messages or as replies to your earlier notes on the board — are flagged for your attention, and the system tells you about them when you enter the forum. The Read menu also reminds you of waiting messages. As you see on the bookmarked example of the Read menu, the "(4)" following option 3 means that there are four messages waiting you. Just enter 3 or WAI at the prompt, and the system shows them to you. Speaking of marked messages, remember that messages written to you can be deleted; that means that a seventh option — "DELETE this message" — will be added to the Read Action menu reached through the CHOICES options on any such message.

## Searching for Messages

Another way to group messages for reading is to *search* for them. The remaining three options on the Read menu deal with searching in one way or another. As the bookmarked menu shows you, you can search the board for messages FROM a particular person (option 4), TO a person (option 6), or by the SUBJECT of a particular message or group of messages (option 5). These commands do not search the *text* of the messages, but rather the messages' headers, that is, the words and numbers contained in the "Sb:," "Fm:," and "To:" fields. To see how it works, suppose you want to search the message board for notes about herbs. At the "Read menu" prompt, you enter 5 or the letters SUB to search the subject field. The system prompts:

```
┌──────────────────────────────────────────────────┐
│                                                  │
│   Enter subject:                                 │
│                                                  │
└──────────────────────────────────────────────────┘
```

You enter the word HERBS, and the forum searches the headers for the messages' subject fields, then displays each message it has found that meets the criteria (in this example, perhaps finding the "Wimpy herbs" thread we showed earlier).

The other two options work similarly. If you want to search message FROM or TO Dave Peyton, you select the appropriate option and the system displays either:

```
┌──────────────────────────────────────────────────┐
│                                                  │
│   Enter sender's name or ID:                     │
│                                                  │
└──────────────────────────────────────────────────┘
```

or

```
┌──────────────────────────────────────────────────┐
│                                                    │
│    Enter recipient's name or ID:                   │
│                                                    │
└──────────────────────────────────────────────────┘
```

Now enter the name or User ID number of the person whose messages you are seeking, and the forum performs the search and displays the results.

About searching these fields:

— Use quotation marks to enclose strings that contain two or more words or names. For example, "Dave Peyton" or "Red Apples" or "Charlie Bowen."

— You don't have to enter a complete word or name. In fact, sometimes you probably *won't* want to use a complete name. If you were searching the board for messages from or to your friend David, you might not know if he joined the forum as "David" or "Dave." In that case, you might want to answer the prompt by entering only as much of the name as you are sure of: "DAV." The system then searches the field for all names that contain the letters DAV side by side and in that order. In the same way, if you were searching the subject field of messages for computer-related topics, you might want to enter only COMPUT, which would find "computer," "computers," "computing," "computation," and so on.

— The forum searches the *entire* field, not just the beginning. So, if you were looking for message from Dave Peyton, you could enter PEYTON or PEY as well as DAVID or DAV.

— The "TO" and "FROM" prompts also accept the user ID, as well as the name, of the person for which you are searching. However, there is a difference: while the system accepts partial names and words, user IDs entered at the prompts must be complete. (If you are looking for messages from the users of ID number 71635,1025, you *won't* find it if you enter only 71635 at the prompt.)

## Having It Your Way — the Change Command

Forums have another powerful tool for grouping messages by *age*. Let's look at the Messages menu again, this time looking at the first line following the header:

```
┌─────────────────────────────────────────────────────────┐
│                                                          │
│   Good Earth Forum Messages Menu                         │
│                                                          │
│   Message age selection = [New]                          │
│                                                          │
│     1 SELECT (Read by section and subject)               │
│     2 READ or search messages                            │
│     3 CHANGE age selection                               │
│     4 COMPOSE a message                                  │
│                                                          │
│   Enter choice !                                         │
│                                                          │
└─────────────────────────────────────────────────────────┘
```

A moment ago, we noted that words in the square brackets of menus, such as [New], can be changed with another message board command, namely, CHANGE. Here it is controlled by option 3, "CHANGE age selection," and the concept already is familiar to you. In Chapter 7, when we toured the National Bulletin Board, we pointed out that notices on the bulletin board were posted for two weeks, and when you searched the board you were routinely shown messages that were posted some time during that 14-day period. However, we also noted you could use the bulletin board's AGE command to narrow that period. If you wanted to confine your search to notices posted in the past two days, you could first use the AGE command to set the time frame to 2, then do the searching. In the forums, the CHANGE works in the same way, except that it has more powerful options and is even easier to use. If you select the CHANGE option, by entering 3 or the letters CHA, the system displays:

```
┌─────────────────────────────────────────────────────────┐
│                                                          │
│   Good Earth Forum Change Menu                           │
│                                                          │
│     1 [*] NEW messages                                   │
│     2 [ ] ALL messages                                   │
│     3 [ ] STARTING message number                        │
│     4 [ ] Number of DAYS                                 │
│                                                          │
│   Enter choice !                                         │
│                                                          │
└─────────────────────────────────────────────────────────┘
```

(Please move your bookmark to this menu.)

The asterisk represents the current setting. (As mentioned, after you read at least one message in a forum, the system automatically changes this variable from ALL to the NEW, and keeps that setting for all subsequent visits.) With this menu, you can change that setting manually. If you choose "ALL" by entering 2 or the word ALL and return to the main Messages menu, it would appear as:

```
Good Earth Forum Messages Menu

Message age selection = [All]

   1 SELECT (Read by section and subject)
   2 READ or search messages
   3 CHANGE age selection
   4 COMPOSE a message

Enter choice !
```

Now if you SELECT by section and subject, you collect messages from the entire board, not just those new ones posted since your last reading. This change affects another menu, too. The Read menu now would appear as:

```
Good Earth Forum Read Menu

Read
 1 [ALL] messages
 2 Message NUMBER
 3 WAITING messages for you (0)

Search [all] messages
 4 FROM (Sender)
 5 SUBJECT
 6 TO (Recipient)

Enter choice !
```

This simple CHANGE has far-reaching consequences. Option 1 doesn't collect only the newest messages by threads but *all* threads on the board, and options 4 through 6 now search the entire board, not just new messages.

Notice that option 3 on your bookmarked Change menu allows you to specify a STARTING message number. This feature gives you access to all public messages having a number greater than or equal to the number you specify.

The fourth CHANGE option — Number of DAYS — is particularly handy. It lets you zero in on messages posted within the number of days you specify. Suppose you want to look at messages that have been posted in the past two days. Selecting option 4 (or entering DAY) at the Change menu causes the system to prompt with "# of days" to which you enter 2. After that, the Read menu appears as:

```
Good Earth Forum Read Menu

Read
 1 [Within 2 DAYS]
 2 Message NUMBER
 3 WAITING messages for you (0)

Search [within 2 days]
 4 FROM (Sender)
 5 SUBJECT
 6 TO (Recipient)

Enter choice !
```

This revised menu makes it obvious that the CHANGE is limiting the messages, you read or search, to those posted within two days. Also, if you use the SELECT function on the main Messages menu, the threads collected are limited to those posted in the time limit you have specified.

Remember these two points about the CHANGE functions:

1. CHANGEs are in effect only for your current forum session. When you leave the forum or log off the system, the age option returns to NEW.
2. Except for the ALL setting, CHANGE *limits* the messages you can find, as if you have placed a grid over the material you want to see. That is why the setting is described in square brackets on a number of menus, simply to remind you of the grid presently in effect.

## Other Useful Reading Commands

Not all forum commands are listed on the menus. Here are some more specialized commands you can use.

For instance, speaking of imaginary *grids* that you can place over the message board, one command allows you to limit your reading and searching to a designated section or sections. It is the command SS, which means "Set Section." Entered at a prompt, the command causes the system to respond with something like this:

```
Currently selected: 1 2 3 4 5 6 7 8 10

Enter choice(s) :
```

This message means that you are currently reading messages on sections or subtopics 1 through 8 and on 10. Now you can enter the numbers of one or more sections (separated by commas). From then on, until you enter another SS command, all the messages you read or search will be from those on the designated sections only. When you log off, the system resets you sections to the original number.

**Note:**   Another command allows you to design sections permanently. (Permanently until you change your mind again). We shall learn about that command in the next chapter.

*But what if I forget the names of the sections used in the forum?*

Another useful command is NAME. Entered at a prompt, NAME causes the system to display something like this:

```
Good Earth Forum Names Menu

  1 Message sections
  2 Libraries
  3 Conference rooms

Enter choice !
```

As noted, forums can have different sections in the message board, data libraries, and conference areas, so the system is asking which names you need to see. If you enter 1, you are shown something like this:

```
Message Sections Available:

 1 Homesteading
 2 Vegetable Gardening
 3 Ornamental Gardens
 4 Herbology
 5 Folkways
 6 Nutrition
 7 Pets
 8 Help
10 General Information


Press <CR> !
```

Other commands offer various kinds of summary data about the messages on the board. Each of the following can be entered at the prompt that follows this Messages menu:

```
Good Earth Forum Messages Menu

Message age selection = [New]

 1 SELECT (Read by section and subject)
 2 READ or search messages
 3 CHANGE age selection
 4 COMPOSE a message

Enter choice !
```

BROWSE displays a summary of each message thread, one at a time, then prompts you to read the thread or continue to the next, like this one:

```
#30917 Mushroom Cultivation
  S 2 / Vegetable Gardening
  2 messages
Read? (Y or N) !
```

As the prompt indicates, you enter Y to read the messages in the thread or N to continue to the next thread BROWSE has found for you. Also you can enter X to end the BROwse session and return to the menu.

SCAN also can be entered at this menu to see the list of headers for each message filed on the post, for instance:

```
#: 30917 S2/Vegetable Gardening
     12-Jan-89  13:04:56
Sb: #Mushroom Cultivation
Fm: Paul Stenquist 73210,415
To: All

#: 31122 S2/Vegetable Gardening
     12-Jan-89  07:17:16
Sb: #30917-Mushroom Cultivation
Fm: Lynn Sherman 72057,55
To: Paul Stenquist 73210,415

#: 30927 S8/Help
     13-Jan-89  13:45:47
Sb: #FLEAS!
Fm: Judith F. Smedley 73310,2427
To: Dave Peyton 76703,244 (X)

#: 30952 S8/Help
     13-Jan-89  22:17:54
Sb: #30927-#FLEAS!
Fm: Doug Pratt (ModelNet) 76703,3041
To: Judith F. Smedley 73310,2427 (X)

etc.
```

SCAN QUICK displays a different kind of summary of message threads, listing their subjects, number of replies, etc., like this:

```
30917:  Mushroom Cultivation   S 2 / Vegetable Gardening
        1 reply

30927:  FLEAS!                 S 8 / Help
        4 replies

30929:  Cats and Rain          S 7 / Pets
        3 replies

31123:  Home Schooling         S 1 / Homesteading
```

Also, there are some additional reading commands that can be used at that "CHOICES" prompt that follows messages, the one that looks like this:

```
Press <CR> for next or type CHOICES !
```

They also can be entered at this Read Action menu, which we have also called the "CHOICES" menu:

```
Good Earth Forum Read Action Menu

  1 REPLY with same subject
  2 COMPOSE with new subject
  3 REREAD this message
  4 NEXT reply
  5 NEXT SUBJECT
  6 READ reply

Enter choice !
```

— MARK designates the message you have just read for later retrieval with the command READ MARKED. In other words, as you read the board, you can enter MARK at the prompt following selected messages. Then, later you can return to the Messages menu and enter the commands READ MARKED to see all the messages you have marked. (We have more to say about command sequences, like READ MARKED, later in this chapter.)

— ROOT displays the first message available in the current thread of messages.

— PARENT displays the "parent" or "owner" message of a reply.

— SCROLL causes the system to display the current batch of messages, consecutively, without your having to press the RETURN key between them. In other words, SCROLL causes the suppression of the "Press <CR> for next or type CHOICES !" prompt for the batch of message you are currently reading.

## Composing Messages on the Board

Two ways exist for you to get your own thoughts and words on the message board. The first is by composing original messages (thus starting your own thread or subject) and the second is by replying to other people's messages (thereby making your note part of an existing thread). This section covers original messages; the next covers two ways to make replies.

The last option listed on the forum's Messages menu is COMPOSE, enabling you to write an original message to post on the board. When you enter COM (or 4) at the prompt, the system displays:

```
Good Earth Forum Compose

Enter message. (/EXIT when done)
  1:
```

If this message looks familiar, it is because this is the same LINEDIT editing program you have used elsewhere on the system. It shows the number of the line you are on as you write. There is a limit to the length of your message: about 2,000 characters, but no more than 96 lines. Theoretically, each line can contain 138 characters, though message writers routinely press the RETURN key at the end of each screen line, usually 80 characters or less. Remember to use RETURN at the end of each line, like this:

```
1: Harry, <RETURN>
2: Sorry I missed the conference <RETURN>
3: last night. I didn't realize <RETURN>
4: 'til it was too late that I had <RETURN>
5: to stay late at the office. <RETURN>
6: /EXIT
```

Actually, forums have *both* CompuServe editing programs available, this line-numbered editor and the unnumbered EDIT editor that you used in Chapter 8. As a forum member, you can choose which of the editing programs you prefer, using an option that is discussed in the next chapter.

When you finish the message and close it with the /EXIT command, the system shows you a Post Action menu that lists these options:

```
Good Earth Forum Post Action Menu

  1 POST message on board
  2 EDIT message
  3 TYPE message
  4 MAIL via EasyPlex
  5 CANCEL message compose

Enter choice !
```

(Please move your bookmark to this menu.)

As the menu indicates, options 1, 4, and 5 take some final actions. Option 1 POSTs it on the message board; option 4 MAILs it via EasyPlex; option 5 is the bailout function, CANCELing the whole message if you respond affirmatively to this subsequent prompt:

```
Please confirm.
Do you wish to cancel
this message (Y or N)?
```

We shall come back to options 1 and 4 in a minute. However, you might want to use options 2 and 3 before you actually POST or MAIL anything. Option 2 allows you to edit your message. If you enter 2 or the letters EDI at the prompt, the system displays:

```
Good Earth Forum Edit Menu

 1 CHANGE characters in line
 2 REPLACE line
 3 DELETE line
 4 INSERT new line(s)
 5 TYPE all lines
 6 POST message on board

Enter choice !
```

These options are straightforward and the same as on LINEDIT menus elsewhere on the system. Note the options require that you supply line numbers. For instance, if you choose option 1 (CHANGE), the forum asks you for the number of the line you wish to change. For that reason, it is wise to use the TYPE command (option 5 on this menu or option 3 on the previous menu) to see your message with the existing line number, like this:

```
1: Harry,
2: Sorry I missed the conference
3: last night. I didn't realize
4: 'til it was too late that I had
5: to stay late at the office.
```

With that information, you can use options 1 through 4 here to CHANGE, DELETE, REPLACE, and INSERT lines.

Another command available but not shown here — PREview — allows you to see the message you are in exactly the way it will appear once you have posted it. The command also is often used to see how a message will appear in a specific screen width. For instance, to see how the message will appear to those with computers having a 32-character screen, you enter PREVIEW WIDTH:32.

**Note:** Obviously, references to line numbers applies only when you are using the line-numbered editor. If later on, after reading the material in the next chapter, you decide to switch to the unnumbered EDIT program, you no longer receive the forum Edit menu when you enter the EDIT command. Instead, the system simply reopens the message for editing and expects you to use those slash (/) commands we discussed in Chapter 8, such as /P to print the current line, /L/*string* to locate a word or phrase, and so forth. As you are new to forums, we suggest that for now you continue to use the line-numbered editor, because it provides many menus along the way. After you get comfortable with the forums in general, you might want to review the material on the unnumbered editor in Chapter 8 and in the On-line Survival Kit at the back of the book, then try it out. In the next chapter you will learn how to flip the editor switch to go from numbered to unnumbered lines.

Once you have your message edited the way you want it, you can put it on the message board by entering the word POST or choosing the corresponding numeral on the menu. The system then prompts with:

```
Post for (Name and/or User ID):
```

New subscribers sometimes misunderstand this prompt, possibly because of the "and/or" business. At a minimum you should enter the user ID number of the intended recipient. As an option, you also may enter the recipient's name on the same line. In other words, you could either:

```
Charlie Bowen 71635,1025 <RETURN>
```

or merely

```
71635,1025 <RETURN>
```

Either way, because you have supplied the user ID number, the forum now knows to mark the message for the recipient on their next visit to the forum. When the intended recipient logs in, the system will announce that your message is waiting. However, if you enter the name *without* the user ID number, the system won't know how to notify the recipient. Several ways exist to find user IDs and names. You saw one in the previous chapter, the MEMBER Directory. You also can find ID numbers and names on the message board itself by using the searching facilities to search the TO and FROM fields as illustrated earlier in this chapter.

There are two other ways you can reply to this "Post for (Name and/or User ID):" prompt. You may enter:

1. ALL if you are addressing the note to the entire membership.
2. SYSOP if you want the message marked for the forum's administrators. If you enter the word SYSOP, you don't have to supply a user ID number.

After you have filled in this blank, the system prompts for the subject of your message. The message can be a word or string of words, up to 24 characters and will appear in the "Sb:" line of the message header. You now know how important the subject lines are. They are used by members who are sorting and reading the message by threads. Because you are using the COMPOSE to create an *original* message (rather than a reply), you are also automatically creating a new thread on the board.

Finally, the system needs to know on what section or subtopic of the board to post your message, and displays a menu of the section names, like this:

```
SECTION # REQUIRED

 1 Homesteading
 2 Vegetable Gardening
 3 Ornamental Gardens
 4 Herbology
 5 Folkways
 6 Nutrition
 7 Pets
 8 Help
10 General Information

Enter choice !
```

Once you enter the number of the section which best describes your message's topic, the system posts your words of wisdom and reports the number it has assigned it.

The remaining option on the bookmarked Post menu allows you to MAIL your message from the forum to the recipient via EasyPlex. With it, your message does not appear on the board as a public pronouncement, but instead is privately sent to the recipient's electronic mailbox. With the option, you are prompted for the recipient's user ID number.

## Replying to a Message

Replying to messages is even easier than composing originals. To put it into perspective, here is a quick recap. We have seen that each message on the forum is followed by this prompt:

```
┌──────────────────────────────────────────────────────────┐
│                                                          │
│  Press <CR> for next or type CHOICES !                   │
│                                                          │
└──────────────────────────────────────────────────────────┘
```

When you enter CHOICES (or CHO) at this prompt, you are shown a Read Action menu, something like this:

```
┌──────────────────────────────────────────────────────────┐
│                                                          │
│  Good Earth Forum Read Action Menu                       │
│                                                          │
│   1 REPLY with same subject                              │
│   2 COMPOSE with new subject                             │
│   3 REREAD this message                                  │
│   4 NEXT reply                                           │
│   5 NEXT SUBJECT                                         │
│   6 READ reply                                           │
│   7 DELETE this message                                  │
│                                                          │
│  Enter choice !                                          │
└──────────────────────────────────────────────────────────┘
```

The first two options allow you to *answer* this message in different ways:

— The REPLY option sees to it that your message has the same subject line as the message you are answering — it also is in the same thread as the original. Because it is a reply, the system does not prompt you for a subject or a recipient after you are finished writing the message.

— The COMPOSE options allows you to answer someone on the board, and to specify a new subject line, thus starting a new thread of messages. Obviously, with this option, the system *does* prompt for the subject after you have finished composing.

*Why two ways to answer?*

It is frustrating to readers when a conversation ranges far from the original subject, as they sometimes can. So, when a subject prompts you to think of a brand new topic, you have the latter option available so you can start a new thread.

**Note:**   A shortcut! You don't really have to go all the way to the Read Action menu in order to use either the REPLY or COMPOSE options. Instead, you can enter the commands at the message prompt, like this:

```
┌──────────────────────────────────────────────────────────┐
│                                                          │
│  Press <CR> for next or type CHOICES ! REP <RETURN>      │
│                                                          │
└──────────────────────────────────────────────────────────┘
```

or

```
┌──────────────────────────────────────────────────────────┐
│                                                          │
│  Press <CR> for next or type CHOICES ! COM <RETURN>      │
│                                                          │
└──────────────────────────────────────────────────────────┘
```

This command causes the system to skip the Read Action menu and open the editing prompt for your words.


## Advanced Command Stacking in Forums

That last point should be a familiar concept by now — the idea of skipping menus by anticipating them with lettered commands — and the notion is even more valuable in the forums than anywhere else in the system. Many shortcuts are available by entering command *words* rather than option *numbers* when prompted. (We already have hinted at one such command stack when we noted that you could enter READ MARKED to find those messages previously designated with the MARK command.)

To get into the full swing of command stacking, you should start now by paying particular attention to the words in all caps on the forum messages — READ, SELECT, CHANGE, COMPOSE, etc. — and using them whenever possible (or their three-letter abbreviations) instead of the numbered options. This method will help you learn the command words. Some commands, particularly READ, can be used to leap past several layers of messages. For example, instead of selecting numeric options from four different menus just to read new messages on the board, an advanced forum member usually enters REA NEW at either the main menu or the Messages menu. Similarly, if you want to read messages posted over the past two days, you could do it, as we have seen, through menus, or you could link the commands by anticipating prompts with a sequence such as REA DAY 2.

The beauty of forum is that the same commands that can be used in the simplest form by numbered options on menus, can also be used for rather sophisticated operations. Best of all, the numbered menus actually serve as a teaching aid to illustrate the broad concepts. At the end of this chapter, we shall suggest another on-line practice session that can help you to begin thinking in terms of this advanced command stacking. The best way to learn is to go slowly; use the menus for now, but enter the words rather than the numbers and try to associate that word with the actual operation; this way should help you remember the command. Later you can begin regularly experimenting by linking frequently used sequences. We shall have tips on that in a moment.

## The Forum Boards' "Shorthand"

As you read messages in the forum that you are exploring, you will see that they often employ a kind of shorthand — abbreviations of frequently used words and phrases and odd acronyms that can be intimidating to the uninitiated. Here are some common abbreviations used in some forums:

| | |
|---|---|
| BBS: | Computer "bulletin board system," usually a private dialup service. |
| BCNU: | "Be seein' you." |
| BTW: | "By the way." |
| CIS: | CompuServe Information Service. |
| CO: | Conference, used to refer to real-time conferencing, either as a noun ("At the CO...") or a verb (EWhen we CO..."). |
| config: | configuration. |
| CU: | "See you," as in "CU tomorrow." |
| DBMS: | database management system. |
| FYI: | "For your information." |
| NBD: | "No big deal." |
| OIC: | "Oh, I see." |
| OTOH: | "On the other hand." |
| params: | parameters, that is, communications settings. |
| p.d.: | public domain. |
| PPN: | literally "Programmer Project Number," an old term for a CompuServe user ID number. |
| prog.: | program. |
| WizOp: | the primary (that is, *wizard*) sysop of a forum. |
| w.p.: | word processor. |
| WYSIWYG: | "What you see is what you get." |
| xfer: | transfer, as if file transfer. |

## Becoming a Good Guy

The message board is a powerful utility for asking questions but, of course, its success depends on your getting *answers*. You are most likely to get replies to your forum messages if you think before you type. Here are some tips from the Sadder-But-Wiser Department of Interpersonal Electronic Relationships:

1. *Leave public messages only when you really have something to say.* Boards often get inundated with one- and two-line replies that say only, "I agree" or "Haha... that's a good one" or perhaps a personal message of interest only to one other forum member. As we have seen, each forum message board holds a limited number of messages and each time a new one is posted, the oldest one is removed. It is always a shame when an old message that might be the beginning of a fascinating thread is sent to limbo by a new note that says nothing. So post messages publicly when they contribute to the discussion and are of general interest. For private communication, you should use EasyPlex.

2. *At the same time, you shouldn't be inhibited from asking questions publicly.* Most questions *are* of general interest. For every one questioner who speaks out, there are four or five wishing someone would ask it. Just remember to pick a good place to post the question — the appropriate subtopic of an appropriate forum. (Sysops have the capability to move a message from one subtopic to another, but they appreciate members who already are savvy enough to post it correctly in the first place.)

3. *Don't be a mass-mailer*, by posting the same message in a number of different forums. Your fellow subscribers often visit a number of forums, and it is inconsiderate if you make them come across an identical message on every board they visit. Just pick the one forum that best meets your needs for a specific question or comment.

4. *Research.* Sysops are used to answering the same questions over and over again, particularly when a new piece of major software or hardware is released or a forum project is under way. Repetition is part of the job. On the other hand, you do everyone a favor if you read a little before you write. If it is conceivable that your question already has been raised and answered recently, search, scan, or browse the board using the options discussed in this chapter. Also check in the data library (discussed in the next chapter); perhaps the forum has preserved a thread file that specifically addresses your question. If you don't find an answer on your own, you can raise the issue in a message. Be sure to ask if there is a library file you might have overlooked.

5. *Watch for your answers.* If you raise a question, be sure to check in again within at least 48 hours to see the replies. It is frustrating to those who take the time to answer a question if the questioner doesn't check back in time to read it before it scrolls off into oblivion. It is bad form to ask the members to answer your question again just because you didn't check back sooner.

6. Remember, *don't leave a message that says, "What's this forum all about?"* Find out for yourself. The sysops have put together special files outlining

their goals in the ANNOUNCEMENTS area. Check them to see what the forum's direction is.

7. Finally, *enjoy yourself!* All this talk of conventions and local customs may make the forums sound like stuffy, straight-laced outfits. They aren't. Most forums love good humor and camaraderie. Let your hair down and inject a little of your own personality into your messages. Introduce yourself. People always are interested in other people. You may find others on the forum who have similar backgrounds. After all, on the message boards, talk is what it is all about.

# Side Roads

Because the message board is such a vital part of the forums, you probably should take a break before starting the next chapter and review what you have learned in this one. Go on-line to stretch your new wings. We suggest you go back to Good Earth during the tour and try these things:

— Use the CHANGE command and set your age specification to "All" messages.

— With the READ command, you should search out messages addressed to specific ways. Find messages addressed to "All." Then look for specific subjects using partial or complete words for your search strings.

— Be on the look out for message to which you can send a brief reply or write an original message. At least send a message to the sysop introducing yourself. (Most sysops appreciate a brief message from new members. And if you send Dave a message saying you bought his book, you will brighten his day!)

— Especially become familiar with the concept of message *threads*. They are the key to your full enjoyment of the forum.

— Pay attention to the words in caps in the forum messages, and use them instead of the numbered options. This exercise will prepare you the next practice session.

You might want to try your commands in other forums as well. Here are three ways to find additional forums for exploration:

1. The FIND command lists forum when you enter FIND FORUMS at a "!" prompt.
2. You can enter G FORUMS which takes you to a menu of forum group, like this:

```
┌─────────────────────────────────────────────────────┐
│                                                       │
│   CompuServe                              FORUMS      │
│                                                       │
│    1 Aviation Forums                                  │
│    2 Education Forums                                 │
│    3 Science/Technology                               │
│    4 Entertainment/Games Forums                       │
│    5 Financial Forums                                 │
│    6 Hardware Forums                                  │
│    7 Media/Electronic Publishing                      │
│    8 Home/Health/Family Forums                        │
│    9 Professional Forums                              │
│   10 Software Forums                                  │
│   11 Sports Forums                                    │
│   12 Travel Forums                                    │
│                                                       │
│   Enter choice !                                      │
└─────────────────────────────────────────────────────┘
```

3.  You can jump ahead and peek at Chapter 14, which summarizes most of the forums on the system.

After that, you might want to begin to explore this idea of command stacking. Start off-line by reviewing the On-line Survival Kit at back of the book. Look at the section dealing with forum message board commands. There you will find a complete collection of commands for the forum in various constructions, illustrating how many commands can be followed by additional information.

# CHAPTER 13

# More About Forums — Data Libraries and More

Have you ever noticed that in most tutorial books sooner or later the authors take off the gloves and start giving you the advanced material with little or no sugar coating? We have come to that point. Actually, we won't throw you into the deep end and abandon you, but we are going to cover rather a lot of material in this chapter. Honestly, you probably aren't ready to employ some of the features we shall see this time. For instance, the chapter covers a feature called User Options that lets you turn off the forum menus and run in expert mode. If you have just started looking into these forums, you aren't ready to be an expert — the menus probably still seem quite acceptable. However, in keeping with our goal to help you customize CompuServe to your own liking, we want you to know where these high-level features are so you can use them when you decide the time is right. On the other hand, other features we shall see now — especially the powerful options of the data libraries — can be put to use right away.

## Reaching the Data Libraries

Make yourself comfortable, we don't need to go on-line for this chapter. Just imagine you have logged on, gone to the Good Earth Forum (G GOODEARTH), and reached the main menu:

```
r---------------------------------------------------------7
i                                                          i
i  Good Earth Forum Menu                                   i
i                                                          i
i    1 INSTRUCTIONS                                        i
i    2 MESSAGES                                            i
i    3 LIBRARIES (Files)                                   i
i    4 CONFERENCING (0 participating)                      i
i    5 ANNOUNCEMENTS from sysop                            i
i    6 MEMBER directory                                    i
i    7 OPTIONS for this forum                              i
i                                                          i
i  Enter choice !                                          i
L---------------------------------------------------------J
```

If the message board is the forum's day-to-day communications, then the data libraries are its archives; the repository where sysops and forum members store articles and programs of lasting interest to the group. You reach the libraries from the main menu with the third option, entering LIB (or 3), to which the forum responds with its list of library sections or subtopics, something like this:

```
r---------------------------------------------------------7
i                                                          i
i  Good Earth Forum Libraries Menu                         i
i                                                          i
i  Libraries Available:                                    i
i                                                          i
i    1 Homesteading                                        i
i    2 Vegetable Gardening                                 i
i    3 Ornamental Gardens                                  i
i    4 Herbology                                           i
i    5 Folkways                                            i
i    6 Nutrition                                           i
i    7 Pets                                                i
i    8 Help                                                i
i   10 General Information                                 i
i                                                          i
i  Enter Choice !                                          i
L---------------------------------------------------------J
```

(As we saw in the previous chapter, you also can retrieve this list from a prompt by entering the command NAMES, then selecting the appropriate option from the subsequent menu.)

Like the message board, the library can be partitioned into some 18 subtopics. Often the names of the library subtopics are identical to those on the message board, but they don't *have* to be; sysops may create library subtopics with subjects that are entirely different from those on the message board.

At this prompt, you need to specify which subtopic you want. Suppose you choose the first subtopic and enter 1 at the prompt; the system now says:

```
Good Earth Forum Library 1

Homesteading

 1 BROWSE thru files
 2 DIRECTORY of files
 3 UPLOAD a new file
 4 DOWNLOAD a File
 5 LIBRARIES

Enter choice !
```

More time-saving tips:

— If you are sitting at the main menu and already know which data library you want, you can bypass the listed subtopic names by linking the commands, as simply LIB 1.

— Also that command-linking can be used inside the libraries as well. For instance, if you are currently viewing LIBrary 1 and you want to move to LIBrary 5 ... right you are! Enter LIB 5.

The commands on this menu seem straight-forward enough. Some already are familiar to us. We learned about UPLoad and DOWNload in Chapter 9. We used a DIRectory command in the Personal File Area. And BROwse isn't completely foreign to us, either, is it? We used a BROwse command back on the National Bulletin Board and a different BROswe command on the forum message board in the previous chapter. You will find BROwse works in a similar way here in the libraries.

## Looking at Files

Suppose you enter BRO (or 1) and answer the prompts this way:

```
Enter keywords (e.g. modem)
or <CR> for all: FARM <RETURN>

Oldest files in days
or <CR> for all: <RETURN>
```

In other words, we enter the word FARM at the first prompt and leave the second prompt ("oldest files") blank. Now, the system searches in the keyword area of each file for the string, FARM, and then displays the most recent file found, such as:

```
[76703,244]
SMLFRM.TXT        12-Dec-84 7340       69

     Keywords: SMALL FARM COMMERCIAL

     An article from The Wall Street
     Journal about a man who says
     a farmer with only 25 acres can
     gross 100,000 a year if he thinks
     less about tractors and more about
     marketing.

     Press <CR> for next or type CHOICES !
```

This display provides the user ID number of the person who uploaded the file, the file name, and the date it was uploaded, followed by the size of the file in bytes (7,340 or about 7.3K in our example). The last figure, 69, is the number of times the file has been retrieved. If this is a large number, it is a pretty good indication that the file has been popular. However, a small number doesn't necessarily mean it is a less popular file. That's because the number of downloads is reset to zero when a sysop edits or moves the file from one library to another. Thus, the number can be misleading and shouldn't be used alone in judging whether a text file or a program is "a good one." There is a better way; just read the keywords and brief description, which were written by the person who uploaded the file, to see if it strikes your fancy.

Now, let's see what "CHOICES" are available from this prompt. If you enter CHO, you see:

```
┌──────────────────────────────────────────────────────┐
│                                                        │
│  Good Earth Forum Library Disposition                  │
│                                                        │
│  1 READ this file                                      │
│  2 DOWNLOAD this file                                  │
│  3 RETURN to library menu                              │
│                                                        │
│  Enter choice or <CR> for next !                       │
│                                                        │
└──────────────────────────────────────────────────────┘
```

This isn't very mysterious, is it? You have four alternatives:

1.  If the file is text (ASCII) — identified either by the description and/or a ".TXT" extension, as in our example — you might want to REAd it (option 1). Subsequently, you can stop and start the display with CONTROL S and CONTROL Q as you have elsewhere in the system. If you want to discontinue reading it, CONTROL P interrupts the displays and returns you to a prompt.
2.  If the description indicates that the file is binary, such as a program written to run on your kind of computer, you might want to DOWnload it onto a disk. After you entered the DOW command, you are shown a familiar menu that prompts you to identify a file transfer protocol, such as CompuServe's B Protocol, Xmodem, or Kermit. After you select one, simply follow the downloading procedure outlined in Chapter 9.
3.  If you want to see if the system has found another file for you, press RETURN, as the bottom line says. (The list produced by the BRO command always is in reverse chronological order, meaning the most recent files are listed first.)
4.  Or you can stop BROwsing and return to the Library menu by entering the letters RET or the word RETURN (*not* the RETURN *key*, of course).

Some points about BROwse:

— The display sometimes is interrupted with a "paging" prompt that says, "MORE !" at which you need to press the RETURN key to continue. Some users like to eliminate this prompt and let the BROwsed information scroll uninterrupted. There are two ways to do it: (1) enter the S navigation command (S for "scroll") at the first "MORE !" prompt, or (2) at the "LIB prompt," enter SET PAGE OFF, which, as you saw in Chapter 9, eliminates all paging functions for the current session. With paging turned off, you still can control the display with control keys: CONTROL S and CONTROL Q to freeze and "unfreeze" the display, CONTROL P to interrupt the display and return to the previous prompt. To turn paging back on, enter SET PAGE ON.

— BRO's file descriptions can be misleading. Sometimes a file's description says, "Download with XMODEM." Does that mean it can't be downloaded with another error-checking technique, such as B Protocol or Kermit? Not at all. *Any* file transfer protocol can be used, so long as (1) it is supported by CompuServe (that is, listed on the menu), (2) it is supported by your *own* communications program, (3) you make the appropriate menu selection to tell CompuServe which protocol you intend to use, and (4) you follow the correct command sequence in your own terminal program to initiate the download with the specified protocol.

## Directory for a Quicker List

BROwse isn't the only option available for seeing file names. Let's look again at the main Library menu:

```
Good Earth Forum Library 1

Homesteading

  1 BROWSE thru files
  2 DIRECTORY of files
  3 UPLOAD a new file
  4 DOWNLOAD a File
  5 LIBRARIES

  Enter choice !
```

Option 2, DIRectory, is similar to BROwse, except that it gives only the file names (no descriptions) and doesn't stop after each name to present a disposition menu. If you enter DIR (or 2) at the prompt, you see a directory something like this:

```
 [71340,2503]
 APPROV.TXT        18-Dec-88 8704
 CHANGE.TXT        17-Dec-88 2688

 [71066,1443]
 WOOD.COM          01-Jan-89 12120     1

 [76703,244]
 PICKLE.TXT        05-Jan-89 5685      5
 WINEMK.TXT        05-Jan-89 6490      6
```

And so on. DIR is handy, but... uh, questions?

*You bet! How do I go about downloading or reading these files if there's no stopping for a "CHOICES" prompt after each one, as there is with the BROwse command?*

The answer is one you probably anticipated. At the prompt, you enter REA or DOW followed by the file name, such as REA APPROV.TXT and DOW WOOD.COM. In other words, you can use DIR for a quick look at the files, note the file name or names you want, return to the LIB prompt, and use the REA or DOW command. There is another handy way to use DIR by linking it with another command, as we will see in the next section.

## Command Linking with Switches

This latest idea — using the REAd or DOWnload command followed by a file name — is, of course, another example command linking, which we talked about in the previous chapter. Here in the Libraries, BROwse is a particularly powerful command when it is linked with other information. Suppose you want to search a library for any files with RECIPES as a keyword. The long way is to enter BRO, then wait for the system to prompt you to enter a keyword; the fast way is to link the command, bypassing that menu and getting right down to business by entering:

```
┌─────────────────────────────────────────────────┐
│                                                 │
│   BRO KEY:RECIPES                               │
│                                                 │
└─────────────────────────────────────────────────┘
```

Here is a variation on that theme, one that is popular with devoted forum-hoppers. Suppose it has been five days since you visited the libraries of your favorite forum. You could access each library and enter this linked command:

```
┌─────────────────────────────────────────────────┐
│                                                 │
│   BRO AGE:5                                     │
│                                                 │
└─────────────────────────────────────────────────┘
```

That message means, "Show me everything that has been added to this library in the past five days."

Such linking of commands is done with a space followed by a *switch* (AGE: and KEY: both are called "switches"), followed by the additional information. You can even link a specification for a transfer protocol when downloading, using a command such as DOW GAME.BAS PROTO:B. (Of course, if you use a transfer method other than CompuServe's B Protocol, you would specify *it* after the PROTO: switch, as in DOW GAME.BAS PROTO:XMODEM.)

Another switch — DES (for "description") — is useful with the DIRectory command we just discussed. You can enter DIR DES to receive a description with the file names. It can be added to other switches, too, as in DIR DES KEY:BASIC. (Of course, DES is *not* needed with BRO, as the BROwse command already produces file descriptions.)

*But why use DIR DES when you can use BRO for file descriptions?*

Some users don't like the way BRO pauses with the CHOICES prompt between each file name and description. Instead, they want a nonstop list of file names and descriptions. For them, the command of choice is DIR with a description switch, such as DIR DES AGE:1. The DIR DES command link will list all the files without prompting the user between each one.

**Note:**　As you will see in the next section, the KEY: switch actually can take *more than one* keyword. Because of that, it is wise to always use the DES statement immediately following the DIR command. For instance, DIR DES KEY:MEMORY is recommended instead of DIR KEY:MEMORY DES. (In the latter example, the system would try to find files with keywords of "memory" and "des.")

## Wildcards and Connectors

You can use "wildcards" with the BRO command when you are searching particularly large libraries. Some computer hobbyist forums have literally thousands of articles and public-domain programs on-line. Suppose you wanted to BROwse to find all of the BASIC game programs submitted in the past 30 days. As most forums use .BAS as the extension for BASIC programs, you might enter:

```
BRO *.BAS KEY:GAMES AGE:30
```

The asterisk (*) is the wildcard. This command tells the system to check all files with the extension of .BAS and display a description if they (1) have a keyword of "GAMES" and (2) have an age of 30 days or less.

Because of the way CompuServe uses the asterisk for wildcards, you can search file names in some interesting ways. Suppose you are looking for telecommunications programs and you want to find files with keywords of "telecommunications," "telecommunicate," or "telecomputing," etc. — that is, any keyword beginning with "TELECOM-." To do that, you enter DIR KEY:TELECOM* or BRO KEY:TELECOM*.

In addition, wildcards don't have to be at the end of a phrase. KEY:*XYZ finds files that include keywords ending in "XYZ"; KEY:*XYZ* finds those with keywords containing the letters "XYZ" somewhere in the middle. They also can be used in the file names. If you had heard of a program in a library called "MEMORY," but didn't know the extension, you could use BRO MEMORY.* or DIR MEMORY.* to find "MEMORY.BAS" and "MEMORY.BIN," "MEMORY.ASC," etc.

Another wildcard — the question mark — can be used to limit the number of characters in a search phrase. BRO TEST?.TXT would find "TEST1.TXT," "TEST8.TXT," and "TESTB.TXT," but not "TESTER.TXT" or "TEST10.TXT." The ? is a wildcard for one space only. More than one question mark also can be used, as in BRO TEST??.TXT.

As mentioned, you also can search for files that contain more than one keyword. If you wanted to find BASIC programs dealing with memory checking, you might enter BRO KEY:MEMORY BASIC. (A space means the connector "AND.") Only files that contain *both* the keywords BASIC and MEMORY are shown. You can mix and match these options in some pretty nifty ways, such as: BRO MEM*.* AGE:2 or BRO AGE:5 KEY:DBASE HELP.

Keywords help you search libraries quickly so CompuServe provides an easy way to determine if a particular keyword is in use. It is the KEY command, similar to the KEYWORD command you used in the National Bulletin Board. At a library prompt, you can enter KEY: followed by a word, and the system reports back with the number of files containing that keyword. Then you can follow up with a DIR or a BRO command. You also can get a complete list of *all* keywords used in a particular subtopic by entering KEY <RETURN> (that is, KEY with no specified search word). However, that could produce a long, long list. It is smarter to use a wildcard, such as KEY:TELECOM* to get a report on how many files contain a keyword that begins with those letters.

## Seeing the World by Extensions

A moment ago, we pointed out that most forum libraries use the extension .BAS to denote a BASIC program and the extension .TXT to mean a text file. Names of library files are assigned by the people who upload them (though a sysop can modify a file name before including the material in a subtopic). As noted earlier, file names can have up to six letters and a three-letter extension. In addition to .BAS and .TXT, some other extensions have particular meanings in most forum libraries, for example:

.ASC means ASCII format. Sometimes this extension is used instead of .TXT to indicate text files. It also sometimes is used to indicate a BASIC program saved in ASCII rather than tokenized BASIC. Like any ASCII file, it can be viewed on-line by entering the REAd command at a LIB prompt, or can be downloaded for reading off-line.

.DOC stands for documentation, that is, the instructions for a particular program. Also sometimes used are .MAN for users manual and .INS for instructions. Nearly always .DOC, .MAN, and .INS have been saved in ASCII. Often the extensions are used in connection with another file of a similar name. MEMORY.BAS might be the program, whereas MEMORY.DOC might contain the instructions. Documentation files often contain a general discussion of the program in the first pages, so if you are uncertain about whether a program meets your needs, you might use the REAd command to examine the first part of the file on-line.

.HLP, "Help." These extensions usually are ASCII files written by the sysops that contain answers to commonly asked questions.

.INF, "information." Usually, this extension is an ASCII file containing background information on a topic.

.THD or .THR stands for thread. Important discussions from a forum's message board often are stored in the library with such an extension.

.CNF or .CO or .CON, a conference transcript, discussions that occurred in the real-time conferencing section of the system, saved in ASCII.

.FIX, a file that corrects an error. It might refer to a specific program (MEMORY.FIX might apply to MEMORY.BAS), or it might be a general article with programming tips.

.PAT, "patch," a bit of programming that can be incorporated in another file to change the program.

.BIN means this file is a program in "binary," that is, a machine-language program; should be downloaded with error-checking. **Note:** .BIN isn't used much in the some forums. The sysops sometimes encourage users to upload files with their "correct" extensions, such as .COM or .EXE in the IBM world, instead of .BIN. Also .IMG (for image) is used in some computer-specific forums.

.ASM, a source code listing for an editor/assembler.

## Compressed Files

The most common file extension in many forums these days is *not* on the above list. Instead, it is .ARC or .LBR or .PIT or .SIT, extensions that *file compression*, and to understand that, we need some background.

Software development is more sophisticated today than it was five years ago. Today's public domain and shareware programs often are much longer, taking advantage of the larger memories in our computers. Sometimes, instead of a single program, good software actually is an integrated *system* that requires several linked programs and data files to interact on the same task. This integration used to cause big headaches for sysops and forum members, because one word processing program or complex spreadsheet or communications program might be represented by not one, but four or five lengthy files in a library. This variation made downloading — particularly for those new to on-line communications — complicated.

Fortunately, in the mid-1980s, the on-line programming wizards rode to our rescue. These days, many forums use one or more file compression methods for these large software systems. The new utility programs the wizards came up with solved the problem of long, multiple files by performing two vital operations. They:

1. Pack together several programs into *one* large file.
2. Then "squeeze" (that is, compress) the file as tightly as possible — sometimes up to 50 percent — to prepare it for uploading to the library.

This idea of packed/squeezed files saves other forum members downloading time and, of course, also saves space in the library — one tightly compacted file, rather than four or five files can be contributed to the library. A file that has been uploaded in a compressed format appears in the library with a special extension. In the world of IBM and IBM compatibles, the extension often is ".ARC" (meaning "archived") and, less frequently these days, ".LBR" (meaning "libraried"). In the Apple Macintosh community, the extension is often ".SIT" or ".PIT," referring to files compressed with the Stuffit and Packit programs.

In BROwsing libraries, when you find files with such a special extension, remember to:

1. Download the file with an error-checking protocol (B Protocol, Xmodem, or Kermit).
2. Be prepared to unpack it and unsqueeze it off-line. Of course, for the second step, you will need unarchiving software tools. Almost always, those utilities are available for downloading in same forum in which you found the compressed file. Check with the sysops for specifics.

The concept of file compression has achieved widest acceptance in the IBM world with .ARC-extension files. The IBM New Users Forum (G IBMNEW) has Library 2 set aside for "Data Library Tools." A file in that library called ARC-E.COM should be downloaded for unARCing files. The instructions are in the same library in an ASCII file called ARC-E.DOC, which explains how to use the utility.

**Note:**   The spread of archiving in the MS-DOS world has been a source of consternation among some other computer users. Suddenly, contents of these files (many of which are informational text files, not binary) were no longer accessible, because their non-IBM computers could not run the "deARCer" programs needed to extract the files. However, now wizards in other parts of the computing world have risen to the challenge, developing utilities for unarchiving the contents of IBM ARC'ed files on non-IBM systems. Obviously, this development won't enable an non-MS-DOS Atari to run a program written for an IBM or IBM compatible, but it will open the door to plain vanilla ASCII files that have been ARC'ed. Such non-IBM unpackers/unsqueezers now are found in at least three forums. For users of CP/M systems, there is UNAR16.COM in the CP/M Forum's Library 2 (G CPMFORUM). Members of the Macintosh Personal Productivity Forum (G MACPRO) have a number of de-ARCers to select from in Library 8, including a favorite called ARCPOP.BIN. Atari ST owners can use ARC.TTP in Library 3 of the Atari 16-bit Forum (G ATARI16); the instructions are in ARC.DOC.

# Contributing to the Database

Now that you know the ins and outs of downloading, uploading will be a snap. It is essentially downloading in reverse.

Suppose you have written a text file or a program. You have edited it and polished it, and now you are ready to share it with the world. The first decision is what forum in which to share it and to which of the forum's libraries should it be uploaded. In many forums, specific libraries are reserved for new uploads. Almost always the name of the library — listed with the NAMES command — will tip you off. If the forum doesn't have a library specifically for new uploads, then chose the library subtopic whose subject most closely fits your contribution. After that, make a quick field trip to the prospective forum. Peek into the library subtopics and, with the BROwse or DIRectory command and the KEY: switch, get an idea of the kind of files stored there.

**Note:**   Many busy forums request that all files over a specific length be compressed (packed and squeezed) before uploading, using an archiving utility similar to those discussed in the previous section. Check the ANNOUNCEMENTS section of the forum for details, including where to find the necessary utilities for the packing. If in doubt, consult the sysop.

When you are ready for the actual upload, two methods are available: (1) simply selecting options from menus, and (2) entering a command string that bypasses the menus by anticipating the prompt. We shall look at the menu-driven approach first, in order to see what's going on. Then we shall see the preferred (i.e., faster) command string method.

To have menus available to guide you in uploading, simply enter the command UPL (for UPLoad) at the "LIB" prompt.

The only problem you might encounter at this point is that sometimes a subtopic already is full. If so, you will receive a message that there is not enough room for new files. You might then post a short note to the sysop, advising him or her of the situation. The sysop probably will get back to you when the space situation improves.

Assuming space is available, the system asks you to enter the file name as you want it to appear in the library (up to six letters plus a three-letter extension). You can use a combination of letters and numbers, as long as the first character is a letter. Also check the ANNOUNCEMENTS area to see if the forum has preferred extensions to certain kinds of data.

After entering the file name, you need to tell the system which transfer protocol you want to use for the upload, by picking an option from the usual menu:

```
Library Protocol Menu

Transfer protocols available -

 1 XMODEM (MODEM7) protocol
 2 CompuServe 'B' protocol
 3 CompuServe 'A' protocol
 4 DC4/DC2 CAPTURE protocol
 5 Kermit protocol
 6 CompuServe Quick 'B' protocol
 0 Abort transfer request

Enter choice !
```

As always, you need to make sure that the communications program you are using supports the protocol you specify from the menu. (For uploading program — binary — files, you can use any of these options except number 4. As discussed in Chapter 9, DC2/DC4 CAPTURE is an ASCII dump, and provides no error-checking.)

After determining which protocol you are planning to use, the system sometimes asks, "File name for your computer:.." In other words, what is the name of the file you want to upload as it exists on your disk? If you are using a two-drive floppy disk system, you should specify the drive on which the file resides, as in "B:TEST.TXT". If you are using a hard disk, you should specify the path to the file if it is not on the currently addressed subdirectory.

Finally, CompuServe needs to know the format of the file and displays this important menu:

```
Transfer types available -

 1 ASCII  (7 - bit)
 2 Binary (8 - bit)
 3 Graphic:RLE
 4 Graphic:NAPLPS
 5 Graphic:GIF

Enter choice !
```

These are the same file types we saw in Chapter 9 in the discussion of uploading. The system is asking simply in what format the file should be *saved* in the library. Note that error-checking can be used to transmit files to be saved in any format. The biggest mistake new users make at this point, is uploading a binary file and having it saved on-line in ASCII format. You can avoid mistakes like that, if you keep in mind that your file should be saved:

— In *ASCII*, if it is something that should be readable by the users while they are on-line with the REA command and if it is already saved in ASCII format on *your* disk.

— In *binary*, if it is a program (machine language or a "tokenized" BASIC file) or if it is a compressed file (.ARC, .LBR, .PIT, .SIT) as discussed in the previous section.

So, we would have HOTONE.COM, a program, saved in binary form; we would have HOTONE.DOC, the instructions, saved as an ASCII file; and if the whole package were squeezed and packed into HOTONE.ARC, we would have it saved in binary.

Regarding the other options, "Graphics" pertains to files containing data for high-resolution pictures that can be displayed on-line. We shall be talking about graphics in Chapter 19.

Once familiar with the uploading procedure, you probably will prefer using the faster *command linking* approach, which allows you to bypass menus by using additional information with a PROTO: switch. Suppose you are uploading a text file called HOTONE.DOC using B Protocol and you want it saved on CompuServe in ASCII. You could enter at the library prompt:

```
UPL HOTONE.DOC PROTO:B TYPE:ASCII <RETURN>
```

This command supplies all the anticipated information: PROTOcol B and file TYPE ASCII. If it were a program to be saved as a binary file and you were using XMODEM to transmit, the commands would be strung together as:

```
UPL HOTONE.COM PROTO:XMODEM TYPE:BIN
```

Options available after the PROTO: switch are B, KERMIT, XMODEM, and CAPTURE. (CAPTURE is offered for the ASCII dump.) Following the TYPE:

switch, you can enter BIN (for binary), ASCII, GIF, or RLE. (Actually, the command string can be abbreviated even further to just the first three letters of each element, as in UPL HOTONE.COM PRO:XMO TYP:BIN.)

When you have answered all the system's questions, either through menus or command linking with switches, the upload begins. The operation is virtually the same as a download, except, of course, that your machine now is the sender and CompuServe is doing the listening.

## Keywords and Descriptions

When the upload is complete, the system notifies you with a message about how long the transfer took, then prompts you for the keywords you wish placed on your file when it is made public. Select keywords carefully. Because you now know how valuable they are when you are searching libraries, choose brief keywords that describe the uniqueness of your file and consider several words that describe the same thing. If it is an accounting program, you might use ACCOUNTING, BUSINESS, STATISTICS, etc. You may enter up to 132 characters worth of keywords.

After that, the system requests a description (in up to 500 characters). Tell the users what, if any, additional files are needed, with a line such as, "You will find the instructions in the file called HOTONE.DOC." Also, include a summary of system requirements — color graphics card, hard disk, etc. A good convention recently instituted in some forums is to include specific information about the file in the last lines, like this:

```
Shareware. DL via protocol. Unpack with ARC-E (8-bit)
-Uploader/Author: (your name)
```

Of course, if you are not the author, the last line should say "Uploaded by:" followed by your name, and the description should say who is the author, if known. Of course, even if you leave off this line, interested fellow members can find you through the user ID that will appear with the file, but it is nice to also have a real name associated with it.

When you have finished with the description, press RETURN on a new line. The system then displays what you have written as keywords and as a description and asks you to confirm it. If you reply that they are incorrect (that is, if you enter an N at this point), you are asked to reenter the keywords and description. When everything is okay, the file is "copied" into the library, but it won't be made public immediately. All new files are flagged for the sysops' review. If the file came through properly, the sysops then will "merge" it into the library; if they discover a problem, you will receive word, either on the board or via EasyPlex.

# Good Citizenship and Uploading

That is the technique of uploading to forums, but that is not the whole story; there also are some *citizenship* points that should be made. Because so many people now contribute to databases, we can make CompuServe a better electronic world if we pay attention to these tips, made by many sysops over the years.

### Before You Upload

Is your text edited? Is the program debugged? Perhaps you should look it over again or run the program through its paces a few days to get the kinks out. Some people think that because they are *giving away* the text or their original program, they have no obligation to edit. No legal obligation, to be sure. On the other hand, if you appreciate it when software you download works as described, you should be inspired to reach the same standard. Naturally, when a number of people start using your program, they may find obscure bugs, but they will be happy that you already have swatted the big ones.

Is the program annotated? Whether it is a BASIC program or an assembly language source code, users are pleased when you take time to include remarks and comments in the listing to explain what is going on.

Is the program documented? Beyond the imbedded comment lines, have you written users instructions? Most good library programs are accompanied by documentation, uploaded with the .DOC extension. It doesn't have to be long; some of the most sophisticated programs have only a page or two of instructions that say simply do this and then this and then this... and so on. Here are some tips for preparing instructions: (1) Write the file off-line with your word processor and, at the top, insert a sentence or two that describes what the program does. (2) At the beginning include details of any special requirements for the program, such as a printer, additional memory, color graphics, and so forth. Briefly summarize how to use the program in step-by-step examples, if possible, just as if you were telling a friend who was sitting beside you at the keyboard. (3) At the end, remind the reader of your user ID number, so you can be reached through EasyPlex or on the message board with comments or questions. (4) When the documentation is completed, save it from your word processor *in ASCII*, just as if you were saving a note for later transmission to the message board. You now know why the concern about ASCII; if it isn't saved in plain vanilla ASCII, the downloaders won't be able to read it.

A final question concerns just *how free* your program should be. Not all programs in the libraries are public domain. Some are shareware, that is, the author gives us his or her original software, putting us on our honor to make a suggested "donation" if we like it and intend to use it regularly. Should you plan to make the same appeal for funding from those who use your creation? It is your call. All good programming should be rewarded, with praise certainly, and sometimes with cold hard cash. The shareware phenomenon is a laudable, positive movement in software creation. At the same time, though, it is not in the spirit of these libraries to have *everything* carry a price tag. The libraries are intended mainly for the distribution of the public domain works. If your program is unique and you sincerely think you ought to be compensated, by all means, place it in shareware. That is what it's all about. However, if in doubt, don't.

### After the Upload

When the file has been uploaded, you might enjoy checking in to the library from time to time to see how many people have downloaded it. One of the pieces of information reported by a BRO or DIR command is the number of times the file has been retrieved.

Make yourself available after you have uploaded a file to field questions or comments. Some users may even want to make some revisions of their own. That could be the beginning of a new on-line friendship, as you obviously have found someone with similar interests.

Also, if you later revise your work and want to replace the original, communicate with the sysops. In some forums, the members themselves are asked to erase the old file. Just visit the appropriate subtopic and enter ERA (for "erase") followed by the name of the file — and then upload the new one. (Of course, you can erase only files that you yourself uploaded in the first place.) The file isn't erased immediately; the request goes to sysops for approval. In other forums, the sysops like to handle all erasures themselves. Check with the administrators to determine the local customs.

## Having it Your Way with User Options

Let's switch gears now to look at another part of the forums. Since Chapter 11, we have pointed out shortcuts and time-saving tips for forums, but we have saved the biggest potential time-saver for last, namely, the OPTIONS features. As you recall, it is the last numbered item on the main menu:

```
r----------------------------------------------------------------
|
| Good Earth Forum Menu
|
| 1 INSTRUCTIONS
|
| 2 MESSAGES
| 3 LIBRARIES (Files)
| 4 CONFERENCING (0 participating)
| 5 ANNOUNCEMENTS from sysop
| 6 MEMBER directory
| 7 OPTIONS for this forum
|
| Enter choice !
|
L----------------------------------------------------------------
```

If you enter OPTIONS (or 7 or OPT) at this prompt, the system takes you to a new, powerful area of the system with an introductory menu that looks like this:

```
r----------------------------------------------------------------
|
| Good Earth Forum Options Menu
|
| FORUM OPTIONS
|  1 INITIAL menu/prompt [Forum]
|  2 Forum MODE [MENU*]
|
| MESSAGES OPTIONS
|  3 PAUSE after messages [Always]
|  4 NAME [Charlie Bowen]
|  5 Prompt CHARACTER []
|  6 EDITOR [LINEDIT*]
|  7 SECTIONS [...]
|  8 HIGH msg read [32007]
|  9 REPLIES info [Count]
| 10 TYPE waiting msgs [NO]
| 11 SKIP msgs you left [NO]
|
| Enter choice !
|
L----------------------------------------------------------------
```

(Please bookmark this page, for we shall return.)

To understand the importance of OPTIONS. let's briefly recall two ideas from earlier discussions. First, in Chapter 9 we took a quick trip into a part of the system called Profile, which stores *defaults* for displays throughout the entire system. Of course, so far we have used Profile very sparingly — only to set screen widths and upper and lowercase — but we have made a date to look at the area in much greater detail in a later chapter. Second, we have commented about how forums are a microcosm of CompuServe itself. In that sense, this OPTIONS area does for a forum what Profile does for the system as a whole, that is, it allows you to make choices that determine how forum information is delivered to your screen.

Notice, too, that the OPTIONS menu uses another convention with which we now are accustomed: it sets off in square brackets the *current settings* (that is, defaults) for each of its 11 options, such as "[Forum]" in the first item. By the way, the asterisks beside some of these settings — such as Forum MODE [MENU*] — indicates the forum is using a setting defined in your Profile area. More about that in Chapter 19.

## Forum Options

As the menu subheadings tell you, the first two options here determine aspects of the forum structure itself, where it should put its front door and how it should look inside.

*Option 1*, INITIAL menu/prompt, tells the system at what point you want to enter this forum. Right now, the front door of this forum — the default, as specified in the brackets — is the main forum menu that we have seen all along. However, you can have it your own way. Suppose you have changed your mind and now, when you enter G GOODEARTH, you want the next menu you see to be, not the main menu, but the Message menu, or the Libraries menu or the Conferencing menu. If you enter INITIAL, INI or 1 at the prompt, the system gives you this list:

```
Good Earth Forum Initial Menu

   1 Forum
   2 Messages
   3 Libraries
   4 Conferencing

Enter choice !
```

Now you indicate with a number where you want the *starting point* to be in this particular forum. For instance, if you select option 3, you are telling the system that from now on when you log into Good Earth Forum, you want to begin in the Libraries with that menu.

*Option 2*, Forum MODE, is more powerful; it determines whether you are shown full menus or abbreviated prompts in this forum. Earlier we noted that some experienced forum users turn off most menus and run in a kind of expert mode. This option makes that possible. If you enter 2 (or MODE) at the prompt, the system displays:

```
Good Earth Forum Mode Menu
Forum mode is MENU

 1 Use PROFILE setting
 2 MENU
 3 COMMAND

Enter choice :
```

Three settings are possible: (1) MENU — the current setting, which allows detailed menus, (2) COMMAND — or abbreviated expert mode, and (3) a setting retrieved from the Profile area of the system. (Again, we look at Profile in depth in Chapter 19.) If you change this variable to COMMAND mode by entering COM or 3 at the prompt, the entire look of the forum changes. No longer are you presented with full numbered menus at every turn in this forum, instead you see abbreviated prompts such as:

```
Forum !
```

or

```
Message !
```

or

```
Libraries !
```

etc.

Instead of selecting numbered alternatives from a menu, you are expected to remember the letters of the commands you want to use (REA NEW to Read New messages, SELECT to chose sections, and threads, etc.).

You probably aren't ready to make a full switch to abbreviated prompts, but you *are* ready to experiment. At the end of the previous chapter, we suggested you take a field trip to the forums to experiment on your own with READ commands, using both the numeric options and the letter commands as exhibited in the chapter and in the On-line Survival Kit at the back of the book. That experience lays the groundwork for getting by without menus. At the end of this chapter, we shall suggest another such field trip.

## Message Options

As the bookmarked OPTIONS menu indicates, the remaining options on this menu deal with how messages in this forum are displayed on your screen.

*Option 3*, PAUSE after messages, tells the forum whether to (1) stop and display a prompt after every message you read, (2) stop only after messages addressed to you, or (3) never stop between messages (keep displaying the messages until it reaches the end and returns to the main menu or prompt). **Note**: if you were to disable the PAUSE with option 3, you could use a slightly different method to reply to messages: at a "!" prompt, you would simply enter the word REPLY (or the letters REP) followed by the message's number.

*Option 4*, NAME, allows you to change the way your name appears in the header of any message you post. This option is important because some forums request that members sign up with full names. If you sign up with first name only or a nickname, the sysops may ask you to use the NAME variable option to provide a full name. Incidentally, this name is the one under which you appear when you log into the forum's conference area.

*Option 5*, Prompt CHARACTER, lets you change the forum prompt. As a rule, this function isn't used by most members. However, some specially designed communications program use it. Some, for instance, direct you to change the CHARACTER variable to a Control-G (the ASCII code for the sounding of a "bell" on your computer). Once changed, a tone sounds each time you reach the a major menu or prompt in that forum.

*Option 6*, EDITOR, deals with writing messages, letting you specify which of CompuServe's two editing programs — LINEDIT or unnumbered EDIT — you wish to use for writing your messages. (This option, like option 2, also allows you to defer to a setting in the Profile area.)

*Option 7*, SECTIONS, lets you specify your defaults for subtopics. In the previous chapter, we discussed the SS command that allows you to Set Sections so that only messages on designated sections subtopics will be searched and read. The SECTIONS opinions allows you to make such a setting more permanent. Enter SEC and the system displays all the subtopic names with an asterisk beside your current defaults followed by an "Enter choice" prompt, where you have three alternatives. You can enter the numbers to "toggle" the settings for subtopics. If a section currently is "on" (that is, marked with an asterisk, as is subtopic 2 in the example), you can turn it "off" by entering its number (2) at the prompt. Or you can enter the letter C to *clear all* (remove) the currently marked defaults, or the letter A to *add all* available subtopics. Setting your permanent defaults this way means that from then on when you enter this forum, the system "knows" your interests in advance and displays messages only on the sections you have marked. However, even with the defaults established, you can override them the SS command, such as SS ALL if you decide on one particular visit that you want to view the entire board.

*Option 8*, HIGH message read, is the variable that contains the number of the last message you read in the forum. This option allows the system to "know" where to start reading if you enter a command to read or scan *new* messages. Note you can change the HIGH variable, raising or lowering it. If you leave it alone, it automatically updates itself as you read messages. You also can set it to L, meaning the *last* message you read on the current session.

*Option 9*, REPLIES info, lets you specify how you want to be told about replies to messages you are reading. At the end of messages you can have a *count* of the replies, a *list* of the *numbers* of all replies, or *no* reply information at all.

*Option 10*, TYPE waiting messages, determines how the system will behave when you enter a forum. If TYP is set to Yes, the forum displays messages addressed to you; if TYP is set to No, then it simply informs you of the numbers of the waiting messages.

Finally, *option 11*, SKIP messages you left, lets you indicate whether during a routine reading of the board you want to see or skip the messages you wrote and posted.

## Permanent or Temporary

Each time you change one of these defaults, the system displays the revised menu. Finally, when you have changed everything you wish to change, you enter T to return to the top of the forum and you see this message:

```
Would you like current settings
to apply to this Session only,
or to be Permanent?

Enter S or P, or H for help:
```

Earlier we talked about how things are "permanent" on this system, it now bears repeating. CompuServe realizes that sometimes a customer wants to test-drive possible changes before accepting them. So, any time you make changes in defaults, the system gives you an option to make them either "temporary" (meaning, for this session only) or "permanent" (that is, permanent until we change them again).

## Practicing with Expert Mode

Now that we have wrapped up our discussion of forums, why not take another trip on-line, as we suggested, to practice with some of the OPTIONS features? Just log on and return to Good Earth Forum (G GOODEARTH), but this time, see what the forum looks like *without* menus. To do that:

1. Enter OPTIONS at the main prompt.
2. Select MODE at the next menu.
3. Choose COMMAND from the final menu.
4. Enter T to return to the top of the menu and, when prompted, enter S to tell the system you want the change in effect for the current session only.

Immediately, you see the change. When you return to the top of the forum, the main forum menu is gone, replaced by:

From this prompt you can enter all your commands. Want to go to the message board? Enter MES (or MESSAGE). Want to go the library? The command is LIB (or LIBRARY). To the conferencing area? Try CON. And so forth. Try going to the message board and see how many commands you remember. (Hint: try REA NEW.) Refer to the forum commands in the On-line Survival Kit if you get stumped. If you get really stuck, you can enter a question mark at the prompt and the system will display what options are open to you at that point. Finally, when you are finished looking around, you can get your menus back by returning to the User Options — enter OPT at a prompt — and select option 2 from this menu:

```
┌──────────────────────────────────────────────────────┐
│                                                        │
│   Good Earth Forum Options Menu                        │
│                                                        │
│   FORUM OPTIONS                                        │
│    1 INITIAL menu/prompt [Forum]                       │
│    2 Forum MODE [COMMAND]                              │
│                                                        │
│   MESSAGES OPTIONS                                     │
│    3 PAUSE after messages [Always]                     │
│    4 NAME [Charlie Bowen]                              │
│    5 Prompt CHARACTER []                               │
│    6 EDITOR [LINEDIT*]                                 │
│    7 SECTIONS [...]                                    │
│    8 HIGH msg read [32007]                             │
│    9 REPLIES info [Count]                              │
│   10 TYPE waiting msgs [NO]                            │
│   11 SKIP msgs you left [NO]                           │
│                                                        │
│   Enter choice !                                       │
│                                                        │
└──────────────────────────────────────────────────────┘
```

If you want to call it a day, just log off. Because you have specified that the changes are for this session only, the next time you come to the Good Earth Forum you will be given your original defaults, including menus.


## Automated Terminal Programs

Forums are so popular that some modern communications programs actually have been designed to work exclusively with them, aimed at fully automating many forum tasks. Typically with such software, the user starts making selections off-line from a menu to tell the program what tasks to perform, such as checking news in specific forums and retrieving EasyPlex messages and so on. Once the user has laid out the jobs, the program automatically logs on and, like a faithful assistant, carries out the assignments, quickly saving new messages to disk files as it goes. The user later reads the saved files at his or her leisure, composes replies off-line, and instructs the program to log on again and post them.

We strongly believe that users ought to *first* learn how to navigate the system themselves, in order to get the most out of their subscriptions. CompuServe has such a variety of features, the subscriber ought to take time to explore them. However, it is also noteworthy that such automated terminal programs can save connect time dollars in the forums by allowing so much of the work to be done off-line. Of course, they are not available for all computer types, but the list is constantly growing, and the forums are your best contacts for new developments in the field.

Fully automated terminal software is the brain-child of a Maryland man named Howard Benner, who has been instrumental in three such programs so far. It all started one Saturday afternoon when he walked into a Radio Shack store to buy batteries. It was spring 1983 and the store was displaying its latest computer, the Model 100, which Benner immediately recognized as an ideal communications machine. With its self-contained modem and built-in communications program, the 100 was a laptop born for the electronic byways. That summer Benner wrote a program called SUPER.SIG, which automated much of the reading and writing of messages in forums. SUPER.SIG let the Model 100 log on and automatically handle a number of preselected chores. When Benner placed his creation in the forum's library for downloading by other members, it was a hit. New versions followed, incorporating refinements suggested by the program's enthusiastic public. Today an enhanced version of that first automated program still is maintained in the Tandy Model 100 Forum (GO M100SIG) in its Library 3. The program is a file called SMART.SIG, and the instructions are contained in SMART.DOC.

Later that year, word of Benner's baby spread to neighboring forums where resident programmers began thinking of how they, too, could create such programs for other kinds of computers. Before long, a new incarnation of the program — *AutoSig* — was born in the IBM Users Network (GO IBMNET). To design it for what was then the relatively new IBM PC, Benner assisted programmers Vernon Buerg, Frank Lipschutz, Don Watkins, and others. These days, *AutoSig* has hundreds of dedicated users. Sysop Don Watkins took on the regular update of the program as a personal project and one entire subtopic of the IBM Communications Forum (GO IBMCOM) is now devoted to it. For the latest copy of *AutoSig*, see Library 1 of IBMCOM.

Meanwhile, Benner moved on. Believing that the SUPER.SIG/*AutoSig* idea was outgrowing the language in which it was written (BASIC), Benner turned to Turbo Pascal for his next creation, *TAPCIS*, his most ambitious automated program yet. Whereas SUPER.SIG and *AutoSig* are public domain software, free for the downloading, the IBM-oriented *TAPCIS* (originally called "ZapCIS") is a shareware program, meaning Benner asks those who download and like it to pay a registration fee. Also, SUPER.SIG and *AutoSig* are offered under the umbrella of general-purpose forums, but *TAPCIS* now has its own support forum. Benner opened TAPCIS Forum (GO TAPCIS) in early 1988, where registered users could have access to special private areas.

Benner's idea of automated software continues to spread to other machines. One of the newer ones arrived recently in the on-line Atari computer world. It's a program called *ST/Forum*, written by Charles McGuinness, a highly regarded programmer who has designed software for a number of different kinds of computers over the past half dozen years. McGuinness' public domain program is available in

Library 13 of the Atari Development Forum (GO ATARIDEV) under the name STFRM.ARC, with the documentation saved in STFRM.DOC.

The Apple Macintosh community has not been left out. At about the same time as McGuinness was writing his Atari program, White Plains, New York, programmer Mike O'Connor created a shareware automated program that took advantage of the Mac's mouse and its "point and click" structure. O'Connor's program later was picked up by CompuServe itself and today is marketed by the company as *Navigator*. The primary source of information and support for this program is the Macintosh Personal Productivity Forum (G MACPRO).

## Side Roads

If you become a dedicated data library enthusiast, here are a couple more features you will be interested in:

— Online Today's "Uploads" column, written twice a month by Dave Peyton as a regular feature of *Online Today*'s electronic edition. Uploads carries reports on some of the hot new additions to data libraries in various forums, giving specific file names, the direct addresses for the forums and the libraries from which the files can be downloaded. Back issues also are available from a menu. To see Uploads, enter G OLT-3700 at any prompt. Also, a compiled version of the Uploads column appeared in the monthly printed *Online Today* magazine mailed to all CompuServe subscribers.

— File Finders, a new keyword-searchable database for quick reference to files in assorted data libraries of the multiple IBM and Apple Macintosh forums. Instead of having to search databases in each forum, subscribers can make one stop at the File Finder and search them all. Mac File Finder (G MACFF) is a database of files from Macintosh-related forums, including the forums of the Micronetworked Apple Users Groups (G MAUG), Aldus, Adobe, and MicroSoft. IBM File Finder (G IBMFF) offers file information from the IBM Users Network, Microsoft, Borland, and Ashton-Tate. At this writing, the File Finders are in use only in the IBM and Macintosh communities, but look for the idea to spread to other forums as well.

# CHAPTER 14

# The Forum Roundup

From the start, we must accept that what we propose to do in this chapter is impossible: to provide a comprehensive list of *all* the forums and their administrators. The problem is, of course, that things never stop evolving. New forums are introduced, new sysops and assistants come on-line, some forums merge or expand to spin off new ones. No printed list, whether here or published by CompuServe itself, can keep up with changes.

Given these limitations, though, we can take a stab at it. This chapter lists nearly 100 forums that were active at the time we put this edition together. It provides the direct access address of each forum, as well as the names and user IDs of the sysops and a description of each forum. Look over the list. You might be surprised at the variety of interests covered by forums.

Beyond that, remember that you have on-line resources for updating this list and keeping abreast of new forums. The system's What's New bulletin is posted each Thursday. In addition, the Community News section of *Online Today*'s Electronic Edition (G OLT) covers forum news. And for a little independent research, you can use the FIND command. FIND FORUMS entered at any "!" prompt will give you the names and addresses of them all, and you can use FIND to locate specific forums, such as FIND IBM or FIND APPLE. Also, you can find some groups of forums by entering G FORUMS, G HARDWARE, or G SOFTWARE.

The forums described in this chapter are divided into five groups:

I. Hardware-specific, those devoted to users of specific systems, such as Apple, IBM and IBM compatibles, Commodore, and so on.

II. Software-related, those operated by, or in cooperation with, software publishers such as Ashton-Tate, Lotus Development Corporation, Microsoft, and others.

III. Publication-sponsored, including forums operated by magazines, such as *Dr. Dobb's Journal*, *PC Magazine*, and more.

    IV. Professional, forums for various occupations, such as law, medicine, aviation, journalism.

    V. General Interest/Home and Recreation, for hobbies, games, cooking, sports, sex, travel, and more.

Keep in mind, though, that some forums don't fit neatly into a specific category. One person's hobby is another person's profession. It is best, then, to read the entire chapter to be sure you don't overlook one that could serve your needs.

# I. Hardware-Specific Forums

The computer is what we all have in common, so it is no surprise that computer-related forums are the most popular on the system. Front-runners include the IBM Users Network, the Micronetworked Apple Users Groups, the Commodore Network, AtariNet, and the Tandy Network. Also popular are smaller forums that support "orphaned" computers.

*Micronetworked Apple Users Groups (G MAUG)*

New York writer/editor Neil Shapiro is well-known in Apple computing circles and has created one of the most successful networks of forums on CompuServe. MAUG, Micronetworked Apple Users Groups, is made up of seven forums, serving early Apples like the Apple II to the latest versions of the Apple Macintosh:

*Apple II and III Forum (G APPLETWO)* serves the venerable veterans of the Apple line.

*Apple Developers Forum (G APPDEV)* caters to discussions about programming and software designs and related issues.

*Apple Vendor Forum (G APPVEN)* is for those who market Apple-related products.

*Apple Hyper Forum (G APPHYP)* is devoted to the applications of HyperCard in Apple Macintosh.

*The Mac Personal Productivity Forum (G MACPRO)* is for those with a specialty in software.

*The Mac Arts and Entertainment Forum (G MACFUN)* concentrates on entertainment and graphics applications of the Macintosh.

*Macintosh Business Forum (G MACBIZ)* emphasizes business applications for the Mac.

In addition, Shapiro and his assistant sysops produce a regular electronic magazine called *Apples Online*. The publication and all the forums are accessible from a menu reached by entering G MAUG at any prompt.

Shapiro's user ID is 76703,401. His assistant sysops are Bill Steinberg, 76703,1027, who is primary sysop of the Mac Productivity Forum; Russ Wetmore 76703,2010, primary sysop of Apple Development Forum; Shawn Goodin, 76703,1034, primary sysop of the Apple 2/3 Forum; Bradley Poulson, 76701,227, primary sysop of the Mac Arts and Entertainment Forum; Robert Wiggins, 76703,4054, primary sysop of Macintosh Business Users Forum; Bill Cook, 76703,1030, primary sysop of the Hyper Forum. Also assisting are Dennis Brothers, 76703,2067; Don Brown, 76703,4221; Harry Conover, 76703,4220; Linda Custer, 76703,4054; Jason Harper, 76703,4222, and Larry Miller, 76703,1031.

MAUG is a registered trademark owned by MCU, Inc. of Bethpage, New York. The organization also provides a voice help line in the evenings between 7:00 p.m. and 10:00 a.m. Eastern Time at (516) 735-6924.

### The Atari Users Network (G ATARI)

Another New Yorker, Ron Luks, is known equally well in the Atari computing world. Since 1982, Ron (user ID is 76703,254) has built the Atari Users Network from a single subtopic in a general computing forum into a network of four separate forums:

*The Atari 8-Bit Forum (G ATARI8).*
*The Atari 16-Bit Forum (G ATARI16).*
*Atari Developers Forum (G ATARIDEV).*
*Atari Vendors Forum (G ATARIVEN).*

In creating the network, he has attracted the attention of a number of computing publications, including the Atari-oriented *Antic* magazine, which now offers an electronic edition in conjunction with the forums. The magazine and all three forums are accessible from a menu you can reach by entering G ATARI at any prompt.

Assisting him are Mike Schoenbach, 76703,4363; Dick Brudzynski, 76703,2011; Dave Groves, 76703,4223; Keith Ledbetter, 76701,124; Tom Hudson, 76703,4224; Dan Rhea, 76703,4364; Charles McGuinness 76701,11; Bill Aycock, 76703,4061 and Don LeBow, 76704,41.

### CD-ROM Forum (G CDROM)

One of the exciting new storage technologies on the horizon for PC users is CD-ROM, holding millions of bytes of data on a surface smaller than a traditional floppy disk. On-line, the new CD-ROM Forum is the gathering place for the fans as well as those who are merely curious about the technology.

Administrating the forum are Ty Wait 76701,231, who has an extensive background in data processing, and Joel Nagy 76701,232, who has worked in various areas of a professional video and audio production company.

### Commodore Users Network (G CBMNET)

Commodore computers always have had a big following on CompuServe and users these days have seven forums at their disposal.

The newest of the Commodore forums serve the newest computer, the colorful, musical Amiga. These include The Amiga Arts Forum (G AMIGAARTS) and the Amiga Tech Forum (G AMIGATECH), operated by Steve Ahlstrom, 76703,2006, of Littleton, Colorado. Ahlstrom is a long-time CompuServe subscriber who cut his on-line administrative teeth as an assistant in the Atari forums. Assisting him here are Don Curtis, 76703,4321; Richard Rae, 76703,4253, Larry Phillips, 76703,4322; and Marlene Zenker, 76701,250.

Another Amiga-oriented group is the Amiga Vendor Forum (G AMIGAVENDOR), operated by the Canadian Transactor Publications, Inc., which publishes *Transactor*. The same publication sponsors two other related forums, for other Commodore computers besides the Amiga. These include the Commodore Communications Forum (G CBMCOM), devoted to telecomputing, and the Commodore Programming Forum (G CBMPRG), for software development. The publisher's on-line management team includes Nick Sullivan, 76703,4353; Gary Farmaner, 76703,3050; Richard Evers, 76703,4243; Chris Zamara, 76703,4245; Jim Kuratomi, 76703,4033; Charlie Lutz, 76703,4034, and Marte Brengle, 76703,4242.

For those who think Commodores mean recreation, there is Betty Knight's Commodore Arts and Games Forum (G CBMART), aiming to serve a variety of Commodore 8-bit machines, including the Commodore 64, C128, the VIC-20, the Pet, the C-16, the Plus 4, and the B-128. Knight, 76703,4037, is a Snohomish, Washington, resident who has been a mainframe computer programmer/systems analyst since 1960. She is assisted by Todd Heimarck, 76703,3051; and Steve Sileo, 76703,4244.

All of the above forums are independent of Commodore International. Meanwhile, the company does have an on-line presence itself. Its staff maintains the Commodore Service Forum (G CBMSERVICE), operated by the company's Telecommunications Department along with in-house engineers, customer support, and service staff members. All staff members are located in the Commodore's headquarters in West Chester, Pennsylvania.

### Computer Club (G CLUB)

One of the oldest forums on CompuServe, the Computer Club has the distinction of being the starting place for many other forums. In fact, the entire Atari User

Network and the IBM Users Network have their roots in this special interest group, starting out as just single subtopics on this old-timer.

These days, CLUB has evolved into a major source of information about so-called orphaned computers. At this writing, the forum provides discussion areas and data libraries for systems such as Sanyo, Eagle, Timex/Sinclair, Actrix, Quantum, and Panasonic. One of the most active sections is devoted to users of the Coleco Adam computer, for which CLUB is the main source of on-line information. CLUB also is the primary on-line source of information for users of Kaypro computers.

Among CLUB's sysops are Dave Yaros 76703,4332; Jon Jacobs, 76701,120; Irv Hoff, 76701,117, and Rick Trethewey, 76703,542. Incidentally, CLUB doesn't forget its own roots: still listed on its roster as a "retired sysop" is Stan Veit who created the forum in the early 1980s for the now-defunct *Computers and Electronics* magazine. Veit now edits *Computer Shopper* magazine from Florida.

### DEC PC Forum (G DECPC)

This forum is dedicated to understanding and using Digital Equipment Corporation's line of personal computers, (including but not limited to, the Rainbow, VT-180, DECmate, and VAXmate).

The sysop here is Bill Leeman, 76703,3055, who works for a software and timesharing service in Tucson, Arizona, as system manager for a VAX 11/750 and 11/780. He has been in the data processing field since August of 1977 and owns a Rainbow 100B, which he uses for communications, word processing, and writing programs in GW-BASIC.

### Epson Forum (G EPSON)

Operated by employees of Epson America, Inc., this forum supports all Epson products, from its line of printers to its MS-DOS computers. Topics identified for discussion include telecommunications, hardware and software, and systems such as the QX-10 and QX-16, the PX-8, HX-20, HX-40, and others.

The forum also gives advice on use of add-ons, such as Titan expansion boards.

The Epson Forum is operated by John Ross, 76703,551, of Prairie Village, Kansas, who has been an active computerist since 1980. He has experience with a variety of computers, from early Tandy systems to the IBM PC, XT, and AT, as well as Sanyo and Epson systems.

Helping out as assistant sysops are Mike Morra, 76703,4051, who works in Epson's New York branch; Jill Bauhs, 70003,3044, a former Epson employee who now works for CompuServe; Chris Hopkin, 76703,4374, and Jim Jeter, 76703,2012.

### Hewlett-Packard PC Forum (G HP)

Sponsored by Hewlett-Packard Company, this forum is a component of the company's HP/ONLINE service and gives customers an on-line link to its support division. Its subtopics include those on data communications, word processing, data management, system utilities, and programming.

The primary sysops are Bill Crow, 76703,632, who specializes in the HP150, the Portable, the Vectra and the LaserJet printer; and Mark Horvatich, 76703,4163, who fields questions on the Touchscreen II, the Portable PLUS, the Vectra and the HP150. Also in the forum is Teri Woolworth, 76703,2023, who coordinates HP/ONLINE.

For questions dealing with the forum or HP equipment, ask Crow and Horvatich. Questions about HP-supported products should be directed to Woolworth.

### IBM Users Network (G IBMNET)

Along with the Micronetworked Apple Users Groups and the Atari Network, one of the most popular collection of forums on the system is the IBM Users Network.

These forums make up this network:

*New Users Forum (G IBMNEW)* fields questions from people new to computing, new to IBM computing, and new to computing on CompuServe. It is also the place to find leisure-time software and discussions of recreational computing, such as games and puzzles.

*Applications Forums (G IBMAPP)* is for application software for business, home, school, fun and more.

*Programming Forum (G IBMPRO)* is devoted to the programming enthusiasts in the MS-DOS and Personal System/2 world.

*Systems/Utilities Forum (G IBMSYS)* is for questions and answers about operating systems and data libraries and is stocked with handy utility programs.

*Hardware Forum (G IBMHW)* covers everything from printers and monitors, hard disks and other peripherals.

*Communications Forum (G IBMCOM)* deals with the ins and outs of telecomputing with the IBM.

*PC Junior Forum (G IBMJR)* serves users of IBM's original "home" computer, the Jr.

Management of these forums is shared by four sysops. They are Don Watkins, 76703,750; Conrad ("Connie") Kageyama, 76703,1010; Chris Dunford, 76703,2002, and Vern Buerg, 70007,1212. Assisting are Dave Hoagland, 70007,3352, and Stephen Satchell, 70007,3351.

Incidentally, for a detailed look at the IBM Users Network and telecomputing with IBMs and IBM compatibles, you might want to take a look at our book, *Advanced CompuServe for IBM PC Power Users* (Bantam Books, 1987).

### Tandy Professional Forum (G TANDY)

Four forums for Tandy Corporation products are associated with a national organization, the independent Tandy Users Network, sponsored by Golden Triangle Corporation of Fort Worth, Texas, the home of Tandy Corporation. These include:

*TRS 80 Professional Forum (G TRS80PRO).*
*Color Computer Forum (G COCO).*
*Model 100 Forum (G M100SIG).*
*The OS-9 Forum (G OS9).*

The Tandy Pro forum supports most of that company's computers and peripherals, including the more recent IBM compatibles, such as the Models 1000, 1200, and 3000, as well as the older systems, such as the Models I, III, and 4.

The Color Computer is devoted to the earliest as well as the most recent versions of that home system.

The Model 100 Forum actually is intended for the users of the TRS-80 Model 100, Tandy 200, NEC portables, Olivetti M-10, Tandy 600, and compatible portables.

The OS9 forum is dedicated to users of the multiuser, multitasking OS-9 Operating System available for most 6809 and 68000 computers.

Heading up the Tandy network is Wayne Day, 76703,376, who has been prominent in the Tandy and the CompuServe communities for many years.

His associates, in the TRS Pro forum, are Renato Reyes, 76703,3100; and Mike Yetsko, 76703,4312. In the Coco forum, Day is assisted by Mike Ward, 76703,2013; and Steve Wegert, 76703,4255. Running the Model 100 forum are Tony Anderson, 76703,4062; Dennis Thomas, 76701,40; and Eiji Miura, 76703,4311. Assisting in OS9 Forum are Pete Lyall, 76703,4230; and Kevin Darling, 76703,4227.

Two other forums also supporting Tandy equipment, but are not operated by the Golden Triangle Corporation. They are:

*The LDOS/TRSDOS6 Users Forum (G LDOS).* Long-time Tandy computer users know LDOS as an outstanding alternative to the standard TRSDOS operating system of the company's 8-bit machines. This forum, serving users of LDOS/TRSDOS6, is operated by Joe Kyle-DiPietropaolo, 76703,437, and the forum is sponsored by MISOSYS, Inc. of Sterling, Virginia, for users of MISOSYS and Logical Systems products.

*The Tangent Group Forum (G TANGENT),* which is an organization of independent business computer users of Tandy equipment, with a special emphasis on Unix, Xenix, and other multi-user systems. Among the regular participants here are numbered hardware designers, value-added resellers (VARs), software designers, consultants, and just plain old-style computer hobbyists. The sysop is John Esak, 76703,746, president of Nexus Inc. of Washington, D.C.

### TI Forum (G TIFORUM)

This forum serves users of Texas Instruments personal computers, including the 99/4A, the TI Professional, CC-40, TI Semiconductors.

At the helm is systems analyst Jim Horn, 76703,603, who has been sysop here since the creation of the forum in 1983. Prior to that, Horn ran the TI subtopic in the CLUB forum. He is affiliated with a data research firm, Tele*Data Guide and a software distribution company, DOS.

Assisting him in managing the forum is Jonathan Zittrain, 76703,3022, who is the editor of *TINEWS* and a regular columnist in computer publications.

# II. Software-Related Forums

In the mid-1980s, some of the fastest-growing collections of new forums have been those in the "software-specific" group, particularly those operated by software companies themselves, like Borland International, Lotus Development Corporation, Ashton-Tate, and others. Programmers and users of sophisticated applications software now have on-line connections for questions and answers.

### Adobe Forum (G ADOBE)

This forum is operated by the Adobe Technical support staff to provide on-line support for users, dealers, service bureaus, third-party developers, and others.

The data libraries include utilities, technical support notes, PostScript files, and text files of information about Adobe and non-Adobe Software products, printers and other hardware, desktop publishing, training, press releases, and new product announcements.

The sysop is Esther Kletter, 76701,26, who is assisted by members of technical support, engineering, and marketing.

### Aldus Forum (G ALDUS)

Aldus, creators of publishing software, supports users of its Aldus PageMaker for the Apple Macintosh, IBM PC/AT, and AT-compatible computers. The forum is managed by the Aldus technical support staff. The sysop is David "Zak" Williamson, 76703,4357, who is assisted by company officials in technical support, engineering, and marketing departments.

Message areas have been set aside for both novice and expert users and the data libraries contain technical support notes, design formats (templates) for publications, and utility programs.

### Ashton-Tate Forum (G ASHFORUM)

Questions about *dBase*? *Framework*? *MultiMate*? You have a direct link to the people who publish these major products. The Ashton-Tate Forum is open for business around the clock by the company's software support center.

At this writing, the forum has topics set aside for *dBase II*, *dBase III*, *dBase Plus*, *MultiMate*, *Framework*, *Runtime*, as well as general areas for subjects such as networks. As Ashton-Tate software is available for a variety of computers, you will find library files utilities that will work with several different types of systems.

The forum is directed by Kent Irwin, 76703,3007, who is Ashton-Tate's supervisor of telecommunications. His assistants are Steve Silverwood, 76703,3035; Susan Schafer, 76703,4217; Chip Boyle, 76701,24; Quinn Wildman, 76703,3033; Mina Nichols, 76702,255; and Jeffrey Moore, 76702,254. You also can write directly to the company's customer service with messages to 76701,101.

In addition to the forum, the company operates the menu-driven "Ashton-Tate Support Library," which offers answers to commonly asked questions, official company announcements, contact numbers for customer services people, lists of authorized training centers, and more. To reach this area, enter G ASHTON.

### Autodesk Forum (G ADESK)

If you are part of the exciting world of computer-aided design/manufacturing, be sure to put this one on your list. Autodesk, Inc. opened the first on-line service devoted to CAD/CAM. Its members include engineers, architects, facilities managers, consultants, designers — anyone who uses a computer to shape the real world.

The forum is primarily set up for users of Autodesk's own products — *AutoCAD, AutoCAD AEC, CAD/camera* — but also hosts general discussions on the industry and has subtopics set aside for messages about third-party software, new developments, news and reviews, and education.

Administering the forum is Jamie Clay, 76703,4204, of Autodesk's product support center, who is assisted by specialists in the company's software, quality control, and marketing divisions.

### Borland International Forums (G BORLAND)

Philippe Kahn's Borland International has taken the computer world by storm. Programs like *Turbo Pascal*, *SideKick*, *SuperKey*, *Turbo Lightning*, and *Turbo Prolog* have created entire subcultures of users, and the smartest of them have on-line connections.

Borland operates three forums; one for its application programs and two for its program-development software. They are:

- *Borland Applications Forum (G BORAPP)* offers discussions on *SideKick, SuperKey, Lightning*, and the *Reflex* database system. The sysops are Gail Meisner, 76703,4162; Celeste Robinson, 76701,126, and Anthony Lee, 76704,32.
- *Borland Programming Forum A (G BPROGA)* is devoted to the big areas of *Turbo Pascal* and *Turbo Basic*. The libraries are filled with programs written by the members in these languages and problems in programming are solved daily on the message board. The sysops, also members of Borland's technical support staff, are Larry Kraft, 76703,764, and Joe Schrader, 76703,4161.
- *Borland Programming Forum B (G BPROGB)* is devoted to the new artificial intelligence systems, *Turbo Prolog* and *Turbo C*. Heading the forum are Schrader along with Robert Goosey, 76701,47.

The Borland forums also create "teams" of experienced users in a number of areas of specialization. The names of the team members and their user IDs are displayed in the bulletin areas of the respective forums.

Borland also provides a menu of general information. If you enter G BORLAND at a prompt, you will have access to company statements, information on the product line, and information about product support.

Also, President Kahn himself is a frequent visitor to the forums and even has moderated on-line panel discussions in the conference areas.

### CADKEY Forum (G CADKEY)

CADKEY Inc. develops three-dimensional Computer-Aided Design and Drafting products for the PCs used in manufacturing, government, and education. The forum is designed to support users and to inform potential customers.

The forum is administered by the company with support from its various dealers. The primary sysop is Steven Chin, 76701,276, with the assistance of Reed Vickerman, 76701,252.

### *Crosstalk Forum (G XTALK)*

One of the best-known names in communications software is Digital Communications Associates' *Crosstalk*. The company operates this forum as a support facility for CompuServe subscribers. The data libraries contain utilities, script files, information about DCA products, and so forth. The message boards are used to answer general and technical questions.

Two DCA/Crosstalk Communications employees manage the forum. They are Shel Hall, 76701,103; and Maria Forrest, 76701,104.

### *Digital Research Forum (G DRFORUM)*

Digital Research, Inc., designers of the popular *GEM* collection of computer utilities, operates DRFORUM for its current and prospective customers.

Running the show are Connie M. Paul, 76703,4147; Tim Mills, 76703,1064; Chuck Brewer, 76703,455; Stephanie Horoszko, 76703,615; and Garry Silvey, 76703,4146.

The forum also is an on-line meeting place for CONUG (The ConCurrent User's Group).

### *Javelin Software Forum (G JAVELIN)*

The technical support staff of Javelin Software Corporation runs this forum for users of its business applications software.

Hosting the activities are Margaret Levine, 76703,4402, representing Javelin, and independent consultant Conrad Smith, 76701,107. The service is geared toward technical support, training, and other on-line help in taking advantage of Javelin's analytical capabilities.

### *Living Videotext Forum (G LVTFORUM)*

The Living Videotext forum has areas set aside for its best known programs — the "idea processor," *ThinkTank*, and *PC Ready!* — and it has a general brain-storming area called "Software Design Lab."

The forum is administered by Bob Hung, 76703,4047, Living Videotext's director of technical services, who also is an expert on making third-party software compatible with LVT products. If you are a software developer, he is a good man to get to know.

### Lotus Development Forum (G LOTUS)

Lotus Development Corporation offers more than one forum. Each of the "World of Lotus" forums has its own focus.

The Lotus Integrated Products Forum (G LOTUSA) cover *Lotus 1-2-3* and *HAL*, *Symphony*, and *Jazz*. The message board covers issues from general information to communications, macro languages and graphics, and lists users groups around the country. The libraries offer utility programs and background articles.

Lotus Stand-Alone Products Forum (G LOTUSB) covers all other Lotus products, including *Manuscript*, *Metro*, *Express*, graphics and information services software, and so on.

The forums are administered by Miguel Caldera, 76703,4342, of the Lotus Product Support group. He is assisted by program specialists. Assisting is Kathy Carbonneau, 76703,4342.

Enter G LOTUS for the overview of the World of Lotus. Company statements are available at the menu, as well as a summary of new entries in the data libraries, lists of software and books recommended, descriptions of drivers and add-ons available for downloading, and so forth.

### MicroPro Forum (G MICROPRO)

Best known for its mighty *WordStar* word processors, MicroPro International Corporation is served on-line by this forum, which attracts users of IBM- and Apple-compatible systems. Its subtopics cover *WordStar 2000* and other members of the *WordStar* family, and questions dealing with specific printers and other add-ons, etc.

The forum is not produced by MicroPro itself, but is operated by Software Support Associates of Forrest Knolls, California, which was organized by its two sysops, Morris Jones, 76703,1071; and Ed Greenberg, 76703,1070. Jones and Greenberg both have been programmers at MicroPro.

Members of the forum share knowledge and utilities for an assortment of MicroPro products, including *WordStar, MailMerge, Easy, CorrectStar* (which sysop Jones designed), *CalcStar*, and others.

### Microsoft Connection (G MSCON)

Two forums, run by Microsoft Corporation's retail division product support group, are the on-line gathering place for users of Microsoft programs. Microsoft is the company that created IBM's BASIC programming language and its PC-DOS/MS-DOS operating system.

Microsoft customer service runs the forums. Debbie Pilgrim handles domestic problems and Mindy Miles takes care of international problems. They share 76701,245. Their forums are Microsoft Applications Forum (G MSAPP) and Microsoft Systems Forum (G MSSYS).

Assisting in the forums are Scott Smith, 76701,160; Brad Peterson, 76701,151; Matt Crinklaw, 76701,270; William Jones, 76701,244; Clay Stevens, 76701,243; Kraig Brockschmidt, 76701,152; Kyle Sparks, 76701,155; Michelle Akins, 76701,156; and Tony Huang, 76701,266.

Topics for boards reflect Microsoft's diversity — *Microsoft Word, Excel, Multiplan, the Flight Simulator, Windows*, and *Access* — and there is always a healthy amount of discussion about programming languages. The forum is particularly popular with experienced users because Microsoft has used its on-line connections to find qualified beta testers for new products. News of new products abounds on the message board.

### Monogram Software Forum (G MONOGRAM)

Monogram Software, which produces a number of financial products, including *Dollars and Sense* and *Moneyline*, opened this forum for on-line support of its customers.

The data libraries contain application programs, answers to common questions, and information about hardware compatibility for Monogram products. The forum is maintained by the company's technical support and analysis department and the primary sysop is Richard West, 76703,4340.

### Nantucket Forum (G NANFORUM)

This forum is operated in conjunction with the on-line Nantucket Reference Center (G NANTUCKET), which provides articles and reference materials about the Clipper database development system and the McMax relational database management system for the Apple Macintosh computer. Support notes with undocumented Clipper facts, including Support Log excerpts and anomaly listings, and articles from Nantucket's bi-monthly technical journal, *Nantucket News*, are also available.

Nantucket Corp.'s technical staff runs the forum, which is administed by Renee Gentry, 76702,300. Assisting are Monier Anvari, 76702,277; Ed Bell, 76702,276; and Gerry Braganza, 76702,301.

### Novell Users Forum (G NOVUSER)

The forum was established for users to exchange tips, techniques and other information related to use of Novell software. Forum operators are John T. McCann (70007,3430), Bart Mellink (76702,256), Dave Kearns (76704,62), Glenn Fund (76704,63), and Jeff Grammer (76704,64). Offical responses from Novell can be found in the Novell Forum (GO NOVFORUM) where an $8 per hour surcharge applies.

**On-line Picture Support Forums** *(G GRAPHICS)*

One group of forums concentrates on graphics, dealing with on-line high-resolution pictures called RLEs ("Run-Length Encoded") and GIFs ("Graphics Interchange Format"), which we shall discuss in a later chapter. The three forums are:

— *The Graphic Support Forum (G GRAPHSUPPORT)*, which provides support for hardware and software used to create and view graphics.

— *The Art Gallery Forum (G GALLERY)*, home for graphics picture files (and their artists) aimed at medium-to-high end-users and elaborate 16-color pictures.

— *The Quick Pictures Forum (G QUICKPICS)*, which supports subscribers who want to view smaller, simpler on-line graphics files.

Operating the forums are administrator Larry Wood, 76703,704 and primary sysop Tom Potocki, 76703,1012. Assisting them are Tom Mitchell, 76701,273; Doug Quinn, 76703,4352; and Warren Gold, 70007,3462. The forums concentrate on how to create and download/upload graphics files for viewing on-line.

*PC Vendor Support Forum (G PCVEN)*

A number of software and hardware vendors, in the world of IBM and IBM compatibles, have come together to create the PC Vendor Support Forum. They are:

— ButtonWare provides support for its *PC-File+* software and its word processing, graphics, and communications products. Its support staff can be reached with messages to 73230,1363, with staffers Blair Cooper, Kevin Smith, and Barbara Wilson answering the questions.

— Mansfield Software supports its REXX programming language originating on mainframes using IBM's VM/CMS operating system, and the KEDIT text editor for the IBM PC. Nico Mak, 70056,241, a software developer at the company, handles the questions.

— The Software Group offers support for its *Enable* integrated software package for the IBM PC, with Joe Sheridan, 76077,2453, answering messages.

— Broderbund supports its various entertainment and productivity software. Representing the company is Dave Ross, 70006,512, manager of Broderbund's support department and a member of its technical support team.

— Laser Friendly Inc. answers questions with development coordinator Mark Skapinker, 76703,207.

— Magee Enterprises, developers of *Automenu*, is represented by members of the technical support staff, Randal DePriest, and Karren Hill, and answers questions sent to 76004,1541.

— Custom Technologies is represented by Tim Bougan, 76515,1555, head of programming.

— Knowledge Garden, Inc.fields questions with Bev and Bill Thompson, John Slade, and Meredith LeClair at 76004,1603.

— Mustang Software, producer of *WILDCAT!* software answers questions with programmer Jim Harrer and Tech support manager Rick Heming at 76004,1552.

— Toshiba America Inc. sponsors Keith Comer, senior product specialist, 76004,1551, to answer questions about Toshiba portable computers.

— MathSoft's manager of technical support Mariann Ivey, 76004,1553, answers queries, along with Faustino Lichauco, applications engineer.

### Software Publishing Forum (G SPCFORUM)

Software Publishing opened this forum for users of its well-known products, *PFS:FILE, PFS:REPORT, PFS:WRITE, PFS:PLAN, PFS:GRAPH, PFS:ACCESS*, and others. It also is in touch with the company's latest news. For instance, when the firm introduced two major new desktop publishing products in 1986 — the *ClickArt Personal Publisher* and the *Harvard Professional Publisher* — discussions began in the forum before news even reached traditional print publications.

The forum is run by Storey La Montagne, 76703,3054, who fields questions on SPC programs as well as forum usage. The company also provides a menu-driven service called Software Publishing Online (G SPC). Files include the company history, lists of new products (with prices and descriptions), and answers to common questions.

### TAPCIS Forum (G TAPCIS)

*TAPCIS* is the name of a rare and popular communications program for IBM and IBM-compatible computers that actually *automates* much of the on-line operations for its users. The software was written by Maryland programmer Howard Benner, and it has been taking a certain segment of the CompuServe community by storm ever since.

Benner, 76704,44, opened this forum in 1988 as an on-line support system for his users. He is assisted by Joan Friedman, 76701,145; Marilyn Ratcheson, 76702,260; and Richard P. Wilkes, 76701,23.

### Unix Forum (G UNIXFORUM)

This forum is dedicated to discussing issues relating to the multiuser, multitasking operating system that was created by AT&T and is considered by many to be The Next Big Thing in the computer world.

Running the forum are David Moskowitz, 76701,100; and Noel Bergman, 76704.34.

### WordPerfect Support Group (G WPSG)

This forum is an independent group designed to support users of the *WordPerfect* word processor for various computers. It is operated by professional writers/editors Richard P. Wilkes, 76701,23; and Sandy B. Wilkes, 76701,22. They are assistant by Joan Friedman, 76701,145.

The forum is dedicated to finding more powerful ways to use *WordPerfect* and related products in various fields, and it is the electronic meeting place for the support group, which has more than 15,000 members worldwide.

### Programming, Languages and Operating Systems

Some of the forums already mentioned cater to programmers. In fact, the word *development* or *developers* in a forum name — such as "Atari Developers Forum" — usually is a tipoff that this is a gathering place for the software authors.

Meanwhile, one forum that represents no single company but rather software development in general is the Programmer's Special Interest Group (G PROGFORUM). This forum is the electronic connection for wizards and would-be wizards, and hosts conversations on many topics: the software business in general, communications and local area networks, applications programs, high-level programming languages, assembly language, software tools, operating systems, and database management.

Holding it all together is a San Francisco-based programmer, teacher and veteran CompuServe subscriber named Brad Paulsen, 76703,1005, who has been in the programming business since 1968. He has experience in COBOL and FORTRAN systems, database management, and consulting. The forum has scored several innovations over the years, including top-rate on-line seminars on database languages, BASIC, assembly language, and others.

Here are some other forums for programmers and serious computer hobbyists:

CP/M: One of the oldest forums on the system, CP-MIG (G CPMFORUM) is devoted to users of the CP/M operating system on various computers. Running the show are John Ross, 76703,551, and Irv Hoff, 76701,117.

FORTH: The CSI Forth Net (G FORTH), has operated since October 1984 thanks to Creative Solutions, Inc.; it is an on-line support group for its Forth language products. The primary sysop is CSI president/founder Don Colburn, 76703,4160, who implemented the first Forth system on the 68000 processor in 1979. He is assisted by Zach Zachariah, 76703,4160, CSI product manager, who also mans the company hotline.

LOGO: The Young Peoples' Logo Association provides the LOGO Forum (G LOGOFORUM) for students of any age. The sysop (and "Chief Turtle") is Jim Muller, 76703,3005, who says that while the group's main interest is the many versions of Logo, there are other languages and other technologies discussed in the forum.

# III. Publication-Sponsored Forums

Regardless of what some say about electronic communications being a "threat" to the printed word, some publications have set up on-line extensions, particularly computer- and science-related magazines.

*AI Expert (G AIE-100)*

Artificial intelligence is perhaps the hottest field in advanced computing, and Craig LaGrow's *AI Expert* magazine seeks to keep us posted on the newest of the new developments. LaGrow, 76703,756, and his staff use the AI Forum to interact with readers and would-be readers on topics such as languages like LISP and *Turbo Prolog*, expert systems in general, reviews, and utilities.

Running the forum is Susan Shepard, 76703,4326, who writes the magazine's regular "AI Insider" column. She is an AI consultant for private business and educational institutions and works with the New York-based Academy for Educational Development. Among her assistants are *AI Expert* editors Marc Rettig, 76703,1037, and Philip Chapnick, 76703,756.

*Computer Language Forum (G CLM)*

Craig LaGrow's original publication, *Computer Language Magazine*, also is represented on-line. Here, advanced computerists discuss languages such as C and FORTH, upload and download public domain utilities, and swap programming tips and techniques.

The forum also provides an outlet for distribution of programs mentioned in the magazine's monthly "Public Domain Software Review" column. In effect, it is building a public database of utilities for virtually all major operating systems.

Heading the forum is Jim Kyle, 76703,762, of Oklahoma City, a 20-year veteran in the programming business, who is a systems analyst for a major manufacturer. He also writes technical articles and books. (Radio enthusiasts may recognize his name from *73 Magazine*, where he was associate editor for the magazine's first ten years.) The assistant sysop is Jeff Brenton, 76703,1065, who is president of his own commercial equipment business in Woodstock, Illinois. Overseeing it all in San Francisco is J.D. Hildebrand, 76701,32, editor of the magazine.

### Dr. Dobb's Journal (G DDJFORUM)

One of the oldest names in technical publications, *Dr. Dobb's Journal*, has been on-line for several years now with a forum that encourages discussions on programming languages, techniques, tools, utilities, and algorithms. The forum's primary purpose is to make available, in electronic form, the programming code published each month in the magazine, and to give its readers a communications link to its editors and writers.

Managing the forum is Tom Genereaux, 76703,4265, who is head of systems programming for the Computer Graphics Lab at the New York Institute of Technology. His assistant is Levi Thomas, 76703,4060, who works out of the magazine's offices in Palo Alto, California.

At present, the message board is subdivided into discussions on C, CP/M, ALGOL, FORTH, 68000 programming, artificial intelligence, and more.

### Online Today's Readers Forum (G OLTFORUM)

Sponsored by the editors and writers of CompuServe's *Online Today* magazine, this forum is different from most forums in that it focuses on CompuServe itself. The forum, administered by Pamela Bowen, 70007,2141, is part traffic cop and part welcome wagon, in that it was established to help subscribers locate various services and also to answer newcomers' questions about use of the system in general. If your other sources of information fail you, try OLTFORUM.

Also you can usually find a few editors and writers of the publication's print and electronic editions hanging around if you have questions or suggestions for them.

Assisting is the sysop chores are OLT columnist John Edwards, 70007,412; and OLT reviews editor Ernest E. Mau, 70007,1255. Other *Online Today* editors and writers are also regular users of this forum.

An added advantage is that OLTFORUM has provided Dave and Charlie a section of the message board for questions from readers of *How to Get the Most Out of CompuServe*.

*PC Magazine's PCMAGNET Forums (G PC MAGNET)*

One of the best-known magazines in the world of IBM and IBM-compatible computers is Ziff-Davis' *PC Magazine*. The magazine now has opened a successful collection of forums on the CompuServe network as an electronic extension of the publication. The features are:

— Editorial Forum supports the magazine's feature stories, as well as "First Looks" and "After Hours" and the regular columnists.
— Utilities Forum is an extension of the magazine's PC Utilities and PC Lab Notes features.
— Programming Forum covers environments, power programming and computer languages.
— Applications Forum supports the "Spreadsheet Clinic" and "Power User" features.
— Tips and Techniques Forum covers the "User-to-User," "PC Advisor," "PC Tutor," and "Connectivity Clinic" features.

Administering the forums are Chris Barr, 72241,13, and Ross Greenberg, 72241,36, with assistance from Mitt Jones, 72241,35; Wendy Huang, 72241,32; Charles Petzold, 72241,56; Ray Duncan, 72241,52; Sal Riccardi, 72241,34; and Erik Bailey, 72241,105.

Incidentally, PCMAGNET is a little different from most forums on the system in that you travel through a kind of gateway to reach them. When you finish in the forums, you must enter G CIS to return to the regular CompuServe features.


# IV. Professional Forums

The forum concept was probably about four hours old when somebody said, "Hey, this would be *great* for keeping up with other lawyers (doctors, teachers, writers) across the country." Indeed, and the healthy number of "professional forums" is proof of the wisdom of those words. But don't assume that a *professional* forum wants nothing to do with "serious amateurs" in the same field. Many of them, such as the Photography Forum, have a standing invitation to those working in the field, as well as others who are interested in it.

### *Aviation Special Interest Group (G AVSIG)*

The aviation forum deals with all topics relating to airplanes and flying, including weather, navigation, air traffic control, safety, maintenance, legal issues, etc.

John B. Galipault, founder and president of the Aviation Saftey Institute of Worthington, Ohio, is the sysop. His ID number is 76703,402. Assisting him are Alan

Bose, 76703,3044; Andy Dulay, 76702,261; Johnny Sewell, 76701,254, and Bob Kaputa, 76701,300.

### Broadcasters and Engineers (G BPFORUM)

John Hoffman, 76703,1036, a broadcast engineer at the NBC Television Network in New York, runs the Broadcast Professionals Forum (BPFORUM) and presents an electronic magazine called *InCue OnLine*. The forum is open to individuals and companies involved in radio, television, cable television, professional audio and video communications, etc. It also provides on-line services for two professional organizations, the Audio Engineering Society and the Society of Broadcast Engineers.

Assisting him are Joe Bartlett, 76703,4225; Chris Hays 76703,4257; and John Reiser, 76701,105.

### Computer Consulting (G CONSULT)

The Computer Consultant's Forum is the electronic arm of the Independent Computer Consultants Association (ICCA), a St. Louis group that, since its inception in 1976, has grown from 11 member firms to more than 2,300, representing more than 5,000 data processing professionals.

The forum is open to all, but has special reserved areas for ICCA members. Administering the forum is Nick Cvetkovic, 76703,4414, president of N.B.C. Associates, Inc., of Cherry Hill, New Jersey. He is assisted by Belva Carr, 70007,1407, ICCA's administrative assistant and David Moskowitz, 76701,100, president of Productivity Solutions, a Norristown, Pennsylvania, consulting firm.

### Education Forums

CompuServe has a number of on-line meeting places for teachers, administrators, students, and parents, starting with Chuck Lynd's Education Forum (G EDFORUM). Lynd, 76703,674, is a former classroom teacher with experience in both regular and special education settings. He also has more than ten years experience in education and computer-based retrieval systems. An assistant is Georgia Griffith, 76703,266, a Columbus, Ohio, music educator.

Other forums in the area on education are:

*Education Research Forum (G EDRESEARCH)* was set up to share, compare, and comment on research findings in the field. Many of its regular members are associated with the American Educational Research Association. The sysop is Dr. Jean W. Pierce, 76703,445, an associate professor at Northern Illinois University, and past president of the Mid-Western Educational Research Association.

*Foreign Language Forum (G FLEFO)* is for teachers and students of all languages. The sysops are Bette and Jerry Ervin, 76703,2063, who both hold Ph.Ds in foreign language education from Ohio State University. Their languages are French, Spanish, German, and Russian.

*Science/Math Forum (G SCIENCE)* is operated by Rick Needham, 76703,627, chairman of the Science Department of the Mercersburg Academy in Mercersburg, Pennsylvania., as a gathering place for teachers, students, and other subscribers with an interest in science and math. Among the items in the data libraries is an extensive collection of practice problems for students studying for college board achievement tests in math, physics, chemistry, and biology.

*Space Education Forum (G SPACEED)* is largely associated with the Teacher In Space Education Foundation, an organization founded by participants in the NASA Teacher In Space Program. In fact, the foundation's board of directors, drawn from the ten national finalists selected to undergo mission training at NASA's Johnson Space Flight Center, have all been given access to the forum. The chief sysop is Dick DeLoach, 76703,303, a NASA research scientist, who also involved in two other CompuServe forums.

*Students' Forum (G STUFO)* is intended for students of all ages, from the early grades to college, and teachers also are welcome. The sysop is Dave Winslow, 76703,2033, who has devoted more than 20 years to teaching high school and middle school, and currently teaches math and computer science at the Columbus Academy in Gahanna, Ohio.

Also, the Association for the Development of Computer-Based Instructional Systems, headquartered at Western Washington University in Bellingham, Washington, runs the ADCIS-Net Forum (G ADCIS). The service, operated by Ron Comer, 76703,564, and Alan Rowberg, 76703,4421, explores computer-based education and training.

The Association for Education in Journalism and Mass Communication also has an on-line connection through the AEJMC Forum (G AEJMC). The sysop is Lucinda Davenport, 76703,3020, an assistant professor in the School of Journalism at Michgan State University. Some of the courses she teaches include videotex and on-line databases, print news writing, broadcast news writing, ethics, and public relations. The forum is dedicated to professionals, researchers, teachers, and students in journalistic areas.

**Health-Related Forums**

One of the first professional forums on the block was MedSIG (G MEDSIG), which is sponsored by the American Association for Medical Systems and Informatics (AAMSI). The forum is open to medical people as well as interested lay people. The sysop is Dr. Alan Rowberg, 76703,4421. Assisting is Dr. Rick Jelovsek, 76703,612.

Since the beginning of consumer computing a decade ago, disabled people have found special significance in personal computers. They can be powerful tools for them. That has been particularly true of computers linked to national computer systems like CompuServe.

Disabled computerists also have their own forum. The Disabilities Forum (G DISABILITIES) is operated by Dr. David Manning, 76703,237, who has been a special educator for the past 23 years, and is the director of the Mainstream Center at the Clarke School for the Deaf in Northampton, Massachusetts. The forum is not directed solely to the disabled, he says, but is open to all people interested in disabilities, from those with handicapping conditions and their families to those who assist, train, educate, or employ the disabled.

The Consumer Health Forum (G GOODHEALTH) is operated by Dr. Mark Riaboy, 76703,650, an optometrist in Dallas, as a meeting place of the public and health professionals (physicians, pharmacists, counselors, nurses, therapists, and others). Topics discussed range from nutrition to mental health, child care, and sexuality. He is assisted by Dana Schmidt, 70007,3461.

The newest health service on-line is the Cancer Forum (G CANCER), administered by Ross & Associates, Communications Management, as a resource for support and information to people with cancer, as well as their relatives and friends. The primary sysop is John Ross, 76703,551, who receives assistance from volunteers of the Cancer Hot Line in Kansas City.

**Investing and Financial**

There is a lot more to telecomputing than telephones and computers. Like money. Several forums now cater to those who have a little left over after the telecomputing bills are paid.

*Investors Forum (G INVFORUM)* is operated by Harry Knutowski, 76703,4214; Mike Pietruk, 76703,4346, an assistant vice president with Preferred Savings and Loan in Chicago, and West Coast computer consultant Larry Ettelson, 76701,202.

*International Entrepreneurs Network (G USEN)*, the electronic arm of the Entrepreneurship Institute of Columbus, Ohio, a national nonprofit organization. Keeping it running is Bruce J. Kullberg, 76703,2032, the institute's national network director.

*National Association for Investors Corporation (G NAIC)* is designed for "value-oriented long-term investors, not market timers." According to a statement from the sysops, "Membership will be worthwhile for investors who aren't concerned with day-to-day changes in market prices, but who focus on finding quality companies and buying them at good prices." The sysops — who include Ed Chiampi, 76703,4354; Don Danko, 76703,4372, and Bob Kalischer, 73047,375 — also note that the service is aimed at education, not investment advice.

**Journalists and Writers**

Journalists and writers have a number of forums to serve them.

*Journalism Forum (G JFORUM)* was established by Jim Cameron, 76703,3010, who is president of Cameron Communications, Inc., a New York City consulting firm specializing in radio news and program syndication. He also is the anchorman for newscasts on the United Stations (RKO) Networks several days a week. The forum is designed to serve professional journalists, those in related fields and students considering careers in the profession. Assisting Cameron are Dan Hamilton, 76701,13, and Tony Russomanno, 76703,4164.

*Literary Forum (G LITFORUM)*, meanwhile, is an information exchange for writers of fiction, poetry, and non-fiction. It is open to working writers and as aspirants alike. The sysop is CompuServe veteran, Alex Krislov, 76703,243, of Cleveland, Ohio.

*Public Relations and Marketing Forum (G PRSIG)* began in January 1984 as a medium for electronic dialogue between professional publicists (as well as students) in the communications field. The founding sysop is Ron Solberg, 76703,575, who is a vice president for corporate affairs with Continental Illinois Bank of Chicago, started the PRSIG program. He has more than 20 years in the public relations industry. Assisting him is writer/editor Michael Naver, 70007,621, of Baltimore.

## *Law (G LAWSIG)*

Legal Forum has been the scene for many heated debates (Get more than one lawyer on the same network and just see what happens.) Also, more than once has a computer-smart attorney called on his on-line colleagues for suggestions on sticky points of law.

The sysop here is Noel D. Adler, 76703,264, a member of the New York State Bar. He is principal law assistant of the Suffolk County, New York, Supreme Court and author/editor of a number of publications including *The Copyright Kit — How to Copyright Your Computer Software*, *New York Civil Motion Citator*, and *Attorneys' Computer News*.

## *Military and Veterans (G VETSIG)*

Those who have been in the armed forces often find the Military Veterans Forum a major stop. It is designed for vets and nonvets to exchange ideas on common problems and issues. A limited-access section for Veterans Online also is offered. Recent discussions have included matters such as veterans benefits, Vietnam veterans, MIA/POW issues, the Veterans Administration, etc.

Running the forum is computer systems analyst Jim Horn, 6703,603, a Rockville, Maryland, retired officer who served in the First Infantry Division in 1966 in the Pacification Task Force Headquarters.

### Photography Forum (G PHOTOFORUM)

Mike Wilmer, 76703,4400, a professional free-lance photographer working out of northern California, established this forum as an electronic connection for professional and amateur photographers. Assisting him are Gabriel Unda, 70007,2532, a senior staff photographer at University of California, Davis, and Jon Jacobs, 76701,120, an Atlanta photographer with more than 18 years professional experience.

The forum has sections devoted to such subjects as darkroom techniques, new products, photographic art, travel pictures, multiimage production, cinematography, medical and scientific, and photojournalism. The service also is affiliated with a number of photographic associations.

### Safety Forum (G SAFETYNET)

Safetynet is devoted to information on safety-related issues and primarily is of interest to professionals in related fields, such as occupational health, safety engineering, or fire prevention. One purpose is to keep members updated on new tools in the profession.

"When we need to locate the latest information on a particular subject, we often make use of networking — we call up someone we know who is familiar with the subject, and ask the relevant questions," says the sysop, Dr. Charles M. Baldeck, 76703,2005. He is assisted by Leonard Wilcox, 76701,115, an industrial Hygienist and author.

### Working From Home Forum (G WORK)

"Take a coffee break with us," say Paul and Sarah Edwards, a California couple who run the first forum for "worksteaders." It is called the Working From Home Forum, devoted to those who presently work from home and those who aspire to. Members includes those who are self-employed, full-time and part-time, as well as salaried telecommuters. They routinely exchange information about making contacts, resources and solutions to problems, tax information, marketing ideas, etc.

The Edwards, 76703,242, are nationally recognized seminar developers and leaders, authors, and speakers. For Tarcher Books, they have written *Working From Home: Everything You Need To Know About Living and Working Under the Same Roof.*

# V. General Interest/Home and Recreation

Some information is vital to getting your computer running properly or working more efficiently in your jobs. Other information is just for the joy of it. A host of forums support recreations, from games to hobbies, from science to science fiction.

### Aquaria/Fish Forum (G FISHNET)

Wondering why your angelfish seemes to have lost the will to live? Can't figure out how to get your aebras interested in each other? You and your modem have come to the right place.

Alabaman John R. Benn, 76703,4256, of Muscle Shoals runs this forum. In addition to home hobbyists, the forum attracts public aquarium administrators, aquarium product manufacturers, and fish farmers and breeders.

In fact, members of a number of organizations use the forum as an on-line meeting place, including the International Betta Congress, Federation of American Aquarium Societies, North American Discus Society, American Cichlid Association, American Killish Association, and American Catfish & Loach Association.

### CB Forum (G CBFORUM)

If the CB Simulator becomes your main interest on CompuServe, then you will certainly want to get to know CBFORUM, one of the first general-interest forums ever brought on-line. It is operated by CompuServe's own CB regular, Pat Phelps, 70006,522, known to thousands of CB'ers as LooLoo. The forum is is a meeting house for a large number of CB users to swap messages and stories, usually related to their CB exploits.

Among the forum's libraries is the "CB Personal Ads," designed to help members find electropenpals. The forum also has a "CB Handle Index," where members can have their favorite handle listed and carved in stone for all to see.

### Comic and Animation Forum (G COMIC)

Members of this forum, operated by Washingtonian Doug Pratt, 76703,3041, take their funnies seriously. The forum features news, reviews, and conferences with some of the greats of comic books and animation. In fact, more than 25 professional comic authors are on-line to answer questions and mail.

### Consumer Electronics (G CEFORUM)

Consumer Electronics Forum was established to provide information about a wide range of topics, including consumer audio, video, software, satellite systems, telephone equipment, and more. In the past, it has been a place where some of the most exciting gadgets of our lives and times are first discussed.

Sysop Dawn Gordon, 76703,204, has been a free-lance journalist and consultant since 1981. Her work has appeared in such diverse publications as *High Fidelity*, *Rolling Stone*, *Popular Mechanics*, *The New York Post*, *Stereo Review*, *Popular Photography*, *Penthouse*, and *Savvy*.

## Food and Drink Forums

Two forums concentrate on the sensual delights of food and wine.

*Cooks Online (G COOKS)* is open to anyone interested in cooking, eating, and drinking. Members exchange their favorite recipes, cooking tips, information on new products and recommendations on favorite restaurants aren't exactly unheard-of there.

*The Bacchus Wine Forum (G WINEFORUM)* is run by aerospace industry manager Jim Kronman, 76703,431, who also is a West Los Angeles wine lover. He and his wife, Diane Ward, publish a wine newsletter, *The Informed Enophile*, which is frequently displayed on-line. The forum also features information about various wines and computer programs for the wine consumer.

### Genealogy Forum (G ROOTS)

This new forum is devoted to helping people all over the country who are interested in tracing their family trees. It asks all members to leave their names and the surnames of interest in the forum's member directory.

The data library offers programs of interest to genealogists, as well as how-to text files on related subjects. In addition, many of the forum's visitors are members of the Federation of Genealogical Societies.

The sysop is Dick Eastman, 76701,263, of Billerica, Massachusetts.

### Good Earth Forum (G GOODEARTH)

Here is Dave Peyton's on-line hangout, a forum that has become a friendly electronic community with a variety of interests, mostly having to do with farming, gardening, and the good life. In the past subjects have included things like how to build an earth-sheltered home, vegetable and ornamental gardening, and nutrition (and how suppliments can improve your health).

Besides being coauthor of this book, Peyton, 76703,244, is a columnist with Gannett News Service and *The Herald-Dispatch* of Huntington, West Virginia. His columns appear in many Gannett newspapers across the country.

**Games Forums**

Games are a big part of CompuServe. For the devoted game player, there are several forums of note operated by Patti Fitzgibbons, 76703,657, also known to her on-line friends as "Nightshift."

*Gamers' Forum (G GAMERS)* focus on all kinds of games, especially those played on a microcomputer. The forum members exchange hints, reviews, and product information on adventure, war/strategy, chess, Diplomacy, role-playing, arcade/action, and play-by-mail games. It is famous for its live, on-line role-playing games conducted in conferencing and via the message board. It also hosts regular chess tournaments.

*Multiplayer Games Forum (G MPGAMES)* is the place to discuss, comment on, and obtain information about the various Multiplayer Games on CompuServe, including MegaWars I and III, SeaWAR, Island of Kesmai, Multiplayer SpaceWar, Terrestrial, Air Traffic Controller, and Multiplayer Casino. Members help each other with answers and tips about playing the games.

*Play-by-Mail Games Forum (G PBMGAMES)* is devoted to a wide variety of imaginative games that can be played by electronic mail.

*Role-Playing Games Forum (G RPGAMES)* focus on various games that have players stepping into new personalities and new roles.

*Ham Radio Forum (G HAMNET)*

Almost from the start, microcomputers have had a big following in the ham radio community, so you would expect a forum like HAMNET to be an oldtimer in their neighborhood. You are right.

Ham Radio Forum has been around since the early 1980s as a meeting place for all sources of amateur radio buffs. The forum has subtopics devoted to short-wave listening, satellite television, packet radio, and much more.

Running the show is Scott J. Loftesness (call letters, W3VS), 76703,407. His assistant is Vern Buerg (N6MG), 70007,1212.

*Issues Forum (G ISSUESFORUM)*

Georgia Griffith, a Columbus, Ohio, music teacher, 76703,266, is one of CompuServe's earlier supporters and has been holding down the fort in Issues Forum for five years now. A blind subscripter who uses a Versabrailler to communicate over the system, Griffith serves on the advisory board of the Center for Special Education

Technology Information Exchange for the Council for Exceptional Children and on the board of directors of the National Braille Association.

Issues Forum is a platform for debate on a wide range of topics, including politics, handicapped issues, human rights, and more.

### Model Building Forum (G MODELNET)

Modelnet Forum was established to serve builders of all kinds of models — airplanes, cars, boats, railroads, and rockets. It has subtopics on such diverse things as model railroading and plastic modeling. The forum's message boards and data library provide information on various kits, tips on construction, shows, and so on.

Running the forum is Doug Pratt, 76703,3041, who is special projects director of the Academy of Model Aeronautics, the model airplane fliers' national organization. He has been on the editorial staff of two national model magazines, and writes regular columns for three. Also he has written several books, including *Basics of Model Rocketry* and *Basics of RC Cars*, published by Model Airplane News.

### Music Forums

Music — playing it, listening to it — has three forums on the system.

*General Music Forum (G MUSICFORUM)* is for musicians and music-lovers of every type, from classical and jazz to country and rock. It is operated by Jon F. Carleton and Sheryl Wickum, 76703,326.

*Rocknet (G ROCKNET)* was created by two Californians, former disk jockeys Les Tracy, 76703,1061, and Jim Palozola, 76703,3027. In addition to running the forum, they provide a daily newsletter on-line, concert information, news and gossip, and nightly gabfests in conference.

*The MIDI Forum (G MIDI)* is devoted to computerized music and music software. It is operated as Music, Computers & Software magazine, and the sysop is Bill Lewis, 76701,35, who is a songwriter, keyboardist, and MIDI musician.

### Religion Forum (G RELIGION)

Religion Forum is open to all religions and denominations for discussions of religious topics. Two educators operate it. They are Dr. Donald K. McKim, an associate professor of theology at the University of Dubuque Theological Seminary, and Dr. Linda Jo McKim, a lecturer in ministry at the University of Dubuque Theological Seminary and pastor of the Community Presbyterian Church of Cascade, Iowa. They can be reached with messages to 76703,547.

## Science and Science Fiction Forums

Dick DeLoach, 76703,303, who has been a NASA research scientist for more 20 years, is a legend on CompuServe. He has been a sysop since 1982, known for his helpfulness in guiding new members. Also, under his direction, Space Forum (G SPACEFORUM) has grown from a single forum to a system of three forums. The newest additions have been to the Space Education Forum (G SPACEED), which was discussed in the education section earlier this chapter, and the Astronomy Forum (G ASTROFORUM).

DeLoach also pioneered new uses of forums. In 1985, he hosted the first international real-time computer conference, allowing members to communicate with science fiction author Arthur C. Clarke, who visited with the forum while sitting at his computer — in Sri Lanka.

Meanwhile, speaking of sci-fi, fans of that genre should keep in mind the Science Fiction and Fantasy Forum (G SCI-FI), operated by San Francisco resident Wilma Meier, 76701,274. The forum specializes in news from the fields, reviews of new books, and conferences with authors.

## Sex Forums

Sex on-line? You bet. Howard and Martha Lewis, 76703,267, are editors/publishers of Human Sexuality Information Service, and on CompuServe, provide the Human Sexuality Support Groups (G HUMAN). This group includes *two* forums and a database of frequently-asked questions. Because the forums are very popular, the Lewises have one of the largest groups of assistant sysops of any forum on CompuServe. The team of assistants is led by Cathy Davis, 70007,2270.

The Lewis', who operate Clinical Communications, Inc. of Shady, New York, have written a number of books, including *Sex Education Begins at Home*, *The Parent's Guide to Teenage Sex and Pregnancy*, *Psychosomatics: How Your Emotions Can Damage Your Health*, and *The People's Medical Manual: Your Practical Guide to Health and Safety*. They also authored *The Electronic Confessional* about their on-line experiences, and they edit *Sexuality and Disability* journal; their articles on health and sexuality have appeared in *Reader's Digest*, *Good Housekeeping*, *Consumer Reports*, and *Family Circle*.

## Sports and Outdoors Forums

Telecomputing essentially is an indoor recreation (though we do know a few folks with batter-powered portables and celluar phones). Nonetheless, some of your fellow modemers use the system to talk about their love of the great outdoors.

In fact, that is the name of Joe Reynolds' corner of the system — the Great Outdoors Forum (G OUTDOORFORUM) — which specializes in information about pastimes like hiking, backpacking, outdoor photography, and wildlife. Reynolds, 76704,37, is northeast regional editor for *Field & Stream* magazine, and an avid fly fisherman and bird hunter. He is a Marylander who has traveled widely in the United States, Canada, and Central and South America in search of fishing and hunting opportunities. His forum invites campers, fisherman, hunters, backpackers, boy or girl scouts, nature lovers, sailors, cyclists... well, you get the picture.

And CompuServe isn't just for landlubbers. Sailing Forum (G SAILING) is operated by John Lovell, 76703,1013, who grew up in Westchester, New York, and as a member of the Larchmont Yacht Club, earned his credentials in the waters of Long Island Sound. Later, he sailed and raced and, during the bicentennial in 1976, was part of the staff crew on the Florida Bicentennial Ship, Brig Unicorn. The forum also gets special support from the staff of *SAIL Magazine*, 70007,2347.

If you like getting even wetter, try the Scuba Forum (G DIVING), open to certified divers as well as those interested in learning more about the sport. Also the forum invites professional divers to join. Subjects cover topics from finding out where and how to look for scuba training to care for equipment. The chief sysop is Richard C. Drew, 76701,123, who has been diving since 1974 and teaching scuba since 1978.

If your sporting interest run toward racing machines, don't miss Auto Racing Forum (G RACING), operated by Michael F. Hollander, director of Operations for Racing Information Systems in Santa Monica, California. Hollander, 76703,771, has been a motorsports journalist for more than a decade. He is the author of two books, *The Complete Datsun Guide* and *The New Mazda Guide* and is the television editor for *On Track*, the auto racing news magazine, whose staffers also regularly appear in the forum.

Finally, for general athletics topics, there is the Sports Forum (G FANS), which specializes in talking and playing sports. In addition to ongoing discussions of all types of athletic events, the forum regularly conducts contests and games based on real sporting events. Among the regular contests are Fantasy Football Leagues, Rotisserie-style Baseball Leagues, College/Pro Football Handicaping Contest, and the Super Bowl Contest. Running the affair is Harry Conover, 76701,220, who is assisted by Tony Brown, 76704,45; Walt Kirspel, 76702,247; Joe Feinstein, 70007,3375; and Steven Rubio, 70007,3374.

**Travel Forums**

Want some help with your vacation or business travel plans? At least two forums stand ready.

*Travel Forum (G TRAVSIG)*, is offered by John Matura (76702,342). The forum is devoted to all manner of travel questions. What tales of adventure or advice do you have to share with the other members? Discovered a particularly good restaurant or hotel? Need to know where to get a good cheeseburger in Tunisia? These are just some of the questions the forum seeks to handle.

If Florida is in your travel plans, note there is a forum devoted to that state alone. The Florida Forum/Discover Orlando (G FLORIDA) is operated by Larry Wood, 76703,704, with assistance from Dave Shaver, 76703,4355; David Pool 76701,25; and John and Pat Mullin, 76703,4352 in conjunction with the Florida Tourism Office, 76703,1011. Many of the forum's staff work for the Florida Department of Commerce, Tourism Division, and are ready to answer about visiting their state. The forum also provides educational assistance to schools, teachers, students, and parents planning visits to Florida.

### At Wit's End (G WITSIG)

At the end of the Forum Roundup is the wit's end, or rather, Wit SIG, a forum that is just for fun. According to the sysop, known only as "Lance," 76703,542, the forum shoots to "put a smile on your face after a tough day... or even after an easy day."

He notes that members of this particular forum "often hide behind pseudonyms (like 'Lance'), to save their families undue embarassment."

Upon entering, deposit your sanity at the door.

# CHAPTER 15

# To Market, To Market

Being benevolent taskmasters, we now begin to feel a little guilty about the paces we have put you through in recent chapters. You have worked hard and deserve a break. How about a shopping spree?

So far, you have seen how the system lets you send and receive messages, download and upload data, talk to people all around the world, and find valuable information instantly. This chapter changes the pace by visiting the system's marketplace to learn how goods can be purchased electronically and how some very specific kinds of information can be retrieved for travel, finance, and shopping. We will take a quick look at The Electronic MALL, an on-line weather service, some stock market information, an electronic travel agency, and more.

## Let Your Fingers Do the Shopping

Since the beginning of the personal computer phenomenon, talk has been of how computers one day would be used to buy goods and services without your having to leave your home or office. CompuServe subscribers don't have to wait. Let's go on-line to find where those products are available right now. Please log on and see the TOP menu:

```
 ------------------------------------------------------------
|                                                            |
|  CompuServe                                         TOP    |
|                                                            |
|    1 Subscriber Assistance                                 |
|    2 Find a Topic                                          |
|    3 Communications/Bulletin Bds.                          |
|    4 News/Weather/Sports                                   |
|    5 Travel                                                |
|    6 The Electronic MALL/Shopping                          |
|    7 Money Matters/Markets                                 |
|    8 Entertainment/Games                                   |
|    9 Home/Health/Education                                 |
|   10 Reference                                             |
|   11 Computers/Technology                                  |
|   12 Business/Other Interests                              |
|                                                            |
|  Enter choice number !                                     |
|                                                            |
 ------------------------------------------------------------
```

This tour samples features in a large area of the system, from options 4 through 7 on the TOP menu. For starters, choose option 6 — The Electronic MALL/Shopping — which prompts:

```
 ------------------------------------------------------------
|                                                            |
|  CompuServe                                    SHOPPING    |
|                                                            |
|  THE ELECTRONIC MALL/SHOPPING                              |
|                                                            |
|    1 The Electronic MALL (R)                               |
|      CompuServe's Electronic                               |
|      MALL saves time and money.                            |
|    2 SHOPPERS ADVANTAGE Club                               |
|    3 SOFTEX (sm) Software Catalog                          |
|    4 Order From CompuServe                                 |
|    5 New Car Showroom                                      |
|    6 Online Inquiry                                        |
|    7 Boston Computer Exchange                              |
|    8 Consumer Reports                                      |
|                                                            |
|  Enter choice !                                            |
|                                                            |
 ------------------------------------------------------------
```

Choosing option 1 takes you from this general SHOPPING page to the specific Mall menu:

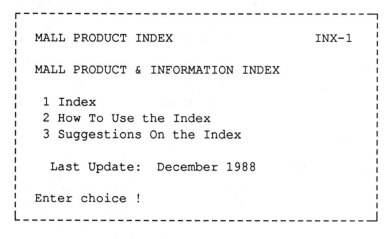

```
The Electronic Mall                      EM-18

     __/__/ T H E
     __/__/ E L E C T R O N I C
         M A L L (R)

    1 — Shop The MALL
    2 Index to Products
    3 SHOPPERS ADVANTAGE Club
    4 How to Shop
    5 Talk to the Mall Manager
    6 Go Mall Online
    7 Mall News/Free Shopping
    8 Catalog of Catalogs

  Enter choice !
```

Think of this as the outer concourse of our on-line shopping mall, from which you can find an overview of the facility's general setup and the entrance to the shopping area itself. Notice there is an introduction to the Electronic Mall concept giving you directions on "How to Shop." Other options list the latest happenings among the mall merchants and allow you to communicate with the mall manager. The easiest way to find merchandise is to browse the Index To Products, option 2 in our example. Select the index option and you see:

```
MALL PRODUCT INDEX                       INX-1

MALL PRODUCT & INFORMATION INDEX

    1 Index
    2 How To Use the Index
    3 Suggestions On the Index


   Last Update:  December 1988

  Enter choice !
```

Now enter 1 and the first page of the index appears:

```
,--------------------------------------------,
!                                            !
! MALL PRODUCT INDEX                 INX-5   !
!                                            !
! PICK A CATEGORY                            !
!                                            !
!   1 Apparel/Accessories                    !
!   2 Audio Equipment                        !
!   3 Automotive                             !
!   4 Books                                  !
!   5 Children's Clothes/Merch.              !
!   6 Collectibles                           !
!   7 Computer Hardware                      !
!   8 Computer Peripherals/Acc.              !
!   9 Computer Software                      !
!                                            !
! Enter choice or <CR> for more !            !
!                                            !
'--------------------------------------------'
```

Press RETURN at this, and each subsequent menu that ends with an "Enter choice or <CR> for more !" prompt, to get a overview of products and services available. Eventually, you come back to the main Index menu:

```
,--------------------------------------------,
!                                            !
! MALL PRODUCT INDEX                 INX-1   !
!                                            !
! MALL PRODUCT & INFORMATION INDEX           !
!                                            !
!   1 Index                                  !
!   2 How To Use the Index                   !
!   3 Suggestions On the Index               !
!                                            !
!    Last Update:  December 1988             !
!                                            !
! Enter choice !                             !
'--------------------------------------------'
```

Now let's go on a short shopping expedition for a book. Choose option 1 to reach the first page of the index.

```
r-------------------------------------------------r
|                                                 |
|  MALL PRODUCT INDEX                     INX-5    |
|                                                 |
|  PICK A CATEGORY                                |
|                                                 |
|    1 Apparel/Accessories                        |
|    2 Audio Equipment                            |
|    3 Automotive                                 |
|    4 Books                                      |
|    5 Children's Clothes/Merch.                  |
|    6 Collectibles                               |
|    7 Computer Hardware                          |
|    8 Computer Peripherals/Acc.                  |
|    9 Computer Software                          |
|                                                 |
|  Enter choice or <CR> for more !                |
L-------------------------------------------------J
```

To begin the actual search, you should choose option 4, which produces:

```
r-------------------------------------------------r
|                                                 |
|  MALL PRODUCT INDEX                     INX-11   |
|                                                 |
|  BOOKS                                          |
|                                                 |
|    1 Advice/Self Help                           |
|    2 Bibles                                     |
|    3 Biographies/History                        |
|    4 Business/Finance                           |
|    5 Classics                                   |
|    6 Computer/Technical                         |
|    7 Cookbooks                                  |
|    8 Children                                   |
|    9 Fiction/Non-Fiction                        |
|   10 Gift Books                                 |
|                                                 |
|  Enter choice or <CR> for more !                |
L-------------------------------------------------J
```

Although there is more to this list of book types (note the prompt), let's search for a computer book. Choose option 6 — Computer/Technical — to see which on-line stores offer such books:

```
MALL PRODUCT INDEX                    INX

1 CompuServe Store                 [ ORD ]
2 Computer Express                 [ CE  ]
3 Marymac Industries Inc.          [ MM  ]
4 McGraw-Hill Book Company, The    [ MH  ]
5 Small Computer Book Club         [ BK  ]
6 Some Things Special              [ SP  ]
7 Time-Life Books                  [ TL  ]
8 Waldenbooks                      [ WB  ]

Enter choice !
```

Some are small regional companies; others, like McGraw-Hill and Walden-books, are nationally known. The codes in the right column are direct addresses for the stores, so from anywhere in the system you could reach one of them by entering GO followed by a code, such as G WB or G BK. Let's see what Waldenbooks offers. Enter 8 (or G WB), and the system says:

```
Waldenbooks

WELCOME TO WALDENBOOKS!!!

Offering you the best in
* Videos * Computer Books
* Free Catalogs *

Enter choice or <CR> for more !
```

Consider this message to be an electronic version of a window display. To enter the kiosk itself, press RETURN and see the main Waldenbooks menu:

```
┌──────────────────────────────────────────────┐
│                                                │
│   Waldenbooks                                  │
│                                                │
│    1 About Waldenbooks Online                  │
│    2 Ordering/Shipping Info                    │
│    3 ** ONLINE SHOPPING **                     │
│    4 Request FREE Catalog                      │
│    5 Waldensoftware Store                      │
│       Locations                                │
│                                                │
│   Enter choice !                               │
└──────────────────────────────────────────────┘
```

Most mall merchants' electronic stores are designed like this, with an introductory menu of options for an overview of the store, one or more catalogs (often searchable by keywords or topics), and ordering and customer service information. To go directly to the book catalog, you enter 3, which causes the system to respond:

```
┌──────────────────────────────────────────────┐
│                                                │
│   Waldenbooks                        WB-19     │
│                                                │
│    1 CURRENT COMPUTERS BOOKS                   │
│       Selected for First New                   │
│       Direct by Waldensoftware                 │
│       Experts                                  │
│    2 VIDEOSELECT                               │
│       New Releases and Classics                │
│                                                │
│   Enter choice !                               │
└──────────────────────────────────────────────┘
```

Here are the computer books that the Index told us Waldenbooks offered. Choose option 1.

```
Waldenbooks

COMPUTER BOOKS selected by
Waldensoftware Experts

THE BEST OF CURRENT COMPUTER BOOKS

Waldensoftware, is a growing chain
of storesbringing you the finest in
computer books and software. Their
staff of experts designed this list
for First New Direct with the needs
and interests of the Compuserve
customer in mind.

Waldensoftware's selections cover
a wide range of interests, offering
titles that reach the novice,
intermediate and advanced user. This
list will continue to grow and change,
reflecting thediversity and cutting
edge elements in the computer market.

Press <CR> for more !
```

Press RETURN to see the menu:

```
Waldenbooks

COMPUTER BOOKS AND VIDEOS

   1 Hardware
   2 Online
   3 Operating Systems/Utilities
   4 PC Videos
   5 Programming
   6 Software

Enter choice !
```

Let's see what they have in the way of books about on-line communications, which is option 2 in our example.

```
-----------------------------------------------------

  2 articles selected

  Waldenbooks                                 WB

    1 How to Get the Most Out of Compuserve
    2 How to Look It Up Online

  Enter choice !
-----------------------------------------------------
```

Well, well — would you look at that! The very book you hold in your hands is listed here. Kind of makes you want to go out and buy another copy, doesn't it? (Nervous grin.) Choose 1 on this menu and read the description of the book. Go ahead! We love those words. There *is* a reason for all of this, besides assuaging our egos. Notice after the description comes a prompt like this:

```
-----------------------------------------------------

  Enter "O" to order.

  !
-----------------------------------------------------
```

This is a common prompt in the Electronic MALL. If you want to order a product you have read about, simply enter O (that is, capital "o", not a zero), and the system notes it. The O command is universal in the MALL. It isn't the only thing you do to order something, but it is the beginning. Here is the rundown on ordering:

— You browse through a single store's database, ordering as many things as you like with the O command.

— As you exit the store, you are taken to an order area (the electronic version of the check-out clerk with a cash register) where you are asked for information such as name, address, phone number, and your method of payment (which often is a credit card number but can vary depending on the merchant with which you are dealing).

— There are stopping places all along the way to make corrections to the ordering information and even to cancel the entire order. In other words, the O command *isn't* a final commitment, so a slip of the fingers won't get you in trouble.

Right now we shall assume that for some reason you don't want to take advantage of the marvelous offer to purchase another of our books, so enter G MALL at the ! prompt, which takes you back out in the concourse:

```
The Electronic Mall                    EM-18

    __/__/ T H E
     __/__/ E L E C T R O N I C
          M A L L (R)

    1 -- Shop The MALL
    2 Index to Products
    3 SHOPPERS ADVANTAGE Club
    4 How to Shop
    5 Talk to the Mall Manager
    6 Go Mall Online
    7 Mall News/Free Shopping

Enter choice !
```

Take a good look at this menu. You will probably want to come back later and check it out in more details. CompuServe is proud of this software, because it offers information about a world of products without the hassle often associated with shopping.

## You Don't Need a Weatherman...

Weather touches all of us, whether we are going out the door to the market or hitting the road for vacation or business. But before you head off, you might want to log on. CompuServe has tapped into the National Weather Service database of local and state forecasts to provide one of the most complete and extensive on-line forecast delivery services. To go there for the next leg of our tour, enter G WEA and, after a "One moment please" message, see:

```
r--------------------------------------------------------r
¦                                                        ¦
¦  CompuServe                              WEA-1         ¦
¦                                                        ¦
¦  PUBLIC WEATHER                                        ¦
¦                                                        ¦
¦   1 (SF)  Short Term Forecasts                         ¦
¦   2 (EF)  Extended Forecasts                           ¦
¦   3 (SW)  Severe Weather Alerts                        ¦
¦   4 (PP)  Precipitation Probability                    ¦
¦   5 (SS)  State Summaries                              ¦
¦   6 (CL)  Daily Climatological Reports                 ¦
¦   7 (SP)  Sports and Recreation                        ¦
¦   8 (MF)  Marine Forecasts                             ¦
¦   9 (AW)  Aviation Weather                             ¦
¦  10 (WM)  Weather Maps                                 ¦
¦                                                        ¦
¦  Enter choice!                                         ¦
¦                                                        ¦
L--------------------------------------------------------J
```

The menu illustrates you can search for all sorts of forecasts, from short-term and extended forecast to those in areas of sports and recreational events. The letters in parentheses after each number are direct-access codes for each functions; that is, you can use them instead of number if you choose.

Let's start out by checking for a short-term forecast for Huntington, West Virginia, where Dave and Charlie live. At the prompt, enter 1 or SF and the system displays:

```
r--------------------------------------------------------r
¦                                                        ¦
¦  SHORT TERM FORECASTS                                  ¦
¦                                                        ¦
¦  Enter city, state,                                    ¦
¦  or H for Help                                         ¦
¦                                                        ¦
¦  SF ID:                                                ¦
¦                                                        ¦
L--------------------------------------------------------J
```

Now at the colon prompt, enter HUNTINGTON. In a moment, the system displays a list for named Huntington (or something like Huntington):

```
Multiple matches for 'HUNTINGTON'

ID          Meaning
-----  --------------------
AR004  HUNTINGTON            AR
FL009  HUNTINGTON            FL
GA008  HUNTINGTON            GA
IN006  HUNTINGTON            IN
IA001  HUNTINGTON            IA
MA006  HUNTINGTON            MA
MO007  HUNTINGTON            MO
NV002  HUNTINGTON            NV
NY016  HUNTINGTON            NY
OH002  HUNTINGTON            OH
OR011  HUNTINGTON            OR
TX033  HUNTINGTON            TX
UT005  HUNTINGTON            UT
VT001  HUNTINGTON            VT
VA005  HUNTINGTON            VA
HTS    HUNTINGTON            WV
WI006  HUNTINGTON            WI

Choose ID(s), reenter location,
 or <CR> to ignore:
```

Searching the list, we find that the Huntington we want is second from the bottom and has a code of HTS. This code can be used in this and other features of the weather service to mean Huntington, West Virginia. Enter HTS at the prompt and this causes the system to display its forecast:

```
FQUS1 KHTS 161622
WVZ003-KYZ006-OHZ009-170100

HUWV-AHKY-
HUNTINGTON ASHLAND AND VICINITY FORECAST.
NATIONAL WEATHER SERVICE HUNTINGTON WV
1120 AM EST FRI JAN 20 1989

.THIS AFTERNOON...PARTLY CLOUDY WITH
LINGERING SNOW FLURRIES...HIGH IN  THE LOW
30S.  LIGHT WIND.

.TONIGHT...INCREASING CLOUDINESS WITH A 30
PERCENT CHANCE OF LIGHT  SNOW TOWARD
DAWN...LOW AROUND 20.  LIGHT SOUTHWEST WIND.

.SATURDAY...SNOW SHOWERS LIKELY...HIGH
AROUND 30.  THE CHANCE OF SNOW  IS 60
PERCENT.

$$
TRI STATE AREA EXTENDED FORECAST...SUNDAY
THROUGH TUESDAY...
CHANCE OF LIGHT SNOW SUNDAY. CLEARING
MONDAY. MOSTLY SUNNY TUESDAY.
DAYTIME HIGHS AROUND 20 SUNDAY...NEAR 30
MONDAY...UPPER 40S TUESDAY.
MORNING LOWS IN THE MID TEENS SUNDAY AND
MONDAY...MID 20S TUESDAY.

SF ID:
```

Just think — no more waiting through 20 minutes of Top 40 music just to hear the latest weather from the radio. We often use this feature when we are planning trips by car or plane since it is important to know what nature has in store for you up the road.

To get back to the main weather menu, press RETURN.

```
PUBLIC WEATHER

 1 (SF) Short Term Forecasts
 2 (EF) Extended Forecasts
 3 (SW) Severe Weather Alerts
 4 (PP) Precipitation Probability
 5 (SS) State Summaries
 6 (CL) Daily Climatological Reports
 7 (SP) Sports and Recreation
 8 (MF) Marine Forecasts
 9 (AW) Aviation Weather
10 (WM) Weather Maps

Enter choice!
```

If weather is an interest of yours, we urge you to return to this main menu later and read some of the other forecasts.


# On-Line Stocks and Bonds

Now we make one of our famous quantum leaps over tall buildings and broad databases to the MONEY page of the system. At the prompt, enter G MONEY to reach:

```
r---------------------------------------------------------¬
¦                                                         ¦
¦  CompuServe                                  MONEY      ¦
¦                                                         ¦
¦  MONEY MATTERS/MARKETS                                  ¦
¦                                                         ¦
¦    1 Market Quotes/Highlights                           ¦
¦    2 Company Information                                ¦
¦    3 Banking/Brokerage Services                         ¦
¦    4 Earnings/Economic Projections                      ¦
¦    5 Micro Software Interfaces                          ¦
¦    6 Personal Finance/Insurance                         ¦
¦    7 Financial Forums                                   ¦
¦    8 MicroQuote II ($)                                  ¦
¦    9 Business News                                      ¦
¦   10 Instructions/Fees                                  ¦
¦   11 Read Before Investing                              ¦
¦                                                         ¦
¦  Enter choice !                                         ¦
¦                                                         ¦
L---------------------------------------------------------J
```

This menu is the entrance to most of the financial information on-line. We shall use this menu to find a searchable database that puts the power of a stock broker in your computer. With it you can gather the latest stock and bond quotes from the major markets. This database is under the first option, so enter 1 and the system responds with:

```
r---------------------------------------------------------¬
¦                                                         ¦
¦  CompuServe                                  QUOTES     ¦
¦                                                         ¦
¦  MARKET QUOTES/HIGHLIGHTS                               ¦
¦                                                         ¦
¦    1 Current Quotes ($)                                 ¦
¦    2 Current Market Snapshot ($E)                       ¦
¦    3 Historical Stock/Fund Pricing                      ¦
¦    4 Highlights - Previous Day ($)                      ¦
¦    5 Commodity Markets                                  ¦
¦    6 No-Load Mutual Funds                               ¦
¦    7 Investment Analysis                                ¦
¦    8 Issue/Symbol Lookup                                ¦
¦    9 Instructions/Fees                                  ¦
¦                                                         ¦
¦  Enter choice !                                         ¦
¦                                                         ¦
L---------------------------------------------------------J
```

From this menu, you can find a variety of searchable databases and text information to help you research investments you have made or are planning to make. As we shall be looking at the current price of a stock issue, choose option 1.

*Hold it right there, fellows! Doesn't that "$" at the end of the choice mean it is a surcharged service? You promised not to lead me into any extra-cost items, didn't you?*

My, my, grandma, what big eyes you have! You are right, of course. That dollar sign symbol *does* means the Current Quotes database is a surcharged feature. Fortunately, we have a way to get you in and out without additional charges.

After you enter 1, the system provides this introduction to the current Quick Quotes (QQUOTE) service:

```
Quick Quote                                    QQUOTE

Quotes are delayed over 15 minutes. CompuServe does not edit this
data and is not responsible or liable for its content,
completeness, or timeliness.


DOW 30 was up 10.27 on 1/22

Quotes are surcharged (7 cents each if the market is open, 2
cents if closed).

Enter ticker symbols (i.e. HRB, IBM), or an asterisk followed by
beginning of a company name (i.e. *BLOCK), /H for HELP or /EXIT.

Issue:
```

There is a surcharge for nearly every stock quote you get from this database, but one is free. It is the quote for H&R Block Incorporated, the company that owns CompuServe; we shall search for Block's latest quote in a moment.

When you see the "Issue:" prompt, you may enter either a stock ticker symbol or a "CUSIP" (a number assigned to each stock and bond issue). Perhaps you don't know either. Fortunately, QQUOTE also allows you to search for a ticker symbol. If you enter an asterisk (*) and any part of a company name, you see a list of companies whose names contain those letters. For example, if you enter *INTER for International Business Machines, you see a list of more than a hundred companies with INTER in their names. If you enter *INTERNATIONAL, you see fewer; the more complete the name you supply, the smaller the resulting list and the closer you get to the company whose stock you want to study. Let's use this method to find H&R Block's ticker symbol. Enter *BLOCK at the "Issue:" prompt to see:

```
Quick Quote

27 Issues begin with BLOCK

 1 Market Indexes/Exchange Rates
 2 Mutual Funds
 3 Options
 4 Stocks/Other

 Enter choice or ALL !
```

We are looking for stocks, so enter 4 at this prompt and the system displays:

```
Quick Quote

    Ticker Company Name                 Issue
    ------ ------- ----                  -----
 1 BLOCA   BLOCK DRUG INC               CLASS A
 2 HRB     BLOCK H & R INC
 3 BBEC    BLOCKBUSTER ENTMT CORP

Enter choice !
```

You learn here that the ticker symbol for H&R Block Incorporated is HRB, and the database gives you a menu from which you can choose the Block stock quote. It is item 2 in our example. Enter the appropriate number and you are shown the most current quote, something like:

```
r---------------------------------------------------------------¬
¦                                                               ¦
¦  Name              Volume   Hi/Ask  Low/Bid  Last   Change  Update ¦
¦  ---------------    ------   ------  -------  ------  ------  ------ ¦
¦  BLOCK H & R INC    842      28.375  28.000   28.000  -0.250  11:58 ¦
¦                                                               ¦
¦    Issue:                                                     ¦
¦                                                               ¦
L---------------------------------------------------------------⌟
```

Now that you are back at the "Issue:" prompt, you can enter the ticker symbol — HRB — to see the quote again. This method is quicker, of course, as you don't have to call up a menu to find the quote you want. Obviously, if you become a regular user of the QQUOTE feature, you should search and memorize (or jot down) the symbols for your particular interests.

At the "Issue:" prompt, press RETURN to go back to the Quotes menu:

```
r---------------------------------------------------------------¬
¦                                                               ¦
¦  CompuServe                                         QUOTES     ¦
¦                                                               ¦
¦  MARKET QUOTES/HIGHLIGHTS                                      ¦
¦                                                               ¦
¦    1 Current Quotes ($)                                       ¦
¦    2 Current Market Snapshot ($E)                             ¦
¦    3 Historical Stock/Fund Pricing                            ¦
¦    4 Highlights - Previous Day ($)                            ¦
¦    5 Commodity Markets                                        ¦
¦    6 No-Load Mutual Funds                                     ¦
¦    7 Investment Analysis                                      ¦
¦    8 Issue/Symbol Lookup                                      ¦
¦    9 Instructions/Fees                                        ¦
¦                                                               ¦
¦  Enter choice !                                               ¦
¦                                                               ¦
L---------------------------------------------------------------⌟
```

# On-Line Travel Services: the Only Way to Fly

No on-line market has grown more rapidly in recent years than the travel services. They let you be your own travel agent, planning your business and pleasure trips on-line, when you want to plan them. What's more, in many instances, you can use these services to reserve airline seats, hotel rooms, and even rental cars.

Our next stop is a feature called Eaasy Sabre. From the "!" prompt where you are located, type GO TRAVEL to see the main travel menu:

```
CompuServe                                    TRAVEL

TRAVEL AND LEISURE

  1 What's New in Travel
  2 Air Information/Reservations
  3 Hotel Information
  4 Car Information/Routings
  5 U.S. Domestic Information
  6 International Information
  7 Travel Potpourri
  8 Forums
  9 Aviation
 10 Electronic Mall Merchants

Enter choice !
```

There is much to look at here. In fact, you can find information about nearly any kind of travel that interests you. Perhaps you will want to return here to check out all the services available. Right now, we want you to pretend you are going on a plane trip. Choose 2 to see this FLIGHTS menu:

```
CompuServe                                    FLIGHTS

AIR INFORMATION/RESERVATIONS

  1 Travelshopper
  2 EAASY SABRE
  3 OAG Electronic Edition

Enter choice !
```

The system is telling you there are three resources for searching airline schedules. We are heading for Eaasy Sabre, option 2 in our example.

```
EAASY SABRE                          EAASYSABRE

   1 Introduction
   2 How to Use
   3 Quick Path and FAASTRACK Help
   4 Access EAASY SABRE
   5 Talk to EAASY SABRE

** HELP DESK 800-331-2690 **

Enter choice !
```

Eaasy Sabre enables you to look for scheduled flights on all major airlines, as well as for hotels and even rental car agencies in major cities. Not only that, you can make reservations for flights, hotels, and rental cars if you sign up for the service. Although you won't be signing up this time, you still may search the databases as much as you like. The database is a service of American Airlines (which, incidentally, solves one of the great mysteries on-line, that is, why the funny spelling of "EAASY"? We now know what the "AA" stands for, don't we?)

**Note:**    Once you enter the Eaasy Sabre area, you actually are leaving the CompuServe computers in Columbus, Ohio, through what is called a *gateway*. (We shall have more to say about gateways on CompuServe in Chapter 20.) For now, what it means is that Eaasy Sabre serves several different on-line services from a central location. You are connected to Eaasy Sabre through CompuServe, but the information you receive is located elsewhere.

Choose option 4 to access Eaasy Sabre and see something like this:

```
EAASY SABRE                                EZS-4

One moment please...

Connected to 14SABRE

 CMP Access, Session  24
X25Mpx REV *4.1, 8/13/87
 SID_APPL SESSION  21
Welcome     COMPUSERVE User
Session 1-1

  MAKE THE MOST OF THE MILES YOU FLY!

Did you know you can earn the mileage
credit you deserve on EAASY SABRE
— regardless of the frequent flyer
program to which you belong?

Simply type your frequent flyer number
when prompted.  EAASY SABRE will forward
it automatically as part of your
reservation record, to your selected
airline.

So, go on!  Make the most of the miles
you fly.  It's EAASY!  Select option 9
from the MAIN MENU for free membership
and immediate booking privileges.

Press <CR> to continue
>
```

That stuff at the beginning that looks like secret code actually is the Eaasy Sabre computer recording your entry from CompuServe into its own network. The

">"prompt at the bottom is unfamiliar, but not particularly unsettling. As the message above it says, merely press RETURN to see some more information:

```
EAASY SABRE is a service supplied
exclusively by American Airlines
Inc.

EAASY SABRE and the SABRE system are
the property of American Airlines,
Inc., and much of the data relating
to schedules and fares is a copy-
righted work of Official Airline
Guides, Inc.  Neither EAASY SABRE
nor any of such data may be
reproduced, sold, transferred, or
modified without the express advance
written permission of American
Airlines, Inc. and, where necessary
Official Airlines Guides, Inc.

Press <CR> to continue
>
```

Now that we have all the wherefores and to-wits out of the way, press RETURN and finally you see an important menu:

```
┌─────────────────────────────────────────────────────┐
│                                                       │
│   EAASY SABRE MAIN MENU                               │
│                                                       │
│    1  System Quick Tips                               │
│    2  Flights                                         │
│    3  Hotels                                          │
│    4  Cars                                            │
│    5  Airline Fares                                   │
│    6  Weather Information                             │
│    7  AAdvantage                                      │
│    8  Itinerary Review                                │
│    9  Application                                     │
│   10  Profile Review And Change                       │
│   11  Sign on For Reservations                        │
│   12  Sign off                                        │
│                                                       │
│   Enter choice, or from any display..type             │
│   Help or ? for assistance, or                        │
│   Top  or /T to return to Main Menu or                │
│   Exit or /E to return to System Operator             │
│   >                                                   │
│                                                       │
└─────────────────────────────────────────────────────┘
```

You can search a flight database, hotel database, or car rental database. Also, you can apply for that service to make on-line reservations. You can use all three databases for a complete itinerary, then review that itinerary. The Quick Tips menu choice (option 1 in our example) contains complete on-line documentation on how to use Eaasy Sabre. Later, if you decide to use the service for reservations, return here and select option 11 to begin the application process. For our tour, we shall look at the airline flight schedules just for information.

**Note:**   Don't be concerned that you might accidentally order a ticket to Rangoon or Newark; it is impossible to spend any money until you actually have signed up for that option.

Before we move on, note the two navigation commands available, both led by a slash (/): /T to return to the main menu and /E to exit, that is, to go back through the gateway and return to CompuServe.

Let's pretend you are going to take a flight with Charlie and Dave from their hometown of Huntington, West Virginia, to The Big Easy, New Orleans. Choose option 2 from the menu and you see:

```
PLEASE ENTER YOUR REQUEST:

DEPARTURE POINT

EXAMPLE:   LOS ANGELES OR LAX

QUICK PATH EXAMPLE:
   DFW,DEN,JUN3,6A,3   OR
   DFW,DEN,JUN3,AA521,3
  >
```

About the note at the bottom of the display: The "Quick Path" way of entering information is to enter codes separated by commas. You learn how to do that by choosing option 1 "System Quick Tips" on the main menu. Because we are new to these parts, let's take things slowly and see how this system works at a basic level.

Enter the name HUNTINGTON as the city of departure at that prompt. Next you are asked for your destination:

```
DESTINATION

EXAMPLE:   LOS ANGELES OR LAX

  >
```

Enter NEW ORLEANS at this prompt, and see:

```
 ┌──────────────────────────────────────────────┐
 │                                                │
 │   TRAVEL DATE:                                 │
 │                                                │
 │   EXAMPLE:   JAN 01                            │
 │                                                │
 │   >                                            │
 │                                                │
 └──────────────────────────────────────────────┘
```

Choose a date about ten days from today and enter it by typing the first three letters of the month, a space, and the date in two digits, which leads to:

```
 ┌──────────────────────────────────────────────┐
 │                                                │
 │   SELECT                                       │
 │                                                │
 │   1   ALL AVAILABLE FLIGHTS                    │
 │   2   SPECIFIC AIRLINE & FLIGHT NUMBER         │
 │                                                │
 │   >                                            │
 │                                                │
 └──────────────────────────────────────────────┘
```

Tell the system you want to see all available flights by choosing option 1. Now see:

```
 ┌──────────────────────────────────────────────┐
 │                                                │
 │   ENTER DESIRED                                │
 │   DEPARTURE TIME                               │
 │                                                │
 │   EXAMPLE: 630A                                │
 │                                                │
 │   >                                            │
 │                                                │
 └──────────────────────────────────────────────┘
```

To keep everyone together, let's all enter 700A for 7 a.m. That doesn't restrict the list to those flights leaving at 7 a.m, but presents flights closest to that time first. Now you should see something like this (though, of course, expect some changes in the actual schedule information):

```
FROM (HTS) HUNTINGTON
TO (MSY) NEW ORLEANS  LA        JAN-15-89
     FLT  DPTR        ARVL         D M ST EQP
1AL  383 HTS   700A PIT   741A 9      0 D9S
     CLASSES:    Y  B  H  Q  M  K  V
 AL   83        955A MSY 1125A 7 B    0 73S
     CLASSES:    Y  Q
2PI  787 HTS   635A CLT   725A 8      0 F28
     CLASSES:    F  Y  B  H  Q  M  K  V
 PI  259        812A MSY  902A 8 B    0 733
     CLASSES:    F  Y  B  H  Q  M  K  V
3DL 3173 HTS   755A CVG   835A        0 SWM
     CLASSES:    Y  B  M  H
 DL  971        920A MSY 1020A 8 S    0 73S
     CLASSES:    F  Y  B
FOR RESERVATIONS, ENTER LINE NUMBER, OR
 8 MORE FLIGHTS        11 FARES
 9 CHANGE FLT REQUEST  12 CODES
10 FIRST FLT DISPLAY   13 DEPENDABILITY


>
```

If you are a regular flier, you know that airlines don't run on jet fuel; they run on codes. And there are lots of codes here. Before we show you how to solve that mystery, let's talk about how to read this screen full of information, using our printed example as our guide. Look first in the left column at the numbers 1, 2, and 3. Each represents a different series of flights we could take from Huntington to New Orleans through various "hubs." No nonstop flights are available between Huntington and New Orleans, but this example shows three flights from Huntington to hub cities for continuing flights to New Orleans. The first flight leaves Huntington Tri-State Airport (HTS) at 7 a.m. and arrives at PIT at 7:49 a.m.

*Hmmm, question: How do I find out what airport is represented by the PIT code?*

Glad you asked that. To find out, you choose option 12 ("CODES") on this menu, which produces:

```
r---------------------------------------------------------¬
|                                                         |
|   SELECT THE CODES NEEDED.                              |
|                                                         |
|   1   CITIES AND AIRPORTS                               |
|   2   AIRLINES                                          |
|   3   EQUIPMENT                                         |
|   4   RETURN TO FLIGHTS                                 |
|                                                         |
|                                                         |
|   >                                                     |
|                                                         |
L---------------------------------------------------------J
```

This area is for unscrambling these and other codes. As the menu says, it is prepared to explain codes for cities, airports, airlines, and equipments — all the codes you see on the flight schedule. Choose option 1 here and see:

```
r---------------------------------------------------------¬
|                                                         |
|   ENTER THE CITY/AIRPORT NAME OR CODE.                  |
|                                                         |
|   EXAMPLE:   LOS ANGELES OR LAX                         |
|                                                         |
|   PRESS <CR> TO RETURN TO FLIGHTS                       |
|                                                         |
|   >                                                     |
|                                                         |
L---------------------------------------------------------J
```

Now just enter PIT to see the airport associated with the code:

```
r---------------------------------------------------------¬
|                                                         |
|   PIT — PITTSBURGH    PA                                |
|                                                         |
|   1   CITIES AND AIRPORTS                               |
|   2   AIRLINES                                          |
|   3   EQUIPMENT                                         |
|   4   RETURN TO FLIGHTS                                 |
|                                                         |
|   >                                                     |
|                                                         |
L---------------------------------------------------------J
```

Notice the menu stands ready to translate other codes with its numbered options.

So, we now know the first leg of the first flight begins in Huntington and ends in Pittsburgh, Pennsylvania. Choose 4 from the menu to return to the previous list of flights.

```
FROM (HTS) HUNTINGTON
TO (MSY) NEW ORLEANS  LA          SEP-15-88
     FLT  DPTR        ARVL        D M ST EQP
1AL   383 HTS  700A PIT  741A 9       0 D9S
          CLASSES:   Y  B  H  Q  M  K  V
 AL    83        955A MSY 1125A 7 B   0 73S
          CLASSES:   Y  Q
2PI   787 HTS  635A CLT  725A 8       0 F28
          CLASSES:   F  Y  B  H  Q  M  K  V
 PI   259        812A MSY  902A 8 B   0 733
          CLASSES:   F  Y  B  H  Q  M  K  V
3DL  3173 HTS  755A CVG  835A         0 SWM
          CLASSES:   Y  B  M  H
 DL   971        920A MSY 1020A 8 S   0 73S
          CLASSES:   F  Y  B
FOR RESERVATIONS, ENTER LINE NUMBER, OR
 8 MORE FLIGHTS          11 FARES
 9 CHANGE FLT REQUEST    12 CODES
10 FIRST FLT DISPLAY     13 DEPENDABILITY

>
```

Continuing to read the schedule in our printed example, you note that Flight 83, the second Huntington to New Orleans flight, leaves PIT at 9:55 a.m. and arrives at New Orleans (MSY) at 11:25 a.m. The number under the D is the dependability of the flight where you see numbers from 1 to 10. The higher the number, the more times that flight has arrived on time in recent months. (Later, if you want to learn more about dependability ratings, return to this menu and choose 13, "DEPEND-ABILITY," from the menu.) Under M you see the meal, if any, served on the flight. Under S you see the number of stops on each leg of the flight. For interpretation of the equipment codes, choose option 12. Finally, classes are explained in the Quick Tips option you saw on the main menu.

Now, let's check the fares of these flights. Choose option 11, and you will see:

```
FROM: HUNTINGTON           HTS
TO: NEW ORLEANS  LA      MSY
ALL AIRLINES-REGULAR AND DISCOUNT FARES
WEDNESDAY   JAN 15 1989
   ONE   RND FARE        AIRLINE
   WAY   TRIP CODE        CODES
1         158 KECOMNR    AL PI
2         198 KHLE2NR    AL PI
3         218 KXE7NR     AL PI
4         258 KWE7NR     AL PI
5         258 QXE2P25    AL
6         268 QXE2P25    PI
7  139   278 MZ6NR       AL
FOR RULES, ENTER LINE NUMBER OF
DESIRED FARE, OR:
 8 MORE FARES            11 FLIGHTS
 9 CHANGE FARE REQUEST 12 SPECIFIC
10 FIRST DISPLAY            AIRLINE

>
```

Here is a presentation of what you would pay for the flights you have seen in the previous display. If you want to examine any fare more closely, choose the number of the flight to see if any special rules apply to obtain the fare. Note that option 11 takes you back to the flight schedules.

Now, let's go back to the main menu. To get there you enter Eaasy Sabre's own navigation command, /T, at the prompt, which brings you to:

```
EAASY SABRE MAIN MENU

 1  System Quick Tips
 2  Flights
 3  Hotels
 4  Cars
 5  Airline Fares
 6  Weather Information
 7  AAdvantage
 8  Itinerary Review
 9  Application
10  Profile Review And Change
11  Sign on For Reservations
12  Sign off

Enter choice, or from any display..typethe
Help or ? for assistance, or
Top  or /T to return to Main Menu or
Exit or /E to return to System Operator

>
```

Once we are in New Orleans, let's see what hotels are available. Remember, if you elect to sign up for on-line reservations, you can actually make hotel reservations through Eaasy Sabre; but for the tour, we shall just take a quick look at how the system displays such information. Choose 3 from the main menu, and you will see:

```
ENTER THE CITY IN WHICH THE
HOTEL IS REQUIRED

EXAMPLE: LOS ANGELES, OR LAX.
QUICK PATH EXAMPLE:
  SJC,JUL01,JUL06,1

>
```

Enter NEW ORLEANS (or the code MSY, as you already know that it is Eaasy Sabre's code for that city). Next, you are asked a series of questions about when you

are arriving, when you are leaving, and how many people are in your party, beginning
with:

```
CHECK IN DATE.

EXAMPLE: JUL 02

>
```

Choose a date about ten days in the future. Next, see:

```
CHECK OUT DATE

EXAMPLE: JUL 06

>
```

Plan on staying one day at least. Hotels don't give special rates for people who check
out in the middle of the first night. In fact, the management frowns on that. Now, see:

```
NUMBER OF ADULTS IN ROOM

1  ONE ADULT
2  TWO OR MORE ADULTS

>
```

Choose 1 at this prompt. Next:

```
PLEASE ENTER NUMBER OF NAMES IN
PARTY, UP TO 4, OR PRESS <CR> FOR 1:

>
```

*Wait a minute. Why does the system want names?*

Remember, this is the same menu you see if you use the system to make reservations on-line. In this case, just press RETURN.

```
NUMBER OF ROOMS DESIRED

1 ONE ROOM
2 TWO ROOMS
3 THREE ROOMS
4 FOUR ROOMS


>
```

Choose option 1 from this menu. Finally, the system displays:

```
QUALIFIERS MAY BE SELECTED.  ONLY
HOTELS WHICH MEET SELECTED REQUIREMENTS
AND HAVE ROOMS AVAILABLE WILL BE SHOWN.

1   HOTEL CHAIN
2   HOTEL NAME
3   LOCATION SELECTION
4   TRANSPORTATION
5   MAXIMUM ROOM RATE (I.E., $64)
6   CORPORATE RATE
7   NO QUALIFIERS DESIRED

FOR PREFERENCES ENTER ONE OR MORE
LINE NUMBERS.

EXAMPLE:  1,2,4


>
```

You can limit your choices to a specific hotel chain, hotel name, location (in town or in the suburbs), whether or not the hotel has transportation to and from the airport, maximum room rate, and whether or not it has a corporate rate. You can choose more than one limitation by separating the numbers with commas and, in that case, are asked to provide more information to narrow your choices. For this tour, choose 7, which means we aren't quite so picky. When you do that, you see the first page of a list of hotels:

```
HOTEL ROOM SELECTION
NEW ORLEANS   LA
PREFERENCES -

   HOTEL CODE       NAME    MILES FROM MSY
  ─────────────────────────

1   IT FRENCH MARKET INN
               NEW ORLEANS LA        18W
2  HY HYATT REGENCY NEW ORL
               THE HOTEL IS CONNEC  14W
3  BW BW WEST BANK
               HARVEY, LA           17SE


FOR DETAILS OR RESERVATIONS
ENTER LINE NUMBER OR :
  8 MORE HOTELS          11 CHANGE HOTEL
  9 CHANGE HOTEL REQUEST    PREFERENCES
 10 FIRST DISPLAY

 >
```

The hotel name is accompanied by information about the number of miles is it located from MSY airport and the direction it is located from the airport. For example, the French Market Inn is located 18 miles west of the airport. For details about one of the hotels, you choose the corresponding number. If you had the capability of making reservations on-line, you would choose the same number.

Now enter the /T navigation command to get back to the main menu. Notice that no matter where you are in Eaasy Sabre, you can get back to "System Operator" — that is, CompuServe — by entering /E. Try that now. Type /E at the prompt and see:

```
THANK YOU FOR USING AMERICAN AIRLINES
EAASY SABRE SYSTEM
ONE MOMENT PLEASE...


>


EAASY SABRE                                          EAASYSABRE


  1 Introduction
  2 How to Use
  3 Quick Path and FAASTRACK Help
  4 Access EAASY SABRE
  5 Talk to EAASY SABRE


** HELP DESK 800-331-2690 **


  !
```

You are out of the Eaasy Sabre system and back with CompuServe. You can tell that because of the familiar "!" prompt. Notice, too there is more information about how to use Eaasy Sabre here as well as an "800" number in case you just can't figure out how to use the system.

This is a good place to stop for a moment and reflect on what you saw. Perhaps it looked vaguely familiar. If you have ever looked over a travel agent's shoulder while he or she was making reservations, this system may have been the one you saw — because it is used by many professionals, sometimes in a slightly modified form.

Now, let's wrap up this tour (enter OFF or BYE to log off the system), and we shall take care of some more business.

# Side Roads

Now that the tour bus has stopped and we can relax a bit, you ought to know that we only scratched the surface of the business, financial, and travel services. You might want to continue your research on your own. Here are some pointers for independent study.

### Collecting Data for Spreadsheets

Data from the Quick Quotes stock quotations (G QQUOTE) can be saved on-line in a file that then can be downloaded and used in a spreadsheet such as *Lotus 1-2-3*. The operation is possible because of the little-known /OUTPUT command. Entered at the "Issue:" prompt we saw during the tour, /OUTPUT causes the system to ask for the name of the online file in which you wish the results of subsequent commands to be stored. This allows you to (1) create a new file, (2) overwrite an existing file with the same name or (3) append data to an existing file. After you have entered a file name, you are returned to the "Issue:" prompt where you may enter stock symbols. Here is how it works:

Suppose you enter the /OUTPUT command at QQUOTE's "Issue:" prompt and, when asked for a file name, you instruct the system to store data in a file called STOX.TXT. Now you are returned to the "Issue:" prompt and you enter four stock symbols: AAPL,HRB,GCI,IBM. The requested data does not display on the screen, but rather is transmitted directly to your new STOX.TXT file, which is stored in a part of the system called MicroQuote II, which we shall see in a moment.

Like most CompuServe file names, it can be one to six characters and (optionally) a period (.) and a one- to three-letter extension. In our example, STOX.TXT would produce a file like this:

```
APPLE COMPUTER INC          857   39.250   38.875   38.875  0.375   9:39
BLOCK H & R INC              38   29.500   29.250   29.375  0.000   9:38
GANNETT INC                 256   33.500   33.500   33.500 -0.250   9:34
INTERNATIONAL BUSINESS MA  1171  121.500  121.250  121.500  0.375   9:39
```

(These figures from QQUOTE represent the volume so far today, the High/Ask, the Low/Bid, the last quote, the change and the time of the update.)

One file name extension has a special function. The extension .PRN causes the /OUTPUT from QQUOTE or PRICES to in a format that can be imported into *Lotus 1-2-3* and compatible spreadsheets after it is downloaded. In our example, if we specify the file name as STOX.PRN, the /OUTPUT looks like this:

```
"AAPL",857,39.25,38.75,38.75
"HRB",38,29.5,29.25,29.375
"GCI",256,33.5,33.5,33.5
"IBM",1171,121.5,121.25,121.5
```

To download STOX.TXT or STOX.PRN, visit MicroQuote II by entering /G MQUOTE at the "Issue:" prompt (or the same command at any ! prompt but without the initial slash), which brings you to:

```
MquoteII !
```

In addition to a number of inter-related financial databases, MicroQuote II provides a storage area similar to your Personal Files Area (G PER) except that it is set aside specifically for financial data.

To retrieve the file, you need to summon MicroQuote's file transfer program by entering the command FILTRN at the prompt. The system displays:

```
File Transfer

TRANSFER PROTOCOL

1 XMODEM (MODEM7) protocol
2 CompuServe 'B' protocol
3 CompuServe 'A' protocol
4 DC2/DC4 (CAPture) protocol
5 MACintosh XMODEM protocol

Enter choice !
```

Select the protocol you wish to use for the transfer (making sure it is one that also is supported by your communications program). After that, the system asks for the *direction* of the transfer (download or upload), the file *type* (ASCII or binary) and, finally, the *name* of the file to retrieve. You then instruct your communications software to retrieve the file as it is transferred by CompuServe.

**Creating a Ticker File**

If you check the same stocks frequently, you can save time by creating a *ticker* file in the MicroQuote II work area. To do that, enter GO MQUOTE to reach the MquoteII "!" prompt and enter EDIT MYSTOX.TIC. (Actually, it can be any six-letter name with an optional three-letter extension.) Now enter the ticker symbols, one per line. You also may enter an OUTPUT command to have the information automatically put into a file. For example, you might enter:

```
IBM
//OUTPUT = STOX.PRN
AAPL
HRB
GCI
/EX
```

In this example, the stock quote for IBM would go to the terminal, then the quotes for Apple, H&R Block and Gannett Inc. would go to the STOX.PRN file in your MicroQuote area. Note the *two* slashes before the OUTPUT in a ticker file, compared with only one slash when entered manually. Also notice that the ticker file is closed with the /EX command.

To use your ticker file at the Issue: prompt of a financial service, simply enter @MYSTOX.TIC. The @ sign tells the system to look for its instructions in your MicroQuote file area. For more on ticker files, see the online documentation by entering GO TICFILE.

A few more points to know. Besides /OUTPUT, the QQUOTE feature has several additional commands, including:

— /ITEMS, which displays a menu of the available data items and lets you choose which ones to send to the file, including ticker symbol, volume, high/ask, low/bid, close/average/last, change, date of the quote.

— /OPTIONS, which provides formatting alternatives for the data, allowing you to select between two- and three-digit decimal precision, between including and omitting the decimal point, between fixed-length and variable-length items separated by spaces or commas and to place or to not place quotation marks around a ticker symbol.

— /DATA, which adds lines numbers to the data items so that they can be used as DATA statements in a BASIC program. The system prompts for a starting line number and the number by which to increment the lines.

Finally, for help with using the financial services, importing data to spreadsheets, setting up ticker files and related matters, visit CompuServe's Investors Forum (G INVFORUM).

**Financial Features:**

On the MONEY menu, we saw ten entries. Each leads to other pages of menus dealing with subjects ranging from the latest reports on the performances of big and small corporations to stock analysis programs with which you can track an issue's performance for ten years or more. Many of these additional stock services carry surcharges, as the stock quote service does. The "Instructions/Fees" selection from the MONEY menu gives you not only the latest surcharges associated with these databases, but also on-line documentation on how to use the features. If you are interested in keeping on top of business news and changes in the markets, you ought to explore the business services on your own.

— Also, if you are interested in the stock market, you might want to check out "The Quick Way" (G QWK-1) and "Tickerscreen" (G TKR-1). Both of these are discount brokerages, which offer on-line purchasing of stock. In other words, you actually can buy securities through your computer. The Quick Way is operated by Quick and Reilly; Tickerscreen is operated by Max Ule and Co., Inc., one of the largest discount brokerage firms in the United States. By signing up for either services, you can get quotes on stock, options, market indexes, and even mutual funds. For a premium, you can get "real-time" quotes rather than those delayed 20 minutes, as in QQUOTE. Both services let you place orders for stock and options on-line and receive confirmation when your orders are executed. You can review your portfolios, value, income, and unrealized gains and losses. Both services allow you to read more about them, take demonstration tours, read about the current terms and prices of the service, and even begin the process of opening an account on-line. No waiting. No salesman will call.

— *Historical stock databases*, including G PRICES for a price/volume reporting on individual securities, G CPRICE for price/volume information on commodities, G PRISTATS for performance summaries of individual stocks, G DIVIDEND for a divident-distribution and interest-reporting service, G OPRICE for a single-day options pricing service, G QSHEET for multiple quotes for a historical date, and G EXAMINE for a detailed issue examination.

**Note:**  On some of these features, you can use special commands to redirect the output to a file that can be downloaded for use in spreadsheets. You can review on-line information about these and other capabilities by enter a question mark (?) at the "Issue:" prompt.

For financial news, here are some features of note:

— Market Snapshot (G SNAPSHOT) is used to get a quick review of current market trends, a one-page report on the direction and breadth of market indicators and so on.

— OTC NewsAlert (G OTN) is used for news of the over-the-counter securities market.

— News-a-tron (G NAT) is used for news and analysis for selected commodities, market indices, and financial instruments.

— Agri-Commodities (G ACI) includes a weekly electronic magazine called *Futures Focus.*

### Demographics

CompuServe also offers resources for demographic information for business or general research, among them:

— Neighborhood Reports (G NEIGHBOR) lets you find age, income, occupation, and household statistics, searching by zip code, county, or state.
— CENDATA (G DEMOGRAPHICS) is an on-line service of the U.S. Census Bureau that includes reports on population, manufacturing, foreign trade, agriculture, business, and so on.
— Business Demographics (G BUSDEM) is for material on assorted business markets in specific geographic areas.

### Travel

Travel services are numerous, and the number is growing all the time. From the main TRAVEL AND LEISURE menu, you can book tours and cruises, read U.S. State Department reports on conditions in other countries, and even socialize with other travelers in the Travel Forum. As this form of communication matures, the on-line buying power of goods and services increases as well. Business and travel are two on-line marketplaces where the potential is virtually unlimited. You might be interested in comparing Eaasy Sabre with two other major flight and reservation services:

— Travelshopper (G PARS) is a product of TWA Airlines, features a low fare finder, has information for the frequent flight bonus programs, and has national and international scheduling. It also offers a currency conversation feature, and provides weather information for cities around the world.
— The Official Airline Guides, Electronic Edition (G OAG) is the oldest airline information service of its kind and still is touted by many as the most extensive database around. In fact, OAG supplies schedule data to more than 250 world airline reservation systems. It also offers low far finders and performance ratings, as well as data on hotels and car rentals. Unlike Eaasy Sabre and Travelshopper, OAG is a surcharged service. An average ten-minute session for prime time (daytime) hours is $4.70, while nonprime (evening and weekend) time is $1.70.

Also of interest to travelers:

— ABC Worldwide Hotel Guide (G ABC) provides descriptions, rates, phone numbers, and facilities for 34,000 domestic and international hotels. It also lists miles to airports, local and toll-free phone numbers, Telex machine identification numbers, credit card information, and more.

— Worldwide Exchange (G WWX) is the electronic extension of an organization dedicated to real estate and holiday facility, renting/chartering, exchanging, buying or selling. It has thousands of listings from all over the world in a database that is updated twice a week. Most of the listings of real estate and holiday facilities are offered for sale, rent, charter, exchange, trade, or to share.

### Shopping

Speaking of buying and selling, in addition to the Electronic MALL, you on-line shoppers might want to look into:

— Shopper's Advantage (G SAC) is a discount shopping club for members (formerly called Comp-U-Store). All CompuServe subscribers can browse, but you must sign on as a member to make purchases. Options on the main menu give details of membership. The advantage of Shopper's Advantage is that you can comparison shop for more than 250,000 brand name products at discount prices. The store also operates a staff hotline for questions and assistance. Like Eaasy Sabre, this is a gateway from CompuServe to computers elsewhere.

— The New Car/Truck Showroom (G NEWCAR) lets you view and compare features of passenger cars, vans, and trucks to help you make buying decisions. The database has information on more than 850 cars, vans, special-purpose vehicles, and light-duty trucks. The feature is surcharged; you may look at models one at a time for 90 cents or two at a time in a side-by-side comparison format for $1.20.

— Softex (G SOFTEX), CompuServe's own software catalog, with which you can purchase software on-line and download it immediately, having the charges placed on your regular CompuServe bill. The database lets you search catalogs of software for your machines by computer type, publisher, title, or Softex catalog number.

## Go Order for "the Good Stuff"

CompuServe offers its own on-line ordering service. You get there by entering G ORDER at any system prompt. To some, that command sounds a bit threatening because it appears as if once you get there, you will have to order something. Actually, the command doesn't commit you to anything. As a new user, you owe it to yourself to invest a little time browsing the ordering service to see the helpful and entertaining products CompuServe has to offer. Perhaps the best news for those on a budget is that there are no connect charges while you are in the On-line Ordering Service area. You aren't charged for connect time while viewing descriptions or placing an order.

A fear among new users, perhaps, is that some unwanted item will be ordered inadvertently. That shouldn't be a problem, though. Anytime you are in the ordering service, you can view items chosen during that session by entering DIS (for DISplay) at a prompt. After the items are displayed, you are asked if you want to make a change in the order. If you have made a mistake, you can correct it on the spot. Finally, when you complete your on-line order, the entire list is displayed for verification. At that point, you can change it or confirm it. Then you are given an order number for you to jot down so you can check on the order later if necessary.

If you are interested in what you can find in the On-line Ordering Service, look in the On-line Survival Kit at the back of the book where we list in the "Further Reading" section a number of the products available.

# CHAPTER 16

# The Executive Option — A Business Edge

In late 1983, CompuServe introduced a system called the Executive Information Service for business people with personal computers in their offices and/or homes. In mid-1985, these features were incorporated into the main CompuServe system as extra-cost services for all. This tier of extra features — collectively called the Executive Option — is becoming increasingly important for those wanting to get and keep a business edge. After all, information is what business is all about, whether keeping up with the competition, scanning the news about what Congress and regulatory agencies are doing, browsing the Wall Street reports for the latest on securities, or doing in-depth research on a business prospect.

Several perks attract subscribers to the Executive Option, including a 50 percent increase in the amount of on-line storage space in the personal file area (PER), along with an invitation to acquire more storage space at a reduced weekly rate. Option subscribers also get a ten percent discount on CompuServe products and direct marketing offers for goods and services from the system's affiliated merchants and manufacturers. Also they have a six-month (rather than 30-day) storage period for unaccessed personal and financial files, and they aren't charged a monthly minimum for the Checkfree billing option. What's more important about the Executive Option, however, is that it opens the door to some exclusive databases, including high-powered demographics, stock market information and analysis, connections to Securities and Exchange Commission documents, sophisticated news gathering, and more.

This chapter, while staying off-line, highlights these databases to help you decide if you want to pick up the option — cost considerations are involved. For one thing, a one-time $10.00 upgrade fee is charged. In addition, surcharges are levied in most of the special databases. Finally, Executive Option users also are subject to a $10.00 monthly minimum charge. (When the monthly CompuServe charges exceed $10.00, no extra fee is levied for that month. All connect-time charges, surcharges, and on-line CompuServe product purchases apply toward the minimum.) After reading this chapter, you may want to enter G EXECUTIVE at any prompt to get more information or to sign up for the Executive Option.

**Note:** If you sign up for the option and later decide you want to cancel it, enter visit Feedback (G FEEDBACK) and choose the category "Account cancellation."

## Supersite: Demographics on Demand (G SUPERSITE)

Demographic information is a cornerstone for many businesses. Whether you are searching for a location for a new regional office or finding the best areas in which to sell your wares, the characteristics of various parts of the country are all important. The same information can be invaluable if you are considering a move to a new city and want to compare it with your current home. At the end of the previous chapter, on-line addresses for several general statistical services were listed, but a more sophisticated demographic resource called SuperSite is open to Executive Option users.

SuperSite provides demographics for the United States as a whole, as well as every individual state, county, Standard Metropolitan Statistical Area (SMSA), Arbitron TV Market (ADI), Nielsen TV Market (DMA), and zip code area. Fourteen reports are available for each area, covering general demographics, income, housing, education, employment from the latest census along with updates and forecasts. In addition, sales potential reports for 16 major types of retail stores and consumer potential for three types of financial institutions. ACORN (A Classification of Residential Neighborhoods), available as part of SuperSite, classifies all households in the United States into one of 44 market segments based upon the demographic, socioeconomic, and housing characteristics of the neighborhood in which they live.

What is best about SuperSite is that it is easy to find the information you are looking for, as easy as answering prompts from a menu. All you have to do is indicate the kind of geography and report you need and turn on your printer for an 80-column printout. (In the event of a printer problem, the reports can be redisplayed immediately at no additional charge.)

Here is a typical report for a single ZIP code area, showing population, number of households, and the income:

|              | 1980 CENSUS | 1986 UPDATE | 1991 FORECAST | 1986-1991 CHANGE | ANNUAL GROWTH |
|--------------|---------|---------|----------|--------|--------|
| POPULATION   | 38946   | 45648   | 50920    | 5272   | 2.2%   |
| HOUSEHOLDS   | 12370   | 15190   | 17597    | 2407   | 3.0%   |
| FAMILIES     | 10260   | 12328   | 14025    | 1697   | 2.6%   |
| AVG HH SIZE  | 3.05    | 2.92    | 2.82     | -0.10  | -0.7%  |
| AVG FAM SIZE | 3.42    | 3.33    | 3.26     | -0.07  | -0.5%  |
| TOT INC (MIL$) | 317.8 | 598.6   | 781.3    | 182.7  | 5.5%   |
| PER CAPITA INC | $8160 | $13113  | $15344   | $2231  | 3.2%   |
| AVG FAM INC  | $27589  | $42298  | $47586   | $5287  | 2.4%   |
| MEDIAN FAM INC | $25809 | $40667 | $46106   | $5438  | 2.5%   |
| AVG HH INC   | $25692  | $39405  | $44400   | $4994  | 2.4%   |
| MEDIAN HH INC | $34080 | $37850  | $43004   | $5153  | 2.6%   |

Most charts give actual 1980 census information, a current update based on interim figures gleaned from several sources, a forecast for 1991, the percentage of change expected between now and 1991, and the annual growth or decline predicted in the various categories.

Only a few years ago, this kind of information was reserved for those who could pay big bucks to research firms. Even then, it sometimes took weeks or even months to gather. SuperSite can be an equalizer between those businesses that can afford to have their own research staff and those businesses that can't but need the information to stay competitive.

SuperSite reports, which are surcharged from $20.00 to $100.00 depending on the information, include:

— Demographic Reports for housing, Hispanic population, education, energy, employment, income and component area and forecast summaries, housing value by age, combined demographic, and income forecast, age by sex, age by income.

— Sales potential reports for various businesses, including appliance store, consumer finance, dry cleaner, hair salon, ice cream store, optical center, photo outlet, retail bakery, savings and loan, apparel store, automotive aftermarket, commercial bank, department store, drug store, footwear store, grocery store, home improvement, restaurant, and shopping center.

— ACORN Target Marketing Reports for population profile, household profile, financial services, investment services, convenience store, restaurant, shopping center retail, and media analysis, media.

An option on the main SuperSite menu provides the current costs for specific reports.

# Taking the Mystery out of OTC (G OTCNEWS)

Ask security traders about today's stock market and many say the over-the-counter (OTC) market is where it's happening. But they also tell you in the same breath that it is often difficult to get information about the thousands of stocks traded in this growing market loaded with small or obscure companies. But not any more. Information about these stocks is available through OTC NewsAlert, a searchable database of articles pertaining to the over-the-counter market. By using OTC NewsAlert, you not only can get company news but you also have access to a wealth of information about the OTC market in general.

OTC NewsAlert is divided into two parts:

1.  Recent OTC News is where articles remain for varying time periods, depending on the type of news. All articles may be retrieved when searched by company name or ticker symbol. Recent articles are intended to provide an overview of the OTC market and as a beginning to additional searches. Because some companies have not yet been assigned a ticker symbol, this is a good place to find them.
2.  Recent/Historical OTC News may have up to a year's worth of articles on a company, including summary earnings reports, large sales contracts and new products, acquisitions and takeover bids, and significant stock transactions by corporate insiders. These, of course, are the types of events that usually have an impact on stock prices.

Even OTC NewsAlert doesn't contain information about all OTC companies. But certain happenings in a company will cause news about the company to appear in the database, such as:

— Filings of certain documents with the Securities and Exchange Commission.
— New issues of securities, also known as Initial Public Offerings (IPOs).
— Appearance or disappearance of a company from the OTC market.

Sometimes a company is added to the database because of earnings and financial performance summaries, legal matters of importance, and acquisition processes.

**Note:**   Perhaps thoughts of searching a huge database such as OTC News-Alert for information about a specific company is not very pleasant. Fortunately, that problem is solved with another service of the Executive Option. All news articles that go into the database also go through a service called the Executive News Service, an exciting new idea in on-line news gathering that lets you create your own personal folders to catch news as it becomes available. This feature saves time and gives you virtually immediate access to news of financial markets and other matters. The Executive News Service will be discussed in detail at the beginning of Chapter 20.

## Disclosure II: On-Line SEC Information (G DISCLO)

When a company decides to make a stock offer, the Securities and Exchange Commission (SEC) requires the company to file a considerable number of forms. That information can be vital to those contemplating the purchase of securities. Before the age of telecommunications, this information was difficult to obtain. Today, SEC filings are reported on-line in the Disclosure II database, which provides information on reports from approximately 8,500 publicly owned companies. The database includes descriptive information; financial information (three years of income statement data and two years of balance sheet data); corporate officers' names, ages, titles, and annual remuneration; directors' names, ages, titles and annual remuneration; stock ownership information; subsidiary information; exhibits; other corporate events, and the full text of the management discussion. CompuServe receives weekly updates from Disclosure Incorporated, the database supplier.

In order to get company reports, you need to know the ticker symbol, the first six digits of the CUSIP number or the Disclosure number for the company. These are available elsewhere on the system (such as in QQUOTE, the stock quote feature we toured in the previous chapter). After entering the identifying code, a menu item appears if the company is listed in Disclosure II.

The following is a list of the reports available and their prices at the time this book was updated:

1. Full company record, $10.00. (The full report includes the next seven reports listed. Prices below are the price of the reports if requested separately.)

   a. Company name and address, $2.30.
   b. Company profile, $4.70.
   c. SEC filings, $2.30.
   d. Officers and directors, $4.70.
   e. Ownership and subsidiary summary, $4.70.
   f. Exhibits, other corporate events, $2.30.
   g. Management discussion, $4.70.

2. Full financial information, $6.00. (The next five reports are listed. Prices below are the price of the reports if requested separately.)
   a. Balance sheet for two years, $4.70.

    b.  Annual income statement, three years, $4.70.
    c.  Quarterly Income statement, $4.70.
    d.  Business segment data, $2.30.
    e.  Five-year summary, $2.30.

  3.  Ratio report, $4.70.

# Company Screening for the Best Deals

Searching through data on several thousand securities isn't an easy task, but with two special searchable databases, the drudgery is reduced. Company Screening (G COSCREEN), an adjunct of the Disclosure II database, and Securities Screening (G SCREEN) both work in much the same way. You provide the characteristics of the security for which you are looking and the computer gives you a list of securities that meet your criteria. Both are menu driven. You choose the menu items that most interest you and give values when asked. For example, the Disclosure II Company Screening menu is:

```
 1 SIC Code                13 Debt/Equity Ratio
 2 State                   14 Market/Book Ratio
 3 Total Assets            15 Current Rat
 4 Book Value              16 Return on Assets
 5 Market Value            17 Return on Equity
 6 Sales                   18 Return on Sales
 7 Net Income              19 Earnings/Share
 8 Cash Flow               20 Cash Flow/Share
 9 Latest Price            21 Price/Earnings Ratio
10 4 Yr Growth Rate-Sales  22 Yield
11 4 Yr Growth Rate-Net    23 Price Position
12 4 Yr Growth Rate-EPS    24 Price Volatility
```

    You may choose one or more of these options and, through a series of prompts, enter your limiting factors. When you finish, the program lists the securities it finds that meet your specifications.

    Surcharges for Securities Screening is $5.00 per screen plus 25 cents per issue displayed. Disclosure Company Screening is $5.00 per screen and 50 cents per company displayed.

# Return Analysis: Charting Gains and Losses (G RETURN)

The Return Analysis Program lets you determine the rate of return for a security or a group of securities over a period of time. If you choose a group of securities to be analyzed simultaneously, the report lists them alphabetically, either from the lowest to the highest or from the highest to the lowest return.

Suppose you want to know how the stocks of IBM, Digital Equipment Corp., and Apple Computers stacked up against each other during 1983. By entering information at the menu prompts, such as the ticker symbol or CUSIP number of the securities, the period of time you want analyzed, and the way you want the report displayed, you can see something like:

```
Returns on Selected Issues

                                                    %         %
Symbol Company name    1/01/83   12/31/83  Value   Change    Return
------ ------------    -------   --------  ------   ------    ------
IBM    INTL BUS MACH   88 1/2    115 7/8   1,309     31.0      31.0
AAPL   APPLE COM INC   29 7/8     24 3/8     815    -18.4     -18.4
DEC    DIGITL EQ CORP  99 1/2     72          723   -27.6     -27.7

       Total 3 Issues                      2,849     -5.0      -5.0
```

# I/B/E/S: Wall Street's Best Guesses (G IBES)

Your broker calls with a hot prospect. "This one can't lose," he says. Earnings are high and everyone — absolutely everyone — says the only way is up. With the Institutional Brokers Estimate System, you can check to see if, in fact, the Wall Street prognosticators are as impressed with the stock as your broker says they are. I/B/E/S is a database that provides consensus earnings estimates on more than 3,400 publicly traded corporations. Consensus Earnings Estimates are arrived at by compiling earnings forecasts made by more than 2,500 professional securities analysts at 130 brokerage and research firms.

The system takes more than 100,000 individual earnings estimates and groups them by company and by fiscal period. Then the database produces average or mean earnings estimates for the current fiscal year, the next fiscal year, and the five-year projected average annual growth rate. An extended I/B/E/S report also prints the highest and lowest earnings estimate among the analysts. What does this mean for you? Perhaps a clearer idea of the earnings expectations, which may relate to the current and future price of a stock. It also means you won't have to take the word of your broker, unless you want to.

## Ticker Retrieval: One-Stop Shopping (G TICKER)

So far you have found that there is information galore on-line about securities, but perhaps you are getting an uneasy feeling that the searching is just too time-consuming. CompuServe proposes to solve that with a program called Ticker Retrieval, which allows you to find financial information quickly from a single menu. Once you enter the company's ticker symbol or CUSIP number, you see the current market price quotations, followed by a menu listing sources of additional information on the company. Selecting an item from the menu transfers you to another program to obtain additional reports on the company. Surcharges vary according to the report that is received.

The following is a list of menu items available and the costs of the reports at this writing:

1. Company synopsis, 25 cents.
2. Pricing history, 3 cents for daily prices for the most recent trading day and 5 cents for other days. Weekly prices cost 10 cents per week, and monthly cost 15 cents per month.
3. Dividend history, 15 cents per distribution.
4. Pricing statistics, $1.25 for 52 weeks.
5. Descriptive information on issue, $1.25.
6. Annual financial reports, $3.20 for four financial statements.
7. Forecasts, $1.60 for Value Line forecasts; $2.00 for expanded IBES forecasts; 50 cents for abbreviated IBES forecast.
8. Quarterly financial reports, $1.60 per report, regardless of number of quarters displayed.
9. Redisplay of current-day price, no charge.
10. Bonds for issuer, 5 cents per bond listed.
11. Options profile, $1.25 per report, regardless of number of options listed.

## Side Roads

You can supplement this chapter's discussion with your own on-line research. Entering G EXECUTIVE at any prompt provides an overview of the service and its surcharges. In addition, you can visit most of the Executive Option databases for additional information *before* signing up, including Ticker Retrieval (G TICKER), Disclosure II (G DISCLO), I/B/E/S (G IBES), Company Screening, (G COSCREEN), Securities Screening (G SCREEN), SuperSite (G SUPERSITE), and OTC NewsAlert

(G OTCNEWS). In each instance, a message tells you that the service is reserved for those with the Executive Option; after you press RETURN, you are shown a menu from which you can choose an overview or sample report.

# CHAPTER 17

# The Games People Play

"It's a funny thing," a CompuServe official mused to us one day. "We have got a good idea of the demographics of the people who use CompuServe. And while they probably won't admit it, there are a lot of professionals who get on the system late at night and play games — a lot of games."

It's not that CompuServe monitors who's playing games and who's not, but it is clear from the usage reports that a lot of people spend a lot of time having fun on-line. And why not? Computers are for recreation as well as for more serious pursuits. If you bought a lot of games for your micro, you would have a lot of money tied up in them; you would wind up playing with most of them for a few hours and putting them aside. By contrast, you never own CompuServe's games; you sort of rent them for the amount of connect time you spend playing them. How many games are there on CompuServe? By actual count... uh, lots. In fact, many probably have been added since this book was updated.

The system's games section is divided into two groups:

*Player-against-computer games*, in which you match wits with a game program. They range from the simplest (such as the old game, Hangman) to complex adventure games in which the player explores the depths of a cave (or a temple, or a pyramid and so on) and tries to retrieve treasures while fighting off horrible creatures.

*Multiplayer games*, in which subscribers from all over the system gather to play the computer and each other at the same time. Many believe this type of game is the most exciting form of play that the home computer and the modem have opened to millions of people. It is now quite common to log on and play a game with someone you have never met who lives in another state or even around the world.

In this chapter there is a list of some of the single-player, or player-against-computer, games offered in the system's games section and information about several forums for game enthusiasts. (The next chapter is devoted to the multiplayer games, providing information about how they are played, where to find more about how they are played, and how to find people on CompuServe to play them with you.) We don't have the space to give complete instructions, but we do point the way to on-line introductions for each. Browse our catalog and see if you find some that strike a chord with you. Most of the descriptions were borrowed directly from CompuServe.

A note about a time saver: each description has the direct-access page number and gives you an idea of whether the game will display properly on your system. (Some suggest specific screen sizes and others require players to be using CompuServe's *Professional Connection* or *VIDTEX* software or at least a program that can emulate *Vidtex*.)

By the way, we hope you appreciate the effort that went into bringing you these game descriptions. After all, Dave lost his shirt in the on-line blackjack casino and Charlie was devoured by some unspeakable entity in a cave. ...

# Hangman

| | |
|---|---|
| Suggested Age | :Children |
| Classification | :Word Game |
| Players (Min/Max) | :1/1 |
| Special Requirements | :None |
| Minimum Screen Width | :32 |
| Direct Access Page | :GO GAM-212 |
| Instructions | :GO GAM-112 |

Here is a computer classic, one of the older games on the system. Hangman is a word-guessing game in which the computer thinks of a word and you try to learn it by picking letters. Each time you come up with a correct letter, the computer shows you where it goes in the word. For each incorrect guess, the computer adds a part of your body to hangman's gallows.

# Golf

| | |
|---|---|
| Suggested Age | :8 and Up |
| Classification | :Simulation |
| Players (Min/Max) | :1/1 |
| Special Requirements | :None |
| Minimum Screen Width | :32 |
| Direct Access Page | :GO GAM-210 |
| Instructions | :GO GAM-110 |

This is an 18-hole computer golf course, but don't expect graphics. The computer "commentator" explains the course as you play. You are given four woods, 8 irons, a wedge, and a putter. Your challenge: choose the right club for the situation as it is explained to you. After each shot, you are told your situation and how far you are from the hole. It is a good game for learning how to choose the right club for varying situations on the links.

# Football

| | |
|---|---|
| Suggested Age | :12 and Up |
| Classification | :Simulation |
| Players (Min/Max) | :2/2 |
| Special Requirements | :None |
| Minimum Screen Width | :64 |
| Direct Access Page | :GO GAM-216 |
| Instructions | :GO GAM-116 |

With this one, two can play at the same terminal or computer. The computer first asks for city and team name information. Here are the commands:

1=DIVE PLAY
2=TRICKY RUN
3=SHORT PASS
4=LONG PASS
5=QUICK KICK
6=PUNT
7=FIELD GOAL

# Advanced Digital Football

| | |
|---|---|
| Suggested Age | :10 through Adult |
| Classification | :Simulation |
| Players (Min/Max) | :1/1 |
| Screen Size | :Any |
| Direct Access Page | :GO GAM-393 |
| Instructions | :GO GAM-439 |

Welcome to the DFL (Digital Football League), a simulation of a football game. You are the coach, calling the plays on offense and defense. At first you may prefer to rely on established plays, then, as you become more experienced, you can create your own plays. A GOLEM is at your side to help, but you always have the option to disregard his advice. It may be fourth and ten, but when the going gets tough, you decide whether to punt or go for it.

# Original Adventure

| | |
|---|---|
| Suggested Age | :12 and Up |
| Classification | :Adventure |
| Players (Min/Max) | :1/1 |
| Special Requirements | :None |
| Minimum Screen Width | :Any |
| Direct Access Page | :GO GAM-200 |
| Instructions | :GO GAM-100 |

Speaking of computer-game classics, this is *the* original text adventure from which all other adventures, both micro and mainframe, evolved. The game understands English words and phrases and attempts to do what you command. The object is to explore a cave, find treasures, and deposit the booty back in the building. A perfect score is 350 points. CompuServe suggests that if this is your first adventure, enter HELP and INFO when the game begins. It is one of a number of text adventures available on-line. For instance....

# New Adventure

| | |
|---|---|
| Suggested Age | :12 and Up |
| Classification | :Adventure |
| Players (Min/Max) | :1/1 |
| Special Requirements | :None |
| Minimum Screen Width | :Any |
| Direct Access Page | :GO GAM-201 |
| Instructions | :GO GAM-101 |

This is the enhanced version of the original adventure game. It was expanded from the original to provide more challenges and more dangers for the skilled player. It also is the one on the tour in Chapter 3.

# BlackDragon

| | |
|---|---|
| Suggested Age | :12 through Adult |
| Classification | :Role play |
| Players (Min/Max) | :1/1 |
| Special Requirements | :None |
| Minimum Screen Width | :Any |
| Direct Access Page | :GO GAM-590 |
| Instructions | :GO GAM-417 |

BlackDragon is a fantasy role-playing game set in a multilevel maze. You use magic and encounter strange and wondrous creatures (most of them deadly). If you survive the first level, nine more await. The object is to accumulate treasure and, by converting gold into experience points, to gain strength. To win, you must be strong enough to conquer the "Arch Demon" on the final level. Skill, experience, and some luck are required.

# CastleQuest

| | |
|---|---|
| Suggested Age | :12 and Up |
| Classification | :Adventure |
| Players (Min/Max) | :1/1 |
| Special Requirements | :None |
| Minimum Screen Width | :Any |
| Direct Access Page | :GO GAM-83 |
| Instructions | :GO GAM-84 |

Search the castle, find the master, and deal with him as needed, while looting the castle of its treasures. You get points for depositing the treasures in the vault. (Note that the descriptions of treasures include an exclamation point.)

# The House of Banshi

| | |
|---|---|
| Suggested Age | :Adult |
| Classification | :Adventure |
| Players (Min/Max) | :1/1 |
| Special Requirements | :None |
| Minimum Screen Width | :Variable |
| Direct Access Page | :GO GAM-219 |
| Instructions | :GO GAM-119 |

Banshi is CompuServe's rendition of the original game of Zork. Some believe it is the most difficult adventure game on any computer. A perfect score is 585 points for the basic game, plus an additional 100 points for the End-Game (second dungeon). The object, as with other adventures, is to explore a series of caverns, solve the puzzles, and return treasures to a trophy case.

## Castle Telengard

| | |
|---|---|
| Suggested Age | :8 through Adult |
| Classification | :Role play |
| Players (Min/Max) | :1/1 |
| Special Requirements | :None |
| Minimum Screen Width | :Any |
| Direct Access Page | :GO GAM-320 |
| Instructions | :GO GAM-395 |

Castle Telengard is another role-playing game. The object is to find the mysterious "Orb of Power" and amass experience and wealth. There are 8,000 locations. In other words, you should be prepared to map your way back out.

## The Multiple Choice

The Multiple Choice isn't one game but many (as well as a touch typing-tutor). Type GO MULTIPLECHOI to see the main Multiple Choice menu:

```
** THE MULTIPLE CHOICE **

1 Adult Tests and Games
2 Kids' Tests and Games
3 Trivia for Everyone
4 Touch-Type Tutor
5 StageII - Two Stage Trivia
6 The Board of Regents Exam
7 Feedback to TMC
```

Adult tests and games include an IQ test, classical quotes, a sports rule quiz, and a personality profile test. Kids' tests and games include fill-ins, a word jumble game, and a state capital quiz. One section provides trivia quizzes for both adults and kids.

## The Whiz Quiz

Direct Access                          :GO WHIZ

The Whiz Quiz is a feature of Grolier's Academic American Encyclopedia (discussed in Chapter 20). Enter GO WHIZ to reach the quiz area where you select from trivia challenges, such as current events, movies, sports, art and architecture, the Bible, music, science, literature, history, myths and legends. No instructions are needed to play this one. Just answer the questions, ma'am (or sir).

## Stage II
## The Two Stage Trivia Game

Suggested Age                  :12 and Up
Classification                 :Trivia
Players (Min/Max)              :1/6
Special Requirements           :None
Minimum Screen Width           :32
Direct Access Page             :GO TMC-8
Instructions                   :GO TMC-10

The object is to earn points by first answering a series of trivia questions and then discovering what the answers have in common. You win by scoring enough points to add your name to the "StageII Spotlight" of high scorers.

## Word Scramble

Suggested Age                  :12 and Up
Classification                 :Word game
Players (Min/Max)              :1/2
Special Requirements           :Vidtex
Minimum Screen Width           :32
Direct Access Page             :GO GAM-232
Instructions                   :GO GAM-198

The computer chooses a word, then scrambles it. Your job is to unscramble it by guessing one letter at a time.

# Biorhythms

| | |
|---|---|
| Suggested Age | :12 and Up |
| Classification | :Charting |
| Players (Min/Max) | :1/1 |
| Special Requirements | :See Instructions |
| Minimum Screen Width | :80 |
| Direct Access Page | :GO GAM-218 |
| Instructions | :GO GAM-118 |

The program plots personalized charts for any year. You may print an individual month or several months. Enter the name of the person for whom you want a chart, then enter the date of his or her birth, the year to chart, beginning month, and number of months to chart. The biorhythm chart also provides text for appropriate days in any given month. This program should be used with an 80-column printer.

# Astrology Calculator

| | |
|---|---|
| Suggested Age | :All Ages |
| Classification | :Charting |
| Players (Min/Max) | :1/1 |
| Special Requirements | :None |
| Minimum Screen Width | :80 |
| Direct Access Page | :GO GAM-239 |
| Instructions | :GO GAM-197 |

This game casts conventional horoscopes. It asks for your birth date, birth time, time zone in effect, and birthplace expressed as latitude and longitude.

# Side Roads

Computer games are so popular that some entire forums are dedicated to playing them, reviewing them, and comparing notes on them. Here are some points of interest.

The Gamers' Forum (GO GAMERS) is devoted to all sorts of on-line and off-line computer games, adventure games, role-playing, games and more. Sysop Patricia Fitzgibbons says there is really no limit to the kind of games discussed on the forum (except for the multiplayer games on CompuServe, which have an entire forum of their own, also administered by Fitzgibbons). It is one of the system's most active forums, proving this form of telecommunications goes hand in hand with recreation. A look at the names of the Gamers' Forum subtopics at the time this book was updated gives some idea of its scope:

```
1 Text Adventures
2 Graphic Adventures
3 War/Strategy Games
4 Chess
5 Diplomacy
6 Sports Games
7 Action/Arcade Games
8 Cartridge Games
9 Computer RPGs
12 Oriental Games
```

If you need help with any of the player-versus-computer games on the system, you usually can get answers here. Also, if you are interested in commercial adventure or role-playing games, computer or noncomputer varieties, you will probably find someone on this forum who shares your interest. If you would like to try your hand at a real-time "dungeons and dragons" type game on-line with other players in widely separated regions, you can do that as well in the forum's conference area. Another popular game is played on the message board and conference areas, one called "Diplomacy" is actually a board game that has been adapted for the forum. Would you like to play a form of mail-chess using electronic mail? You are likely to find a partner in the chess section of the forum. And would you believe on-line bridge? The most popular of all card games has been adapted for play in the conference area. You can read about it in the card games section. Fitzgibbons says no one should feel limited by what is on the message board or in the forum libraries. If you have an idea for playing a game that can involve those in the forum, suggest it. The forum is on-line to help find news ways of playing games electronically.

The Play-By-Mail Games Forum (G PBMGAMES) is exclusively devoted to this popular pastime. The forum offers discussions, file libraries and on-line conferences about all types of commercial play-by-mail games. Members include long-time players, faction leaders, and game designers. In addition, several play-by-mail game companies are members of the forum and accept turns via the forum's private message function. The editors of *Flagship* magazine are also regular visitors to the forum.

The Role-Playing Games Forum (G RPGAMES) is designed for gamers who are into role-playing games. All kinds of board/paper/text role-playing games are topics in the forum, including Dungeons and Dragons, RuneQuest, Gamma World, Traveller, Champion and Justice Inc. (Computer-based role-playing games are discussed in the Gamers Forum.)

In addition, the expansion of game support is expected to continue. As this edition neared completion, CompuServe said a Game Vendors Forum was in the works where game creators and marketers would be on-line to answer questions and give tips.

Gaming also has spawned its own on-line magazine called *The Electronic Gamer*, edited by sysop Fitzgibbons. To read it, enter G EGAMER at any prompt. Among its features:

— Walkthrus: Step-by-step instructions for solving various adventure games. Each is divided into two or more sections so you can zero in on those that deal with your question. These are full solutions to the games listed, not merely hints. (Each contains just one person's solution, not the *only* solution to a game.)

— Hints: If you prefer hints rather than complete answers, this section is for you. It displays a menu indicating which hints are available. Choose the game you are playing, and look on the menu for the spot where you are stuck. Not every obstacle is covered for every game, of course, but the section has clues to the most-frequently asked questions about the most popular games. If the hint you need isn't here, or you would like more help, go to the Gamers' Forum Library 16 where you will find three files that contain names of members who have finished a particular game. These files are entitled: "GAMES1.HLP" "GAMES2.HLP," and "GAMES3.HLP". Leave a message to that person asking for help.

— Reviews: Here you can read about the features of computer or board games before you buy them. The computer game reviews area is divided into several sections (computer games, board games, cartridge games, etc.).

— Company Newsletters: Excerpts from newsletters including Infocom's STATUS onLine, Datasoft's *Alternate Reality*, SSI' *Inside SSI* and Electronic Arts' *Farther*. You will find prerelease reports on new games, interviews with designers, and announcements of special events.

— Teg's Gazette: An on-line minimagazine of articles, essays, interviews, current events, and so forth from The Electronic Gamer.

— Role-Playing Games Annals: Transcripts of episodes of several role-playing games being played on-line via the forum message board (in subtopic 6).

— *Computer Play* Online: Excerpts from *Computer Play* magazine.

— Multiplayer Games Columns: Up-to-date information and reports about several of the system's most popular multiplayer games.

— *Flagship*'s PBM Gaming Guide: News, reviews, hints and more from *Flagship* magazine, the magazine for play-by-mail gamers.

# CHAPTER 18

## A Multitude of Multiplayer Games

Wonder if designers of the first on-line multiplayer games had any idea just how successful they would be? They were creating a recreation on the very cutting edge of high-tech, so they had to worry over what subscribers would think about getting on-line and competing with others around the country. Players would not need to meet face to face, probably would know nothing about each other. As gaming often is a personal pursuit, how could anyone expect strangers to play games together by such computerized long-distance? Would it be like trying to play dominoes via a telephone conference call?

The programmers pressed on and came up with a new way to play; it caught on in a big way. Today, multiplayer games are the fastest growing segment of the CompuServe recreational division. New games are added frequently, and the people in charge say some tantalizing new developments are in store for us.

In this chapter, we go on-line briefly to visit one of the most innovative multiplayer games, "You Guessed It" (YGI), a wacky, addictive simulation of a television quiz show. Offered by the people at Hallmark Cards, YGI tests your knowledge of trivia in multiplayer "shows" that are operated around the clock by a cast of computer-simulated characters, including Dominic the doorman, game show host Bob Illuminati, and faithful sidekick Phil Vox.

After that we log off and collect details on other multiplayer games. How you can learn more about them, and where to find other players from virtually around the world.

## On-Line for YGI

Fire up the computer and, while you are making the connections, think of a really good pseudonym for yourself. Like the CB Simulator, YGI is an area in which you don't really have to be yourself. (There are very few rules about the name you use. If it is obscene or more than 20 characters, you will have some trouble, but those are the only restrictions.) The name you choose for your first trip into YGI is not permanent; if you return to the game later, you can change it.

YGI allows you to watch a game in progress and, while there is a $3 per hour surcharge to *play*, there is no surcharge to be part of the "studio audience." Watching others play is a good way to see how the show works.

To reach You Guessed It, enter G YGI at your first prompt, which takes you to:

```
CompuServe                                YGI

YOU GUESSED IT


  1 To Read Instructions
  2 To Play You Guessed It


Suggested Age         :18 & Up
Classification        :Trivia/Humor
Players (min/max)     :2/6
Special Requirements:None
Minimum Screen Width:Any
Direct Access Page    :Gam-17


Enter choice!
```

This menu is similar to the menus that introduce all CompuServe games. If you want to read the instructions, you can enter 1. Let's forge ahead directly to the game area. Enter 2 and see:

```
3-/ Studios' YGI! (tm)
   Version 2A(115)

   Copyright (c) 1988
CompuServe Incorporated

    <...out of nowhere there appear the
stately columns, gleaming lights, and
well-worn welcome mat of 3-C, a monument to
imagination, communication, and good times
for all who enter... And from an unseen
loudspeaker issue forth the golden tones of
the Voice of Videotext himself, Phil Vox:

    (Phil Vox) Welcome to the studios of
the 3-C Network (Creative Compucasting
Company), owned and operated by CompuServe.
The 3-C Network is the first of its kind,
producing compucasts that combine the
interactivity of computer communications
with the best in broadcast entertainment.
We invite you to participate in our new
interactive, real-time game, "YOU GUESSED
IT!" to meet people and compete for Sponsor
Gifts. New games begin every quarter hour,
but first we encourage you to step inside
the lobby and become whoever you'd like to
be....

    <...the heavy brass doors swing open
as if your arrival has been anticipated by
everyone, including Dominic the Doorman —
and, in fact, it has...>

    (Dominic) Ah! Some friends of yours
told us to watch for you. I must say the
description they gave us hardly does you
justice! Please, if you would do us the
honor of signing our guest book? Any name
you like, just keep it under 20
characters...
```

Here is where you enter the name you have chosen for yourself. After you RETURN, the system displays:

```
Very good. Now remember, the $3 per hour
surcharge is only in effect during the game
itself — not in the Lobby or Lounge. Allow
me to escort you into the Lobby proper...

    <Dominic makes a sweeping gesture
toward a sweeping staircase arcing down
into the fantasy of fountains, foliage, and
fellowship that is the 3-C Lobby>

    (Dominic)<from top of stairs, in his
best Brooklyn accent> Hey, everybody, (YOUR
NAME GOES HERE) is here! <stage whisper>
pssst...before you hobnob with this uptown
crowd, it may be worth your while to check
out the Lobby Signboard, so you know what's
happening. And before you play a game, be
sure to read the rules... holds out hand
for tip>

Press <CR> !
```

That Dominic is a real, uh, character, isn't he? That is, a real *simulation*... Press RETURN to see the main YGI menu:

```
┌─────────────────────────────────────────────────────┐
│                                                       │
│      ***Studio Lobby Signboard***                     │
│      ─────────────────────────────                    │
│   YGI! games start in 10 minutes                      │
│                                                       │
│      1 Instructions & Rules (READ 'EM)                │
│      2 Create & Read Personal Bios                    │
│      3 The Lobby: Get A Game Going                    │
│      4 View Games in Progress                         │
│      5 Visit the Bonus Bunker                         │
│      6 Suggestion Box                                 │
│      7 Unwind in the 3-C Lounge                       │
│      8 Multi-Player Games Forum                       │
│                                                       │
│   Enter choice !                                      │
└─────────────────────────────────────────────────────┘
```

Option 1 offers instructions and rules. Option 2 lets you create a personal biography to store in this area for others to read, or to read biographies of other regular players. If you choose option 3, you go to the lobby. (More about that in a minute. Similar to the CB Simulator or a forum conference area, the Lobby is where you meet people to form teams to play the game.) Option 5 takes you to the area where you can read about the prizes offered for winning YGI games.

The prizes here are real. By playing, you win points that can be converted into prizes. Option 6 is a feedback area where you can make suggestions and comments to the people who operate the game. Option 7 is another conference area you can visit after a game. Option 8 takes you to the Multiplayer Games Forum. (More about this important forum at the end of this chapter.)

Right now, choose option 4, which allows you be a member of the audience and watch computer-generated host Bob Illuminati and his pal, Phil Vox, moderating a game in progress. After entering 4, you should see something like this:

```
Games in Progress
-----------------


     How can Bob be in two places at once,
when he's not anywhere at all? You will
find the answers to this and far more
interesting questions by participating as a
YGI viewer! There's no surcharge and you
get to answer every question! (However, you
earn no points towards those Sponsor
Gifts.) Here are the games going on right
now:

Key <CR> to continue.
```

Press RETURN and you see a brief description of a game in progress in one of the studios followed by:

```
Do you want to <V>iew this game, <C>heck
out the action in another game, or go back
to the <L>obby signboard (V,C,L)?
```

Enter V to see this game in progress, after these words from Phil Vox:

```
(Phil Vox) Remember, as members of the
audience you may answer each and every YGI
question. Your responses are tabulated and
DO influence the Big Board. However, you
may not "talk" openly during the game (this
would distract the players onstage) nor
vote during player challenges. Enter /HELP
if you need it, /LOBBY to leave studio.
```

Now sit back and enjoy the game. When Bob Illuminati asks a question, you enter an answer. As the message said, your answers become part of the official record and have a bearing on the outcome. When you have viewed a little of the show (you don't have to wait until the game is over), we shall take you briefly to the lobby. To get there, enter:

```
/LOBBY
```

Upon entering the lobby, you see this advisory:

```
The use of obscene or abusive language can
result in the suspension of your service.
CompuServe charges Big Bucks to reactivate
suspended users. So don't be obscene or
abusive. It's not worth it. If you plan to
captain a YGI team, use your time in the
Lobby to find teammates and opponents. Your
game will start up more smoothly if you can
pre-arrange with another captain to play
each other.
```

After this message, you will probably see some on-line chatter among people who are organizing teams. Many commands are available in this area. To see them, enter /HELP. (Some may not make any sense to you right now, but they become clear if you read the instructions for playing YGI. Of course, you should read them before you actually begin play.) If anyone says hello to you and asks you to join a game, you might respectfully decline by telling them you are just a tourist for the moment. (Uh, tell 'em about the grand book you are reading while you are at it.... Nervous grins...) When you are ready to leave the lobby and the YGI game, you enter /EXIT and see:

```
(Dominic the Doorman) <holding door open>
Thanks for stopping in. See you later!
```

When you arrive at a Games menu with a familiar prompt, enter OFF to log off the system.

Your quick trip through You Guessed It gave you an idea of the mystique of multiplayer games. People separated by thousands of miles form teams and play a game directed by a central computer. Some players met by chance in the YGI conference area; others met elsewhere on the system and agreed to gather at a specified time. Odds are these people have never met in person.

## Other Multiplayer Games

You Guessed It is only one of many such games. It is in fact one of the simpler ones, and a good one to begin with if you become interested in this new form of recreation. Following is a look at some other multiplayer games available.

# MegaWars
# MegaWars I — The Galactic Conflict

| | |
|---|---|
| Suggested Age | :12 and Up |
| Classification | :War Game |
| Players (Min/Max) | :1/10 |
| Special Requirements | :None |
| Minimum Screen Width | :Any |
| Direct Access Page | :GO GAM-209 |
| Instructions | :GO GAM-109 |

## MegaWars III — The New Empire

| | |
|---|---|
| Suggested Age | :12 and Up |
| Classification | :War game |
| Players (Min/Max) | :1/100 |
| Special Requirements | :None |
| Minimum Screen Size | :32 by 6 |
| Direct Access Page | :GO GAM-105 |
| Instructions | :GO GAM-154 |

MegaWars I, one of the earliest multiplayer games, has proved to be so popular that a similar, more complex game called MegaWars III was added a few years ago. The games were developed by two former University of Virginia students, Kelton Flinn and John Taylor. MegaWars I is a real-time space battle to be played by one to ten people. One person? Yes, if no one else is around, the computer plays against you. In fact, most multiplayer games can be played at a single-player level against the computer, though it is more fun as a group activity. Want a taste of the adventure? Here is a section from the MegaWars I introduction:

```
    From the dark star of Algol they came
— unprovoked and undaunted in their
determination to conquer, enslave and rule.
From Algol, they attacked and enslaved
Perseus, conquered Capella and swept
through Andromeda before we saw them. That
was 700 years ago. MegaWars began without
warning — without regard to peace or
civilization — when they belittled Algol.
For 700 years the Kryons have now exported
their culture of slavery and dictatorship;
and for 700 years we Colonists of the
Galaxy have fought and repelled their every
thrust...
```

Hmmmmm, now *there* is a plot for a shoot-'em-up space movie. The introduction tells you there are the Colonists (the good guys) and the Kryons (the bad guys). When you enter MegaWars, you decide whether you want to be a good guy or a bad guy. What you aren't told is that there is a third force in the galaxy called the Archerons; and they don't like anyone. So even if you wind up in a one-player game or if all the players in the game are of one army, you still have to watch out for the Archerons. As if you don't have enough to worry about, the black holes that the instructions describe as "annoying" exist. Indeed, if you get into one of them, you are dead. Chances are one-in-four a black hole lurks in the game you are playing.

Your mission in MegaWars I is to destroy your enemy, capture planets for your side, stay away from black holes and Archerons, rise in rank from cadet to admiral, and avoid getting zapped by other players.

MegaWars III goes beyond simple (?) warfare. This advanced simulation involves building spaceships to seek new planets, establishing colonies on them, building defenses, creating economic systems, and ruling their people.

"We like to say, 'Here's a universe,' and then sit back and watch," designer Flinn once told The Associated Press. "The players can decide where their warships will go and what taxes will be set at on their planets."

Before you rush on-line to play either game, heed the advice of master players: buy the printed game manuals. For details, enter G ORDER at any prompt.

# Air Traffic Controller

| | |
|---|---|
| Suggested Age | :12 through Adult |
| Classification | :Simulation |
| Players (Min/Max) | :1/9 |
| Special Requirements | :Vidtex |
| Minimum Screen Size | :40-by-24 |
| Direct Access Page | :GO GAM-236 |
| Instructions | :GO GAM-237 |

Programmer Steve Estvanik says his goal with Air Traffic Controller was to create a game not based on warfare and competition but on cooperation among players. It simulates an air traffic controller's duties, and you are responsible for all planes within a sector of air space. Your mission: guide the planes safely through your assigned sector of airspace or to a nearby airport. New planes arrive from other sectors and from the airports. You can influence other sectors by delaying planes or sending them out with inadequate fuel. You also can send messages to other players to notify them of planes you send into their sectors. In other words, if everyone cooperates, you all score better. If there are no other players, you still can play, though you receive only computer-generated planes. If other people are playing, you may get additional planes from them. You have direct contact with as many as four other players, to the north, south, east, and west. Several levels of difficulty are available and score is kept for each 10- to 12-minute "shift" you play.

# Baffle

| | |
|---|---|
| Suggested Age | :8 and Up |
| Classification | :Word game |
| Players (Min/Max) | :1/20 |
| Special Requirements | :None |
| Minimum Screen Width | :32 |
| Direct Access Page | :GO GAM-34 |
| Instructions | :GO GAM-528 |

Baffle is a word-search game. You are given a four-by-four display of single letters. The object is to form words using adjacent letters (horizontal, vertical, or diagonal). For example, your board may look like this:

```
┌─────────────────────────────────────────────┐
│                                             │
│   W   R                                     │
│                                             │
│                                             │
│                                             │
│   P   A                                     │
│                                             │
└─────────────────────────────────────────────┘
```

You could form WAR, RAW, PAR, RAP, WRAP, WARP, and PAW. A letter may be used only once per word, and words must be at least three letters long. You have three minutes to find as many words as you can.

When you enter the game, you are ushered to the library, where you may talk to other players, see who else is available for play, and set yourself up to enter the next available game. While you wait, you may either stay in the library or play by yourself. You are notified when the game begins. The timer starts as soon as you see an asterisk "*" prompt.

# Casino

| | |
|---|---|
| Suggested Age | :12 through Adult |
| Classification | :Casino |
| Players (Min/Max) | :1-4/table |
| Special Requirements | :None |
| Minimum Screen Size | :Any |
| Direct Access Page | :GO GAM-281 |
| Instructions | :GO GAM-238 |

Here is a chance to play blackjack, craps, and roulette with other users for "credits" (which have no value other than as a measure of how successful, or unsuccessful, you are). When you enter the casino, an account is opened for you. Once inside, you can join a game or watch one already in progress. The rules are similar to any casino game. The program also allows you to make comments to those with whom you are playing. We know several users who find this a great way to meet informally with other users while having fun. Incidentally, the system keeps account of your credits from one session to the next, so you can tell how you are doing over a long period of time.

# The Island of Kesmai

| | |
|---|---|
| Suggested Age | :12 through Adult |
| Classification | :Role Play |
| Players (Min/Max) | :1 / 100 |
| Special Requirements | :Vidtex |
| Minimum Screen Size | :40 x 24 |
| Direct Access Page | :GO GAM-26 |
| Instructions | :GO GAM-76 |

In this fantasy role-playing game, you direct your alter ego around the Island of Kesmai, through its catacombs searching for riches and avoiding danger. You can play the game alone or enter the island with others for a group adventure. (The Multiplayer Games Forum is the place to join a group or to learn more about how to play the game.) The Island of Kesmai is complex. Although there is considerable on-line help, veteran explorers on the island say it is best to order the printed Island of Kesmai manual. (G ORDER.)

# Seawar

| | |
|---|---|
| Suggested Age | :12 and Up |
| Classification | :War Game |
| Players (Min/Max) | :1/4 |
| Special Requirements | :Vidtex |
| Minimum Screen Width | :32 |
| Direct Access Page | :GO GAM-319 |
| Instructions | :GO GAM-548 |

SeaWAR is an oceanic combat that may be played singly, against the computer, or in a multiplayer mode against one to three human opponents. The object: to destroy all of your enemy's ships, by commanding an armada of ships more skillfully than your opponents.

# Multiplayer Spacewar

| | |
|---|---|
| Suggested Age | :8 and Up |
| Classification | :War Game |
| Players (Min/Max) | :1/8 |
| Special Requirements | :Vidtex |
| Minimum Screen Width | :32 |
| Direct Access Page | :GO GAM-214 |
| Instructions | :GO GAM-114 |

SpaceWAR is a high-speed multiplayer shoot-em-up. The object is to seek out and destroy all other space ships. Each player competes against all others. Points, awarded for each ship hit, are subtracted each time your ship is hit.

# British Legends

| | |
|---|---|
| Suggested Age | :12 and Up |
| Classification | :Adventure |
| Players (Min/Max) | :1/36 |
| Special Requirements | :None |
| Minimum Screen Size | :32 |
| Direct Access Page | :GAM-153 |
| Instructions | :GAM-166 |

The land of British Legends has rolling pastures, dense forests, mist-swathed graveyards, and evil beings lurking in the shadows. The key is that not all the creatures you encounter are computer-controlled. Some are real people who are also playing. You must conquer more than unknown countryside; you must battle other players as well. Your goal is to become a wizard or witch. Once this goal is achieved, you inherit enviable powers over other players. However, the way is fraught with insidious dangers and ancient evils.

# Off-Line Game Help

Some people love to try to solve computer games without reading the printed documentation. That is fine if you have time and no one else is waiting for you to make a move. If you get serious about on-line multiplayer games, though, we suggest you order the printed documentation. In many instances, on-line help exists, but for the more complex ones — the MegaWars series and the Island of Kesmai in particular — it would take too much time to read all the on-line documentation. In addition, you owe it to your fellow players to be familiar with the game before you plunge in. It is tacky to introduce yourself with, "How do you play this sucker?"

To order gaming manuals, enter G ORDER. You will find manuals, maps, and other goodies to get you involved in some of the more complex games quickly. The cost of your order will be added to your CompuServe bill.

## Side Roads

The Multiplayer Games Forum (G MPGAMES) is a *must* stop on your road to successful gaming. It is operated by the same people who administer the game forums described in the previous chapter. Chief among the administrators is Patti Fitzgibbons (a.k.a. NightShift). The forum is divided into areas that provide training in multiplayer games as well as advanced technical help. The forum also provides places for you to meet other players and create teams. MegaWars I, MegaWars III, SeaWAR, Island of Kesmai, British Legends, and You Guessed It all have their own message and library sections. In addition, veteran gamers host frequent real-time conferences for beginners. These get-togethers provide an excellent place for overviews of specific games and to get basic questions answered. See the forum bulletins for the conference schedule.

# CHAPTER 19

# Advanced Stuff

CompuServe's strength is that it grows with you. When you are a new user, the system has menus to guide you; when you outgrow the menus, you can turn them off like removing training wheels from your first bicycle. So far, this book has illustrated simple ways to customize the system, pointing out that the more you make the service perform the way you want it to, the faster you can navigate and the more money you save. This chapter concentrates on more shortcuts and dramatic customizing options by using:

— Powerful utilities in the Profile area.
— Other SET commands for temporary changes to the system.
— Additional advanced features in EasyPlex, as well as ways to send electronic mail to people outside of CompuServe, through MCI Mail, telex, facsimile machines, and more.
— Special tips for logging on.

In addition, we also introduce an exciting new area of on-line computing, high-resolution graphics.

Before we get started, let's knock down a rumor about Profile: Despite what some people might say, it isn't a tar pit. Just as some subscribers fear the "OK" prompt or the personal file area, others say Profile is mysterious, hard to understand, and moreover, is dangerous to play with because you might inalterably upset the way your screen looks when you are on-line. Balderdash. Profile actually is easy, and even fun. More importantly, it is the heart and soul of customizing the service. In Chapter 13, as we wrapped up the discussion of how to use the discussion forums, we talked about running the forum program as an "expert." We even suggested that you experiment to see how many commands you could remember without the menus to prompt you. Through an option we shall now introduce, it is possible to travel *all* of CompuServe with a minimum of menus. Many subscribers — those who have learned where the "good stuff" is — save connect time by using this mode. They turn off repetitious menus and take the express directly to features they want. Having traveled this far with us, you probably now are ready to think about using these options, or at least to start experimenting with them — just as you tried out the forums' advanced options. This chapter, without actually going on-line, shows you how these major changes are made. Later, at your own pace, you should try it; log on and give the fast lane a try.

## Taking Off the Training Wheels — Slowly, with SET

The easiest way to start abbreviating the system is with the SET command. Chapter 9 introduced SET, showing you how at any "!" prompt you can use it to change your screen width (SET WID 64) and screen depth (SET LIN 24), and to turn off and on the paging option (SET PAG OFF and SET PAG ON, respectively). You also learned that changes made with SET were *temporary*, that is, for the current session only.

Another handy SET command turns on and off the system's *brief mode.* New subscribers automatically receive full menus (or "verbose" prompts) at all features. However, at any "!" prompt, you can enter:

```
SET BRI ON
```

That means "Turn on the BRIef mode (and turn off the menus)." With BRIef mode turned ON, many prompts are shortened. If you SET BRI ON and visit the National Bulletin Board, you receive not a full, verbose menu of options, but merely an abbreviated prompt at which you can enter commands. Most, but not all, system features are affected automatically by the SET BRI ON command. (A few, like Easy-Plex, have their own built-in SET commands; we will look at that later in this chapter.)

The nature of SET — that it affects no *permanent* changes to how things are displayed — makes it ideal for experimentation. As you become bolder about using CompuServe, you can SET BRI ON just to get a feel for how the system looks at a faster pace. Once you are comfortable with the system's new appearance, you can use Profile options to make more permanent changes.

# More about Profile

As you saw in Chapter 9, by entering G PROFILE, you produce this menu:

```
CompuServe                          PROFILE

CHANGE YOUR USER PROFILE

   1 Terminal Settings
   2 Change Your Password
   3 Password Security Guidelines
   4 Change Your Billing Options
      or Credit Card Information
   5 Change Your Billing Address

   Enter choice !
```

Think of this menu as the control center from which you maintain much of your personal data on-line — changing a password, looking at billing options, altering your credit card information on file, and so forth — and it also is the passageway to the powerful Terminal Settings section. If you choose option 1 (or enter G TERMINAL or G OPTIONS at any prompt), you see:

```
TERMINAL SETTINGS/SERVICE OPTIONS

Use this area to change your terminal
type/parameters and/or service options.

   1 Instructions
   2 Change permanent settings
   3 Explanation of session vs. permanent
   4 Show session vs. permanent
   5 Change current session settings

   Enter choice!
```

This area records the setting of your *defaults*. We have defined defaults as settings that tell CompuServe how to send information to you. For instance, "Dear CompuServe: I'd like 24 lines per screen, 80 characters per line, uppercase and lowercase letters..." Using this area, you make your settings temporary or permanent.

**A Word about Words, Digression Part 1:**    We have talked about how the language we use to describe computer concepts can be an obstacle to newcomers. We have contemplated the new meanings we telecomputerists apply to the words "permanent" and "temporary," observing that in setting parameters, a user can make changes permanent, while really meaning, "permanent until I change my mind again" (or, if you will, "temporarily forever maybe"). A similar computer term oddity can be noted in the meaning of *defaults*. Most us grew up with rather negative notions about that word. As we learned it in school, default means *failing* to do something. A loan is in default if we don't pay it. A business loses a contract by default if it neglects it. Even in sports, default is a bad thing, that is, lose a game or a match because of a failure to show up on time or properly to meet the criteria. With such a history, it's little wonder that default has had such a hard time of it on-line; it certainly sounds like something we ought to avoid. Actually, though, in computer parlance, "default" is not negative. In terms of parameters, it simply means the setting that CompuServe *assumes* for a particular option unless you specify a different setting.

At the outset of our tours, we saw how these defaults get their original settings. When you log on for the first time with a new user ID number, CompuServe prompts for a few facts about your hardware and software. The system then stores the answers as your defaults. Those settings and more can be changed in the TERMINAL/OPTIONS area.

When you access this feature, the system may inform that your permanent and temporary settings do not match. As you can see from this menu, TERMINAL/OPTIONS allows you to change settings permanently with option 2 and temporarily with option 5. (The latter option often is called "session," meaning, of course, to remind you that the changes made with it are for the current session only.) Meanwhile, option 4 is a handy preliminary feature, as it compares the settings of both permanent and session parameters.

Questions so far?

*Why would I want to change options only temporarily?*

Well, why do you like to try on new clothes or a drive a new car? To see how it feels. Actually, many options primarily deal with the *display* of information. Depending on your computer and software, you might enjoy a different view of CompuServe that you can discover through tinkering with the settings.

*OK, but why come all the way over to this part of the system to make temporary changes? We have already seen how to do the same thing faster with the SET command, right?*

SET is fine for one or two quick changes. However, if you have a number of alterations to try, come here. With TERMINAL/OPTIONS, you can compare the temporary settings with permanent ones (option 4), then make a number of changes at one time with option 5. But don't get confused; changes made here as "session" are just as temporary as those made with the SET commands. (In fact, there are corresponding SET commands for most of the TERMINAL/OPTIONS defaults, which we shall see as we go along.) Either way — with SET or with temporary defaults made here in Profile's TERMINAL/OPTIONS — you can drive around the system to see how the changes look. If you don't like the results, simply log off and the changes are canceled. If you do like the new look, come to this menu in TERMINAL/OPTIONS and select option 2, "Change permanent settings," to change the options individually. Let's suppose you have selected option 2; that produces:

```
PERMANENT SETTINGS

    1 Explanation
    2 Logon/Service options
    3 Display options
    4 Terminal type/parameters
    5 Transfer protocol/graphic support
    6 Make session settings permanent

    Type EXIT when done

    Enter choice!
```

(Please place a bookmark on this page; we shall refer to it as the "permanent settings menu" several times in this first part of this chapter.)

More than 25 parameters are set and controlled in Profile's TERMINAL/OPTIONS section. This menu shows them divided into several groups: log-on and service options, display options, terminal type and communications parameters, and transfer protocol and graphic support.

For a moment we shall defer discussion of the settings under option 2 "log-on and service options" and look at the display options. If you select option 3 from this menu, you see:

```
┌─────────────────────────────────────────────────────┐
│                                                       │
│   PERMANENT DISPLAY OPTIONS                           │
│                                                       │
│    1 PAGED display                      [YES]         │
│    2 BRIEF prompts                      [NO]          │
│    3 CLEAR screen between pages         [YES]         │
│    4 BLANK lines sent                   [YES]         │
│    5 Line feeds sent                    [YES]         │
│                                                       │
│   Enter choice !                                      │
│                                                       │
└─────────────────────────────────────────────────────┘
```

Each option on this menu is followed by a word in square brackets. As we have come to expect, this represents your current default setting. In this example, each of the display options except the second one has a default setting of "YES."

Changing defaults is easy, because menus guide the way throughout; your current default always is identified and then the other options are explained. Suppose you choose option 1 on this menu — PAGED display — which shows you:

```
┌─────────────────────────────────────────────────────┐
│                                                       │
│   PAGED DISPLAY                                       │
│                                                       │
│   Permanent setting =                   [YES]         │
│                                                       │
│   1 YES                                               │
│     (Output is presented in pages;                    │
│     you are asked to enter <CR> after                 │
│     each page.)                                       │
│                                                       │
│   2 NO                                                │
│     (Output is scrolled continuously                  │
│     to end of article.)                               │
│                                                       │
│   Enter choice!                                       │
│                                                       │
└─────────────────────────────────────────────────────┘
```

This format is typical of TERMINAL/OPTIONS' secondary menus. The line immediately following the header reminds you of the current default setting ("YES"), followed by a brief explanation of each alternative. The subject of this setting is familiar; we have observed that ordinarily CompuServe sends you text in pages; it fills the screen, then pauses with a prompt. Setting this parameter to "YES" means you want CompuServe to continue sending its data in this format, that is, the preset number of screen lines followed by a prompt to press a carriage return ("<CR>") for more. On the other hand, setting the option to "No" means you want incoming text to scroll without such interruption to the end of selected articles.

*Question: Are there "correct" answers to the questions posed in TER-MINAL/OPTIONS?*

A few — an option we shall talk about soon must be handled carefully — but *most* answers are simply a matter of preference. In this case, some users like to have the PAGE option activated so that when they are reading material on-line, the system automatically stops from time to time to let the eye catch up. Others prefer to let the incoming text flow freely and choose to use CONTROL S and CONTROL Q to stop and start the transmission.

Two notes:

1. If you routinely have your communications program capture on-line articles to disk files for off-line reading, you probably want to have this parameter set to NO so that the incoming text will scroll without page breaks.
2. Remember that this default, like most, can be overridden temporarily with the SET command. In this case, from any point in the system, you enter SET PAGE ON or SET PAGE OFF.

Option 2, "BRIEF prompts," asks whether you want verbose or abbreviated prompts. Earlier we talked about the SET command that accomplishes this temporarily (SET BRI ON); with this option you can make the change more permanent. Setting it to "Yes" puts you in expert mode, meaning you receive abbreviated prompts throughout the system. Answering "No" leaves you in novice/intermediate mode, receiving full prompts all along the way. Typical prompts in novice/intermediate mode read:

```
,-------------------------------------------------,
|                                                 |
|   Enter choice !                                |
|                                                 |
'-------------------------------------------------'
```

and

```
,-------------------------------------------------,
|                                                 |
|   Enter <CR> for more !                         |
|                                                 |
'-------------------------------------------------'
```

By contrast, the same prompt in expert mode would be simply "!" in the first example and "More !" in the second. Elsewhere in the system, expert mode suppresses most verbose menus and command prompts that are designed for newcomers. Generally, it is a good idea to leave your permanent setting for BRIEF prompts at NO until you have become familiar with the system.

After that is option 3, "CLEAR screen between pages," which means that if you have the paging option activated, you can have the system clear the screen of your computer before it sends each new page.

The next option is 4, "BLANK lines sent," and... Uh, question?

*Yes! Why in the world would I want to receive blank lines from CompuServe? I can make all the blank lines I want when I'm off-line, right?*

Actually, across the system, blank lines are used to make text more readable, just as white space is used in typography to separate bodies of type on a printed page to make it easier on the eye. Setting this option to NO (that is, "don't send blank lines") saves a little space and tiny bit of time, but it may make the incoming text more difficult to read. This is another option with which you should experiment before you consider abandoning "normal mode" (the YES setting) for the suppression of blank lines. To test drive it, either set the option temporarily through TERMINAL/OPTIONS or just use the SET command sequence, SET BLANK OFF and SET BLANK ON.

The final default, 5, "Line feeds sent," is the only one among the display parameters that needs to be handled with care, because it does have a "correct" answer in a sense, depending on your particular communications software.

Some background: Normally, CompuServe sends a line feed every time it sends a carriage return. (Picture a typewriter; every time the carriage is pushed back to the right, the paper also advances to the next line.) Most communications programs these days anticipate this step, and this parameter can be set to "YES," meaning that CompuServe should continue sending the line feeds. However, a minority of terminal programs take it upon themselves to issue a line feed every time they receive a carriage return. The effect is double spacing: one line feed is provided by CompuServe and immediately another is provided by the terminal program. In that case only, you want to set the Line Feed Sent option to NO, telling CompuServe, "Don't bother; my terminal program loves to do line feeds." Obviously, caution should be exercised with this option because if it is incorrectly set, you wind up with incoming text overwriting itself.

## Terminal Types and Other Parameters

Now look back to the bookmarked example of the permanent settings menu and let's plunge into "terminal type/parameters," listed under option 4. Entered here, 4 produces:

```
r----------------------------------------------------------┐
¦                                                          ¦
¦    TERMINAL TYPE/PARAMETERS                               ¦
¦                                                          ¦
¦     1 TERMINAL type                    [OTHER]           ¦
¦     2 Screen WIDTH                       [80]            ¦
¦     3 LINES per page                     [24]            ¦
¦     4 Form FEEDS                       [REAL]            ¦
¦     5 Horizontal TABS             [SIMULATED]            ¦
¦     6 Chars. received (CASE)            [U/L]            ¦
¦     7 Chars. sent in CAPS                [NO]            ¦
¦     8 PARITY                           [EVEN]            ¦
¦     9 Output DELAYS                       [1]            ¦
¦    10 ERASE when backspacing             [NO]            ¦
¦    11 Micro inquiry sequence at logon [YES]             ¦
¦                                                          ¦
¦    Enter choice !                                        ¦
¦                                                          ¦
L----------------------------------------------------------┘
```

**A Word about Words, Digression Part 2:**   Some computer terms aren't native to computers at all, but rather come down from the language of writers and printers, harkening back to mechanical devices like typewriters, linotype, and teletype machines. But, as usual, computer users have created their own meanings for these older phrases. And the words' evolution almost certainly will allow us one day to observe the birth of new anachronisms in our own times. Consider, for instance, the *carriage return*. On an old manual typewriter, the carriage is the moving unit that contains the platen and its associated parts. Its job is a simple one, to carry the paper across the point at which the keys strike through the inked ribbon. The carriage return, then, is a physical part of the machine, an arm with which the operator returns the carriage (usually, at the end of a line) so that when the next letter is typed, it appears on the left margin. Of course, computerists use "carriage return" to mean a code (or its symbol) that causes the cursor to behave the same way, that is, to be returned to the left margin. The point is that all of us understand this phrase in both its historic and current sense because we grew up within hailing distance of the Typewriter Age. Having seen the slow change in the word's usage, we can make the necessary mental leap to connect the references. However, it is likely that sometime within our lifetimes we shall be asked by a youngster to point out his or her computer's "carriage." All of this is long-winded way of saying that the some of the terms on this menu already are familiar from our typewriter heritage, words and concepts like *tabs*, *backspace*, *caps lock*, and *form feeds*.

Meanwhile, other menu terms represent new concepts, such as "terminal type," mentioned in option 1. CompuServe supports a number of specialized terminals and software, each with its own features. Selecting this option produces a list such as:

```
┌───────────────────────────────────────────────────┐
│                                                     │
│   TERMINAL TYPE                                     │
│                                                     │
│   1 VIDTEX (Professional Connection)                │
│   2 ANSI                                            │
│   3 VT100                                           │
│   4 VT52                                            │
│   5 Heath (Zenith)                                  │
│   6 ADM                                             │
│   7 CRT                                             │
│   8 Other                                           │
│                                                     │
│   Enter choice !                                    │
│                                                     │
└───────────────────────────────────────────────────┘
```

The first option — VIDTEX compatible — is the one you select if you are using one of CompuServe's own terminal programs, such as *The Professional Connection* or *Vidtex*. Generally, the others on the list represent different ways of dealing with control and escape codes on-line. For instance, ANSI-compatible systems conform to certain escape and control sequences defined by the ANSI standard; VT52 and VT100 are commercial terminals that have special control or escape sequences of their own; CRT is a plain vanilla setting used for terminals or micros that respond to a form feed signal by clearing the screen but have no other special control or escape codes in use. Most of us can set either option 1 — Vidtex — or the general purpose "Others," but if you think your system conforms to one of the other standards, you should check your manual or call your salesperson. If that doesn't help, you can use Feedback (G FEEDBACK).

**Note:** Many modern communications programs also offer "terminal emulations" that can give you a new view of CompuServe. You might be able to instruct your software to emulate a VT100 terminal, for instance, then use this menu to select terminal type 4 and see how the system looks to users of that system. If interested, check your software manual to see if any of the above terminal emulations are supported.

As we saw in Chapter 9, the next default concerns screen width. CompuServe often displays its information in lines that are a maximum of 32 characters long. This length is just right for some computers, but what if you are using a system with a different line length? In that case, you need to tell the system how you want text displayed. Similar to the setting of a right margin on a typewriter, "Screen WIDTH", option 2, is simply the number of characters that fit on a screen line. When you select this option, the system prompts:

```
┌─────────────────────────────────────────────────┐
│                                                   │
│   WIDTH:                                          │
│                                                   │
└─────────────────────────────────────────────────┘
```

Here you enter the number of characters that can be accommodated on a single line on your screen, such as 32, 40, 64, 80.

"LINEs per page" (option 3) means the number of lines that fit on one screen. As mentioned, CompuServe can send text in pages, filling the screen with text and pausing to prompt you to press RETURN. This option tells CompuServe how *many* lines to a page for your particular screen. (This applies only to video; if you use a printing terminal, this option should be set to zero unless form feeds are desired.)

"Form FEEDS" (option 4) can be either *real* or *simulated*. Real form feeds use your computer's control to clear the screen and move the cursor to the upper left corner (if your communications software can accomplish this); simulated ones merely print out eight blank lines between pages. (On a printing terminal, a real form feed causes the paper to advance to the top of the next page on a continuous sheet.)

"Horizontal TABS" (option 5), like form feeds, also can be real or simulated. Real horizontal tabs can be transmitted if your terminal has tab stops and your communications software recognizes them. Otherwise, they are simulated by eight spaces.

The next two options, which were also examined in Chapter 9, deal with upper-case and lowercase text. Some computers can accept one style only, uppercase or lowercase.

"Chars. received (CASE)" (option 6) has three possible settings — U/L (normal mode) means that the text you receive from CompuServe will be in capital and lowercase letter as available on the host computer; UPPER means you will receive the text from host in uppercase letters only; LOWER means you will receive the text in lowercase.

"Chars. sent in CAPS" (option 7) can be set as either NO or YES. If you set it to YES, then whatever you enter on the keyboard will *always* be sent in capital letters, regardless of whether you hold down the shift key. Set at NO (the normal mode), then whatever you enter will be in the case you have selected. It helps to think of this one as a "caps lock" on a typewriter. When on (YES), all letters that you type are upper-case. When the caps lock is off (NO), letters are uppercase or lowercase, depending on whether you hold down the shift key. (Note that the caps lock setting does not affect the case of letters sent *to* your screen; that is controlled by option 6.)

"PARITY" (option 8) refers to a setting in your terminal software, and understanding it requires a little background. Communications programs usually have a number of different parameter settings for parity and data bits, all explained in your software's user manual. Most subscribers log on with a setting of 7 bits/even parity, which is the default setting. If you try to log on with another popular setting (8-bits/no parity), you receive garble at the log-on prompt. However, you can come to this part of the system, choose the PARITY setting and, when prompted, select the option "ZERO." This option informs CompuServe that in the future you will routinely log on with the 8-bit/no parity setting, rather than 7-bit/even parity.

"Output DELAYS" (option 9) are needed when your printer operates at a slower speed than your modem, causing characters to be lost at the beginning of each line. (DELAYS are recognized only if you are logging on through CompuServe's own network, (option 10) not a packet network, such as Tymnet, Telenet, Datapak.)

"ERASE when backspacing" can be set to either YES or NO. A YES setting means that when you transmit a backspace from your keyword, CompuServe sends a space and another backspace (in effect, erasing the last character typed). For almost all modern terminal software, this is the *normal* setting. However, a NO setting is also available, meaning no special processing is done by the system when a backspace is received.

Finally, "Micro inquiry sequence at logon" (option 11) is another new concept. If set to YES, it tells the system to discreetly and silently communicate with your terminal program at log on to determine if it recognizes "Vidtex protocols" (such as B Protocol for uploading and downloading and certain "cursor positioning" codes for graphics). If you are using CompuServe's own communications programs — *The Professional Connection* or *Vidtex* — this option should be set to YES. Otherwise, you should set it to NO.

As noted, most of the display and parameter options have corresponding SET commands available for fast, temporary settings. In addition to the ones already mentioned, you can SET:

| | |
|---|---|
| BLANK | (YES/NO) to send blank lines. |
| CAPS | (YES/NO) to send characters in CAPS. |
| DELAY | (0-255) to output delay. |
| ERASE | (YES/NO) to set erase when backspacing. |
| FEEDS | (YES/NO) to set automatic line feeds. |
| FORM | (REAL/SIM) to set form feeds real or simulated. |
| PARITY | (EVEN/ODD/ONE/ZERO) to change the parity setting. |
| TABS | (REAL/SIM) to set horizontal tabs either real or simulated. |

## Basic Log-on Actions

Okay, ready for some micro magic? With the next section of TERMINAL-OPTIONS you can change what CompuServe thinks is the beginning of the service. Option 2, on the bookmarked example, is where this and other popular options reside. With

"Logon/Service options" you can indicate how you want the system to look when you log on and actually where to "start" in the system. When you select this option, you see something like this:

```
┌─────────────────────────────────────────────────┐
│                                                   │
│   LOGON/SERVICE OPTIONS                           │
│                                                   │
│   1 First service at logon          [MAIN]        │
│   2 EasyPlex waiting       [GO TO EASYPLEX]        │
│   3 Personal menu established         [NO]         │
│      (Select this to create or                    │
│      change a personal menu.)                     │
│   4 TOP goes to                     [MAIN]         │
│   5 Online editor               [DEFAULT]          │
│   6 Forum presentation mode     [DEFAULT]          │
│                                                   │
│   Enter choice!                                   │
│                                                   │
└─────────────────────────────────────────────────┘
```

Let's put a bookmark on this example too, so we can refer back to it quickly.

These six options offer possibilities for many changes. For discussion purposes, we shall take them slightly out of order.

"EasyPlex waiting" (option 2) simply determines the "logon action" when you have received an EasyPlex message. As now set, the system takes you directly to the electronic mail program, as we have seen on our tours. With this option, though, you can specify, alternately, that you want to be informed about new EasyPlex but *not* taken directly to the mail program.

"Online editor" (option 5) is an option at which we have hinted. We have noted several times that two editors are available in various features, LINEDIT (line-numbered editor) and EDIT (unnumbered editor). Earlier we saw how to record a preference in a single forum, but this TERMINAL/SETTINGS option lets you specify a selection for the entire system. The choices are EDIT, LINE, and DEFAULT (meaning no preference).

"Forum presentation mode" (option 6) is a valuable option for forum regulars. It determines the type of presentation you routinely will receive in all forums you visit. You have seen how to change from menu mode to command mode in a specific forum by using the user OPTIONS feature. With this option, you can make the change for *all* forums, even for those you haven't visited yet. The possible settings are MENU (or novice mode), COMMAND (expert mode with gives you one-word prompts), and DEFAULT (meaning no preference.) So, when you are comfortable with the command mode in your chosen forums, you can set this option to have that abbreviated mode waiting for you in all forums you visit.

The remaining three log-on/service options deal with how CompuServe appears at log on.

"First service at logon" (option 1) is another concept we first learned in the forums. Remember how one of the User OPTIONS allowed you to determine what we called "the front door" of the forum, that is, the first feature you see when you visit it? This Profile option is similar, but more powerful, in that it determines the front door of *all* of CompuServe for your account. Selecting this option shows you a menu like:

```
FIRST SERVICE

Permanent setting =                [MAIN]

 1 MAIN menu (Normal setting)
 2 Designated first service
    (You specify which one.)
 3 Personal MENU
    (A menu you have constructed)
 4 COMMAND mode in the personal
    file area

Enter choice or <CR> to leave unchanged!
```

The "normal" setting is MAIN, which is the TOP menu to which we are accustomed. However, the menu gives us three alternate starting points:

1. Something called "Personal Menu."
2. A different designated page number.
3. COMMAND mode of the personal file area (PER).

We shall talk about Personal Menu (option 3) in the next section. Moving on, the designated page number means that you can specify your *own* starting page. If you select option 2, the system prompts for the address of the service you want to see first each time you log on. Suppose you want always to start in CB; you enter CB-1.

If it were the forum we explored together (Good Earth Forum), the page would be GOODEARTH. Any legal system page number can be entered. The final option — COMMAND mode — allows you to have *no opening menu* at all. In other words, it is possible to flip that switch so that your logging on would look something like this:

```
 CompuServe Information Service
   17:26 EST Sunday 22-Jan-89
        (Executive Option)
   Last access: 23:02 19-Jan-89


      Copyright (C) 1988
    CompuServe Incorporated
      All Rights Reserved


   OK
```

No time-consuming menu; just an "OK" prompt, from which you can enter a GO command to take you anywhere you need to go. This option is a particular favorite for veteran electronic travelers because it is so streamlined. If you want to try running the system from the "OK" prompt, you select this option. It causes the system to start you in your PER area and in command mode.

Another log-on/service option on the previous menu is "TOP goes to", (option 4) which also requires some background. All along, we have told you the "top" of the system (that is, the trunk of the information tree) is the page named TOP. We lied. Well, maybe not *lied*, exactly. TOP *is* the page CompuServe makes as its default for the top of the system, meaning it is the one to which you return when you enter a TOP or T command. However, you can change that destination page. If you enter 4, the system lists these options (in a menu almost identical to the previous example):

```
TOP GOES TO

Permanent setting =                    [MAIN]

  1 MAIN menu (Normal setting)
  2 Designated top page
     (You specify which one.)
  3 Personal MENU
     (A menu you have constructed)
  4 COMMAND mode in the personal
     file area

Enter choice or
<CR> to leave unchanged!
```

If wanted to consider the Good Earth Forum as the top of CompuServe, you could select option 2 here and then enter GOODEARTH as the designated page number when prompted. Option 4 allows you to consider COMMAND mode of the personal file area (the "OK" prompt) as the top of the system. Again, there is that "personal MENU" business. Let's talk about that.

## Creating a Personal Menu

Option 3, "Personal menu established," allows you to be particularly creative. Wouldn't it be nice if you could create your own menu to list of your favorite features? Several years ago, CompuServe implemented the Personal Menu to let you do just that by selecting option 3 from the log-on/service options menu (your second bookmarked example). Your personal menu may contain up to ten choices and for each, you enter the system page number you wish to access and a description of the feature. Suppose you want the first option on your personal menu to be the *Online Today* electronic publication. You need to know that its direct page number is OLT or OLT-1. After you chose option 4, and the system prompts:

```
Menu choice 1
Page number:
```

You enter OLT, then CompuServe asks for a description (that is, how you want it to appear on the menu; you might enter ONLINE TODAY). Suppose you also want The Good Earth Forum (GOODEARTH), the CB Simulator, and EasyPlex on your menu. After you answer the questions (supplying a page number and description for each item when prompted), the system displays the choices and gives you a chance to insert, delete, or change the selections. After you have the selections the way you want them, the system sets up the personal menu and places in your personal file (PER) area a new file called MENU.CTL. Suppose you also chose the personal menu as your first service on the previous menu. Then the next time you log in, you are greeted by something like this:

```
  Copyright (C) 1989
CompuServe Incorporated
  All Rights Reserved


CompuServe                    Personal Menu

 1 Online Today
 2 Good Earth
 3 CB Simul.
 4 EasyPlex


Enter choice !
```

To go to any of the selections, just enter the number. To return to your personal menu from elsewhere in the system, you enter G MENU. (If you selected Personal Menu as the "top" of the system, you could return to it by entering T.)

A few more points about the personal menu:

— When you are creating your menu, you might occasionally receive a message that says, "That page is empty," even though you know it is an active page. The customer service people can provide you with a page number that will work in the menu for that particular service. Just send a message via FEEDBACK that includes the page address with which you have had trouble.

— When your personal menu is stored in your personal file area (PER), it is like any other PER file. That means that if you have not accessed it in 30 days (or six months, if you have the Executive Option), the menu may be deleted.

— To disable the personal menu, simply return to the First Service menu in TERMINAL/OPTIONS and pick something other than personal menu, such as MAIN or COMMAND.

## Recording a Preference for a Transfer Protocol

The final options on the permanent settings menu are settings for transfer protocols and graphics support. If you select option 5 on the menu in the first bookmarked example, you see:

```
TRANSFER PROTOCOLS/GRAPHICS SUPPORT

FILE TRANSFER PROTOCOL
  1 PROTOCOL preference         [SHOW MENU]

GRAPHICS SUPPORT
  2 GIF SUPPORT                       [NO]
  3 NAPLPS SUPPORT                    [NO]
  4 RLE SUPPORT                       [NO]

(Note: Please consult your software and
hardware documentation for
graphics support before changing these
settings.)

Enter choice!
```

(Please move your second bookmark to this page.)

So far, when we have talked about uploading to or downloading from the system, we always have shown a menu of possible transfer protocols, like this:

```
Protocol Menu

Transfer protocols available -

  1 XMODEM (MODEM7) protocol
  2 CompuServe 'B' protocol
  3 CompuServe 'A' protocol
  4 DC4/DC2 CAPTURE protocol
  5 Kermit protocol
  6 CompuServe Quick 'B' protocol

  0 Abort transfer request

Enter choice !
```

As the second bookmarked example illustrates, SHOW MENU is the default setting for this parameter. We also have said that by selecting an option from the menu, you tell CompuServe which protocol you want to use for the transfer. However, you can bypass this menu of possible protocols by simply recording a preference for a protocol in this option. If you choose the option 1 "PROTOCOL preference," the system shows you its available protocols (B Protocol, Xmodem, Kermit, etc.) and asks you to pick your favorite (one that, of course, is also supported by your communications software). From then on, whenever you want to download or upload a file (DOW and UPL, respectively), CompuServe doesn't take time to display its menu of protocols, but merely checks the choice you have filed here.

**Note:** If you do decide to register a preferred protocol here, you still can override it with some fancy command linking. If you enter at a prompt, DOW *filename.ext* PROTO:XMODEM, the system understands to download the file with Xmodem, regardless of the protocol you have listed with preference here. You can use the same command structure for the UPL command. (For background, see our Chapter 13 discussion of such command linking in connection with the forum data libraries.)

# High-Resolution Graphics — Rle, Gif, and NAPLPS

When people used to talk about high-resolution graphics on-line, their feelings about ASCII-based services like CompuServe could be summed up succinctly: "Can't be done." They were wrong about that. In recent years, CompuServe has conducted some interesting experiments with hi-res graphics, enabling subscribers to send and receive digitized photographs, line drawings, schematics, flow charts — all kinds of pictures — through three types of files called RLE (that is, "Run Length Encoded" files), GIF (CompuServe's own "Graphics Interchange Format"), and NAPLPS (North American Presentation Level Protocol Syntax). With the final choices in TERMINAL/OPTIONS, you can tell this system if any of these graphic formats are available for your computer system. But, it is not quite that simple. Getting in on the fun requires three things:

1. The hardware. You need a computer that can display high-resolution graphics, either in monochrome or color. For some systems, that is standard equipment; for others, you need a graphics enhancement card.
2. The software. You should be using a communications program that supports the system's cursor-positioning codes. Of course, CompuServe's own *Professional Connection* and *VIDTEX* software does, as does some other commercial and public domain programs.

3. Configuration: You need to have your user ID account set up. This is the easiest part; just set the appropriate options here on the bookmarked example. Options 2, 3, and 4 deal with graphics.

On-line pictures appear all around the system, some from menus, others in forum libraries. Public domain utility programs exist for some computer types that allow you to download the artwork and view it off-line. For that, check with the forums that support your kind of computer. Once you have taken care of your software, hardware, and configuration considerations, the easiest way to look at a picture is to visit one of the menu-driven galleries. For instance, fans of the CB Simulator have established a collection of photos of themselves. To see it, enter G CBPIX. Look over the names, then enter the number of the photo you want to see. The system clears your screen and displays the art, one pixel at a time. RLE pictures are displayed in a 256-by-192 pixel arrangement; when the RLE is accessed, the system displays the top row of pixels, then moves to the next row, and so forth. GIF graphics, introduced in the spring of 1987, are displayed in a larger layout — 320 pixels by 200 pixels — and are destined to people who have color monitors because the pixels can be in one of several colors (depending on the capability of the subscriber's graphics hardware), compared with RLEs that usually are in monochrome. NAPLPS graphics are a protocol being used in other systems.

The on-line graphics also are available in data libraries of some forums, and they are just as easy to display there. But first you have got to find them. A sure bet is to visit the On-line Picture Support Forum (G PICS), a service that specializes in on-line graphics of all kinds. Operated by Larry Wood, the forum has data libraries and a message board full of tips for displaying the artwork with a variety of computers. To check out its galleries, you enter NAMES and will see the names of the library's subtopics. Choose one that sounds interesting, then access it by entering LIB followed by the subtopic number — for instance, LIB 8 to access Library 8. All graphics files have an extension of either .RLE or .GIF, so to browse your chosen subtopic, enter BRO *.RLE or BRO *.GIF. That produces a list with a description of each file. When you have found one that looks interesting, you need only to *read* it. To do that, enter REA followed by the file name. For example, REA MICKEY.RLE would begin the display of a file called MICKEY.RLE.

Graphics files also can be downloaded for off-line use, if you have a utility for displaying them. Programming wizards in the various computer-specific forums have been writing such utilities and contributing them to the public domain. To find out about that, visit the forum that supports your computer and drop a note to the sysop.

## Still more about EasyPlex — The SET Command

By now you probably have come to think of CompuServe as having two basic modes of operation: "verbose mode" (long menus, lots of help) and "brief mode" (short prompts, or no menus at all, sometimes referred to as "expert mode"). However, one CompuServe creation, the EasyPlex electronic mail service, actually has *three* modes — novice (which you have been using), intermediate, and expert — as well as its own SET command to deal with them. The SET option also can manipulate a few other details, such as switching from the line-numbered editor to the unnumbered editor.

You learned most of the EasyPlex system in the first half of this book. We deferred discussion of its special SET command until now so we could put it in perspective. Switching to one of EasyPlex's advanced modes is something you probably will want to consider about the same time you are deciding to use other shortcuts in this chapter. Let's backtrack a bit and see how EasyPlex can be SET. You probably remember seeing SET as option 6 on the main EasyPlex menu:

```
EasyPlex  Main Menu
   *** No mail waiting ***

 2 COMPOSE a new message
 3 UPLOAD a message
 4 USE a file from PER area
 5 ADDRESS Book
 6 SET options

 Enter choice !
```

Selecting it brings you to this menu:

```
EasyPlex  Options Menu

 [ ] Represents Current Setting
     (yes/no options toggle)

 1 EDITOR uses line numbers [NO]
 2 MODE of operation is [MENU]
    (MENU, PROMPT, COMMAND)
 3 Output is PAGED [YES]

 Enter choice!
```

Options 1 and 3 aren't mysterious. Option 1 lets you toggle from the line-numbered editor to the unnumbered editor we have used elsewhere on the system. Option 3 determines whether your messages are "paged" or not. As elsewhere on the system, EasyPlex pauses with a "Press <RETURN> for MORE" prompt from time to time while you are reading your messages — unless you decide to set this Paged option to "Off." Once set, the options stay that way unless you use the SET option to change them again.

Of the three, option 2, "MODE" is the new concept. As the menu indicates, our present mode is "Menu." (Pretty obvious, as we are looking at a menu right now.) In this mode, the start of the EasyPlex feature always looks as it did at the start of this section. However, if you switch to the intermediate Prompt mode, you don't receive a menu upon arrival in EasyPlex, but you get this:

```
SCAn, REAd, COMpose, ADDress or HELp!
```

If you selected the Command mode, your prompt is:

```
EasyPlex!
```

Subsequent functions in EasyPlex, such as the *action* menu and the *send* menu, also are abbreviated in the Prompt and Command modes.

At first, those look substantially different from a friendly menu, but don't forget what experience has taught us: menus on the system are just an illusion. In our first excursion into the PER area, we turned off menus completely and ran around the system from the "OK" prompt. The lesson was that just about anything we can do from a numbered menu, we also can do from an abbreviated prompt. In this case, all we have to do is type in the lettered command. If we want to compose a letter at either of these prompts, we enter COMPOSE (or just COM). If you suddenly forget what options are open to you at one of these abbreviated prompts, enter HELP or a question mark (?) and the system lists them.

The advantage of using the advanced modes is time-saving. You are not asking the system to construct all those menus for you. On the other hand, you won't save time if you move on to them too soon and find yourself sitting at the prompt and scratching your head. We suggest you advance to Prompt and then Command mode at a reasonable pace; don't rush, let menu mode help you learn the letter commands. Because EasyPlex, like most menus, can accept either numbers or letters at the prompt, get in the habit of typing COM rather than 2 at the main menu. Then when you move up to abbreviated prompts, COM will already mean "compose" to you.

Finally, some people are reluctant to experiment with advanced modes of Easy-Plex because they are afraid they will somehow get trapped in the expert mode and be unable to get back to the menus. Don't worry about that. For one thing, EasyPlex asks you to confirm most major changes (with a message such as "Make changes permanent for future EasyPlex sessions (Yes or No)." Also, if you find yourself in

Prompt or Command mode and want to go back to menu mode, enter SET MODE
MENU at an EasyPlex prompt and you are in business.

One more thing about EasyPlex: CompuServe occasionally adds new options.
From time to time, you should enter NEW at the main EasyPlex prompt to be brought
up to date.

## EasyPlexing to Different Systems

With EasyPlex you also can write electronic messages for delivery to people who are
*not* users of CompuServe's consumer service, that is, to users of MCI Mail and the
InfoPlex electronic mail systems and to Telex and facsimile (FAX) machines around
the world. These are surcharged (extra-cost) features.

To send to any of these other systems, you simply write the message or upload
it to EasyPlex as you ordinarily would, close it, and issue the SEND command to
reach this prompt:

```
    Send to (Name or User ID):
```

Here you enter a ">"character followed by the address of the recipient on the
other system. The ">" character is essential, because it tells EasyPlex that the message is going to a *remote* electronic mail service.

Incidentally, extra costs are quoted in the following discussion, but note they
are subject to change. To get the latest charges, check on-line by entering G TRANS-
ACTIONS at any prompt.

**MCI Mail:**   To send your message to an MCI Mail address, you must enter
the words "MCI MAIL:" followed by the MCI address of the intended recipient, such
as:

```
    Send to (Name or User ID):>MCI MAIL:123-4567
```

You also may use an MCI Mail registered name (such as "MCI MAIL:Charles
Bowen"), but the MCI user ID number is preferred because it is unique to the
recipient, while there could be several MCI Mail users with the same name. If your
message is not uniquely identified, it cannot be delivered.

Costs of sending messages to MCI Mail vary, depending on the length. For
messages up to 500 characters, the cost is 45 cents. Messages of 501 to 7,500 characters cost $1. An additional $1 is charged for each additional 7,500 characters.

**Sending to TELEX:**    After you have written and closed your EasyPlex message and gone to the send prompt, you can post it to a Telex I or II machine by entering the ">"symbol followed by the letters TLX and the machine number, such as:

```
Send to (Name or User ID): >TLX 1234567
```

You also may follow with an answer-back code, like this:

```
Send to (Name or User ID): >TLX 1234567 ABCDEF
```

The answer-back code is optional, but if used, it must be correct and complete for the delivery. In other words, if you are not sure, don't use it.

Telexes sent to MCI Mail subscribers require a special prefix — 650 — before the Telex number. Telexes sent to destinations within the continental United States are considered domestic, whereas those sent to destinations outside of the United States (regardless of point of origin) are international and require a three digit country code before the Telex machine number. For more on that, you should enter HELP TELEX SEND at the EasyPlex Main Menu.)

The cost of sending EasyPlex to Telex varies depending on the type of machine and the destination. For domestic mail, the cost is 60 cents per 300 characters sent to Telex I machines and 65 cents per 300 characters sent to Telex II machines. For international Telexes, the costs vary depending on the country. The exact charges are displayed before the message is sent for your verification.

**Receiving from TELEX:**    You also can have Telex I or II machine messages sent to your EasyPlex mailbox. The information the sender needs is your user ID number and the number of the machine to which to send the message, 3762848, which has the answer-back of COMPUSERVE. The sender must specify on the first nonblank line of the message a "TO:" followed by "EASYPLEX:" and then your user ID number. If a subject is desired, the sender also may add a "RE:" after the "TO:" line in the message. In other words, the format looks like this:

```
TO: EASYPLEX:71635,1025      (This is Required)
RE: TEST MESSAGE             (optional)

(begin text)
```

Note the required use of the two colons in the first line.

Also the sender can direct that the message be delivered to more than one mail-box simply by appending additional user ID numbers separated by semicolons on the "TO:" line, as in:

```
TO: EASYPLEX:71635,1025; EASYPLEX:70475,1165
```

**Facsimile (FAX) Machines:**    EasyPlex messages can also be routed to Group 3 FAX machines. Write or upload the machine as usual and get to the "Send" prompt. To send to domestic recipients, enter the ">" symbol followed by the letters FAX and the domestic machine number, (the area code and the phone number) as in:

```
Send to (Name or User ID):>FAX 614-5551234
```

To send to an international facsimile machine, you include the international ac-cess code (such as 011), followed by the country and city codes before the phone number, as in:

```
Send to (Name or User ID): >FAX 011-44-1-12345
```

This example would reach Great Britain (44), city of London (1).

CompuServe makes several attempts to deliver your message within a 24-hour period and returns the message to you if it is undeliverable.

The cost of messages sent to domestic FAX machines is 75 cents for the first 1,000 characters and 25 cents for each additional 1,000 characters. The cost of inter-national messages is determined by the country of destination and the length of the message.

**InfoPlex:**    Finally, EasyPlex also can be sent to users of another CompuServe electronic mail system called "InfoPlex," which is used by some corporations and in-stitutions. The charge is 45 cents per message.

To send to InfoPlex, simply write or upload the message and go to the "Send" prompt. Then enter the ">" symbol, followed by the letters ORG and the organization's on-line address in this format:

```
>ORG:address
```

"ORG" represents the organization's unique InfoPlex identifier and "address" as the user's mailbox name. Incidentally, you also store the mailing address in your EasyPlex Address Book.


## Alternate Log-on Parameters

Finally, back to shortcuts. In addition to the SET commands and the options of Profile, other features will let you change the way information appears on your screen. One, called *alternate log-on parameters*, is especially useful if you have more than one computer with which you log on.

Suppose your main machine is an IBM PC compatible and you have already used Profile to establish parameters that best serve your 80-column by 25-line screen. However, let's say you also periodically use a laptop computer with a 40-column by 7-line screen such as a Tandy Model 100. A set of alternate parameters allows you to inform CompuServe *at log on* that you are using the other machine. A special command causes the system to automatically set up different screen widths and page depths to accommodate.

We do our work from Command mode (the "OK" prompt) of your personal file area (PER in command mode). To display the *existing* set (that is, the parameters you are currently using), you enter the command TER PAR (for TERminal PARameters) at the "OK" prompt to see something like this:

```
*** Active terminal parameters ***

RATE = 1200
MODEL = TTY
HORIZONTAL = Real
VERTICAL = Simulated
FORMFEED = Real
PARITY = Zero
Switches :
  ALF = Off   ALT = Off   BCR = Off
  BDF = On    BSE = Off   DBL = Off
  FCR = Off   FIL = On    LCT = Off
  NIM = Off   SBL = Off   SCR = Off
  SYN = Off   XLF = Off
Delays :
  BSD = 0   CRD = 1
  FFD = 0   HTD = 0
  LFD = 1   MCL = 0
  VTD = 0
CASE = Standard
SENDS = Standard
WIDTH = 80
DELETE = Rubout
SPCTAB = 8
PAGSIZ = 0
```

*Now, wait a minute! Where did all those variables come from if I've never used this feature before?*

The values assigned in your main set of parameters were placed there by the system itself when you indicated your "terminal type," either when you signed up as a member or when you last used the TERMINAL/OPTIONS to make adjustments.

All these codes can be set on or off or can be given a specific numeric value. Most, such as the set of DELAYS, are esoteric and can be left unchanged between computers. Others, like the WIDTH variable (referring to the width of a screen line), are useful to change.

(If you want to find out what each variables means, you can enter the command HELP TERMINAL at the "OK" prompt. You will see a general explanation and "Subtopic?" prompt. You then enter the variable about which you are curious. You also can enter "Introduction at the "Subtopic?" prompt for a further overview. If you enter the variable WIDTH at the "Subtopic ?" prompt, the system tells you the code "sets width of terminal line to *n* characters." In the example of our existing set of parameters, the WIDTH is 80. In our alternate set, we want to set WIDTH to "40." You can look up any of the variables in the example for further explanation. Once you have all the answers you want, press RETURN at the "Subtopic ?" prompt, and you come back to the "OK" prompt.)

To change a variable, such as the WIDTH variable, enter this at the "OK" prompt:

```
TER WIDTH 40
```

The system makes the change and again displays "OK."

You might also want to change the Page Size (PAGSIZ variable) to 7 for the 7-line screen with the command TER PAGSIZ 7.

After you have set all the variables as you want them, you need to save the new file. To do that, at the "OK" prompt enter this:

```
TER DEF name
```

That is, TERminal DEFinition followed by a name. It can be up to six letters, such as TER DEF LAPTOP. The system now saves the alternate parameters in a file called LAPTOP.

From then on, you can call on your new alternate parameters at log on by appending its name to your user ID number, like this:

```
71635,1025*LAPTOP
```

Note the asterisk (*) between the user ID and the file name. Without the asterisk and the file name, the system assumes you want to log on with your main parameter set as established at the TERMINAL/OPTIONS menu.

If you forget the procedure at log on, you can switch parameter sets after connection by going to the "OK" prompt and entering:

```
TER IS LAPTOP
```

Also, once you have activated an alternate set of parameters, if you enter G TERMINAL and take the "Show session vs. permanent" option, you can see the changes as they appear on your current user record.

**Note:**   Another way to override the defaults on file for your system at log on is to append a semicolon and the switch "TTY" to your user ID number, such as 71635,1025;TTY. This adjustment causes the system to log you on in a plain vanilla fashion.

## Other Log-on Tips

Here are two more tips for special applications that can be used at various times during an on-line session:

1.  If you have more than one user ID account and want to check in with each during a single connection, you don't have to disconnect and redial the network number. Instead, just enter LOG at a "!" prompt. That causes the system to log you off the current account, keep the connection, and return you to the "User ID:" prompt.
2.  You also can bypass the password prompt at log on if you have a backward slash (\) on your keyboard. Just enter your user ID, followed by the backward slash, followed by your password, such as:

```
71635,1025\BOAT%TOUCH
```

The system zips you right past the "Password:" prompt. (The password doesn't display on the screen after you type the backward slash.)

## Side Roads

This chapter introduced the area of on-line graphics and told you about the On-line Picture Support Forum (G PICS) which specializes in questions and answers about RLE and GIF pictures. In addition, here are other places on the system that now have high-res pictures for viewing:

— Hollywood Hotline Art (G HHA)is a gallery of more than a hundred film stars.

— The FBI Ten Most Wanted posters (G TEN) is a collection of bad guys.

— The National Weather Service daily weather map (G MAP).

— MegaWars I Pictures (G MW1PIC) is for those who want to see quadrant maps and pictures of the various fighting ships in the game.

— Biorhythms (G BIORHYTHMS) is for an illustration of the generated biorhythms chart.

— The Missing Children Database (G MIS-1) provides photos of missing children.

— TREND (G TREND) is a financial feature that charts the price/volume history of a stock.

To stay up to date on the latest RLE and GIF offerings, enter FIND GRAPHICS at any "!" prompt.

# CHAPTER 20

# ... And There's Even More in Reference Materials

Have you ever wished you had the resources of your local newspaper or television station working *just for you*? You could have an editor on call to sort the daily news — even when you are asleep — and set aside only the stories that might interest you personally. While we're at it, what about having a librarian on call as well, one who not only can give you access to an enormous amount of material, but also has time to *help* you search for what you need? Futurists tell us that someday we shall be able to do that. On CompuServe, someday has arrived.

During the past few years, a number of value-added (extra-cost), keyword-searchable services have been brought on-line to provide news and general information. This chapter focuses on:

— The Executive News Service, which provides an electronic "clipping" service for stories from the Associated Press, *The Washington Post*, the Reuter Financial News Service, McGraw-Hill News, and other resources.

— IQuest, is a gateway to more than 700 databases from a dozen top vendors, including such well-known names as Dialog, BRS, NewsNet, Vu/Text.

— Grolier's Academic American Encyclopedia is a ten-million-word reference work, which is updated four times a year.

— Microsearch is a searchable collection of reviews and technical information about assorted computer-related topics.

## The Executive News Service (G ENS)

The Executive News Service (ENS) provides access to current news from the Associated Press, today's *Washington Post*, OTC NewsAlert, Reuter Financial News

Service, McGraw-Hill News, and other resources, as many as 4,000 fresh stories daily. It automatically saves any stories containing keywords about subjects that you want to follow in your electronic "clip folders." Even when you are not on-line, ENS works around the clock, instantly clipping stories and offering them to you the next time you visit the feature. You can browse ENS's wires yourself in real-time as well.

To use ENS, you must first sign up for the Executive Option, which, as you learned in Chapter 16, provides a number of additional services. (For more details, enter G EXECUTIVE at any prompt.) Once signed up, you can use the news feature by entering G ENS, which displays:

```
Executive News Svc.

  1 Introduction to the
    Executive News Service
  2 Review Current News
  3 Review Late Breaking News
  4 Create/Change/Delete a Folder

  Enter choice !
```

Here we see the two ways to use ENS. Options 2 and 3 represent one way: browsing the current and late-breaking news from the various resources. Choose either option and the system prompts you to identify the wires you wish to scan, using a menu like this:

```
  Executive News Svc.     Wire Selection

  1 AP US & World
  2 AP Sports
  3 AP Financial
  4 Reuters Financial Report
  5 McGraw-Hill News
  6 OTC NewsAlert
  7 The Washington Post

  Enter choices separated by commas :
```

The Associated Press offers its national and world news wires, as well as its sports and financial wires. Reuters is a British wire service offering financial reports with a decidedly international flavor. McGraw-Hill is a major publisher of news and business journals and magazines, including *Business Week*, and McGraw-Hill News Service specializes in news analysis. OTC NewsAlert is a business wire concentrating on news of companies traded over-the-counter in the stock market. *The Washington Post*, the main newspaper in the nation's capital, offers selected stories from the day's morning edition. (Of course, look for this menu to change as Compu-Serve adds new resources to ENS.)

After you have entered your selection or selections, ENS finds the stories you have requested and asks how you want to see them, prompting with a menu such as:

```
Executive News Svc.

   48 stories selected

 1 Scan by story titles
 2 Scan by story leads
 3 Read all stories

 Enter choice !
```

Option 1 produces a menu of stories with titles — a word or two or perhaps a screen line — about each one; you then select the stories you wish to read. Option 2 shows you more information, the opening three lines of each story ("leads"), and prompts for the numbers of the ones you want to read. Option 3 skips the intermediate step by displaying ("Read") the text of each story already found.

Browsing the wires this way is fine for some applications, but that isn't where the feature shines. What ENS does best is its second method of news gathering: electronic clipping.

Suppose election fever has hit your household and you want ENS to follow news of your favorite candidates. You can set up a folder to capture election news as it is transmitted over the various wires. The stories then can stay in the folders until you next visit the ENS. To create a folder, start by selecting option 4, "Create/Change/Delete a Folder," from the main ENS menu, and the system displays this folder maintenance menu:

```
Executive News Svc.

   1  Create a Clipping Folder
   2  Change a Folder
   3  Delete a Folder
   4  List a Folder

Enter choice !
```

After you choose option 1, "Create a Clipping Folder," the system asks you to name the folder, using up to ten characters, such as ELECTIONS. Now the system asks:

```
Folder Expiration Date (MM/DD/YY):
```

How long do you want the folder to exist? Enter the date in the common numbers/slashes format, as in 11/30/89. A folder can exist for up to one year. (However, that date can be extended with a revision option we shall see later.) After that, you are prompted for "Number of days to retain clipped stories." If you plan to check in every other day, enter 2.

Now ENS gets down to the most important part of the work, choosing the news resources and subjects to clip, starting with this menu:

```
Executive News Svc.

 Folder GENERAL           Mode is INCLUDE

News Wires Selection

   1 AP US & World
   2 AP Sports
   3 AP Financial
   4 Reuters Financial Report
   5 McGraw-Hill News
   6 OTC NewsAlert
   7 The Washington Post

 Enter choice or <CR> to continue !
```

You may select a single wire service or more than one; enter the numbers separated by commas. For our ELECTIONS folder, we might select 1,4,5,7.

Next ENS prompts for up to seven keywords or phrases, such as the candidates' names. Phrases may be up to 80 characters long and may be enclosed in parentheses (LEAGUE OF WOMEN VOTERS). Also some powerful commands are available for linking them. For example:

— An asterisk (*) is a wildcard, so VOT* clips stories containing "vote," "votes," "voters," and so on.

— You also may qualify your phrase with a plus sign (+) to require two or more words or phrases be clipped. This means "AND" as in SMITH+VOTERS and SMITH+ELECTION.

— To indicate that a story should be clipped if it contains one keyword but *not* another, use a minus sign (-), such as ELECTION-NATIONAL.

— To chip a story that matches any of two or more phrase, use the I sign to mean OR, as in ELECTION I VOTE I RUN-OFF.

Actually, sophisticated commands for narrowing and broadening keywords and phrases, in ENS clipping folders, can be mixed and matched in some interesting ways by using parentheses to enclose complex concepts. Here are some examples Compu-Serve has offered on-line:

OHIO ST* + FOOTBALL finds stories containing both the phrase Ohio St AND the word football.

MERRILL LYNCH - (DAILY TREASURY INDEX I TELERATE) lets you follow Merrill Lynch announcements, such as initial public offerings it is underwriting and corporate news on itself, but NOT daily reports on its bond index.

MERRILL LYNCH - (CAPITAL MARKETS) finds stories on Merrill Lynch but NOT those regarding the initial public offerings it is underwriting.

APPLE + COMPUT* finds any story containing both the word apple AND any variation of comput. Since both combinations are required, it avoids stories dealing with apple growers and those about computers other than Apple's computers.

COMPUT* + (SECUR* I CRIME I PRIVACY) finds stories containing variations of the word comput, AND one OR more of the words secur*, crime and privacy.

COMPUT* + (VIRUS - DISEASE) finds stories containing variations of the word comput AND the word virus, but NOT the word disease.

After you have answered all the questions, the system stores the ELECTIONS folder and is ready to go to work. From now until the folder's expiration date, ENS monitors your specified wires and news categories, setting aside any stories that contain at least one of your keywords or phrases. You can read the clipped news any time you are on-line by entering G ENS. Notice the system has revised the main ENS menu:

```
┌─────────────────────────────────────────────────┐
│                                                 │
│   Executive News Svc.                           │
│                                                 │
│    1 Introduction to the                        │
│       Executive News Service                    │
│                                                 │
│    2 Review Current News                        │
│    3 Review Late Breaking News                  │
│    4 Create/Change/Delete a Folder              │
│    5 Review folder ELECTIONS   (6 stories)      │
│                                                 │
│   Enter choice !                                │
│                                                 │
└─────────────────────────────────────────────────┘
```

If you choose option 5, "Review folder ELECTIONS," the system gives you this menu from which to scan and read your clipped stories:

```
┌─────────────────────────────────────────────────┐
│                                                 │
│   Executive News Svc.                           │
│                                                 │
│     6 stories selected                          │
│                                                 │
│   1 Scan by story titles                        │
│   2 Scan by story leads                         │
│   3 Read all stories                            │
│                                                 │
│   Enter choice !                                │
│                                                 │
└─────────────────────────────────────────────────┘
```

You can revise or delete a folder by choosing the "Create/Change/Delete" option on the main ENS menu. The option provides an opportunity to add and delete key phrases and news wires and categories. Note the revision option also lets you change the expiration date and the number of retention days.

ENS carries a surcharge of $15 an hour over the base connect rates at all times.

## IQuest (G IQUEST)

One of the latest innovations in on-line communications already seems familiar to us: A technology called *gateways*. That's because there is a bit of the old-fashioned librarian in it, someone who can help us find our way through the rows and rows of reference materials. A gateway links one entire computer system with another. Users go through this electronic portal to use other systems, whether the destination computers are in a building next door or in a city on the other side of the world.

In mid-1985, CompuServe introduced IQuest, a joint gateway project with Telebase Systems Inc. of Narberth, Pennsylvania. IQuest puts CompuServe subscribers in touch with more than 700 databases provided by such major vendors as Dialog, BRS, Vu/Text, and NewsNet. With IQuest, you pay your usual CompuServe connect time as well as for material retrieved through the gateway. We reach the IQuest gateway by entering G IQUEST at any prompt, and see this introductory menu:

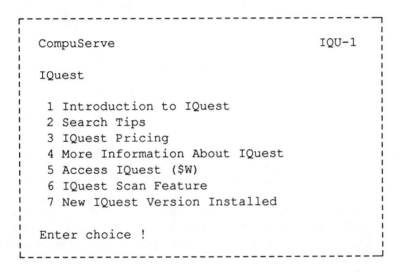

```
CompuServe                          IQU-1

IQuest

  1 Introduction to IQuest
  2 Search Tips
  3 IQuest Pricing
  4 More Information About IQuest
  5 Access IQuest ($W)
  6 IQuest Scan Feature
  7 New IQuest Version Installed

Enter choice !
```

Option 5 begins the search with a main menu like this:

```
┌─────────────────────────────────────────────────────┐
│                                                       │
│    Welcome to IQuest                                  │
│                                                       │
│   (c) 1988 Telebase Systems, Inc.                     │
│         Patent Pending                                │
│                                                       │
│   PRESS    TO SELECT          * Main Menu *           │
│                                                       │
│    1  IQuest-I   System helps select the              │
│   database                                            │
│    2  IQuest-II  You name the database                │
│    3  SmartScan  Scan a group of databases            │
│    4  Instructions                                    │
│    5  Announcements                                   │
│    H  for Help,   C  for Commands                     │
│                                                       │
│   Total charges thus far:    $0.00                    │
│                                                       │
│   ->                                                  │
│                                                       │
└─────────────────────────────────────────────────────┘
```

Immediately we find there really are three ways to use IQuest:

1. IQuest-I, designed for inexperienced subscribers, is menu-driven and actually helps you select an appropriate database. It does that by first prompting you to make selections from a series of categories listed by menus, then you are asked to enter your question in the form of a keyword or keywords. After that, IQuest-I takes you through the gateway to the database it has chosen for you and automatically translates your query into a command language which that particular database understands.
2. IQuest-II is for more experienced searchers and offers a larger selection of databases. It asks you to name the database you wish to search and to enter the keywords that make up your query. IQuest-II then takes over, making the call to the remote service, and, again, it translates your question into the database's own language.
3. SmartScan is a relatively new convenience feature that lets you make a preliminary scan of several relevant databases at one time to see which ones contain information on your search topic.

For starters, let's suppose you are new to all this, so you choose IQuest-I to let the system handle more of the work. That produces this menu:

```
r----------------------------------------------1
I                                              I
I   PRESS    TO SELECT                         I
I                                              I
I     1  Business                              I
I     2  Science & Technology                  I
I     3  Medicine & Allied Health              I
I     4  Law, Patents, Trademarks              I
I     5  Social Sciences & Education           I
I     6  Arts, Literature, Religion            I
I     7  Entertainment & Travel                I
I     8  Persons                               I
I     9  News                                  I
I     H  for Help,   C  for Commands           I
I                                              I
I   Total charges thus far:    $0.00           I
I                                              I
I   ->                                         I
I                                              I
L----------------------------------------------J
```

The system seeks to narrow the search to one of nine broad areas of interest. Note, too, the service keeps a running tab of your charges. Generally, IQuest bills only for the searching and the information actually retrieved from a database. As we have not yet gone through the gateway to a database, our charges are "$0.00."

About costs:

— $9 is charged for searching and retrieving information from a database. However, if a search turns up no files that meet your search specifications, the charge may be only $1. (Some databases charge nothing at all for unsuccessful searches.)

— Some 30 of the 700 databases carry an additional $4 to $25 in surcharges. These databases are identified on-line to alert users in advance, and you are given an opportunity to back out of a search before incurring such an extra charge.

— Standard CompuServe communications connect time charges are also in effect in IQuest.

— Any additional on-line purchases, such as abstracts of references or full-text of articles, are charged on a per-item basis.

Let's assume you want information about a business, so you choose option 1 from the current menu. That leads to further narrowing of the subject:

```
PRESS    TO SELECT

    1   Accounting
    2   Banking & Finance
    3   Companies
    4   Economics
    5   Industries
    6   Insurance
    7   Management
    8   Marketing
    9   Real Estate
   10   Taxation
    H   for Help,    C   for Commands


Total charges thus far:    $0.00


->
```

If you are looking for company information, you should select the third option here, which produces something like:

```
PRESS    TO SELECT

    1   Company fact sheet
    2   Financial reports
    3   Management, ownership, affiliations
    4   Company news
    H   for Help,    C   for Commands


Total charges thus far:    $0.00


->
```

Each menu gets more specific about the information for which you are looking, giving the system the background it needs to decide which database to access for you. The surcharges remain zero until after the actual trip through the gateway to a database. (However, you are incurring the usual CompuServe connect charges during this time.)

Information in IQuest is available in two forms:

1. *Bibliographic*: Basic information about published material, such as the name of the publication, date, author, and title of the article. Many bibliographic databases also provide abstracts (brief summaries) of the cited articles, for an extra charge.
2. *Full-Text*: The complete text of the articles you have located.

Most of the databases accessible to IQuest contain only bibliographic references or only full-text articles. When there is a choice, IQuest asks which you prefer.

After you have made your selections on all the menus, IQuest-I is ready to determine your question with a prompt that says:

```
┌─────────────────────────────────────────────────────┐
│                                                     │
│   Enter your specific topic.                        │
│                                                     │
│   (type H for important examples)                   │
│   or B to back up)                                  │
│                                                     │
└─────────────────────────────────────────────────────┘
```

The system is searching for a keyword or keywords to describe what you are looking for. (More about keywords in a minute.) Also, notice that you could enter other options:

— H for Help, which provides examples of search strategies. Some databases have their own syntax for searches, and examples are useful.
— B to back up (return to the previous menu).

H and B can be used at virtually any IQuest prompt. There are two other commands: T (for TOP) that returns you to the main IQuest menu and L (for "Leave") to log off IQuest and return to the main CompuServe system.

After verifying your keyword, IQuest-I reports the name of the database it has selected for the job and makes its way through the gateway. This process could take a few minutes because IQuest has rather a lot to do. It:

— Accesses a communications network and dials into the chosen database vendor.
— Submits a password for admission (as IQuest is your representative, the password is sent from the gateway to the host computer; it isn't displayed to you).
— Navigates to the database it has selected.
— Translates your query into a language that particular database understands.

Once the search is finished, IQuest reports a number of "hits," that is, the number of references it has found that meet the specifications. If your destination is a bibliographic database, your $9 charge provides a list of up to ten of the most recent references. Each is displayed with a heading number and basic information, including the title of the article, the name of the author and the publication, the publication date, volume number, and usually the page number. For additional charges, you sometimes can see abstracts of selected articles ($2 apiece), the next ten headlines in the catch ($9), or you can order reprints of the selected articles to be mailed to you directly ($12 by U.S. mail, $28 via overnight courier).

On the other hand, if the destination database is a full-text service, your initial $9 provides up to the latest 15 references. For no extra charge, you may enter a heading number to view the complete text of one article. Usually for extra charges you also may order mailed reprints, display the text of another article, or see the next 15 references from the search.

A typical menu following a search looks like this:

```
PRESS       TO SELECT


   1      Review results again
   2      See abstracts
   3      Order reprints
   4      See additional headings
   5      Start a new search
   6      Leave System


Total charges thus far:     $9.00


->
```

The bottom line informs us that so far the charges amount to $9.00. Should you order additional services — the next collection of headings, another search, reprints — the amount goes up.

After you become familiar with IQuest-I, you might want to step up to the advanced service, IQuest-II. It is faster because it provides fewer menus to study, and it offers access to a wider variety of databases. The difference with IQuest-II is that you select the database you wish to search, rather than turning that responsibility over to the system. You can request the names of specific IQuest databases at the "->"

prompt. Just enter DIR followed by a subject, such as DIR MUSIC, to find databases devoted to a specific subject, and IQuest responds with something like:

```
MAGAZINE ASAP                                        1614


Provides the full text of about a quarter of the
popular American magazines contained in MAGAZINE INDEX.


Format:             full text
Field Searching:    available
Time Span:          from 1983 to present
Updating:           monthly
Reprints:           available
Host:               DIALOG Information Services, Inc.


Press (return) to continue...->
```

Pressing RETURN causes IQuest to show you other music-related resources.

Suppose you decide to search the publication in the example; select IQuest-II and, when prompted to enter the name of the database to search, enter MAGAZINE ASAP. IQuest prompts for keywords that describe your subject, logs on, and makes the search. Incidentally, you also can enter DIR LIST at the "->" prompt to get a list of IQuest's various search areas.

As mentioned at the beginning of this chapter, SmartScan provides a preliminary scan of several relevant databases at one time. It then lets you choose from a menu, the databases from which you want to retrieve the data.

To start, enter the word SCAN followed by the name of one of IQuest's database groups. (You can get a complete list of IQuest's database groups by entering SCAN LIST.) For instance:

```
-> SCAN ACCOUNTING
```

This command scans selected databases that include coverage of accounting principles, applications, and the accounting industry. The system then prompts for keywords and ultimately produces an *occurrence menu*, like this:

```
PRESS     TO SELECT                    Occurrences   Data Type
  1       Database A.........................152       abstracts
          Database B                         0         abstracts
  2       Database C.........................20        abstracts
  3       Database D.........................7         full text
  4       Database E.........................439       reference
  5       Database F.........................2         reference
  H       Explanation of databases
  M       Main menu


  ->
```

The "Occurrences" column shows you how many records relevant to your keywords can be retrieved from each database. You know up front where the coverage is — and isn't — for your particular topic. Pressing H (for Help) retrieves database descriptions.

Once you have reviewed the menu, you can retrieve references from the databases by making your selection from the SmartScan menu. The system then conducts a standard search, after which, if you choose, you may start a new search.

The cross-database scan and resulting occurrence menu are billed as one standard search, $9 at current rates. Each subsequent access to a database from the SmartScan menu is billed as a separate standard search, including any applicable database surcharges.

With IQuest-I, IQuest-II, or SmartScan, the key to successful searching is in defining keywords. The best place to start your search strategies for IQuest and other extra-cost, keyword-searchable features is off-line. Before you log on, give some thought to what you want to specify at the keyword prompt, it will save you money.

Here are some guidelines for entering IQuest keywords:

— Omit such common words as OF, THE, FOR and AT. (Instead of "the Department of the Interior," make it DEPARTMENT INTERIOR.)

— Think of words and phrases that are unique to your subject. "Convertible," for instance, is a more specific term than "Automobile."

— Don't worry about capitalization. IQuest views uppercase and lowercase letters the same.

— The slash (/) character is a wildcard and can be used at the end of a keyword to retrieve references to text that includes words beginning to specified letters (COMPUT/ to retrieve COMPUTER, COMPUTERS, COMPUTING, COMPUTATIONS, and so on). The slash also can be used in the middle of words, such as PRACTI/E retrieves both "practice" and the British spelling, "practise."

IQuest also recognizes three connectors:

AND to narrow your search. (APPLE AND IBM to fetch only those files that contain *both* keywords.)

OR to expand your search. (APPLE OR IBM retrieves files containing *either* the word "Apple" or the letters "IBM.")

NOT to exclude a specified topic from your search. If you are looking for references to the country of Libya that do not deal with the political violence, you might enter LIBYA NOT TERRORIS/. That collects files that mentioned "Libya" but do *not* mention words that begin with "terroris," such as "terrorism" and "terrorist."

Finally, you can combine (or *nest*) searches by using parentheses around groups of words you have connected with AND, OR, or NOT. (LIBYA OR SYRIA OR IRAN) AND TERRORISM retrieves files that contain a mention of at least one of the three countries *and* the word "terrorism."

Here are the major database vendors represented in IQuest:

Dialog Information Services, Inc. of Palo Alto, California, provided by Knight-Ridder Company, offers more than 200 databases. It was originally conceived by Lockheed Corporation as a tool for NASA researchers. The databases deal with a wide range of topics from law and government to medicine and science, engineering and technology, patents and agriculture.

BRS (Bibliographic Retrieval Service) of Latham, New York, has some 80 databases. It was designed in the mid-1970s as a dialup service for research librarians. Since then, it has been expanded to cover science and medicine, business and finance, references, education, and humanities.

SDC/Orbit of Santa Monica, California, is a subsidiary of Burroughs Corporation and is considered the oldest modern database vendor. Brought on-line in 1965, it has about 80 databases, including some not found anywhere else: SDC, the provider of Accountant of the American Institute of CPAs; MONITOR, an index of *The Christian Science Monitor* newspaper, and SPORT, covering sports literature.

NewsNet of Bryn Mawr, Pennsylvania, brings together more than 300 newsletters from 34 industry groups, including computing, telecommunications, electronics, as well as medicine, business, education, law, social sciences, and others. The publications are daily, weekly, monthly, and quarterly.

Vu/Text of Philadelphia, Pennsylvania, is another Knight-Ridder service and offers full-text of a number of major newspapers, including *The Washington Post*, *The Boston Globe*, *The Miami Herald*, and others.

DataTimes of Oklahoma City, Oklahoma is another newspaper service with full-text of additional papers.

Questel of Washington, D.C., is a subsidiary of the French Telesystems and contains more than 40 databases, including its best-known DARC chemical files.

DataSolve of London is a product of the British Broadcasting Corporation. It offers summaries of world radio broadcasts from 120 countries and foreign news agencies, as well as BBC news.

In addition, IQuest has added Datastar of Switzerland, G. Cam Serveur of Paris, QL Systems of Kingston, Ontario, Canada, and Timeplace of Waltham, Massachusetts.

# Grolier's Academic American Encyclopedia (G AAE)

Isn't it frustrating when you turn to a trusted reference work only to find the entry you need is outdated? These days you can have an encyclopedia on-line that is updated and revised four times a year. Grolier's Academic American Encyclopedia (AAE) has more than 31,000 articles, fact boxes, bibliographies and tables. If you were to have it in print, it would be a 21-volume work containing some ten million words.

Besides its timeliness, what is special about Grolier's AAE is that:

— It is flexibly searchable by keywords. You can enter something quite general, like HORSE, then zero in on the specific subject by examining the menu of articles it retrieves; or you can start by entering something like ITALY, HISTORY OF and get right to heart of the matter.

— It is a "quick read" because of how complex subjects are organized. If you ask AAE for its article on FRANCE, it produces an outline with a menu that lets you jump into the middle, directly to portions dealing with "Land," "People," "Economic Activity," "Government," and so on. In addition, some topics are broken down even further. Under the "Land" section is usually a submenu to take you to the discussions of soils, climate, vegetation, animal life, resources, and so on.

You can subscribe to AAE for one month, six months, or a year and use the service as often as you like during the period. For details on subscriptions, including the latest rates, enter G AAE at any "!" prompt.

As a subscriber to the encyclopedia, an express lane is opened to you. You can enter G ZZX-4 to go directly to the encyclopedia, bypassing its introductory menu.

AAE recognizes all the usual system navigation commands, plus one. At any "!" prompt inside the encyclopedia, you can enter SE (for search) followed by a keyword. Then the service sorts its entries and displays, in menu form, a list of titles matching the term.

With most searches, the encyclopedia finds all entries beginning with the letters you enter, so CAT finds CAT, CATS, CATERPILLAR, CATACOMB... well, you get the idea. The service also recognizes a pound sign (#) to specify a search term. If you enter "#" at the end of a keyword — as in SE CAT# —the system finds only articles that match the term exactly. Also, with keywords shorter than three letters, AAE retrieves only those entries that match exactly. Thus, searching for "OZ" would find "The Wizard of Oz," but not OZONE.

Here are some tips for planning a search:

— Have alternate terms in mind. If you can't find an entry under MOVIES, be prepared to try MOTION PICTURES or FILMS.

— Include in your plans broad, categorical terms. No AAE entry exists for BALD EAGLE, for example, but information about the bird can be found under EAGLE.

— If in doubt about spelling, enter only as much of the word as you are certain of. If you enter BRZ, the service finds BRZEZINSKI.

— Don't let that get to be a crutch. It doesn't hurt to check the spelling before going on-line to make the search. A misspelled keyword is the most common reason for failure to find entries. We once grumbled at Grolier's because we couldn't find an entry on "John Erhlichman." Later we found out why. Darned if the Watergate character's name isn't "John Ehrlichman." Spelled correctly, the search worked just fine.

Having access to such an up-to-date encyclopedia is particularly valuable if current statistics are important to you. Many AAE articles are accompanied by fact boxes that summarize material. Expect to find fact boxes with all articles about countries, continents, states, Canadian provinces, and U.S. presidents. Several hundred entries also display statistic tables such as sports records, awards and prizes and industry production data. (AAE displays all its tables in 39-character lines.) If an article has an accompanying table, the system calls your attention to it on a menu displayed before the text begins.

Finally, if you are curious about the on-line encyclopedia but aren't yet ready to commit any money for a subscription, take advantage of free demonstrations. AAE has pulled out about a hundred entries from various subjects — sports, arts, biographies, issues, history, science — to let you have a free look. After you select a general category, the service lists a dozen or two topics you can view. For example, under arts and entertainment, you can look at sample entries ranging from English literature to Mozart to Sam Shepard to Michael Jackson. To get on the tour bus, enter G AAE at any prompt and look for a "Demo the Encyclopedia" option on the introductory menu.

## Microsearch (G MICROSEARCH)

Microsearch is a searchable database of microcomputer information provided by Information Inc., a Washington, D.C., electronic services and publishing company. It contains more than 20,000 abstracts of product reviews from some 200 microcomputing magazines and newspapers, as well as product literature from more than 4,500 hardware and software manufacturers. To use it, you enter G MICROSEARCH and reach this introductory menu:

```
CompuServe                        MICROSEARCH

MICROSEARCH

  1 Introduction/Search Tips
  2 Software Information ($)
  3 Hardware, Services, and
      Accessories Information ($)
  4 Directory of Manufacturers($)
  5 Feedback

Enter choice !
```

The database is organized into three categories. Software Information gives abstracts of reviews on programs for business and games, as well as educational, scientific, and health-related applications. Hardware, Services, and Accessories Information includes data on various kinds of microcomputers as well as related products and services. The Directory of Manufacturers provides company names, addresses, contact names, toll-free numbers, and so forth. Choosing any category produces:

```
Search Hardware By:

  1 Subject
  2 Micro or Operating System
  3 Product Name
  4 Manufacturer
  5 Publication
  6 Date
  7 Document Type

Enter choice !
```

About these terms:

*Subject search* allows for a keyword search of the abstracts. Each abstract is associated with descriptive terms about the product.

*Micro or Operating System* lets you specify a computer type. Use the standard spelling or format, such as IBM PC, IBM PC AT, APPLE IIE, APPLE II PLUS, or APPLE MACINTOSH.

*Product Name* has two applications. If searching software information, enter the name of the product (correct capitalization is not required); for hardware, always search by the name of the manufacturer and the product name, as in COMMODORE AMIGA.

*Manufacturer* lets you enter the name of the manufacturer or software publisher. If you are not sure of the spelling, enter only the first few letters of the name.

*Publication* accepts the name of the periodical desired. The database also includes publications that now are out of print.

*Date* lets you specify a range of publication dates back to 1982. The date of a software review refers to the date it appeared in the magazine. The date associated with product literature refers to the date the product was abstracted, not the date it was released.

*Document Type* refers to whether the article is an abstract of a magazine review (product review) or a description of a product based on information supplied by the manufacturer (product literature).

After you have selected the term, Microsearch prompts for a keyword. Be as specific as possible. The feature doesn't support wildcard searches, but it does search all entries that *begin* with the search term used; therefore, if you enter the subject term WORD, the database will find all abstracts that have subject terms beginning with those four letters (*WordStar, WordPerfect, word processor,* etc.) Also try a different spelling if a search does not find any articles (DATABASE instead of DATA BASE, for instance). Always use the most obvious search term first, such as ACCOUNTING for accounting packages.

A convenient feature of Microsearch is that once a collection of abstracts is located with the first search word, the database displays this "Next Action" menu:

```
┌──────────────────────────────────────────────────┐
│                                                    │
│  CompuServe                              MHD-18    │
│                                                    │
│  Next Action                                       │
│                                                    │
│   1 Display Selected Titles                        │
│   2 Narrow Selection Set                           │
│   3 Expand Selection Set                           │
│   4 Begin New Search                               │
│                                                    │
│  Enter choice !                                    │
│                                                    │
└──────────────────────────────────────────────────┘
```

Option 1 lets you display a menu of your located abstracts, whereas options 2 and 3 let you continue searching by narrowing or expanding the collection.

Microsearch is updated twice a month, and the surcharge for using the service is $10 an hour.

## Side Roads

To find other reference and news features on the system, enter FIND REFERENCE and FIND NEWS at any prompt.

Here are a few more reference features that might interest you:

**PaperChase** (G PCH-1) is a searchable, surcharged database called MEDLINE that features references from biomedical literature. The database contains more than five million references from 4,000 journals, all references indexed for MEDLINE since its inception in 1966. Each month some 25,000 more references are indexed and abstracted. The service is provided by Boston's Beth Israel Hospital.

**Rare Disease Database** (G NORD) provides on-line reports by the the National Organization for Rare Disorders, a nonprofit, voluntary health agency dedicated to the identification, control, and cure of rare "Orphan Diseases." The database is funded by the Generic Pharmaceutical Industry Association (GPIA) with additional aid from the Pharmaceutical Manufacturers Association (PMA), REVCO Drug Stores Foundation, and the Robert Leet and Clara Guthrie Patterson Trust.

**Hollywood Hotline** (G HOLLYWOOD) is a daily collection of news items from the entertainment world, including TV, films, stage, and recordings.

**Newsgrid** (G NEWSGRID) is a **non**surcharged news feature and compiles news reports from major wire services throughout the world. The feature is searchable and the main menu provides detailed tips and how to search it.

**Information USA** (G INFOUSA) is an on-line product by author Matthew Lesko, whose *Information USA*, published Viking Penguin Books is a 1,250-page reference to nearly everything. The on-line service specializes in telling Lesko's techniques for getting questions answered, with tutorials such as "The Art of Obtaining Information from Bureaucrats."

**Consumer Reports Magazine** (G CONSUMER) which compares and recommends appliances, cameras, electronics, and other products for the home, is now available on CompuServe. The articles have been edited to conform to the on-line environment. There is a $2.00 surcharge to review each article, plus applicable connect-time charges.

**Computer Database Plus** (G COMPLIB) features 11 search methods for retrieving articles from more than 120 computer-related magazines. It carries a $24-an-hour surcharge, a $1-an-article summary surcharge and a $1.50-per-article full-text surcharge.

# CHAPTER 21

# On Your Own

The journey isn't over. Although we have come to the end of our tours and Charlie and Dave are preparing to take their leave, your real exploration is just starting. You won't be left empty-handed. Following this chapter is the On-line Survival Kit, a section full of command summaries and tips to sustain you in your electronic travels. Having taken these tours, you have camped on CompuServe turf long enough to consider yourself a patron of the on-line arts and have learned important facts about CompuServe's style of electronic communication, among them:

— What may appear at first to be a system held together with baling wire and black magic actually is a logical network of related features. If services appear unrelated, it is only because of their diversity.

— Several ways exist for navigating. The simplest is slow, through menus; the faster is by direct (GO) commands at markers known as prompts. Methods of moving about the system are interchangeable and available to all, no matter what level of expertise, meaning you can progress from one approach to the next at your own pace.

— Once you learn commands in one area of the system you can use them in similar services elsewhere. Commands used in a computing-related forum also work across the system in a forum devoted to gardening. Moreover, similar *concepts* also are at work in entirely different parts of the system. A compelling similarity was observed between the commands of the National Bulletin Board and those of the libraries in the forums, between commands for message-writing in the forums and those in EasyPlex and elsewhere.

— Fears of getting lost, though natural because of the system's sheer size, are groundless. No matter where you are, a simple command or two takes you back to the system's front door or gets you out of the system entirely. Help files abound, and are available from almost any prompt if you press RETURN or enter HELP or a question mark.

— You can't "break" CompuServe. Many a new user has feared that if he or she enters a wrong command or hits the wrong key at the wrong time, CompuServe will come to a grinding halt, bells and whistles will sound, and the CompuServe police will be dispatched. It only happens that way in the movies. The system has withstood full frontal attacks from hundreds of thousands of computers and still is humming alone quite nicely, thank you.

— Things change often, but the more they change the more they stay the same. New services come on-line almost weekly, but commands for operating them — and basic concepts behind those commands — seldom are drastically different from those in existing features.

## In the Crystal Ball

Speaking of change, what does the future hold for CompuServe? Has it reached the end of its development? Absolutely not. On the contrary, we still are in the very first stage of this medium. Much like television in the early 1940s, CompuServe and similar services are just now beginning to explore their potential.

In the years to come, look for *gateways* to become increasingly important. When we talked about gateways in the previous chapter, we defined them as links between CompuServe and the massive resources of other systems, such as the databases of Telebase Systems Incorporated's IQuest service. This linking of large services obviously is appealing to us modem users, because it represents an ever-expanding world of retrievable information. Look for gateways to possibly become important for accessing CompuServe itself as well. In 1988 U.S. District Judge Harold H. Greene of Washington, D.C., authorized the seven AT&T spinoff companies, the so-called Baby Bell firms, to launch their own gateway services. Each of these new gateways is intended to allow access to several information services through a single phone call. Recently CompuServe announced that it would participate in some of the Baby Bells' gateway experiments.

Interconnectivity is important on another front, *electronic mail*. Chapter 19 talked about how EasyPlex messages can now be sent to electronic mail users of other systems, including MCI Mail and InfoPlex, as well as to telex and facsimile machines. Industry watchers anticipate further growth in the area of interconnected electronic mail services. To that end, electronic mail providers have adopted new standards aimed at someday producing a universal directory assistance service that will provide electronic mail addresses around the world.

# Vision and the Host Micro Interface

Perhaps the most exciting new development at CompuServe is in the area of the *user interface*. In early 1988, CompuServe programmers began working with a new idea — called "the host-micro interface" (HMI) — that soon may enable a much greater teamwork between CompuServe's computers and the terminal software on our own PCs. The company also announced a new series of communications programs called *CompuServe Vision* that incorporate this interesting new convention.

To understand HMI's potential and how it will work in the *Vision* software, we need to see it in perspective. When CompuServe started a decade ago, most PCs were no more than a step or two above "dumb terminals." They could display ASCII data received from the host computers, but little else. In fact, that's why CompuServe designed the existing system as it did: the tree of connected ASCII menus that we have looked at throughout this book. There were disadvantages to this approach. It was slow and inefficient to have the powerful minicomputers on CompuServe's host end constantly transmitting all those complete menus over and over again. At least it was a system with which virtually any kind of microcomputer could communicate. No special software was required; *any* terminal program — from plain vanilla to state-of-the-art — could be used. This approach was essential for the period, because numerous types of PCs were being used with precious few standards among them.

This past decade, of course, has seen phenomenal growth in personal computers. In speed, graphics and processing power, PCs have surpassed the best predictions of the early industry seers, leading to a whole new generation of fast, colorful and powerful software. Only in data communications has the growth been less obvious. That's because no matter how sophisticated communications programs themselves become, they still are communicating with a generic host interface that was designed to accommodate the least common denominator. You can have the hottest terminal program on the electronic road, but most on-line services — including CompuServe — treat you as if you got there on the bus. However, hints of a change are in the wind. Some observers say the next era in on-line computing will come from capitalizing on the PC's new-found power. The new idea in interfaces is to make this business of communications a more equally shared task between the micro and host.

CompuServe's host-micro interface and its *Vision* programs hope to do that by changing the basic way the system transmits its data. Instead of sending all that time-consuming ASCII data in the form of menus and prompts, the new thinking is to transmit compressed *binary* data, which then could be translated by the receiving microcomputer that is running the *Vision* terminal program, which recognizes HMI's conventions. Several advantages are apparent. First, speed. Receiving compressed binary data (even with the time it takes to convert it to something readable on the receiving end) is considerably faster than receiving the thousands of bits of data needed to construct a single ASCII menu. Also phone line static becomes less of a problem; HMI sends the binary data with an error-checking routine, much like CompuServe's B Protocol, Xmodem or Kermit, now used in file transfer.

But more importantly, *Vision* with HMI allows CompuServe to interact with the powers in the user's microcomputer. It coordinates the PC's resources with those of the host computers in ways that have never been seen before on commercial information services. We saw on the tours that if you walk through a series of menus and then need to back up to one or two of them, CompuServe must take the time to *re-transmit* the data to you, even though you already have received it once. However, with HMI, the *Vision* terminal software you use in your micro could simply keep in memory all previously viewed menus. It then could save you time and money by flashing the previously-seen menus onto the screen without having to ask the system to resend them.

Also, contemporary programming features so common in other software these days — windows, pop-up secondary screen, pull-down menus, bar cursors, sound and graphics enhancements, mouse interfaces — not only could be widely used in terminal programs, but also could interact with CompuServe through binary signals sent back and forth. Instead of having to enter numeric menu choices or three-letter commands, the subscriber could routinely make selections with a bar cursor on a windowed menu.

CompuServe began testing the HMI idea in the spring of 1989 with some IBM and Apple Macintosh programs. Also software toolkits were made available to assist major third-party software publishers in designing communications programs that recognize the new conventions. Look for more on-line discussion of *Vision* and the HMI concepts in the months and years ahead. Also, at present we are writing a new book for Bantam Books about seeing CompuServe through the Vision software. This book, called *Vision: CompuServe As You've Never Seen It Before*, will be published in 1989.

**Note:** Of course, not everyone will be sampling HMI right away. Obviously, the current ASCII version of the host interface will still be available for those systems that don't yet support the new convention.


# A Citizen of Micropolis

Meanwhile, despite an ever-changing digital landscape, some things never change on CompuServe. For instance, in the future, as today, your attitude about CompuServe has a profound effect on the system. The very first time you logged on, you became a citizen of an on-line *community*. The system's highly interactive nature — from the CB Simulator and EasyPlex to the on-going conversations in the forums — means that what you do and say affects others. Much of the "good stuff" on-line wasn't put there by CompuServe, but rather by the subscribers themselves. Everything from recipes in one forum to elaborate public-domain programs in others were contributed by subscribers sharing what they have and what they know. CompuServe provides the framework, but the heart of the system is its people.

Anyone who spends time on-line learns, like any good citizen, that you get more out of a system if you also put something into it. You will find you can enrich your on-line time if you enhance the system. If you simply prowl as a nameless subscriber with nothing to say, you will likely become dissatisfied, impatient, frustrated. That's because the genius of CompuServe is its two-way communication on a human, personal level.

So, now that you know the way, *participate*. Get to know the forums. Reexamine the list in Chapter 14 and choose a few you think might be of interest. Set aside time to explore each one on your list. Check the section names, choose some messages, and read their threads. If someone asks a question publicly and you know the answer, jump in. Leave an introductory message to the sysop just to say hello. If you want some specific information and don't see it, leave a message to ask. Questions and answers are the life's blood of the forums. Be sure to return in a day or two to read the responses, and don't wait too long or your replies may scroll off the message board.

Be *self-reliant*. Don't ask the sysop to explain what the forum is all about. Read the announcements and files in the libraries. And, please don't ask a sysop to go above and beyond what he or she already is doing for the forum. You would be surprised how often we see messages to sysops that say, "Please call me on the phone and tell me..." Now, that isn't necessary. Your computer has put you in touch with one of the most amazing communications tools of our time, so let's allow the harried sysop to work in that environment.

Try to *contribute*. If you have a special program you have written and you think someone else might be interested in it, leave it in a forum library. If you find someone else's public program that you really like, write an EasyPlex message to its creator expressing thanks. Always think of new features you would like to see. CompuServe isn't exactly flying by the seat of its pants, but employees acknowledge that, as no one has ever given birth to an animal quite like this before, no one is sure just what it should look like. The company looks to its subscribers for suggestions and provides the Feedback area for communications. Feedback is so special, the company doesn't charge you for the time you spend there. Extensive changes in the system have been made because one subscriber had a better idea.

Be *responsible*. Report wrongdoings. Did someone try to trick you into divulging your password? Is someone leaving messages that smack of false advertising? Have you run across a program on-line that you know is copyrighted rather than in the public domain or shareware? Report it through Feedback.

*Protect* yourself. Change your password regularly. If someday you try to log on and find out that your password no longer works with your user ID, report it immediately to customer service. Your number and password may have been stolen. Unless you report it, you might be charged for the time the thief spent on-line with your number.

There are very few hard-and-fast rules laid down by CompuServe; they can be viewed on-line by entering G RULES at any prompt. You will find it is a short list and the reason is simple. The company seems to have the philosophy that rules shouldn't be made until they are necessary. An enlightened attitude, in our opinion. The fact is that the majority of people who use CompuServe regulate themselves and thereby regulate the system, rewarding kindnesses and friendship with more kindness and friendship.

## This, Above All ...

We want to leave you with this message. Have *fun* on CompuServe; however you define fun, whether it's playing a game, chatting with the world on CB, talking technical in a forum, or retrieving financial information that will just set the office on its ear. Don't feel guilty when you begin feeling like a child with a new toy. There is nothing wrong with a little wide-eyed enthusiasm. We hope the excitement never fades for you, although your priorities for using CompuServe are likely to change with your experience, moods, and needs. That's all right, too. As you grow, CompuServe grows too.

Prophets of the new age say information services and telecomputing are likely to play a major role in what all of us do. Winners will be those who keep abreast of both the technology and the information it brings to the home, business, and marketplace. No one can predict what CompuServe will be like tomorrow, next week, or next year. "We don't make predictions. They make us nervous," one CompuServe official said. In this slightly wacky world of developing computer technology, nothing is forever. But those who don't keep abreast can easily fall behind. We feel that, although it isn't the ultimate computer service yet, CompuServe is the best training grounds around for those who want to keep on top of what's happening with computer communications.

Now, it is time you were on your way by yourself. Good luck. See you around the system!

# APPENDIX

# On-line Survival Kit

Smart travelers, no matter how street savvy they are, always have a first-aid kit handy. It is the same with electronic travelers. Now that you have toured the system with us and have seen the sights, we want to leave you with this On-line Survival Kit to help solve problems that come up in your future treks through CompuServe's assorted neighborhoods. We have collected lists of important addresses in the system and commands for major services, and have tried to anticipate your questions. Of course, no one guide can foresee all questions that might arise, so we also are leaving you with some phone numbers for reaching other helpful folks, like the CompuServe customer-service representatives and the good people at Feedback. Naturally, much of this material has been covered in the body of the book. However, when you are on-line and have a question, you don't want to retrace the steps of your tours. Perhaps you will find the answers here.

We have organized this kit into these major parts:

I. Making the Connection: phones, log-on numbers, and the like.
II. Command Compendium.
III. Troubleshooting and Getting Help.
IV. Your Electronic Address Book: page addresses for major services.
V. Further Reading.
VI. CompuServe Rules and Regulations
VII. Reaching Us.

# I. Making the Connection

In this section we have:

— Log-on procedures for CompuServe, Tymnet, Telenet, DataPac, local access transport area (LATA) networks, and the Computer Sciences Corp. (CSC) network that is used by many overseas subscribers. (Note: if you currently are referring to the survival kit from Chapter 3, *this* is the part you need to check.)
— How to find telephone access numbers throughout the country.
— Acceptable communications configurations for CompuServe.
— How to protect your password.
— Tips for international access of the system.

### Logging On

The best way to connect to CompuServe is through one of its own local phone numbers. Most metropolitan areas in the contiguous United States now have them. There is a 30-cent surcharge if you connect directly through a CompuServe number. Most other connections carry a surcharge of $2 an hour. For details on specific rates, enter G RATES at any prompt.

### *CompuServe*

To log on directly to CompuServe:

1. Dial the CompuServe network phone number and make the modem connection.
2. Press CONTROL C (that is, hold down the control key and the letter C together).
3. At the User ID: prompt, type your ID number and press RETURN.
4. At the subsequent "Password:" prompt, type your password and press RETURN.

Occasionally at log on, a user receives a "Host Name:" prompt. If this happens to you, type CIS <RETURN>, which takes you to the "User ID:" prompt.

### *Tymnet*

To reach CompuServe through Tymnet, follow these steps:

1. Dial your Tymnet number. The system responds with "PLEASE TYPE YOUR TERMINAL IDENTIFIER." (If you are logging on at any speed

other than 300 baud, this message is garbled, but don't let that throw you; just continue to step 2 and everything will work out.)
2. Type the letter A (uppercase or lowercase), but *don't* follow it with the RETURN key. The system responds with PLEASE LOG IN:.
3. Type CIS and press RETURN. If you make a typo but catch it *before* you press the RETURN key, press the ESCAPE key instead. Next, just reenter the host name, CIS.

Now Tymnet logs you into the system and gives you the "User ID:" and "Password:" prompts. Follow steps 3 and 4 in the direct CompuServe log-on instructions above.

### Telenet

To reach CompuServe through Telenet, follow these steps:

1. Connect with your Telenet number and press the RETURN key twice. Telenet will announce itself and display the terminal "port address," followed by a TERMINAL=.
2. Type D1 and press RETURN. Now Telenet displays the symbol @.
3. Type either C 202202 or C 614227 and press RETURN. You will be connected with CompuServe and will see the "User ID:" and "Password:" prompts.

Follow steps 3 and 4 in the direct CompuServe log-on instructions above.

### DataPac

Canadian subscribers to CompuServe often connect through DataPac, a network provided by Bell of Canada, to connect to Tymnet or Telenet in the United States. To log in through DataPac:

1. Dial the DataPac number and make the modem connection.
2. Type the appropriate service request signal — one period (.) for 300 baud or two periods (..) for 1200 baud — and press RETURN. The periods won't print on your screen. DataPac will display a message like "DATAPAC: 9999 9999." The numbers are a port address.
3. To specify you want to use the CompuServe network, enter CompuServe <RETURN>.
4. DataPac may prompt you for ":Host Name." If it does, enter CIS. You will then be taking to the user ID and password prompts.

Follow steps 3 and 4 in the direct CompuServe log-on instructions above.

### Local Access Transport Area (LATA) Networks

Some regional Bell phone companies now offer access to CompuServe through local access transport area (LATA) networks with surcharges that often are lower than those of other networks, except a direct connection to a CompuServe line. To see where LATA service is available, enter G PHONES at any CompuServe prompt and then look for the networks by area code or by city and state. LATA connections differ slightly from network to network. To find information on a specific LATA network, enter G LOG at any prompt and see option 2, Log-on/Log-off instructions. In general, here are the log-on steps for a LATA:

1. Dial the LATA network telephone access number and make the connection.
2. After the welcoming message, enter .CPS at the "*" prompt and press RETURN. CPS *must* be typed in uppercase.
3. Type CIS when prompted for "Host Name:" press the RETURN key. You then are prompted for your user ID number and password. Follow steps 3 and 4 in the direct CompuServe log-on instructions above.

### Computer Sciences Corporation (CSC) Network

Some overseas subscribers make connections with CompuServe through the Computer Sciences Corporation (CSC) network, a surcharged service. To find various CSC numbers for reaching CompuServe, enter G CSCNET at any prompt. To log on:

1. Dial the CSC network phone number and make the connection.
2. Press RETURN. CSC displays a pound sign (#) and determines your baud rate. If you have a block mode terminal, set the switch to character mode for baud rate detection.
3. At the pound sign prompt (#), enter the letter C and press RETURN. CSC responds by displaying the "CENTER" prompt.
4. Type CPS at the "CENTER" prompt and press RETURN.
5. Enter CIS at the "Host Name:" prompt. This leads to the user ID and password prompts.

Follow steps 3 and 4 in the direct CompuServe log-on instructions above.

### Finding Phone Numbers

A searchable database of telephone access numbers across the country is available on-line to help you locate direct CompuServe lines, as well as indirect connections through services like Tymnet and Telenet. The database, which you can reach by entering G PHONE at any prompt, also reports any recently changed network number or planned additions, and where the nearest 300-, 1200- and 2400-baud access numbers are for you. The menu looks something like this:

```
┌─────────────────────────────────────────────┐
│                                               │
│   CompuServe                       PHONES     │
│                                               │
│   COMPUSERVE NUMBERS                           │
│     1 Search by area code                      │
│     2 Search by City and State                 │
│     3 List all CompuServe Numbers              │
│                                               │
│   ALL NETWORK NUMBERS                          │
│     4 Search by area code                      │
│     5 Search by City and State                 │
│     6 List all network numbers                 │
│     7 Help and Information                      │
│     8 Number changes/additions                 │
│                                               │
│   Enter choice !                               │
│                                               │
└─────────────────────────────────────────────┘
```

If you use any of the search utilities here, the database identifies with a code (in parentheses) whether the lines are operated by CompuServe, Tymnet, Telenet, Data-Pac, local access transport areas, or others.

**Note:**   Codes differ slightly, depending on whether you are accessing the system with an 80-column screen width or a system with a narrower screen. The codes are CS or C for CompuServe lines, TYM or T for Tymnet, TEL or G for GTE's Telenet, DPC or D for DataPac, L or LAT for local access transport areas, and so forth.

The PHONES database is particularly useful in this age of portable computers. Many CompuServe subscribers take a computer with them on the road to log in from Aunt Molly's house or from a hotel room. With so many access numbers available, it is a local call from just about anywhere in the country.

**Communications Parameters**

If your screen is filled with garbled words when you are communicating with CompuServe, it may be that your computer isn't speaking in the right dialect. Data communications depend on visiting computers' having the same configuration as the host computer. CompuServe supports two set of parameters:
— 1 stop bit, even parity, 7-bit words.

— 1 stop bit, no parity, 8-bit words.

Any other setting results in garbled communications.

Also note that when you are using the 8-bit setting, the first prompt received from the system usually is garbled. That is because CompuServe is "expecting" the 7-bit setting. Just enter your user ID as usual; the system recognizes the 8-bit setting and makes the necessary adjustments.

If you are having trouble with garbled communications, you should check the terminal transmission characteristics set up in your terminal, computer, and modem. If in doubt, consult your computer store representatives, or call CompuServe's customer service toll free at (800) 848-8990 (or in Ohio, (614) 457-8650) from 8:00 a.m. to midnight Eastern Time weekdays and 2:00 p.m. to midnight Eastern Time weekends.

**Note:**   As we saw in Chapter 19, one of the TERMINAL/OPTIONS settings allows you to record your preferred PARITY setting. See the "Terminal Types and Other Parameters" section of Chapter 19 for details.

### Password Protection

We have said it before; we shall say it again. Protect your password, because it is the key to your account. Never discuss it on the system. Never make your password anything easily associated with you (such as your name or nickname). Change your password regularly. To do that, enter G PASSWORD at any prompt. (That takes you directly to the TERMINAL/OPTIONS area of the system.) You are asked to confirm your present password and type in your new password. Most passwords are two unrelated words connected with a symbol. After you have typed in the new password, the system confirms that the change has been made.

If you ever forget your password or think it has been stolen, you should contact the customer service people immediately at (800) 848-8990 or in Ohio, (614) 457-8650. The representative there won't be able to give you a new password over the phone, but can mail it to you at the address on file with your account number.

### International Access

Outside the United States and Canada, some subscribers access CompuServe through PTTs ("postal, telephone and telegraph agencies"), government bureaus that control the public data networks in various countries. To find out how to log in through such a system, contact the country's PTT representative and say that you want to communicate with CompuServe, whose DNIC (data network identification code) is 3132. The PTT should provide the log-on steps to reach CompuServe's "Host Name:" prompt. At this point, you enter CIS and the system should prompt for user ID and password.

CompuServe itself has information on access from nearly 200 countries. To see it, enter G IAI at any prompt.

# II. Command Compendium

Various commands are used throughout CompuServe, depending on which services you are using. We have covered all the major commands in the course of our tours, but it might be useful to have them all together in one neat stack. Here is the stack.

In this section, we summarize:

— A. Navigation commands.
— B. Control codes.
— C. CB and forum conferencing commands.
— D. Editing commands.
— E. Forum library commands.
— F. Other forum commands, especially those for reading the message board.

(Note: if you currently are referring to this section from Chapter 12, *this* is the section to check.)

— G. National Bulletin Board commands.
— H. Profile's TERMINAL/OPTIONS settings.

### A. Navigation Commands

CompuServe's navigation commands are the same almost everywhere in the system. (In the few services using special or addition commands, on-line help messages explain them to you.) Here are the commands that can be entered at the bottom of any menu or at an abbreviated prompt.

- T — TOP menu page. From virtually anywhere in the system, this command will take you directly to the first page of CompuServe, the menu labeled top, unless you have specified a different "top" through Profile options.
- M — Previous Menu. This command goes back to the menu page that points to the current page.
- G *n* — Go to *n*. The GO command takes you directly to page *n*, which is an address, as in G OLT-1. These days the GO command is more often used with a quick reference word, as in G IBMNEW and G PHONES.
- H or ? — HELP gives elaboration from the system on the current command.
- S *n* — Scroll from *n*. This command continuously outputs pages until the last page in a series is reached. If you are at a menu page, you can use S in connection with a menu item, as in S 1 to scroll item 1.

- N — (Next) can be entered at any prompt within related pages of information. This command selects the next menu item from the most recently used menu without redisplaying the menu.
- OFF or BYE — Disconnects you from the service immediately.
- F — (Forward) moves you forward a page, that is, displays the next page in a series of pages. A single carriage return (the RETURN or ENTER key) will do the same thing.
- B — (Backward) returns to the page preceding the current page.
- P — (Previous) goes to the previous item from last selected menu. For example, if 5 was the last choice, the P command will display item 4.
- R — (Resend) redisplays the current page. This command is useful if the current page has scrolled off the screen or after a HELP command.
- FIND — Follow this by a keyword and you can locate other features on the system. For instance, FIND IBM would cause the system to locate any features it has on file that deal with IBM. FIND builds a special menu for you, from which you can access any of the features found by simply entering a numbered option.

### B. Control Codes

What if you begin reading a long document on the system only to find it isn't what you were looking for at all? Is there any way to interrupt it? What if the display is going too fast? Can you make it wait until you catch up? Yes, on all counts, with control keys. Control characters are entered by holding down the control key on your keyboard and pressing a specific letter key. (Most keyboards these days have a key labeled "CONTROL" or "CTRL." If yours doesn't, consult your users manual. Some computers require a sequence of alternate keys to signal the CONTROL function.) In on-line messages about control functions, the system often uses the character "^," as in "^C Interrupt."

An important thing to remember about control keys is that you shouldn't use them to show your impatience. If you enter a bunch of CONTROL C's, it only causes you more delays later when you start moving again. That is because CompuServe has a "type-ahead" capability — the system "remembers" what you type. In other words, one CONTROL C should do the trick.

The control codes most often used on CompuServe are:

- CONTROL C interrupts the display so that you can enter another menu selection or command. Often it results in the display of a ^C Interrupt Menu from which you can cancel the current operation, continue at the point before the CONTROL C was enter, or go to the previous menu or prompt.
- CONTROL U deletes the line that you are typing. This code is similar to pressing the Backspace key repeatedly. It removes all characters that you

(such as /WHO 71635,1025) to get the handle currently being used by that account, and (3) with a handle (/WHO Bluegrass) to get the user ID number of that handle-holder.

- /DISPL UID displays a CB user's ID number with his or her handle. /DISPL NOUID turns off the /UID option so all you get is the handle.
- /DISPL JOB displays a user's job number with his or her handle, and /DISPL NOJOB turns off the function.
- /DISPL ALL displays both the user IDs and job numbers with all transmissions, whereas /DISPL NONE turns both off.
- /WHERE followed by a user ID number, job number, or handle locates another user on CB and reports his or her handle, job number, node, and current channel.
- /HANDLE allows you to change your CB name or "handle" while in the CB Simulator.
- /SQU *handle*, where handle is the name of the user, squelches a subscriber so that you no longer receive messages from him or her. /SQU *ID number*, where ID number is the user ID, has the same effect, except that you are squelching by user ID. /SQU *job*, where job is the job number of the person you want to squelch.

### Private CB Conversations

- /JOB displays the special number ("job number") assigned to you when you logged into the conference area. Job numbers are needed for establishing TALK sessions.
- /USERS TLK shows you the user status information on those people currently in "talk."
- /TALK *job* allows you to talk privately with another user. (/TALK 43 would notify the person with Job 43 that you wanted to talk.)
- /BREAK ends a TALK session and returns to the public channels.
- /NOTALK suppresses /TALK requests from other users.
- /SCR *code* places you in scramble mode and enables you to send and receive messages from any other user who had scrambled on the same code word on that particular channel.
- /XCL *code* allows you to monitor a scrambled channel while transmitting and receiving on a public channel.
- /SMC *code* allows you to monitor a public channel and transmit and receive on a scrambled channel.
- /UNS unscrambles a previously scrambled transmission.
- /PAGE *job* "pages" another user on CB, that is sends a private message that you are looking for him or her.
- /NOPAGE disables pages for your number temporarily.

### CB/Conferencing Control Codes

- CONTROL V key redisplays what you have typed before you actually send it.
- CONTROL U erases everything you have just typed if you haven't pressed RETURN yet.
- CONTROL P breaks off a /TALK session; it is the same as /BREAK.

## D. Writing and Editing Commands

Two text editors are in use throughout the system: LINEDIT, a line-numbered editor, and EDIT, an unnumbered editor. In many features, such as the forums and EasyPlex, you may choose which editor you want to use. Also, a preference for editors can be specified in the Profile area of the system. In the forums, a preference can be specified in the OPTIONS area of individual forums. In EasyPlex, you can choose an editor with the SET options on the main menu. In the National Bulletin Board, you can enter SET EDIT LINEDIT or SET EDIT EDIT to switch from one editor to the other.

Here are characteristics that both editors share:

— You must press the RETURN key at the end of each screen line.
— You cannot use your computers cursor-positioning arrow keys to edit the document.
— To close a document and leave the editor, you use the command /EXIT.

Now, here are tips for using each of the editors.

### LINEDIT, the Line-Numbered Editor

For newcomers, LINEDIT is the easier of the two available editors because it prompts for each line with a new line number, and it uses menus for editing changes, like this:

```
┌─────────────────────────────────────────────────────┐
│                                                       │
│   Edit Menu                                           │
│                                                       │
│     1 CHANGE characters in line                       │
│     2 REPLACE line                                    │
│     3 DELETE line                                     │
│     4 INSERT new line(s)                              │
│     5 TYPE all lines                                  │
│                                                       │
│                                                       │
│   Enter choice !                                      │
│                                                       │
└─────────────────────────────────────────────────────┘
```

It is recommended that you use the TYPE option first to see the numbered lines of your message, because all other commands, such as REPLACE and DELETE, will ask for line number references.

### *EDIT, the Unnumbered Editor*

Every command begins with a forward slash. If a line does not begin with a slash, the computer assumes it is text. It is helpful to think in terms of an invisible pointer that marks the position of the current line. You can direct the line pointer to move up or down your file. The pointer can be directed to move downward line-by-line from the first line of your text file searching for information to be displayed, changed, or erased.

- /EX exits the writing/editing service and returns to Command Mode. (Incidentally, you don't have to be at the bottom of the file to close with this command.)
- /T positions the line pointer at an imaginary line just before the first line of the file; and allows you to insert new lines above the current first line of the file.
- /P *n* displays a specified number (*n*) of lines in the file. If *n* is omitted, only the current line will be displayed. For example, a "/P3" will display three lines starting with the current line. (*Tip:* /T followed by carriage return and a "/P1000" will display the entire contents of the file, unless it is more than 1,000 lines long.)
- /L/*string* scans the lines following the current line one-by-one until the first occurrence of the specified string is located. To display the line located, give the /P command. (Incidentally, if you terminate the /L/*string* command with an ESCAPE key, the located line will be displayed immediately.) Your pointer must be on a line *above* the line for which you are searching in order

to use /L/. It always searches downward in the file. (*Tip:* If you give the "/T" command just before the "/L/String command," you will be able to locate a string above the current line.)

- /C/*oldstring*/*newstring*. This command replaces any specified string in the current line with a new string where: *oldstring* = the string to be replaced and *newstring* = the replacement string. If omitted, then *oldstring* will be erased.
- /(GC/*oldstring*/*newstring*, meaning "global change," is the same as the /C command, except that all occurrences of the old text are changed to the specified new text. If *newstring* isn't specified, then the command removes all occurrences of *oldstring*.
- /A/*string* adds the specified string to the end of the current line. The line pointer will remain on that line after the command is executed.
- /D*n* deletes the number of lines (*n*) specified starting with the current line. The pointer will be positioned at the line following the last line erased. If omitted, only the current line is erased.
- /B moves the line pointer to the last line of your file.
- /N *n*, meaning Next, moves your line pointer down the file a specified number of lines from its current position. If you enter *n* as a positive number (/N2), the line pointer advances down your file *n* (2) lines. If you enter *n* as a negative number (/N-3), the line pointer retreats up the file *n* (-3) lines.
- /TYPE displays the contents of the work space.
- /HELP gives more information about editing commands.

## E. Forum Data Libraries

Public Access and the data libraries of the forums both are databases of programs and text files. They share many of the same commands, including:

- BROwse — lets you see a summary of information about each file, one at a time, pausing with a prompt to download or read the file. The command also can be BROwse AGE:*age* to see files uploaded within the specified number of days and BROwse KEY:*keyword* to see files that contain the specified keyword or keywords.
- DIRectory — lets you see a briefer list of files in the database. The command also can be DIRectory DEScription to receive further description of the files. Unlike BROwse, this command does not pause with the prompt after each file to allow you to read or download the file.
- REAd — reads a file whose name you specify. This command can be used with ASCII text files.
- DOWnload — copies the file whose name you specify from the library to a disk in your personal computer.
- UPLoad — copies a file from your personal computer to the library.

- HELP — displays addition information.
- KEYword — displays an alphabetized list of keywords and number of files that use each keyword in the database.
- ERASE — removes a file that you contributed to the database.
- LIBrary *number* — takes you to the library whose number you specify. Entered by itself, the command displays a menu of the available libraries.

## F. Other Forum Commands

CompuServe's forums have their own specialized commands. They can be entered either at the bottom of the menus (in novice mode) or at function prompts (in expert mode). Here are the commands and how to use them.

### Global Commands

These can be entered at nearly any prompt in a forum:

- CONference — to reach the real-time conference area.
- HELp — for addition information.
- LIBrary — to go to the data libraries.
- MESsages — to reach to message board.
- OPTions — for the menu of user-settable options.
- USERS — to see the user IDs, job numbers, and location of other members current in the forum.
- WHO *user ID* — to see the name on file with a specific user ID number.

These may be entered at the forum's main menu or secondary menu prompts:

- ANNouncements — to see bulletins from the sysops.
- DEScriptions — for a menu of descriptions of message board sections, libraries and conference rooms.
- INStructions — for lengthy on-line help files.
- NAMe — for a list of section names in the message board, library, and conference area.
- NEW — to list the latest enhancements in the forum software.

### Main Menu Commands

- CONference *room-number* — to reach the specified room of the real-time conference area.
- MESsage — to reach the message board.
- MEMber — to reach the Member Directory menu.

- ULOg — for a list of the names of each person who accessed the forum in the last 24 hours, along with the date and time.

### Message Menu Commands

These can be entered at the Message menu prompt:

- BROwse *age sections* — for a summary of each message, one at a time. You can read a message or go on to the next summary. Entered by itself, BRO browses through new messages.

**Notes:** The *age* specification here and in the *following* commands can be either:

- NEW — meaning all message not read before.
- ALL — all public messages.
- DAYS: — *number-of-days*, selecting messages posted within the number of specified days.
- START: — *message-number*, starting with the specified message number.

Also, the *sections* specification follows this format — SECTIONS:*section-number(s)*, to display messages posted in the section or sections whose numbers you specify. For instance, REA SECTIONS:1-2,4,11

- CHAnge *age sections* — to specify the age and section of message you access. Entered by itself, CHA displays the message board's Change message.
- DELete *message-number* — to delete the message whose number you indicate. Of course, you can delete only messages you have posted or those posted to your user ID number.
- REAd *direction age section* — to read messages. Entered by itself, REA will display the Read Menu.

**Note:** The *direction* specification here and in the following commands can be either:

- FORward:*message-number* to display messages in the order they were posted
- REVerse:*message-number* to display them in reverse chronological order
- THRead:*message-number* to see messages in thread order, starting with the specified message. As noted, the system automatically displays message in thread order unless directed otherwise by one of the previous two specifications.
- REAd *age search-criterion sections* — to see messages.

**Note:** In this and following commands, the *search-criterion* specification can be either:

- FROm:*name* to see messages posted from the person names or the user ID number listed.
- SUBject:*text* to display messages whose subject line in the header contains the specified text.
- TO:*name* to see messages posted to the person names or the user ID number listed.
- NUMber:*message-number* to see messages beginning with the specified number.
- MARked to display message you have marked during your current forum session.
- WAIting to see messages posted to you that you have not read yet.
- SCAn *direction age sections prompt* — to display summary information about each message. Entered by itself, SCA scans new messages.

**Note:** The *prompt* specification here displays summary information about each message, one at a time. You can read a message, then mark it for later retrieval, or skip it and all messages related to it.

- SCAn *age search-criterion sections prompt* — to display summary information about each message.
- SCAn QUIck *age sections* — for a brief summary of message threads, name and number of the section where the messages are posted.
- SELect *age sections* — to see a Sections Menu that offers messages having the age you specify.

### Read Actions Menu Commands

- CHOices — re-displays the Read Actions Menu or prompt.
- REPly — allows you to write and post a message in response to the message you just read, with the same subject line in the header.
- COMpose — allows you to write and post a message in response to the message you just read, but with a *different* subject.
- DELete — deletes the message you just read (assuming it was either written by or to you).
- MARk — designates the message you just read for later retrieval with the REAd MARked command.
- NEXt — displays the next message in a thread.
- NEXt SUBject — skips the unread messages in the current thread and shows you the first message of the next thread.

- PARent — displays the parent message of a reply.
- ROOt — shows the first available message in the current thread.
- REAd REPly — shows the first reply to the message you just read.
- RERead — redisplays the current message.
- SCRoll — causes the messages to display consecutively, without pausing with a prompt between them.

### Post Action Menu Commands

- CANcel — aborts the message you are writing without posting it.
- EDIt — allows you to edit your message before POSting it, using either LINEDIT or EDIT.
- MAIl — sends the message to the recipient's EasyPlex mail, rather than posting it on the message board. This command also can be entered as **MAIl UNFormatted**, meaning to mail the message exactly as it appears in your writing work space. This "unformatted" option is available to allow you to retain columns of figures, for instance, that the forum ordinarily might reformat to the screen width of the recipient.

POSt *options* — posts the message on the message board. The *options* here can be:

- TO:*name/user ID* to post a message to the person specified.
- SECtion:*number* to post it on the specified section of the board.
- SUBject:*subject* to post it with the specified subject.
- PRIvate, to post the message privately, so that only you and the recipient will see it. (Note: This option isn't available in all forums.)
- UNFormatted to post it exactly as it appears in your writing work space. As with MAIl UNFormated, above, this option is available to allow you to retain columns of figures, for instance, that the forum ordinarily might reformat to the screen width of the recipient.

PREview — displays the message exactly as it will appear once it is MAIled or POSted. This command also can be used with a width designation, such as **PREview WIDth:32** to see how the message will look to a reader with a 32-column screen.

- TYPe — displays the entire message in the work space.

## *User Options*

The user option commands let you specify certain settings for your account, either "permanently" (that is, as your "default settings) or for the current visit only. Here are the options:

- INItial *menu/prompt* — tells the system at what point you want to enter this forum, main function menu, message board, libraries or conferencing area.
- PAUse (after messages) — tells the forum whether to stop and display a prompt after every message you read, stop only after messages addressed to you, or never stop between messages.
- NAMe — allows you to change the way your name appears in the header of any message you post.
- CHAracter — lets you change the forum prompt.
- EDITor — tells the systems which text editor you are using, LINEDIT, EDIT, or the one you have specified in the Profile area of the system.
- SECtions — lets you specify your defaults for subtopics.
- HIGh *message read* — is for "High Message Number," the variable that contains the number of the last message you read in that forum.
- REPlies — lets you specify how you want to be told about replies to messages you are reading, with a list of the numbers of all replies, a count of the replies, or no reply information.
- TYPe — determines how the system will behave when you enter a forum. If TYP is set to Yes, the forum displays messages addressed to you; if No, then it simply informs you of the numbers of the waiting messages.
- SKIp — lets you indicate whether during a routine reading of the board you want to see or skip the messages you yourself have posted.

## G. National Bulletin Board

The following commands are used in the National Bulletin Board.

- HELP — gives you help on all the other commands used in the bulletin board.
- SCAN — offers a quick look at the numbers and keywords of all the messages posted.
- BROWSE — is similar to SCAN, except that it pauses after each message and asks if you'd like to read it.
- READ — allows you to read a message. For example, READ 124 displays message number 124 on your screen.
- COMPOSE — is the command that lets you write a message for the board.
- EDIT — after you have written the message, allows you to change it, using the same edit commands you use in EasyPlex.

- POST — lets you place the message on the board.
- ERASE — removes one of your messages.
- EXIT — leaves the bulletin board and returns to the regular service.
- CHECK — to see the status of messages you have posted.
- KEYWORD — to search the keywords of messages on the bulletin board.
- AGE — to change the age range of messages being scanned and read.

### H. Profile's TERMINAL/OPTIONS Settings

Chapter 19 concentrated on the *default* settings controlled by the Profile area's TERMINAL/OPTIONS section. Here are the some 25 options controlled there:

### A. LOGON/SERVICE OPTIONS

— First Service can be set to either MAIN menu (Normal setting), a designated first service (you specify which one), personal MENU (a menu you have constructed), or COMMAND mode in the personal file area (PER).

— EasyPlex Waiting can be set to Go to EasyPlex (takes you to EasyPlex when you have messages waiting) or notify only (notifies you that you have messages waiting, then takes you to your first service).

— Personal Menu Established can be set to YES (which you select to *create* or *change* your personal menu) or NO (when you haven't created a personal or what to delete an existing personal menu.)

— TOP Goes To can be set to MAIN menu, a designated top page, a Personal MENU you have constructed or COMMAND mode in the personal file area.

— Online Editor Preference determines the editor you will normally use. You may change this for a specific forum via the forum options or for EasyPlex via the EasyPlex options. The possible settings here are EDIT (which doesn't use line numbers), LINEDIT (uses line numbers), or DEFAULT (no preference).

— Forum Presentation Mode determines the type of presentation you normally receive in each forum you visit. You may change this for a specific forum via the forum options. The settings are MENU mode (novice/intermediate), COMMAND mode (expert), or DEFAULT (no preference).

### B. DISPLAY OPTIONS

— Paged Display can be set to YES (output is presented in pages; you are asked to enter after each page) or NO (output is scrolled continuously to end of article.)

— Brief Prompts can be YES for expert mode (you receive abbreviated prompts such as "!" or "More!") or NO for novice/intermediate mode (you receive full prompts such as "Enter choice!" or "Enter <CR> for more!").

— Clear Screen Between Pages can be either YES or NO. The latter suppresses screen clear and use of cursor positioning.

— Blank Lines Sent can be YES (the normal mode) or NO. (Note: Not sending blank lines can save space but may make output more difficult to read.)

— Line Feeds Sent the normal setting is YES. Choose NO *only* if your terminal or software always adds a line feed to a carriage return. Not sending line feeds may result in text writing over itself.

## C. TERMINAL TYPE/PARAMETERS

— Terminal Type can be either VIDTEX (Professional Connection), ANSI, VT100, VT52, Heath (Zenith), ADM, CRT, or Other.

— Screen Width determines the number of characters per line on your screen.

— Lines Per Page determines the number of lines per screen for your system.

— Form Feeds can be either REAL (uses your micro control to do new page form feeds) or SIMULATED (prints out 8 blank lines between pages).

— Horizontal Tabs also can be either REAL (uses your micro control to move to tab stops across the page) or SIMULATED (uses spaces to simulate tabs).

— Characters Received (CAPS) can be set to U/L, the normal mode (the output to you is in uppercase or lowercase depending on how it is sent by CompuServe), UPPER only (you receive only uppercase output) or LOWER only (you receive only lowercase output.)

— Characters Sent in CAPS can be NO, the normal mode (meaning that whatever you input is in the case you send it) or YES (whatever you input is always in CAPS regardless of how you send it.)

— Parity can be either EVEN, ODD or ZERO.

— Output Delays is normally set to 1, but can be increased if your printer operates at a slower speed than your modem and characters are lost at the beginning of each line. (Note: Delays aren't recognized, however, if you are accessing through a supplemental network such as Tymnet, Telenet, Datapak, or a LATA.)

— Backspace Erase can be set to YES, the normal setting (when a backspace is received, CompuServe sends a space and another backspace, which has the effect of erasing the last character typed) or NO (with which no special processing when a backspace is received).

— Send Micro Inquiry Sequence at Logon should be set to YES if your software is *The Professional Connection* or another of CompuServe's own communications programs.

## D. TRANSFER PROTOCOLS/GRAPHICS SUPPORT

— File Transfer Protocol Preference can be set to record a preferred transfer protocol — B Protocol, Quick B protocol, Xmodem, Kermit — or set to SHOW

MENU (which causes the system to present a menu of available protocols when you request a file transfer).

— GIF Support should be set to YES only if your communication software supports CompuServe's Graphic Interchange Facility.

— NAPLPS Support should be YES if your terminal software supports NAPLPS, the North American Presentation Level Protocol Syntax.

— RLE Support should be YES if your terminal software supports RLE, that is, Run-Length Encoded graphics.

# III. Troubleshooting and Getting Help

Even after your tours, we expect that from time to time you will run across a problem that we didn't address. Here are some places for answers.

**FEEDBACK**

FEEDBACK is a special area of CompuServe where you can leave your comments and questions, a kind of on-line letter to the editor. You are invited to write a message to the Customer Service representatives, just as you might in EasyPLex. To reach the area, enter G FEEDBACK from any prompt in the system. You are not billed for the time you spend in FEEDBACK and you receive answers to your questions either through EasyPlex or direct contact.

Also, you can order written documentation for most of the services from FEEDBACK. If the documentation you want isn't listed, you can ask about it in a message in FEEDBACK directed to Customer Service.

Finally, FEEDBACK recently added a section for answers to common questions. It is a menu-driven area accessible from the main FEEDBACK menu. So far, the area has discussions on topics such as billing, log on, EasyPlex, forums, Personal File Area, setting up first services, and creating Personal Menus, using on-line ordering, navigating the CB Simulator, market quotes features, National Bulletin Board, and much more.

**Online Today's Electronic Edition**

You receive *Online Today*, a monthly magazine, as part of your CompuServe membership. Note, too, that OLT has a daily electronic edition as well, which includes an active letters to the editor department. To read or write letters to OLT, enter G OLT-30 at any prompt.

## Online Today Readers Forum

Speaking of *Online Today*, remember that members of the magazine's staff frequent a special forum called the Online Today Readers Forum, which is set up for questions and answers about the system, a sort of combination Welcome Wagon and traffic cop. To reach it, you enter G OLTFORUM at any prompt.

## Questions in the Forums

Most good forums have a subtopic set aside for "Ask the Sysop." Of course, this section is primarily intended for forum-related questions, but if you can't seem to find the answer to something that is troubling you about the system as a whole, ask a sysop. Most forum administrators are members of a private CompuServe-sponsored forum where they are kept up-to-date on systems enhancements. Maybe the sysop can find the answer.

## Customer Service

If all else fails, talk to a human being. Customer Service can be reached by a toll-free line. The number is (800) 848-8990; in Ohio, call (614) 457-8650. The Customer Service office is open from 8 a.m. to midnight Eastern Time Monday through Friday, and 2 p.m. to midnight on weekends.

## Operator and Network Messages

Occasionally CompuServe may send you a message to notify you to log off before a host computer is taken down. It is important — especially if you are using your data library files — to log off promptly. If you don't, you may lose some of the information you were entering.

In addition, if there is a problem with the system, you may receive a "network message," such as:

```
? NTWCCN - Cannot Connect
? NTWLCP - Lost Connect Path
? NTWSPR - System problem, please try again later.
```

If you receive any of these, hang up your telephone and try again later. Meanwhile, this message:

```
%NTWCPR - Communications Problem, PLEASE wait.
```

means that the network path which your terminal was using to connect to Compu-Serve Information Service has been disrupted. The network will try to reconnect your terminal to the system. Often you will see a message advising you to enter Control Q to resume. If it does not appear, hang up and try again.

**Glossary**

Some of the terms used in this book and other computer-related manuals are clear in context. However, it never hurts to have a brief glossary of frequently used terms, particularly those dealing with networking.

**ASCII** — American Standard Characters for Information Interchange. This is a common communications convention for computer-to-computer communications. In the coding scheme, letters, numbers, and special symbols are represented as unique 7-bit values, thus allowing for standardization between computers.

**Baud rate** — the number of times the signal on a transmission line changes state. Properly, baud rate is the inverse of the bit time, the time within which a bit is sent. For most communications via telephone lines with databases, information services, and Bulletin Board Systems (BBSes), transmissions are either 300 or 1200 baud. However, for direct computer-to-computer connections, 4800 or 9600 baud is possible.

**Buffer** — A contiguous block of memory for temporary storage. Characters are collected in a buffer prior to being processed. For example, in a communications program, a buffer is an area of memory in your computer where incoming information can be stored for saving on disk or printing. Usually buffers also are available for information that you want to transmit to the host computer.

**Carriage return (ENTER) or RETURN** — The specific key on the keyboard that enters the current line into the computer.

**Control characters** — Codes that can be used to control the flow and display of data being passed to and from the host computer, and for other signaling functions.

**Default** — The action that takes place unless you specify another action. For instance, an information service or database may "default" to displaying 80-character lines, but may have a section of the service that allows you to specify a different display, say, 64-character lines.

**Download** — The process of transferring a file of data from CompuServe to your own computer. Opposite of "upload."

**FEEDBACK** — Area of CompuServe that allows you to ask questions and order documentation.

**Host computer** — Large computer at CompuServe to which you are connected. The term also is used to mean the primary or controlling computer in a multiple computer operation upon which the smaller computers depend to do most work.

**Job** — A user's individual session while logged onto a CompuServe computer. In some on-line features, such as real-time conferencing, users each have a "job number."

**Log off** — Sequence that disconnects you from the system.

**Log on** — Sequence that connects you with the system.

**Menu** — List of options from which you may select in a system. Most information services are "menu-driven." That means that you navigate the system by selecting options from menus on the screen.

**Network** — A general term for the system communications link and equipment that enables you to connect to CompuServe in Columbus, Ohio. CompuServe operates its own network in most major cities in the United States. Access from other cities is available via a supplementary network (such as Tymnet) at an additional charge.

**Node** — Specialized communications computer that allows many terminals to communicate through the same line to CompuServe's computer complex in Columbus.

**Off-line** — In telecomputing, when your computer is not communicating with a remote computer or host computer. The opposite is on-line, meaning that you are communicating via modem with another machine.

**Packet-switching** — Transmission of data into standard-sized pieces for greater efficiency. Many networks are referred to as "packet-switching networks."

**Parity** — Scheme to detect errors in data transmission. An extra bit is added to each character being transmitted to force an odd (if "odd parity" is being used) or even (if "even parity" is being used) number of 1 bits in the transmitted character. The receiving computer performs its own calculation of the number of 1 bits received, and if different from what is expected, indicates that an error has occurred.

**Password** — A set of characters that secure entry into the service for a unique user ID.

**Premium service or value-added service** — Service that has an additional charge for the data retrieved. You will always be notified in advance if a feature is a premium service.

**Prompt** — Message displayed when the computer is waiting for input.

**Protocol** — Agreements between transmitter and receiver about how the data shall be formed.

**Upload** — The process of transferring a file from your computer to CompuServe. (This is the opposite of "download.")

**VIDTEX** (tm) — Terminal emulator program that is specially designed for use with CompuServe. Sometimes the term is used also to describe the IBM-compatible CompuServe program, *The Professional Connection*.

## IV. Your Electronic Address Book

We want you to be able to avoid on-line traffic jams by knowing all the shortcuts you can. The GO command is your ticket into the expressway. To help you use it, we have devoted this section to some of the more popular page address and *quick reference words*. To access the services, enter G followed by the page number or quick word, as in G EASYPLEX or G OLT or G GOODEARTH.

The only problem with talking about specific page addresses is, of course, that the system is constantly changing, being updated and improved. So it may be that a few of these addresses are outdated. Gives you something on which to test your explorer's instincts.

Here are a few tips for using updates from the system itself:

— You can get a list of the latest quick words by entering G QUICK at any prompt. At last count, there were some 500 of them, so if you plan to collect them, open a buffer and make yourself comfortable.

— The FIND command. At nearly any prompt, if you enter FIND followed by a keyword, such as FIND NEWS, the system will produce a customized menu for you of relevant features.

— G INDEX will take you to a searchable database of features that works much like FIND. (In fact, INDEX is an older version of the FIND command.)

CompuServe's list, produced by G QUICK, is alphabetized by the quick words, which seems backwards to us. So, we have resorted the list by subject to provide the following for your files.

**Most Important Quick Words**

For general navigation and to reach on-line help:

The first menu in the system — TOP.
Users options menu — PROFILE.
Terminal setting area — TERMINAL or OPTIONS.
Command summary — COMMAND.
Help and instructions menu — HELP, HOWTO or USERINFORMATION or INSTRUCTIONS.
Log-on information menu — LOGON.
EasyPlex — EASYPLEX, MAIL or EASY.
A list of available forums — FORUMS.
Subscribers Directory — DIRECTORY.
Electronic Mall — MALL, MALLDIRECTORY, MALLINFO, MALLMANAGER.

## User Information

Billing:

General information — BILL, CHARGES, MONTH, BILLING, BILNIF.
Questions — QABILL.
Options — BILOPT.
Periods — PERIOD.
Limits on CheckFree/Direct — LIMIT.
Disk storage charges — STORAGE.
Connect rate information — CONNECT.
Rates — RATES.
Surcharge information — SURCHARGES.
Transaction program charges — TRANSACTION.
Miscellaneous billing charges — MISCELLANEOUS or MISC.

Feedback and product ordering:

Feedback — FEEDBACK.
Order CompuServe Documentation/Products — ORDER, ORDERING,
DOCUMENTATION, ORDERS.
CompuServe's software exchange — SOFTEX.

Lists and account maintenance:

Change Your Password Program — PASSWORD.
Node List — NODES.
Quick Reference Words List — QUICK.
Subject Index — TOPIC or INDEX.
Telephone Numbers — PHONE or PHONES or NUMBER or TELEPHONE.
Tour — TOURS or TOUR.
Users Directory — USERS.
Users Profile Program — TERMINAL or OPTION or DEFAULT or
DEFALT.
Vidtex Information — VIDTEX or VERSION.

## Summary Menus

Many of CompuServe's features are summarized on menus that collect related features. Here is a list of quick words that take you to summary menus. To reach:
Adventure games — ADVENT.

Arts/music/literature — ARTS.
Aviation — AVIATION.
Brokerage — BROKERAGE or BROKER.
Business — BUSINESS or PROFESSIONS.
Business news — BUSNEWS.
Commodities — COMMODITIES.
Commodity symbols — CSYMBOL.
Communications — COMMUNICATE.
Computing — COMPUTERS.
Corporate reports — COMPANY.
Earnings projections — EARNINGS or PROJECTIONS.
Economic indicators — INDICATORS.
Economics, general — ECONOMICS.
Education — EDUCATION.
Electronic publishing — MAGAZINES.
Engineering — ENGINEERING.
Entertainment — ENTERTAINMENT.
Family — FAMILY.
Finance — FINANCE.
Financial help — FINHLP.
Food/Wine — FOOD or WINE.
Games — GAMES.
Government information — GOVERNMENT.
Handicapped — HANDICAPPED.
Hardware forums — HARDWARE.
Health — HEALTH.
Historical stock/fund pricing — SECURITIES.
Hobbies — HOBBIES or HOBBY.
Home banking — BANK or BANKING.
Home — HOME.
Insurance — INSURANCE.
Investment analysis — ANALYSIS.
Investments — INVESTMENTS.
Issue/symbol look-up — SYMBOLS.
Legal — LEGAL.
Market quotes — QUOTE or QUOTES.
Media services — MEDIA.
Medical — MEDICINE or MEDICAL.
Money — MONEY.
News — NEWS.
Newsletters — NEWSLETTERS.
Professional features — PROFESSION.
Personal menu — MENU.

Reference — REFERENCE.
Shopping — SHOP or SHOPPING.
Software forums — SOFTWARE.
Software interfaces — INTERFACES.
Sports — SPORTS.
Technology — TECHNOLOGY.
Travel — TRAVEL, RESERVATIONS, VACATION, AIRLINES, FLIGHTS.
Weather — WEATHER and BRIEFINGS (aviation weather).

# V. Further Reading

Some people can never read enough on a subject. If you are that way about telecomputing, you are in luck. There are other books and articles and you will start receiving some of them as a CompuServe subscriber.

### Compuserve Publications

CompuServe offers a number of users guides that can be purchased on-line (G ORDER) and charged to your regular bill. Here are the two primary publications:

*CompuServe Information Service Users Guide*, $7.95, the same guide that is contained in the CompuServe Subscription Kit. It includes manuals for EasyPlex and the forums, command summary cards for the most popular features, and a menu poster. It is spiral-bound with a hard cover. (Incidentally, the guide is frequently back-ordered, and it sometimes takes six to eight weeks for delivery.)

*CompuServe Almanac*, $12.95, is a handy publication particularly for experienced users. It provides command summaries of most features, with helpful tips. Along with the spiral-bound book comes an EasyPlex address book and an alphabetized product index with Quick Reference Words.

*Mini-Guide to Online Computing*, $2.95, is a booklet that covers the basics, making it a good gift for a friend who might be curious about what all the shouting is about in this CompuServe thing. It presents answers to common questions about making connections, and includes a cross-referenced glossary of words most frequently used in telecomputing.

*MicroQuote Users Guide*, $6.95, is a reference tool for those using the financial service, MicroQuote. It provides instructions for using the system's historical database of securities, stock quotes features, symbol and CUSIP database, etc. A binder for the 8-1/2-by-11-inch pages is sold separately.

*Let's Talk: The CB Simulator Users Guide*, $4.95, is a manual for learning the ins and outs of CompuServe's most popular general service, real-time conferencing. The guide is directed at learning the CB Simulator, but, of course, the same commands also work in the conferencing areas of the various forums. It contains information on the newest conferencing commands, a node list, and a command reference card.

*National Bulletin Board Users Guide*, $5.95, this guide provides instruction for using the National Bulletin Board with illustrations of different modes of operation and two types of editors available for message-writing.

*Personal File Area Guide*, $10.95, is a manual that tells the uses of the 128K of storage space available on-line in your personal file area. Information can be stored in the PER for 30 days without charge, making it a convenient place to store EasyPlex messages, text for "form letters," etc.

*EDIT Users Guide*, $5.50, is a guide to the unnumbered line editor called EDIT (formerly "FILGE"). The guide shows how to use EDIT in EasyPlex, the forums, the Personal File Area, etc.

Also available with G ORDER are guides to some of CompuServe's most popular interactive games — MegaWars I, MegaWars III, and the Island of Kesmai — and communications software, perhaps the most important merchandise CompuServe has to offer. If you are not satisfied with your current terminal program and the way it allows your computer to interact with CompuServe, you ought to investigate the terminal software CompuServe has to offer. There is *Professional Connection* for IBM machines and IBM compatibles, and *VIDTEX* for non-IBM compatible Tandy machines, the Commodore 64, the Apple family of computers, and the Atari. As this software was developed by CompuServe for use on CompuServe, you may find one of these programs is perfect for your needs.

Back issues of *Online Today* magazine can be ordered there, as well as desk clocks, T-shirts, and more.

**Other Books**

If you enjoyed this tour guide, there are a few other books you might want to watch for.

*Vision: CompuServe As You've Never See It Before* by Charles Bowen and David Peyton, Bantam Books, $21.95, a new look at CompuServe from the perspective of CompuServe's new "host-micro interface" (HMI) and its new *Vision* software for IBM and Apple Macintosh computers.

*Advanced CompuServe for IBM PC Power Users*, by Charles Bowen and David Peyton, Bantam Books, $19.95, which some consider a companion to this book for those using MSDOS-compatible computers. It focuses on the ins and outs of downloading and uploading and introduces you to the wonderful IBM Users Network.

*The Complete Electronic Bulletin Board Starter Kit*, by Charles Bowen and David Peyton, featuring Tom Mack's RBBS-PC software, $39.95. A book-software package for setting up and customizing your own computer bulletin board system (BBS).

*How to Get the Most Out of Dow Jones News/Retrieval*, by Charles Bowen and David Peyton, Bantam Books, $19.95. An on-line tour guide to the nation's main financial network.

*The Complete Handbook of Personal Computer Communications*, by Alfred Glossbrenner, St. Martin's Press, $14.95, one of the first commercial books devoted to dialup services.

# VI. Compuserve's Operating Rules and Copyright Policy

As a CompuServe subscriber, you signed an agreement to abide by the system's rules and regulations. For the record, here is that agreement (which also can be read on-line by entering G RULES at any prompt):

### Compuserve Information Service Operating Rules

The operating rules are designed to protect the data and communications offered by CompuServe information providers and customers. The rules are also provided to make on-line information usage and communications a positive and secure experience for customers.

Customers agree during the on-line sign-up procedure to the terms and conditions outlined in the operating rules.

### *Introduction*

These operating rules are part of the terms of your service agreement with CompuServe, and you are bound by them. CompuServe may modify these rules at any time by publishing the modified rule(s) over the service.

### *Copyright*

The entire contents of the service is copyrighted as a collective work under the United States copyright laws. The copying, reproduction, or publication of any part of the service is prohibited, unless expressly authorized by CompuServe.

Each customer who places data, materials, or other information, including communications, in the public areas of the service grants CompuServe the right to edit, copy, republish, and distribute such data, materials, and other information to its customers and other persons. Each customer who places data, materials, or other information on the service retains any rights the customer may have in such data, materials, or other information.

### Information Content

Customer agrees not to publish on or over the service, any information that violates or infringes upon the rights of any other person or any information that would be abusive, profane, or sexually offensive to an average person, or which, without the approval of CompuServe, contains any advertising or any solicitation of other customers to use goods or services.

### Editing of Public Information

CompuServe reserves the right in its sole discretion to edit any public information appearing on the service, regardless of whether it violates the standards for information content.

### Service Termination

CompuServe reserves the right in its sole discretion to suspend or terminate Service to any customer at any time.

### Indemnification

Customer agrees to indemnify and hold CompuServe harmless from any claims and expenses, including reasonable attorney's fees, related to customer's violation on his service agreement, including these rules.

## More on Copyright

In mid-1986, there was much discussion on-line about what the copyright clause in the operating rules means to those who upload and download files in the forums.

Here is how CompuServe elaborated on its copyright policy in a statement posted on the system in September 1986. (For more on the company's copyright position, enter G COPYRIGHT at any system prompt).

### What is a Compilation Copyright?

CompuServe has copyrighted the contents of the CompuServe Information Service as a compilation copyright, just as many magazines and newspapers reserve such a copyright on the contents of their publications. This copyright is held in accordance with the 1976 Copyright Act of the United States.

A compilation copyright is granted when an organization collects information in a lawful way, adds value to it, and offers it to others. In this case, the CompuServe Information Service is a value-added product; CompuServe Incorporated has committed substantial financial resources to collecting more than 400 databases and offering them in an organized, structured way to a defined user base through a nationwide telecommunications network. The compilation copyright is intended to protect that substantial investment from unauthorized exploitation. This does *not* mean that CompuServe assumes ownership of individual programs and databases provided to the system by subscribers or information providers.

*If I upload a software program I have developed to CompuServe, do I still retain ownership of the program?*

Yes, you do. CompuServe's compilation copyright does *not* supercede individual ownership rights or copyrights to any of the material furnished to the service by subscribers or information providers.

For example, a subscriber who creates a program and uploads it to a CompuServe forum data library *still owns* that program, and may upload it to other information services and bulletin board systems.

It should be noted, however, that CompuServe cannot grant any redistribution rights for materials copyrighted by the author, unless specifically authorized to do so. CompuServe does not own the material or the copyright. These rights must be obtained directly from the author.

*What is CompuServe's stance toward copyrighted, public domain, and shareware programs?*

Each of these types of property have special characteristics, and deserves separate explanation:

**Copyrighted Material** — CompuServe does not allow copyrighted material to be placed on the CompuServe Information Service without the author's permission. Only the owner(s) or persons they specifically authorize may upload copyrighted material to the service.

Any subscriber may download copyrighted material for (his or her) own use. Any subscriber may also noncommercially redistribute a copyrighted program with the expressed permission of the owner or authorized person. Permission must be specified in the document, on the service, or must be obtained directly from the author.

**Public Domain** — Any subscriber may upload public domain programs to the service. Any subscriber may download public domain programs for their own use or noncommercially redistribute a public domain program.

**Shareware** — Only the owner or an authorized person may upload shareware programs. Any subscriber may download shareware programs for their own use, subject to the terms provided by the owner. Any subscriber may noncommercially redistribute a shareware program subject to the provided terms explicitly displayed in the software itself, or with permission of the owner or authorized person.

*As a CompuServe subscriber, can I download public domain information and shareware programs for my own use from CompuServe forum data libraries?*

Yes, you can. Public domain information and shareware programs are uploaded to CompuServe data libraries by their authors for use by other CompuServe subscribers.

*May I download programs from CompuServe forum data libraries and share them with a friend, or upload them to another bulletin board system?*

In keeping with the spirit of the development of public domain information and shareware, it is not CompuServe's current policy to prevent casual redistribution of this type of information — this is low volume and low frequency use or redistribution of information where no commercialism is involved. This means that a customer may download a file and share it with others for no commercial gain — either via a bulletin board service, diskette, or other means.

A subscriber may not, however, download a large number of files for redistribution via any means, nor is it acceptable for a subscriber to update another bulletin board regularly with files obtained from CompuServe.

It is important to note that CompuServe cannot grant redistribution rights for programs clearly copyrighted by the author, unless specifically authorized to do so. Such permission must be obtained directly from the author of the program.

*May I download and resell a program from a CompuServe forum data library?*

Commercial exploitation of material contained on the CompuServe Information Service is specifically prohibited by the CompuServe service agreement, to which each subscriber agrees before being permitted to access the service. Therefore, subscribers cannot lawfully download and redistribute public information or shareware programs for personal gain.

In addition, mass redistribution of public domain information or shareware is also prohibited. Mass distribution is defined as high frequency and/or high volume transfers.

*What are the penalties for violating the compilation copyright or service agreement provisions?*

When a situation involving exploitation is brought to CompuServe's attention, we investigate and, if warranted, remind the violator of the terms of the service agreement. If subsequent violations are reported, access to the CompuServe Information Service may be terminated for the violator and, in extreme cases, a letter is sent from our legal counsel asking that he or she cease and desist, or risk further legal action.

This measure is done as a positive step to protect the value and use of the material for CompuServe Information Service subscribers, and to discourage unauthorized redistribution of that material.

# VII. Reaching Us

Now that you are a seasoned traveler in this electronic world, we hope you will feel free to drop us a line sometime and let us know how you are getting along. We are only an EasyPlex away. You can reach Charlie by writing to user ID 71635,1025. Dave can be reached at 70475,1165.

# Index

# X

# About the Authors

Charles Bowen and David Peyton have been writing about the electronic community since 1982. They have written *The Complete Electronic Bulletin Board Starter Kit* (Bantam Books, 1988), *Advanced CompuServe for IBM Power Users* (Bantam Books, 1987), *How to Get the Most Out of Dow Jones News/Retrieval* (Bantam Books, 1986) and *How to Get the Most Out of The Source* (Bantam Books, 1985), and have written articles and columns for an assortment of computer magazines and journals.

Bowen also was co-author with Stewart Schneider of *Smarter Telecommunications* (Bantam Books, 1985). He is a freelance writer and a former newspaper editor. He and his wife, Pamela, live in Huntington, West Virginia.

Peyton is a regular columnist and feature writer for *The Herald-Dispatch* in Huntington, West Virginia, where he has worked for more than twenty years. He lives in Huntington with his wife, Susan, and their eighteen-year-old son, Davy.